Clashing Views in

American Foreign Policy

FIFTH EDITION

TAKING SIDES

Clashing Views in

American Foreign Policy

FIFTH EDITION

Selected, Edited, and with Introductions by

Andrew Bennett
Georgetown University

George Shambaugh
Georgetown University

 **Higher Education**

Boston   Burr Ridge, IL   Dubuque, IA   New York   San Francisco   St. Louis
Bangkok   Bogotá   Caracas   Kuala Lumpur   Lisbon   London   Madrid   Mexico City
Milan   Montreal   New Delhi   Santiago   Seoul   Singapore   Sydney   Taipei   Toronto

Mc Graw Hill **Higher Education**

TAKING SIDES: CLASHING VIEWS IN AMERICAN FOREIGN POLICY, FIFTH EDITION

Published by McGraw-Hill, a business unit of The McGraw-Hill Companies, Inc., 1221 Avenue of the Americas, New York, NY 10020. Copyright © 2010 by The McGraw-Hill Companies, Inc. All rights reserved. Previous edition(s) 2008, 2006, 2002. No part of this publication may be reproduced or distributed in any form or by any means, or stored in a database or retrieval system, without the prior written consent of The McGraw-Hill Companies, Inc., including, but not limited to, in any network or other electronic storage or transmission, or broadcast for distance learning.

Some ancillaries, including electronic and print components, may not be available to customers outside the United States.

Taking Sides® is a registered trademark of The McGraw-Hill Companies, Inc.
Taking Sides is published by the **Contemporary Learning Series** group within the McGraw-Hill Higher Education division.

1 2 3 4 5 6 7 8 9 0 DOC/DOC 0 9

MHID: 0-07-354564-3
ISBN: 978-0-07-354564-6
ISSN: 1536-3260

Managing Editor: *Larry Loeppke*
Senior Managing Editor: *Faye Schilling*
Senior Developmental Editor: *Jill Peter*
Editorial Coordinator: *Mary Foust*
Production Service Assistant: *Rita Hingtgen*
Permissions Coordinator: *Shirley Lanners*
Senior Marketing Manager: *Julie Keck*
Marketing Communications Specialist: *Mary Klein*
Marketing Coordinator: *Alice Link*
Senior Project Manager: *Jane Mohr*
Design Specialist: *Tara McDermott*
Cover Graphics: *Rick D. Noel*

Compositor: Macmillan Publishing Solutions
Cover Image: U.S. Air Force photo by Staff Sgt. Lorie Jewell

Library of Congress Cataloging-in-Publication Data

Main entry under title:
    Taking sides: clashing views in American foreign policy/selected, edited, and with introductions by Andrew Bennett and George Shambaugh—5th ed.

    Includes bibliographical references and index.
    1. United States—Foreign policy. I. Bennett, Andrew, and Shambaugh, George, *comp.*

                                                        327.73

www.mhhe.com

Clashing Views in
American Foreign Policy
FIFTH EDITION

Andrew Bennett
Georgetown University

George Shambaugh
Georgetown University

Advisory Board

v

Preface

As of this writing, the United States finds itself with well over 100,000 troops deployed halfway around the world in a controversial conflict, trying to establish a democratic government capable of defending itself but facing daily guerrilla-style attacks by opposing forces that take the lives of several Americans every day. It was not so long ago that a very different kind of foreign policy problem—a devastating surprise attack on U.S. territory—dominated public discussion, stimulated a far more assertive U.S. foreign policy, and ultimately led to the creation of vast new national security organizations to deal with a fundamentally changed international context.

The previous paragraph clearly describes the U.S. interventions in Afghanistan and Iraq, and the September 11, 2001, attacks on New York and Washington, but it could just as easily have been written in the early 1960s as the United States built up its forces in Vietnam and looked back to the surprise Japanese attack on Pearl Harbor that precipitated U.S. entry into World War II and that ultimately led to the creation of the Department of Defense, the Central Intelligence Agency, and the National Security Council in 1947.

These parallels, and many others that could be drawn as well to previous U.S. military interventions (in Somalia, Lebanon, Nicaragua, to name just a few) and previous surprise attacks on U.S. territory or forces (including terrorist bombings in the 1980s and 1990s in Lebanon, Yemen, and U.S. embassies in Africa), are a reminder that while the specific issues and countries that dominate U.S. foreign policy continually change, there is some continuity as well in both the foreign policy problems that the United States confronts and the ways in which Americans think about how to address them. True, the current situation in Iraq differs from Vietnam's in the 1960s in some ways that make Iraq a more challenging problem and in other ways that make it more amenable to America's influence. And the implications of the surprise attack on Pearl Harbor were very different from those of the 9/11 attacks. Even so, the study of recent foreign policies, with due attention to how they differ from the current context as well as the ways in which they resemble it, is extremely useful in clarifying the options the United States has as well as the likely costs and benefits of each alternative.

Thus, while much of the 2008 presidential campaign was focused on promoting "change," President Barack Obama is facing many foreign policy challenges similar to those faced by former president George W. Bush and those who preceded him. Whatever the outcome in Iraq, the United States will for the foreseeable future continue to confront the problem of autocratic states seeking, testing, or deploying weapons of mass destruction, including Iran and North Korea. Whether or not Osama bin Laden and other top al Qaeda leaders have been captured or killed by the time you read this book, the United States will continue to face a balancing act between giving law enforcement and intelligence officials a free hand to seek out terrorists and safeguarding civil liberties, and the monumental task of coordinating a vast bureaucratic machinery to protect tens of thousands of civilian and military sites that terrorists might target. These and other issues included in this volume will need to be managed with limited economic resources, an overextended military, increasing energy demands, and growing recognition of the consequences of national behavior on climate change, disease and other emerging concerns for many years to come.

This fifth edition maintains the philosophy of the *Taking Sides* series that debating vital issues is valuable and necessary and can push students and teachers alike to re-examine the assumptions behind their views. In a "fifty-fifty" nation in which each of the last two presidential elections was won by a narrow margin, it is essential to keep in mind that no party or individual is right all the time, ourselves included. It might seem at first glance that the format of this book—one reading on each side of an issue with an oversimplified label of "yes" or "no"—perpetuates the increasing polarization of our public political discourse. Readers will quickly discern, however, that each reading is far more subtle than the simple "yes" and "no" labels used as an organizing device, and the range of additional readings and Web sites suggested in each postscript present a still more diverse set of views.

This book follows a format that has proven successful in helping students come to terms with the complex challenges of American foreign policy. Each issue has two readings, one pro and one con. *Introductions* to each issue provide some background information on the essay authors and provide historical and political context for the debate in which they are engaged. The issues then conclude with *postscripts* that provide further avenues for exploration and suggest additional readings and Web sites. General Web sites are also listed under the heading *Internet References* for each part opener. At the back of the book is a listing of brief biographies for all the *contributors to the volume*. The contributors are a mix of scholars, journalists, practitioners, and noted political commentators.

Changes to the fifth edition   In the years between the fourth edition and the present volume, the basic problems confronting American foreign policy have not changed radically, but there is a pervasive expectation that President Obama will apply different strategies in managing these problems. Reflecting this change, Secretary of State Hillary Clinton emphasizes the use of "smart power," which is the selective use of the full foreign policy tool kit including diplomacy, economic might, military power, culture, and "soft-power" (the ability to persuade others that they should want the same goals we do) to address U.S. foreign policy challenges and meet U.S. foreign policy objectives. The new edition introduces more than 20 new essays on subjects that include withdrawing U.S. forces in Iraq, responding to Iran's nuclear ambitions, managing the Arab-Israeli conflict, fighting the war on terrorism, responding to a rising China, ending sanctions against Cuba, and promoting the best economic strategies for restarting economic growth at home and abroad.

Note to instructors   A general guidebook, *Using Taking Sides in the Classroom*, which discusses methods and techniques for integrating the pro-con approach into any classroom setting, is available. An online version of this guidebook can be found at http://www.mhcls.com/usingts/index.mhtml.

Note for student readers   The debates in this book are not one-sided. Each author strongly believes in his or her position. If you read the debates with an open mind, you will find that each author makes cogent points that are hard to dismiss out of hand. Foreign policy involves trade-offs among competing values, and even when people agree on what values take priority, they may disagree about the best means of attaining them.

Yet to consider competing views with an open mind does not require that you remain neutral in the end. We hope these essays help clarify your own views and motivate you to put your views into action by writing to elected officials, working for candidates, and joining or creating organizations and political parties. Get involved, whichever side of an issue you are on!

Acknowledgments   We would like to thank the colleagues whose essays are reproduced herein. We would also like to thank Jill Peter of McGraw-Hill for her many helpful suggestions and hard work in producing this edition.

Andrew Bennett
Georgetown University

George Shambaugh
Georgetown University

*We dedicate this book to the men and women who have
dedicated their lives since September 11, 2001, in pursuit
of a better life for all Americans.*

Contents In Brief

Contents

UNIT 1 THE UNITED STATES AND THE WORLD: STRATEGIC CHOICES   1

Issue 1.   Is American Hegemony Good for the United States and the World?   2

YES: Michael Mandelbaum, from "David's Friend Goliath," *Foreign Policy* (January/February 2006)   *4*

NO: Jack Snyder, from "Imperial Temptations," *The National Interest* (Spring 2003)   *9*

Michael Mandelbaum, a professor of international relations at Johns Hopkins University, argues that most countries in the world benefit greatly from America's efforts to provide regional stability, limit proliferation of weapons of mass destruction, and maintain a free trading system. As a result, other countries are not responding to America's power by traditional power balancing. Jack Snyder, professor of international relations at Columbia University, argues that U.S. leaders have bought into the myths that entrapped imperial powers in the past, and that American unilateralism is creating nationalist backlashes against the United States, leading to a risk of imperial overstretch in which U.S. commitments would overburden American capabilities.

Issue 2.   Is the United States in Decline?   24

YES: Richard N. Haass, from "The Age of Nonpolarity: What Will Follow U.S. Dominance," *Foreign Affairs* (May/June 2008)   *26*

NO: Robert J. Lieber, from "Falling Upwards: Declinism, the Box Set," *World Affairs Journal* (Summer 2008)   *35*

Richard N. Haass, president of the Council on Foreign Relations, maintains that the world is entering a period of "nonpolarity" due to the relative decline of the United States and the dispersal of power to both other states and nonstate actors. No single rival can match U.S. power, but the general dispersal of power will make it more difficult for the United States to achieve international cooperation on security, environmental, and economic issues. Robert J. Lieber, professor of government at Georgetown University, points out that forecasts of American decline in the 1970s and 1980s proved to be inaccurate. The United States retains a preponderance of power and America's potential rivals face problems of their own that will prevent them from matching U.S. power.

Issue 3.   Should Promoting Democracy Abroad Be a Top U.S. Priority?   43

YES: Joseph Siegle, from "Developing Democracy: Democratizers' Surprisingly Bright Development Record," *Harvard International Review* (Summer 2004)   *45*

Joseph Siegle, Douglas Dillon Fellow at the Council on Foreign Relations, argues that large numbers of countries are continuing to democratize and, because of the increase in accountability associated with democratization, they tend to experience economic growth as fast as, if not faster than, other countries in the same region. Tamara Cofman Wittes, research fellow in the Saban Center for Middle East Policy at the Brookings Institution, argues that U.S. efforts to promote democracy in Iraq and the Arab Middle East are likely to fail unless the U.S. government matches its rhetoric with a credible commitment to promote policies institutionalizing the forward movement of liberalism in Iraq and the region at large.

Marc Lynch, associate professor of political science and international affairs at George Washington University, argues that the situation in Iraq remains fragile, but that the failure to withdraw U.S. troops on the schedule President Barack Obama proposed on the campaign trail would cause renewed instability in Iraq. Gen. David Petraeus, commander of U.S. Central Command and former commander of the Multi-National Force in Iraq, notes that the "surge" policy of increasing U.S. troops in Iraq and changing U.S. strategy and tactics has succeeded in greatly reducing violence in Iraq. This will allow reductions in the level of U.S. troops in Iraq, but further reductions must be contingent on whether Iraq remains stable.

Norman Podhoretz, editor-at-large for *Commentary* magazine, asserts that Iran is continuing to pursue the acquisition of nuclear weapons, that carrots and sticks brandished by the United States and others have failed to slow this effort, and that the United States will soon have no alternative but military force if it is to prevent Iran from attaining nuclear weapons. Scott D. Sagan, professor of political science and director of the Center for International Security and Cooperation at Stanford University, argues that other states have been dissuaded from acquiring or keeping nuclear weapons, and that Iran can be as well if the United States gives up the threat of changing the Iranian regime by force.

Barnett R. Rubin, director of studies and senior fellow at the Center on International Cooperation at New York University, and Ahmed Rashid, a Pakistani journalist and fellow at the Pacific Council on International Policy, propose that the U.S. should pursue negotiations with Taliban insurgents in Afghanistan and Pakistan to establish stability in the region. Joseph J. Collins, a retired army colonel who teaches at the National War College, asserts that many of the diverse groups fighting against the United States in Afghanistan are irrevocably opposed to U.S. goals and that the United States must achieve greater military successes in Afghanistan before pursuing any negotiations with the opposition so that it can bargain from a position of strength.

Nikolas Gvosdev, senior editor of *The National Interest* and adjunct senior fellow at the Nixon Center, suggests that Russia is unlikely to be integrated into the Euro-Atlantic community and cannot be coerced into acquiescing in U.S. policies. The United States must prioritize its core interests vis-à-vis Russia, particularly the need for cooperation on non-proliferation and counterterrorism and allow Russia greater flexibility in policy issues that are more important to Russia than to the United States. Stephen Sestanovich, professor of international diplomacy at Columbia University and senior fellow at the Council on Foreign Relations, rejects calls for a grand bargain with Russia, which in his view would not achieve greater Russian cooperation on Iran and other issues. Instead, the United States should pursue more modest and incremental steps to integrate Russia into a European security framework.

Aaron L. Friedberg is a professor of politics and international affairs at Princeton University and director of Princeton's Research Program in International Security. He served in the Office of the Vice President of the United States as deputy assistant for national security affairs and director of policy planning from 2003 to 2005. He argues that the United States should respond to China's rising strength and soft power with a strategy that includes intensified efforts to maintain a favorable balance of power by reinforcing existing alliances and institutions, building bilateral relations with major states in Asia, and maintaining forces sufficient to deter and if necessary, defeat China militarily. Christopher Layne is a professor at Texas A&M University's George H. W. Bush School of Government and Public Service. He argues that a U.S.–P.R.C. military conflict is certain if the United States tries to maintain its dominance in Asia, but that such a conflict can be avoided if the United States engages in offshore balancing, relying more on regional powers to counter China, and using force only in the face of direct threats to vital American interests.

David C. Kang, associate professor of government at Dartmouth College, contends that the threat posed by North Korea is overblown because North Korea will continue to be deterred from acting aggressively and, consequently, that engagement offers the best strategy promoting economic, political, and military change. Victor D. Cha, associate professor of government and D. S. Song-Korea Foundation Chair in Asian Studies in the School of Foreign Service at Georgetown University and Asian director in the National Security Council of the U.S. government, argues that North Korea remains hostile and opportunistic. Engagement—if used at all—should be highly conditional, and the United States and its allies should remain prepared to isolate and contain North Korea if engagement fails.

Steven A. Cook, senior fellow for Middle Eastern studies at the Council on Foreign Relations, and Shibley Telhami, professor of peace and development at the University of Maryland, assert that Hamas has genuine support from a sufficient number of Palestinians that it must be brought into a Palestinian unity government and included in the peace process, if it is not to be a spoiler in any negotiations. David Pollock, senior fellow at the Washington Institute for Near East Policy, recommends that the United States continue to isolate Hamas unless it first recognizes Israel, renounces violence, and promises to honor past Palestinian agreements with Israel.

nation that upholds its tradition of welcoming immigrants. Mark Krikorian, executive director of the Center for Immigration Studies and a visiting fellow at the Nixon Center, argues that immigration reforms promoting guest workers or amnesty are unrealistic and prone to fraud and paralysis.

Nathan E. Hultman, assistant professor at the University of Maryland, argues that historical patterns of change in the sources of our energy and the increasing efficiency with which we consume it suggest that we can enhance energy security and address climate change without major disruptions to our society. Strategies for doing this include expanding government-sponsored research and development, establishing clear and stable long-term carbon prices, and developing new technology standards. Philip J. Deutch, director of Evergreen Solar and general partner of NGP Energy Technology partners, a private equity firm investing in energy technology companies, argues that U.S. oil imports are so high that it would be impossible to end them in the next few decades, and that U.S. energy use is likely to continue to grow, as will oil prices, even if energy efficiency and conservation increase.

Charles Krauthammer, *Washington Post* opinion columnist, argues the lives saved by information provided by those with information about terrorist incidents justify the use of torture to obtain that information. Andrew Sullivan, senior editor of *The New Republic*, argues against claims of the military utility and necessity of torture.

Kenneth Roth, executive director of Human Rights Watch, argues that while humanitarian intervention is extremely costly in human terms, it can be justified in situations involving ongoing or imminent slaughter, but that it should only be considered when five limiting criteria are met. Alan Kuperman, resident assistant professor of international relations at Johns Hopkins University, argues that the benefits of humanitarian intervention are much smaller and the costs much greater than are generally acknowledged because violence is perpetrated faster than interveners can act to stop it and the likelihood of humanitarian intervention may actually make some local conflicts worse.

Correlation Guide

The *Taking Sides* series presents current issues in a debate-style format designed to stimulate student interest and develop critical thinking skills. Each issue is thoughtfully framed with an issue summary, an issue introduction, and a postscript. The pro and con essays—selected for their liveliness and substance—represent the arguments of leading scholars and commentators in their fields.

Taking Sides: Clashing Views in American Foreign Policy, 5/e is an easy-to-use reader that presents issues on important topics such as *strategic choices, security issues, regional and bilateral relations,* and *economic and environmental issues.* For more information on *Taking Sides* and other *McGraw-Hill Contemporary Learning Series* titles, visit http://www.mhcls.com.

This convenient guide matches the issues in **Taking Sides: American Foreign Policy, 5/e** with the corresponding chapters in two of our best-selling McGraw-Hill Political Science textbooks by Rourke/Boyer and Rourke.

Taking Sides: American Foreign Policy, 5/e	International Politics on the World Stage, Brief, 8/e by Rourke/Boyer	International Politics on the World Stage, 12e by Rourke
Issue 1: Is American Hegemony Good for the United States and the World?	**Chapter 1:** Thinking and Caring About World Politics **Chapter 2:** The Evolution of World Politics	**Chapter 2:** The Evolution of World Politics
Issue 2: Is the United States in Decline?		
Issue 3: Should Promoting Democracy Abroad Be a Top U.S. Priority?	**Chapter 6:** Power, Statecraft, and the National State: The Traditional Structure **Chapter 11:** International Economics: The Alternative Road	**Chapter 13:** International Economic Cooperation: The Alternative Road
Issue 4: Should the United States Withdraw from Iraq Expeditiously?	**Chapter 2:** The Evolution of World Politics **Chapter 9:** Pursuing Security	**Chapter 2:** The Evolution of World Politics **Chapter 10:** National Security: The Traditional Road
Issue 5: Should the United States Preemptively Attack Iran's Emerging Nuclear Weapons Capability?	**Chapter 9:** Pursuing Security **Chapter 10:** National Economic Competition: The Traditional Road	**Chapter 10:** National Security: The Traditional Road **Chapter 11:** International Security: The Alternative Road **Chapter 12:** National Economic Competition: The Traditional Road
Issue 6: Should the United States Negotiate with the Taliban?	**Chapter 6:** Power, Statecraft, and the National State: The Traditional Structure	**Chapter 8:** National Power and Statecraft: The Traditional Approach

Taking Sides: American Foreign Policy, 5/e	International Politics on the World Stage, Brief, 8/e by Rourke/Boyer	International Politics on the World Stage, 12e by Rourke
Issue 7: Should the United States Allow Russia More Leeway in Eurasia in Exchange for Russian Help in Stopping Iran's Nuclear Program?	**Chapter 6:** Power, Statecraft, and the National State: The Traditional Structure	**Chapter 8:** National Power and Statecraft: The Traditional Approach
Issue 8: Should the United States Challenge a Rising China?	**Chapter 2:** The Evolution of World Politics **Chapter 3:** Levels of Analysis and Foreign Policy **Chapter 8:** International Law and Human Rights	**Chapter 2:** The Evolution of World Politics **Chapter 3:** Levels of Analysis and Foreign Policy **Chapter 9:** International Law and Justice: An Alternative Approach
Issue 9: Should the United States Seek Negotiations and Engagement with North Korea?	**Chapter 6:** Power, Statecraft, and the National State: The Traditional Structure	**Chapter 8:** National Power and Statecraft: The Traditional Approach
Issue 10: Should the United States Engage Hamas?	**Chapter 4:** Nationalism: The Traditional Orientation **Chapter 8:** International Law and Human Rights	**Chapter 4:** Nationalism: The Traditional Orientation **Chapter 9:** International Law and Justice: An Alternative Approach
Issue 11: Should the United States Contribute to a NATO Peacekeeping Force to Encourage and Guarantee an Israeli-Palestinian Peace?	**Chapter 3:** Levels of Analysis and Foreign Policy	**Chapter 3:** Levels of Analysis and Foreign Policy
Issue 12: Should the United States Continue Sanctions in Cuba?	**Chapter 6:** Power, Statecraft, and the National State: The Traditional Structure **Chapter 8:** International Law and Human Rights	**Chapter 8:** National Power and Statecraft: The Traditional Approach **Chapter 9:** International Law and Justice: An Alternative Approach
Issue 13: Is Loosening Immigration Regulations Good for the United States?	**Chapter 4:** Nationalism: The Traditional Orientation	**Chapter 4:** Nationalism: The Traditional Orientation
Issue 14: Are Free Trade and Economic Liberalism Good for the United States?	**Chapter 10:** National Economic Competition: The Traditional Road	**Chapter 12:** National Economic Competition: The Traditional Road
Issue 15: Is Fighting Climate Change Worth the Cost?	**Chapter 2:** The Evolution of World Politics **Chapter 12:** Preserving and Enhancing the Biosphere	**Chapter 2:** The Evolution of World Politics **Chapter 15:** Preserving and Enhancing the Biosphere
Issue 16: Is It Realistic for the United States to Move Toward Greater Energy Independence?	**Chapter 2:** The Evolution of World Politics **Chapter 12:** Preserving and Enhancing the Biosphere	**Chapter 2:** The Evolution of World Politics **Chapter 15:** Preserving and Enhancing the Biosphere
Issue 17: Is It Justifiable to Put Suspected Terrorists under Great Physical Duress?	**Chapter 8:** International Law and Human Rights	**Chapter 9:** International Law and Justice: An Alternative Approach **Chapter 14:** Preserving and Enhancing Human Rights and Dignity
Issue 18: Can Humanitarian Intervention Be Justified?	**Chapter 9:** Pursuing Security	**Chapter 11:** International Security: The Alternative Road

Introduction

J ust as economics generally involves competition over scarce resources, pol-icymaking often involves competition over scarce values. Foreign policy deci-sions, in particular, are prone to debate because they affect multiple groups in the domestic and global arenas who often hold different values or have differ-ent sets of priorities. In the context of wars and crises, like the attacks on the World Trade Towers in New York and the Pentagon on September 11, 2001, or the attack on Pearl Harbor in 1942, the country tends to unify around the president and will give him or her extraordinary powers to shape the U.S. policy response. In the immediate aftermath of such events, U.S. national security is given precedence over other concerns. However, the rally-around-the-flag effect does not last long. Within months of these events, other values—like the maintenance of civil liberties, the humane treatment of prisoners, the promotion of democracy abroad, the maintenance of good relations with allies, and concerns about the costs of conducting expansive foreign policy initiatives—begin to reassert themselves. Most people agree that maintaining national security, preserving liberty, achieving a healthy economy, and foster-ing a clean and sustainable environment all matter all of the time. They are likely, however, to disagree about which issue takes precedence when policies designed to promote one goal potentially undermine the others.

How much security, liberty, environmental sustainability, or national wealth is enough? What takes precedence when strategies to enhance national security begin to undercut civil liberties at home or human rights abroad? What should we do when our desire to promote democracy abroad conflicts with the strategic or economic imperatives of maintaining good relations with authoritarian regimes? What economic price are we willing to pay to achieve a cleaner or more sustainable environment, or a higher degree of energy inde-pendence or security? As always, there are compelling arguments for opposing answers to these questions.

In addition, even individuals or groups who share the same values can differ on what they think are the best strategies and tactics for attaining those values. When are diplomacy, foreign aid, trade, economic sanctions, or cul-tural exchanges called for, and when is force necessary? Under what condi-tions can the United States build and use international organizations and alliances, and when must it act unilaterally? Will raising the threat of a preemp-tive attack convince a potential adversary to stop working to obtain weapons of mass destruction, or will it only spur the country in question to accelerate its programs in the hope of acquiring weapons so deadly that the United States will be deterred from acting? There is no easy or universal answer to such ques-tions regarding the widely shared goals of peace and prosperity.

Understanding all sides of an issue is one of the best ways to make a good decision. The contributors in this volume believe passionately in the views they put forth. They present cogent arguments that, when read in the absence of the competing point of view, are often very persuasive. Indeed, it is often easy to be seduced by the persuasiveness of a well-articulated argument and the use of a few illustrative examples—even if the argument is made in a 30-second election campaign commercial! To be an informed consumer, it is important to recognize and understand the viewpoints of those who are most likely to criticize the viewpoint you find most compelling. You might believe that their views are wrong, but do not dismiss them out of hand. You can become an informed consumer only by seeing various sides of an issue. Once you can see multiple sides to an issue, you will no longer be seduced by a flashy presentation. You may, however, be persuaded by a good one.

If, after seeing the issue from multiple perspectives, you still favor the argument that grabbed you in the beginning, so much the better. Now you can make your case stronger by anticipating and responding to those who would most likely challenge you. This will make your position stronger and your foreign policy choices more resilient. The Chinese strategist Sun Tzu once argued that to be successful you must know your enemy. By knowing your critics' arguments, you will better know yourself and be better able to defend your foreign policy position. Beyond the sheer fun of arguing, these are true benefits of a debate.

The debate format is intended to make you think, but it is not intended to neutralize your convictions. In fact, once you are informed, you *ought* to form convictions, and you should try to act on those convictions and to influence international policy to conform better with your beliefs. Ponder the similarities in the views of two very different leaders, a very young president in a relatively young democracy and a very old emperor in a very old country: In 1963, President John F. Kennedy, in recalling the words of the author of the epic poem *The Divine Comedy* (1321), told a West German audience, "Dante once said that the hottest places in hell are reserved for those who in a period of moral crisis maintain their neutrality." The very same year, while speaking to the United Nations, Ethiopia's emperor Haile Selassie (1892–1975) said, "Throughout history it has been the inaction of those who could have acted, the indifference of those who should have known better, the silence of the voice of justice when it mattered most, that has made it possible for evil to triumph."

The point is: Become informed. Then *do* something! Promoting democracy and civil liberties abroad have become centerpieces in U.S. foreign policy. For democracy to have meaning, informed individuals within democracies must act. Write letters to policymakers, donate money to causes you support, work for candidates with whom you agree, join an activist organization, or do any of the many other things that you can to make a difference. What you do is less important than that you do it.

Theories and Assumptions Behind American Foreign Policy

As will become evident as you read this volume, there are a number of ways to study American foreign policy. This reader is organized in terms of substantive topics, but it is important to remember that the competing views on these topics are informed by the theories and assumptions that each of the authors holds about how the world works. People in general tend to keep their theories and assumptions implicit until they are asked to justify why they think or feel the way they do about a particular issue. Academics are trained to be more explicit about the assumptions they make and the theories they use; yet they, too, often make judgments without acknowledging the foundations on which their judgments are made.

The United States faces an evolving set of relatively new challenges abroad, including ongoing conflicts in Afghanistan and Iraq, the possibility that Iran might acquire a nuclear weapon, complex relations with Russia and China that involve elements of cooperation and competition, and the global economic crisis. The advent of a new administration under President Obama provides an opportunity for fresh theoretical analysis of these challenges and innovative policies for addressing them. At the same time, the issues involved in this volume—the nature of sovereignty versus global governance, the costs and benefits of unilateralism versus those of multilateralism, the role of international norms and international law, the management of relations with allies and adversaries, the interaction of global forces and domestic politics in foreign policy, and tensions between security, economic, and environmental issues in the global arena—are all enduring. While the specific states, institutions, and individuals at the center of U.S. foreign policy may change, these issues will remain central. Thus, while they, too, may need to be tweaked to account for new players on the world scene, the basic concepts and theories that we use to explain and understand these issues remain pertinent as well.

American scholars who study international relations generally categorize the field into three theoretical approaches or schools of thought. The first is the "realist" school, which argues that states are the key actors in world politics and that they continually seek to increase their power as a means of ensuring their security and enhancing their prosperity. Realists also maintain that states balance against, or work to constrain, the other states that they find most powerful and threatening. In the process of seeking power and balancing against threats, military capabilities are the ultimate arbiter of which state will prevail at the negotiating table or on the battlefield. Realists believe that international institutions such as the United Nations do not truly constrain powerful states, because these institutions are created by the most powerful states to serve these states' interests, and these states will choose to ignore the institutions they create whenever they feel like it. Also, for realists, the domestic political structure of a state (democratic, authoritarian, communist, and so on) matters far less in determining its foreign policies than the level of military power the state has and the geographic threats and opportunities it faces. In terms of the history of American foreign policy, realism is most closely associated with President Nixon and his secretary of state, Henry Kissinger, while prominent scholars who are realists include Hans Morgenthau, Kenneth Waltz, Stephen Walt, and John Mearsheimer.

The "liberal" school of thought, which should not be confused with the term "liberal" in American politics despite some similarities, disagrees with the realists on several points. Liberals also see states as key actors focused on their own self-interests, but they believe states can use institutions to better serve those interests. In this view, states create international institutions, including formal organizations like the United Nations and the World Trade Organization and agreements like arms-control treaties, to help make international relations more transparent and provide mechanisms for sharing burdens to provide collective or public goods that benefit all states, such as a free trading system. Institutions, in other words, lower the "transactions costs" for states to cooperate on issues where they share goals by making it easier to identify which states have followed agreed-upon rules and which have not, and to punish the latter and reward the former. Liberals also believe that domestic politics greatly influence the foreign policies of states, and that democracies seldom if ever go to war against other democracies. In American foreign policy, Presidents Wilson and Carter are most clearly identified with the liberal approach. To the extent that they sought to maintain the U.S. role in existing multilateral military and economic institutions as a means of addressing U.S. foreign policy concerns, Presidents George H. W. Bush and Bill Clinton fit in this category as well. Scholars who are associated with this approach include Immanuel Kant, Adam Smith, Michael Doyle, Robert Keohane, and G. John Ikenberry.

A third group, "constructivists," differs from both realists and liberals. Constructivists agree that states, for now, are key actors in world politics, but they emphasize that this was not always so and may not remain so. Constructivists are more attentive than liberals or realists to the roles of actors other than states, ranging from international corporations, to transnational human rights movements, to terrorist cells. For constructivists, both the actors in world politics and the principles (like sovereignty) that define them are *socially constructed;* that is, they are the result of social actors' behavior, not immutable entities created by the natural world. Such social structures, including formal and informal international institutions, rules, and patterns of behavior, are created and shaped by the interactions of various actors in world politics but, once created, these institutions also affect their behavior. International institutions in this view have not only intended consequences, which liberals emphasize, but also unintended consequences unforseen by their creators. Such institutions take on a life of their own and do not merely act on the orders of or in the interests of powerful states. Constructivists maintain that social structures, including both states and international institutions, are ideational as well as material. The military, economic, and political capabilities of states affect how other states view them, but so do the ideas, cultures, and values that they hold and that others hold about them. Among U.S. presidents, Theodore Roosevelt and Ronald Reagan best demonstrated an awareness of the importance of shaping ideas, images, and identities of the United States and others in the ways they exercised and promoted U.S. foreign policy in the domestic and global arenas. For example, President Reagan's success in identifying the Soviet Union as the "Evil Empire" was a key component in his foreign policy strategy, but once the reformist Soviet leader Mikhail Gorbachev began to show some success in changing the Soviet Union's identity and its way of government, Reagan moved to improve relations with the Soviet Union much more quickly than the realists in his administration. Scholars who are constructivists include Alexander Wendt and John Ruggie.

Table 1

	Realism	Liberalism	Constructivism
Intellectual Founders	Hans Morgenthau Kenneth Waltz	Adam Smith Immanuel Kant	Alexander Wendt John Ruggie
Academic Scholars	John Mearsheimer Randall Schweller Stephen Walt	Michael Doyle Robert Keohane G. John Ikenberry	Kathryn Sikkink Michael Barnet Martha Finnemore
Foreign Policy Personnel	Richard Nixon Henry Kissinger Colin Powell Condoleezza Rice	Woodrow Wilson Jimmy Carter George H. W. Bush Bill Clinton	Franklin Roosevelt Ronald Reagan

This table is adapted from Jack Snyder, "One World, Rival Theories," *Foreign Policy* (November/December 2004), p. 54.

These dominant approaches are summarized in Table 1. Each of these three approaches has something important to say about the post-9/11 world. Realism helps us understand why the United States has reacted so strongly to perceived threats, why it has largely acted with and through other states to address the problem of terrorism, and why, as the most powerful actor, it felt that it must and could intervene in Iraq even without a UN resolution specifically authorizing the use of force. Liberalism helps illuminate why even though the United States bypassed the UN on the question of a resolution authorizing force in Iraq, it still found the UN useful in setting up and monitoring elections in Iraq. Constructivism helps us understand the cultures and values that motivate not just terrorist groups but the many individuals around the world who do not themselves espouse terrorism but do express deep discontent in opinion polls about America's foreign policies.

Yet these three theoretical approaches only partially and imperfectly capture the schools of thought among the American public and American leaders on foreign policy. Four key questions have been the subject of continual debate through the history of American foreign policy: Should the United States take an active role in world affairs (internationalism), or can and should it confine its actions mostly to domestic matters (isolationism)? When it takes action abroad, should the United States work with and through international organizations and alliances (multilateralism), or should it work mostly through its own devices and avoid becoming entangled in the constraints inherent in working with others (unilateralism)? Should the United States rely heavily on strong military capabilities and the threat and use of force to achieve its ends, or should it emphasize diplomatic, economic, and political instruments? Finally, what relative emphasis should the United States place on preserving its immediate security, fostering democracies abroad, and advancing U.S. economic and environmental goals and the prosperity of U.S. businesses and citizens?

Some combinations of answers to these questions overlap fairly closely with the theoretical approaches outlined above. Foreign policy realists like Henry Kissinger are internationalist, multilateralist in terms of alliances but less so in terms of international organizations, willing to threaten and use force, and focused on security issues. Liberals like President Wilson are internationalist, multilateralist in terms of both institutions and alliances, reluctant to use force but willing to do so to defend the United States and democratic principles, and focused on building democracies abroad as a means of promoting American security as well as American values and economic interests.

Three important schools of thought in American foreign policy do not fall so easily within the three theoretical approaches above, however: Hamiltonians, Jacksonians, and neoconservatives.[1] Hamiltonians, who include to some degree George H. W. Bush, are internationalist and willing to use force for U.S. security and to protect U.S. businesses but less willing to do so to promote democracy abroad, and focused on the economic dimension of U.S. foreign policy. Jacksonians, like President Andrew Jackson, would prefer to focus on domestic matters and are skeptical of international institutions, but when provoked by threats to U.S. security, are highly motivated to use force decisively and victoriously; the Jacksonians' motto is "Don't tread on me."

Finally, neoconservatives are internationalist, deeply skeptical of international institutions and alliances and willing to act unilaterally, and are very focused on building democracies abroad and ready to use force for this purpose as well as for addressing direct threats to American security. This group agrees with the Wilsonians that it matters a great deal whether other states become democracies, and criticizes realists for ignoring this, but it disagrees with the Wilsonians' emphasis on international institutions and alliances and their hesitance to use force to help fledgling or endangered democracies. This neoconservative school of thought has received considerable attention recently because some have characterized President George W. Bush's foreign policies as being neoconservative. Former Bush administration Deputy Secretary of Defense Paul Wolfowitz, for example, is widely considered to be a leading neoconservative. Other Bush administration officials, however, have been more realist in their writings and public statements, including first-term Secretary of State Colin Powell and second-term Secretary of Defense Robert Gates, whom President Obama kept on as his own secretary of defense. President George W. Bush himself espoused realist policies prior to 9/11/2001, but soon thereafter also pursued more liberal policies including ambitious commitments to building democracy in Afghanistan and Iraq.

President Obama's early months in office have exhibited a mix of realist, liberal, and constructivist inclinations. In addition to keeping Robert Gates as Secretary of Defense, he has shown a realist willingness to use force by increasing troop deployments in Afghanistan and continuing missile strikes on suspected Taliban and Al Qaeda targets in Pakistan. As liberal internationalists have urged, Obama has worked to strengthen international institutions in international finance and bolster alliance relationships in NATO. Consistent with constructivism, his first formal interview after taking office was with Al Arabiya, a

---

[1]The description of Hamiltonians and Jacksonians here is borrowed from Walter Russell Mead, *Special Providence: American Foreign Policy and How It Changed the World* (Routledge, 2002).

news organization based in Dubai, where he reached out to the Muslim world. He has also sought to reach out to the people around the world directly through "town hall meetings" during official visits abroad. President Obama's other top foreign policy appointees, including Secretary of State Hillary Clinton and National Security Advisor Gen. James Jones, are also hard to place in any one school of thought based on their policy pronouncements early in Obama's time in office; Secretary Clinton voted as a Senator to authorize the use of force against Iraq but also spoke out strongly on human rights issues in her time as First Lady, while Gen. Jones served in the military for most of his career but also spent time working on energy issues after retiring from the military. In any event, care must be taken in applying any such labels to individuals, as most of us have elements of all these approaches in our thinking. We provide these outlines of various schools of thought to provide a framework for thinking about and discussing foreign policy rather than a straightjacket to place on others or yourself.

Globalization, Domestic Politics, and Foreign Policy

In a vivid and dramatic stroke, the terrorist attacks of 9/11 shattered the illusion of American invulnerability to world events. Neither America's great economic or military resources nor the geographic benefits of being surrounded by large oceans and friendly countries could protect its citizens from the threats posed by nefarious individuals seeking to do them harm. In response to this new global threat, the United States altered policies by promoting preemption and invading Iraq (Issue 4).

Ironically, what these attacks demonstrated in the security arena has long been acknowledged in other areas: that U.S. foreign must anticipate, respond, and adapt to the actors and phenomena operating in a global context. In economic terms, the United States is more reliant upon trade and international financing than ever before (Issue 14). In health terms, the globalization of human and animal movements has increased the spread of new diseases—like AIDS, bird flu, and mad cow disease—and the resurgence of older diseases—like tuberculosis, malaria, and polio—which, though once eradicated, are again sickening many people in U.S. inner cities. In environmental terms, the activities of foreign actors have increasingly devastating effects on our land, people, and economy—through, for example, the depletion of commercial fish stocks by fishing trawlers operating in international waters or the degradation of our buildings, crops, and trees by acid rain produced by powerplants' emissions in other countries (Issue 15). In political terms, the inability of the United States to garner large-scale logistic, financial, and military support for its invasion of Iraq suggests that gaining support for its foreign policy initiatives—even from its allies—requires consideration of their concerns.

As Peter Gourevitch argued in a seminal work in 1978 ("Second Image Reversed: International Sources of Domestic Policy," *International Organization*, Fall 1998), global actors and phenomena also influence the evolution of domestic institutions. For example, the creation of the Department of Homeland

Figure 1

Global Actors and Phenomena ←→ U.S. Foreign Policy and Institutions ←→ Domestic Actors and Politics

Security and the dramatic reorganization and centralization of U.S. intelligence services are both a direct response to the terrorist attacks of 9/11/2001. Less obvious, but perhaps even more profound, the attacks led Congress to adopt the Patriot Act and modify other policies that have broad implications for civil and political liberties and social policy in the United States (Issue 17). As was true following attacks on U.S. soil like the Japanese attack on Pearl Harbor in 1942 and the British invasion of Washington in 1812, Congress has also modified policies in other areas—like immigration and the treatment of prisoners—which have widespread domestic as well as international implications (Issue 13).

The reverse is also true—domestic politics often drive U.S. foreign policy with important consequences in the global arena. Matthew Evangelista ("Institution and Change," in Michael Doyle and G. John Ikenberry, eds., _New Thinking in International Relations Theory,_ Westview Press, 1997) provides a useful review of this perspective on foreign policy. For example, domestic political pressure is driving part of the debate over the U.S. response to the Kyoto treaty (Issue 15) and the treatment of suspected terrorists under interrogation (Issue 17). It also drives much of U.S. policy toward the democratic Republic of China in Taiwan in ways that may run counter to U.S. strategic objectives regarding the People's Republic of China (Issue 8).

Furthermore, global actors and phenomena increasingly exert direct effects on domestic actors who, in turn, demand a compensatory response from their local and national governments. For example, the fear of job loss due to an increase in offshore outsourcing has led several labor groups to lobby the U.S. government to curb outsourcing. In anticipation of a policy backlash, the Indian government and Indian companies are engaging in a variety of strategies to highlight the benefits of outsourcing and calm the fears of those who may be hurt by it (Issue 14).

Thus, as represented in Figure 1, U.S. foreign policy decisions and the institutions in which those decisions are buffeted by competing pressures from global actors and phenomena are on one hand, and domestic actors and domestic politics are on the other. Furthermore, domestic and global actors may influence each other directly and try to shape U.S. foreign policy and policymaking institutions accordingly.

Substantive Issues in U.S. Foreign Policy

Unit 1 (Issues 1–3) focuses on key aspects of the multifaceted question of what the overall role of the United States should be in the world. Michael Mandelbaum makes the case that active U.S. leadership in the world helps solve many collective action problems and bolsters peace, stability, and free trade, benefiting both America and its allies. Jack Snyder, in contrast, worries that American unilateralism is creating nationalist reactions against the United States around the world and leading to excessive American commitments around the world.

A second question concerns whether the United States is in a period of decline relative to other states and relative to a period of almost unprecedented preeminence in the period between the end of the Cold War and the 2001 attacks. Richard Haass argues that the United States must adjust its global strategy for a period of diminished and diluted American power, while Robert Lieber argues that the United States still retains far more power than any potential rival and is likely to continue to do so in the foreseeable future.

A third issue, promoting democratization abroad, has become a prominent long-term strategy for achieving Americas values and protecting its security. Yet democracy is not easy to achieve, especially from the outside. Joseph Siegle offers an optimistic assessment of democratization, whereas Tamara Wittes warns that democratization is not likely to be effective without enhanced and sustained American involvement.

Unit 2 addresses two key security issues. First, on the issue of whether the United States should withdraw its forces from Iraq on a rapid timetable (Issue 4), Marc Lynch argues that developments in Iraq have established sufficient stability to allow such a withdrawal, while Gen. David Petraeus maintains that despite a sharp drop in violence and increase in stability, the situation in Iraq remains tenuous and any U.S. withdrawals have to be conditioned on continuing progress in Iraq. Second, on the challenges posed by Iran's nuclear weapons program (Issue 5), Norman Podhoretz asserts that the United States will soon have no alternative to using force as a means of stopping Iran's program. Scott Sagan, in contrast, argues that multilateral diplomacy may still succeed in convincing Iran to end its pursuit of nuclear weapons.

Unit 3 deals with a wide range of regional and bilateral issues. Issue 6 addresses the question of whether the United States should negotiate with the Taliban rebels who have fought against U.S. forces and the Afghan government since the U.S. removed them from power in 2001. Barnett Rubin and Ahmed Rashid suggest that the United States should negotiate with the less radical members of the Taliban to get them to stop their attacks, while Joseph Collins rejects this approach until and unless the United States can negotiate from a position of strength.

Issue 7 takes on the increasingly difficult relationship between the United States and Russia, with Nikolas Gvosdev arguing that the United States must allow Russia more influence in its immediate region if it hopes to gain greater Russian cooperation on dealing with Iran and terrorism, but Stephen Sestanovich counters that this kind of bargain is neither necessary for achieving American goals nor assured of success in doing so.

Issue 8 concerns what policies the United States should adopt toward China as that country becomes an increasingly powerful regional and even global actor. Aaron Friedberg argues that the United States should reinforce existing alliances and maintain sufficient military forces to deter and, if necessary, defeat China. Christopher Layne warns that military conflict is likely if the United States tries to maintain its dominance in Asia, and that the United

States should instead rely more on regional powers to balance against China and threaten or use force only in defense of vital American interests.

Issue 9 addresses North Korea's nuclear weapons program, which has successfully tested nuclear bombs. David Kang argues that diplomatic engagement with North Korea can be effective in changing its behavior, while Victor Cha insists that the United States must be willing to use sticks as well as carrots to isolate and contain North Korea if its behavior does not change.

Issue 10 takes on the question of whether the United States should engage Hamas, the Palestinian movement that has taken control of the Gaza territory. In the view of Steve Cook and Shibley Telhami, Hamas has sufficient support from Palestinians in Gaza and beyond that it must be included in any peace process if that process is to succeed. David Pollock, on the other hand, recommends that the United States continue to isolate Hamas unless it first recognizes Israel, renounces violence, and promises to honor past Palestinian agreements with Israel. Issue 11 focuses on the related question of whether the United States should be ready to contribute to a peacekeeping force to foster peace between Israel and the Palestinians. Gen. Montgomery C. Meigs warns that any peacekeeping force interposed between Israel and the Palestinians would face difficult requirements and would have to be prepared for attacks by extremist groups. Daniel Klaidman, Christopher Dickey, Dan Ephron, and Michael Hirsh give the contrasting view that NATO, and the United States as a member of NATO, should provide such a force as a necessary part of an overall settlement between Israel and the Palestinians.

Issue 12 concerns U.S. policies toward Cuba. On this front, Otto Reich calls for continuing the existing diplomatic and trade embargoes against Cuba, while a Brookings Institution study headed up by Ernesto Zedillo and Thomas Pickering proposes selectively lifting elements of these embargoes and establishing diplomatic contacts with Cuba.

In Issue 13, former President George W. Bush suggests that the United States can enforce its laws on immigration more rigorously while still upholding America's traditional openness to legal immigrants. Mark Krikorian, in contrast, argues that immigration reforms that offer guest worker programs and amnesty for illegal immigrants are unrealistic and counterproductive.

Unit 4 addresses international economic and environmental concerns. Issue 14 turns to the question of whether free trade or government intervention in the economy is good for the United States. Matthew Slaughter argues that government intervention in the economy will increase the likelihood of trade protectionism in other countries and push down the value of the dollar. Andrew Liveris asserts that sustaining a strong manufacturing base is only possible through a targeted industrial policy that supports key industries.

Issue 15 raises the question of whether steps to address global climate change are worth the costs they would entail. Bill McKidden argues that the science on global warming is clear, that a climate catastrophe is underway, and that the costs of failing to make significant changes to address this crisis will be large and widespread. On the other side of this issue, Jim Manzi asserts that markets can adjust to deal with global warming without requiring a major role for governmental policies. Issue 16 addresses the related issue of whether the

United States can realistically move toward greater energy independence. Nathan Hultman argues that it is indeed possible for the United States to substantially reduce its reliance on oil imports through increased energy efficiency, new technologies, and diversified energy supplies. Philip Deutch is more pessimistic, maintaining that America's dependence on oil imports is so high that it cannot be substantially reduced through conservation or other measures in the next few decades.

Unit 5 addresses U.S. policies that bear upon international norms and institutions. In Issue 17, Charles Krauthammer insists that suspected terrorists are not entitled to the protections afforded to enemy combatants under the laws of war, and that information obtained from suspected terrorists through physical duress can save lives and is therefore justified. Andrew Sullivan disagrees, arguing that torture is neither necessary nor useful in gaining information from captives, and that the use of torture is antithetical to American values and undermines respect for the United States around the world.

Finally, in Issue 18 Kenneth Roth argues that humanitarian intervention is justified in some circumstances, particularly when other approaches have failed. Alan Kuperman, in contrast, maintains that humanitarian intervention is often ineffective or even counterproductive, aggravating rather than resolving local conflicts.

All of the debates outlined above are critical because, regardless of which side of the argument you find more convincing, the norms and expectations of international behavior are changing as a result of U.S. policies. Although the United States cannot by itself define what the new norms will be, its actions as arguably the most powerful state in the contemporary world will clearly shape their evolution, with important implications for the prospects for achieving American values in the foreseeable future.

Internet References . . .

U.S. Department of State Web Site

The U.S. Department of State Web site reflects the department's view that the United States should be internationalist, should seek to play a very strong role in a wide range of international issues, and should usually take a multilateral approach and seek to work with other countries.

http://www.state.gov/

The WWW Virtual Library: International Affairs Resources

To understand U.S. foreign policy, it is important to also be able to explore the world beyond the territorial boundaries of the United States. The WWW Virtual Library is a fine resource to help that exploration. The site has over 1,750 annotated links on a range of international affairs topics.

http://www.etown.edu/vl

Foreign Policy in Focus

This site is a joint project of the Interhemispheric Resource Center and the Institute for Policy Studies and generally takes a liberal point of view. It is subdivided by topic.

http://www.fpif.org

Home Page of the Heritage Foundation

To contrast the foreign policy slant of the Foreign Policy in Focus Web site, you can turn to the conservative views of the Heritage Foundation.

http://www.heritage.org

The Council on Foreign Relations

This site provides an independent and nonpartisan source of research and analysis on the world and the foreign policy choices facing the United States and other governments.

http://www.cfr.org

House Committee on International Relations and Senate Foreign Relations Committee

The House Committee on International Relations and the Senate Foreign Relations Committee are the primary bodies in which Congress debates and provides its input into U.S. foreign policy.

http://www.house.gov/international_relations

http://foreign.senate.gov/

The United States and the World: Strategic Choices

*T*he issues in this section all relate to the multidimensional question of what the role of the United States should be in the world. At its most fundamental, the issue is a debate between internationalists and isolationists over whether or not the United States should be strongly involved in world affairs. Given that the United States is involved, another question that must be addressed involves whether the United States should attempt to play a leading, or perhaps the leading, role on the world stage or whether it should be content to be just one among many actors. Whatever role the nation chooses to play, yet another matter that must be resolved is whether the United States should generally act unilaterally to promote its goals and ideals or whether it should modify its actions to work with others in the international community.

- Is American Hegemony Good for the United States and the World?

- Is the United States in Decline?

- Should Promoting Democracy Abroad Be a Top U.S. Priority?

ISSUE 1

Is American Hegemony Good for the United States and the World?

YES: Michael Mandelbaum, from "David's Friend Goliath," *Foreign Policy* (January/February 2006)

NO: Jack Snyder, from "Imperial Temptations," *The National Interest* (Spring 2003)

ISSUE SUMMARY

YES: Michael Mandelbaum, a professor of international relations at Johns Hopkins University, argues that most countries in the world benefit greatly from America's efforts to provide regional stability, limit proliferation of weapons of mass destruction, and maintain a free trading system. As a result, other countries are not responding to America's power by traditional power balancing.

NO: Jack Snyder, professor of international relations at Columbia University, argues that U.S. leaders have bought into the myths that entrapped imperial powers in the past, and that American unilateralism is creating nationalist backlashes against the United States, leading to a risk of imperial overstretch in which U.S. commitments would overburden American capabilities.

T he Bush administration's policies after 9/11, and most notably the U.S. intervention in Iraq, stimulated discussions in the United States and abroad on whether the United States has become an "empire," or perhaps more accurately a "hegemon," and if so, whether this is desirable. Few argue that the United States has become an empire in the traditional sense of a central power occupying many other lands and providing order and security but exacting tribute and suppressing political opposition. While some argue that the United States has become a new kind of "informal empire," it is probably more instructive to ask whether the United States is a hegemon, or an actor powerful enough to change the formal rules and informal practices of the international system all by itself.

There is no doubt that the United States, with the world's largest economy by a large margin and the only military force capable of projecting conventional forces or using nuclear weapons anywhere in the world, is the most powerful state in the international system. More controversial is whether the United States can, has, or should attempt to change the international "rules of the game" by itself. It remains to be seen how assertive the Obama administration will be in trying to change the formal and informal rules of the international system, and whether it proves to be more (as promised) or less cooperative in adapting to international regimes largely shaped by other states. Key issues to watch include U.S. policies toward the International Criminal Court (ICC), the Kyoto environmental policy process, the International Monetary Fund, the World Bank, the World Trade Organization, and the G-8 and G-20 groups of the world's leading economies.

There are sharply different views on whether it is beneficial to have a system in which one state is far more powerful than others, and how such a powerful state should conduct itself. Michael Mandelbaum expresses the most benign interpretation of American power, known as "hegemonic stability theory." In this view, international peace and free trade are "public goods," or goods that countries can benefit from whether or not they contribute to bringing them about. Because states can enjoy these goods whether or not they help provide them, there is a temptation to "free ride" and not assist in achieving these goods. This leads such public goods to be underprovided or scarce. A hegemon that is both willing and able to provide international public goods even when others ride free can solve this collective action problem.

A second view is that powerful democratic states like the United States find it in their interest to "self-bind," or tie themselves to international rules or institutions that actually reduce their freedom of action. The logic here is that in the absence of such self-imposed restraints, less powerful countries will challenge a powerful state because they fear that state will use its power in the future to exploit weaker states.

A third "preponderance of power" school maintains that the United States is so powerful that even a coalition of other great power states cannot effectively balance against the United States, and so they do not even try to do so. Scholars who make this argument, as Mandelbaum does, often add that because the United States is a democracy with no ambitions to permanently occupy other countries, other states have little incentive and limited capabilities to balance against the United States in the traditional military sense.

Arguing against these benign visions of America's exercise of power are those like Jack Snyder who argue that other states cannot and do not take such a complacent view of America's leading role in the world. Like many great powers in the past, Snyder argues, American leaders have convinced themselves of the "myths of empire" that have traditionally led to imperial overstretch, or a growing gap between commitments and capabilities. These include exaggerated fears of distant conflicts, excessive optimism about the effectiveness of preventive uses of force, and unrealistic expectations that adversaries will bandwagon with or bow down before America's power rather than balance against it. While most other countries are not building up their arms to balance against the United States as they did against great powers in the past, they are finding ways to constrain America's ability to act unilaterally.

YES ⤶

Michael Mandelbaum

David's Friend Goliath

Everybody talks about the weather, Mark Twain once observed, but nobody does anything about it. The same is true of America's role in the world. The United States is the subject of endless commentary, most of it negative, some of it poisonously hostile. Statements by foreign leaders, street demonstrations in national capitals, and much-publicized opinion polls all seem to bespeak a worldwide conviction that the United States misuses its enormous power in ways that threaten the stability of the international system. That is hardly surprising. No one loves Goliath. What is surprising is the world's failure to respond to the United States as it did to the Goliaths of the past.

Sovereign states as powerful as the United States, and as dangerous as its critics declare it to be, were historically subject to a check on their power. Other countries banded together to block them.

Revolutionary and Napoleonic France in the late 18th and early 19th century, Germany during the two world wars, and the Soviet Union during the Cold War all inspired countervailing coalitions that ultimately defeated them. Yet no such anti-American alignment has formed or shows any sign of forming today. Widespread complaints about the United States' international role are met with an absence of concrete, effective measures to challenge, change, or restrict it.

The gap between what the world says about American power and what it fails to do about it is the single most striking feature of 21st-century international relations. The explanation for this gap is twofold. First, the charges most frequently leveled at America are false. The United States does not endanger other countries, nor does it invariably act without regard to the interests and wishes of others. Second, far from menacing the rest of the world, the United States plays a uniquely positive global role. The governments of most other countries understand that, although they have powerful reasons not to say so explicitly.

Benign Hegemon

The charge that the United States threatens others is frequently linked to the use of the term "empire" to describe America's international presence. In contrast with empires of the past, however, the United States does not control, or aspire to control, directly or indirectly, the politics and economics of other

From Foreign Policy, *January/February 2006, pp. 51–56. Copyright © 2006 by the Carnegie Endowment for International Peace. Reprinted with permission. www.foreignpolicy.com*

4

societies. True, in the post-Cold War period, America has intervened militarily in a few places outside its borders, including Somalia, Haiti, Bosnia, Kosovo, Afghanistan, and Iraq. But these cases are exceptions that prove the rule.

These foreign ventures are few in number and, with the exception of Iraq, none has any economic value or strategic importance. In each case, American control of the country came as the byproduct of a military intervention undertaken for quite different reasons: to rescue distressed people in Somalia, to stop ethnic cleansing in Bosnia, to depose a dangerous tyrant in Iraq. Unlike the great empires of the past, the U.S. goal was to build stable, effective governments and then to leave as quickly as possible. Moreover, unlike past imperial practice, the U.S. government has sought to share control of its occupied countries with allies, not to monopolize them.

One policy innovation of the current Bush administration that gives other countries pause is the doctrine of preventive war. According to this doctrine, the United States reserves the right to attack a country not in response to an actual act of aggression, or because it is unmistakably on the verge of aggression, but rather in anticipation of an assault at some point in the future. The United States implemented the doctrine in 2003 with the invasion of Iraq.

Were it to become central to American foreign policy, the preventive war doctrine would provide a broad charter for military intervention. But that is not its destiny. The Bush administration presented the campaign in Iraq not as a way to ensure that Saddam Hussein did not have the opportunity to acquire nuclear weapons at some point in the future, but rather as a way of depriving him of the far less dangerous chemical weapons that he was believed already to possess.

More important, the countries that are now plausible targets for a preventive war—North Korea and Iran—differ from Iraq in ways that make such a campaign extremely unattractive. North Korea is more heavily armed than Iraq, and in a war could do serious damage to America's chief ally in the region, South Korea, even if North Korea lost. Iran has a larger population than Iraq, and it is less isolated internationally. The United States would have hesitated before attacking either one of these countries even if the Iraq operation had gone smoothly. Now, with the occupation of Iraq proving to be both costly (some $251 billion and counting) and frustrating, support for repeating the exercise elsewhere is hard to find.

America the Accessible

The war in Iraq is the most-often cited piece of evidence that America conducts itself in a recklessly unilateral fashion. Because of its enormous power, critics say, the policies that the United States applies beyond its borders are bound to affect others, yet when it comes to deciding these policies, non-Americans have no influence. However valid the charge of unilateralism in the case of Iraq may be (and other governments did in fact support the war), it does not hold true for U.S. foreign policy as a whole.

The reason is that the American political system is fragmented, which means there are multiple points of access to it. Other countries can exert influence on one of the House or Senate committees with jurisdiction over foreign policy. Or countries can deal with one or more of the federal departments that conduct the nation's relations with other countries. For that matter, American think tanks generate such a wide variety of proposals for U.S. policies toward every country that almost any approach is bound to have a champion somewhere.

Even Sudan, which the U.S. government has accused of genocide, recently signed a $530,000 contract with a Washington lobbyist to help improve its image. Non-Americans may not enjoy formal representation in the U.S. political system, but because of the openness of that system, they can and do achieve what representation brings—a voice in the making of American policy.

Because the opportunities to be heard and heeded are so plentiful, countries with opposing aims often simultaneously attempt to persuade the American government to favor their respective causes. That has sometimes led the United States to become a mediator for international conflict, between Arabs and Israelis, Indians and Pakistanis, and other sets of antagonists. That's a role that other countries value.

The World's Government

The United States makes other positive contributions, albeit often unseen and even unknown, to the well-being of people around the world. In fact, America performs for the community of sovereign states many, though not all, of the tasks that national governments carry out within them. For instance, U.S. military power helps to keep order in the world. The American military presence in Europe and East Asia, which now includes approximately 185,000 personnel, reassures the governments of these regions that their neighbors cannot threaten them, helping to allay suspicions, forestall arms races, and make the chances of armed conflict remote. U.S. forces in Europe, for instance, reassure Western Europeans that they do not have to increase their own troop strength to protect themselves against the possibility of a resurgent Russia, while at the same time reassuring Russia that its great adversary of the last century, Germany, will not adopt aggressive policies. Similarly, the U.S.-Japan Security Treaty, which protects Japan, simultaneously reassures Japan's neighbors that it will remain peaceful. This reassurance is vital yet invisible, and it is all but taken for granted.

The United States has also assumed responsibility for coping with the foremost threat to contemporary international security, the spread of nuclear weapons to "rogue" states and terrorist organizations. The U.S.-sponsored Cooperative Threat Reduction program is designed to secure nuclear materials and weapons in the former Soviet Union. A significant part of the technical and human assets of the American intelligence community is devoted to the surveillance of nuclear weapons-related activities around the world. Although other countries may not always agree with how the United States seeks to prevent proliferation, they all endorse the goal, and none of them makes as significant a contribution to achieving that goal as does the United States.

America's services to the world also extend to economic matters and international trade. In the international economy, much of the confidence needed to proceed with transactions, and the protection that engenders this confidence, comes from the policies of the United States. For example, the U.S. Navy patrols shipping lanes in both the Atlantic and Pacific oceans, assuring the safe passage of commerce along the world's great trade routes. The United States also supplies the world's most frequently used currency, the U.S. dollar. Though the euro might one day supplant the dollar as the world's most popular reserve currency, that day, if it ever comes, lies far in the future.

Furthermore, working through the International Monetary Fund (IMF), the United States also helps to carry out some of the duties that central banks perform within countries, including serving as a "lender of last resort." The driving force behind IMF bailouts of failing economies in Latin America and Asia in the last decade was the United States, which holds the largest share of votes within the IMF. And Americans' large appetite for consumer products partly reproduces on a global scale the service that the economist John Maynard Keynes assigned to national governments during times of economic slowdown: The United States is the world's "consumer of last resort."

Americans purchase Japanese cars, Chinese-made clothing, and South Korean electronics and appliances in greater volume than any other people. Just as national governments have the responsibility for delivering water and electricity within their jurisdictions, so the United States, through its military deployments and diplomacy, assures an adequate supply of the oil that allows industrial economies to run. It has established friendly political relations, and sometimes close military associations, with governments in most of the major oil-producing countries and has extended military protection to the largest of them, Saudi Arabia. Despite deep social, cultural, and political differences between the two countries, the United States and Saudi Arabia managed in the 20th century to establish a partnership that controlled the global market for this indispensable commodity. The economic well-being even of countries hostile to American foreign policy depends on the American role in assuring the free flow of oil throughout the world.

To be sure, the United States did not deliberately set out to become the world's government. The services it provides originated during the Cold War as part of its struggle with the Soviet Union, and America has continued, adapted, and in some cases expanded them in the post-Cold War era. Nor do Americans think of their country as the world's government. Rather, it conducts, in their view, a series of policies designed to further American interests. In this respect they are correct, but these policies serve the interests of others as well. The alternative to the role the United States plays in the world is not better global governance, but less of it—and that would make the world a far more dangerous and less prosperous place. Never in human history has one country done so much for so many others, and received so little appreciation for its efforts.

Inevitable Ingratitude

Nor is the world likely to express much gratitude to the United States any time soon. Even if they privately value what the United States does for the world, other countries, especially democratic ones, will continue to express anti-American sentiments. That is neither surprising nor undesirable. Within democracies, spirited criticism of the government is normal, indeed vital for its effective performance. The practice is no different between and among democracies.

Anti-Americanism has many domestic political uses. In many parts of the world, the United States serves as a convenient scapegoat for governments, a kind of political lightning rod to draw away from themselves the popular discontent that their shortcomings have helped to produce. That is particularly the case in the Middle East, but not only there. Former German Chancellor Gerhard Schröder achieved an electoral victory in 2002 by denouncing the war in Iraq. Similarly, it is convenient, even comforting, to blame the United States for the inevitable dislocations caused by the great, impersonal forces of globalization.

But neither the failure to acknowledge America's global role nor the barrage of criticism of it means that the officials of other countries are entirely unaware of the advantages that it brings them. If a global plebiscite concerning America's role in the world were held by secret ballot, most foreign-policy officials in other countries would vote in favor of continuing it. Though the Chinese object to the U.S. military role as Taiwan's protector, they value the effect that American military deployments in East Asia have in preventing Japan from pursuing more robust military policies. But others will not declare their support for America's global role. Acknowledging it would risk raising the question of why those who take advantage of the services America provides do not pay more for them. It would risk, that is, other countries' capacities to continue as free riders, which is an arrangement no government will lightly abandon.

In the end, however, what other nations do or do not say about the United States will not be crucial to whether, or for how long, the United States continues to function as the world's government. That will depend on the willingness of the American public, the ultimate arbiter of American foreign policy, to sustain the costs involved. In the near future, America's role in the world will have to compete for public funds with the rising costs of domestic entitlement programs. It is Social Security and Medicare, not the rise of China or the kind of coalition that defeated powerful empires in the past, that pose the greatest threat to America's role as the world's government.

The outcome of the looming contest in the United States between the national commitment to social welfare at home and the requirements for stability and prosperity abroad cannot be foreseen with any precision. About other countries' approach to America's remarkable 21st-century global role, however, three things may be safely predicted: They will not pay for it, they will continue to criticize it, and they will miss it when it is gone.

Jack Snyder   → **NO**

Imperial Temptations

America today embodies a paradox of omnipotence and vulnerability. The U.S. military budget is greater than those of the next 14 countries combined and the American economy is larger than the next three combined. Yet Americans going about their daily lives face a greater risk of sudden death from terrorist attack than ever before. This situation has fostered a psychology of vulnerability that makes Americans hyperalert to foreign dangers and predisposed to use military power in what may be self-defeating attempts to escape their fears.

The Bush Administration's new national security doctrine, which provides a superficially attractive rationale for preventive war, reflects this uneasy state of mind.[1] In an open society, no strictly defensive strategy against terrorism can be foolproof. Similarly, deterring terrorist attack by the threat of retaliation seems impossible when the potential attackers welcome suicide. Bizarre or diabolical leaders of potentially nuclear-armed rogue states may likewise seem undeterrable. If so, attacking the sources of potential threats before they can mount their own attacks may seem the only safe option. Such a strategy presents a great temptation to a country as strong as the United States, which can project overwhelming military power to any spot on the globe.

In adopting this strategy, however, America risks marching in the well-trod footsteps of virtually every imperial power of the modern age. America has no formal colonial empire and seeks none, but like other great powers over the past two centuries, it has sometimes sought to impose peace on the tortured politics of weaker societies. Consequently, it faces many of the same strategic dilemmas as did the great powers that have gone before it. The Bush Administration's rhetoric of preventive war, however, does not reflect a sober appreciation of the American predicament, but instead echoes point by point the disastrous strategic ideas of those earlier keepers of imperial order.

Imperial Overstretch

Like America, the great empires of the 19th and 20th centuries enjoyed huge asymmetries of power relative to the societies at their periphery, yet they rightly feared disruptive attack from unruly peoples along the turbulent frontier of empire. Suspecting that their empires were houses of cards, imperial rulers feared that unchecked defiance on the periphery might cascade toward

From *The National Interest*, Spring 2003. Copyright © 2003 by National Interest. Reprinted by permission.

the imperial core. Repeatedly they tried the strategy of preventive attack to nip challenges in the bud and prevent their spread.

Typically, the preventive use of force proved counterproductive for imperial security because it often sparked endless brushfire wars at the edges of the empire, internal rebellions, and opposition from powers not yet conquered or otherwise subdued. Historically, the preventive pacification of one turbulent frontier of empire has usually led to the creation of another one, adjacent to the first. When the British conquered what is now Pakistan, for example, the turbulent frontier simply moved to neighboring Afghanistan. It was impossible to conquer everyone, so there was always another frontier.

Even inside well-established areas of imperial control, the use of repressive force against opponents often created a backlash among subjects who came to reassess the relative dangers and benefits of submission. The Amritsar massacre of 1919, for example, was the death knell for British India because it radicalized a formerly circumspect opposition. Moreover, the preventive use of force inside the empire and along its frontiers often intensified resistance from independent powers outside the empire who feared that unchecked, ruthless imperial force would soon encroach upon them. In other words, the balance of power kicked in. Through all of these mechanisms, empires have typically found that the preventive use of force expanded their security problems instead of ameliorating them.

As the dynamic of imperial overstretch became clearer, many of the great powers decided to solve their security dilemmas through even bolder preventive offensives. None of these efforts worked. To secure their European holdings, Napoleon and Hitler marched to Moscow, only to be engulfed in the Russian winter. Kaiser Wilhelm's Germany tried to break the allies' encirclement through unrestricted submarine warfare, which brought America's industrial might into the war against it. Imperial Japan, facing a quagmire in China and a U.S. oil embargo, tried to break what it saw as impending encirclement by seizing the Indonesian oil fields and preventively attacking Pearl Harbor. All sought security through expansion, and all ended in imperial collapse.

Some great powers, however, have pulled back from overstretch and husbanded their power for another day. Democratic great powers, notably Britain and the United States, are prominent among empires that learned how to retrench. At the turn of the 20th century, British leaders saw that the strategy of "splendid isolation"—what we would now call unilateralism—was getting the empire into trouble. The independence struggle of Boer farmers in South Africa drained the imperial coffers while, at the same time, the European great powers were challenging Britain's naval mastery and its hold on other colonial positions. Quickly doing the math, the British patched up relations with their secondary rivals, France and Russia, to form an alliance directed at the main danger, Germany. Likewise, when the United States blundered into war in Vietnam, it retrenched and adopted a more patient strategy for waiting out its less capable communist opponents.

Contemporary America, too, is capable of anticipating the counterproductive effects of offensive policies and of moderating them before much damage is done. The Bush team, guided by wary public opinion, worked through existing UN resolutions during the fall of 2002 to increase multilateral support for its threats of preventive war against Iraq. Moreover, the administration declined to apply mechanically its preventive war principles when North Korea renounced international controls on its nuclear materials in December 2002. Strikingly, too, a December codicil to the *NSS*, dealing specifically with the proliferation of weapons of mass destruction, never mentioned the option of preventive attack.[2] A brief tour through the misguided strategic ideas of previous empires underscores the wisdom of such self-restraint.

Myths of Security Through Expansion

Every major historical instance of imperial overstretch has been propelled by arguments that security could best be achieved through further expansion— "myths of empire," I have called them.[3] Since many of these myths are echoed eerily in the Bush Administration's strategic rhetoric, it is worthwhile recalling how those earlier advocates of imperial overstretch tried to make their dubious cases. Eight themes deserve mention.

Offensive Advantage

The most general of the myths of empire is that the attacker has an inherent advantage. Sometimes this is explained in terms of the advantages of surprise. More often, it relies on the broader notion that seizing the initiative allows the attacker to impose a plan on a passive enemy and to choose a propitious time and circumstance for the fight. Even if the political objective is self-defense, in this view, attacking is still the best strategy. As the *NSS* says, "our best defense is a good offense."

Throughout history, strategists who have blundered into imperial overstretch have shared this view. For example, General Alfred von Schlieffen, the author of Germany's misbegotten plan for a quick, decisive offensive in France in 1914, used to say that "if one is too weak to attack the whole" of the other side's army, "one should attack a section."[4] This idea defies elementary military common sense. In war, the weaker side normally remains on the defensive precisely because defending its home ground is typically easier than attacking the other side's strongholds.

The idea of offensive advantage also runs counter to the most typical patterns of deterrence and coercion. Sometimes the purpose of a military operation is not to take or hold territory but to influence an adversary by inflicting pain. This is especially true when weapons of mass destruction are involved. In that case, war may resemble a competition in the willingness to endure pain. Here too, however, the defender normally has the advantage, because the side defending its own homeland and the survival of its regime typically cares more about the stakes of the conflict than does a would-be attacker. It is difficult to imagine North Korea using nuclear weapons or mounting a conventional artillery barrage on the South Korean capital of Seoul for purposes of conquest, but it is much easier to envision such desperate measures in response to "preventive" U.S. attacks on the core power resources of the regime. Because the Bush Administration saw such retaliation as feasible and credible, it was deterred from undertaking preventive strikes when the North Koreans unsealed a nuclear reactor in December. Indeed, deterring any country from attacking is almost always easier than compelling it to disarm, surrender territory or change its regime. Once stated, this point seems obvious, but the logic of the Bush strategy document implies the opposite.

Power Shifts

One reason that blundering empires have been keen on offensive strategies is that they have relied on preventive attacks to forestall unfavorable shifts in the balance of power. In both World War I and II, for example, Germany's leaders sought war with Russia in the short run because they expected the Russian army to gain relative strength over time.[5] But the tactic backfired badly. Preventive aggression not only turned a possible enemy into a certain one, but in the long run it helped bring other powers into the fight to prevent Germany from gaining hegemony over all of them. This reflects a fundamental realist principle of the balance of power: In the international system, states and other powerful actors tend to form alliances against the expansionist state that most threatens them. Attackers provoke fears that drive their potential victims to cooperate with each other.

Astute strategists learn to anticipate such cooperation and try to use it to their advantage. For example, one of the most successful diplomats in European history, Otto von Bismarck, achieved the unification of Germany by always putting the other side in the wrong and, whenever possible, maneuvering the opponent into attacking first. As a result, Prussia expanded its control over the German lands without provoking excessive fears or resistance. Pressed by his generals on several occasions to authorize preventive attacks, Bismarck said that preventive war is like committing suicide from fear of death; it would "put the full weight of the imponderables . . . on the side of the enemies we have attacked."[6] Instead, he demanded patience: "I have often had to stand for long periods of time in the hunting blind and let myself be covered and stung by insects before the moment came to shoot."[7] Germany fared poorly under Bismarck's less-able successors, who shared his ruthlessness but lacked his understanding of the balance of power.

Because Saddam Hussein attacked Kuwait, the elder Bush enjoyed a diplomatic advantage in the 1991 war. That's why the coalition against Iraq was so large and willing. This advantage is vastly and inherently more difficult to achieve in a strategy of preventive attack, as the younger Bush has learned over the past year. Especially when an adverse power shift is merely hypothetical and not imminent, it hardly seems worthwhile to incur the substantial diplomatic disadvantages of a preventive attack.

Paper Tiger Enemies

Empires also become overstretched when they view their enemies as paper tigers, capable of becoming fiercely threatening if appeased, but easily crumpled by a resolute attack. These images are often not only wrong, but self-contradictory.

For example, Japanese militarists saw the United States as so strong and insatiably aggressive that Japan would have to conquer a huge, self-sufficient empire to get the resources to defend itself; yet at the same time, the Japanese regime saw the United States as so vulnerable and irresolute that a sharp rap against Pearl Harbor would discourage it from fighting back.

Similarly, the Bush Administration's arguments for preventive war against Iraq have portrayed Saddam Hussein as being completely undeterrable from using weapons of mass destruction, yet Secretary of Defense Donald Rumsfeld said he expected that Iraq would not use them even if attacked because "wise Iraqis will not obey his orders to use WMD."[8] In other words, administration strategists think that deterrence is impossible even in situations in which Saddam lacks a motive to use weapons of mass destruction, but they think deterrence will succeed when a U.S. attack provides Iraq the strongest imaginable motive to use its weapons. The *NSS* says "the greater the threat, the greater is the risk of inaction"; but this is a rationale for preventive attack only if we accept a paper tiger image of the enemy.

Bandwagons

Another myth of empire is that states tend to jump on the bandwagon with threatening or forceful powers. During the Cold War, for example, the Soviet Union thought that forceful action in Berlin, Cuba and the developing world would demonstrate its political and military strength, encourage so-called progressive forces to ally actively with Moscow, and thereby shift the balance of forces still further in the favor of the communist bloc. The Soviets called this the "correlation of forces" theory. In fact, the balance of power effect far outweighed and erased the bandwagon effect. The Soviet Union was left far weaker in relative terms as a result of its pressing for unilateral advantage. As Churchill said of the Soviets in the wake of the first Berlin Crisis, "Why have they deliberately acted for three long years so as to unite the free world against them?"[9]

During the 1991 Gulf War, the earlier Bush Administration argued that rolling back Saddam Hussein's conquest of Kuwait was essential to discourage Arabs throughout the Middle East from jumping on the Iraqi bandwagon. Now the current Bush Administration hopes that bandwagon dynamics can be made to work in its own favor. Despite the difficulties that the United States has had in lining up support for an invasion of Iraq, the administration nonetheless asserts that its strategy of preventive war will lead others to jump on the U.S. bandwagon. Secretary Rumsfeld has said that "if our leaders do the right thing, others will follow and support our just cause—just as they have in the global war against terror."[10]

At the same time, some self-styled realists in the administration also argue that their policy is consistent with the concept of the balance of power, but the rhetoric of the *NSS* pulls this concept inside out: "Through our willingness to use force in our own defense and in the defense of others, the United States demonstrates its resolve to maintain a balance of power that favors freedom." What this Orwellian statement really seems to mean is that preventive war will attract a bandwagon of support that creates an *im*balance of power in

America's favor, a conception that is logically the same as the wrongheaded Soviet theory of the "correlation of forces." Administration strategists like to use the terminology of the balance of power, but they understand that concept exactly backwards.

Big Stick Diplomacy

A closely related myth is the big stick theory of making friends by threatening them. Before World War I, Germany's leaders found that its rising power and belligerent diplomacy had pushed France, Russia and Britain into a loose alliance against it. In the backwards reasoning of German diplomacy, they decided to try to break apart this encirclement by trumping up a crisis over claims to Morocco, threatening France with an attack and hoping to prove to French leaders that its allies would not come to its rescue. In fact, Britain did support France, and the noose around Germany grew tighter.

How does the United States today seek to win friends abroad? The *NSS* offers some reassuring language about the need to work with allies. Unlike President Bill Clinton in the Kosovo war, President Bush worked very hard for a UN resolution to authorize an attack on Iraq. Nonetheless, on the Iraq issue and a series of others, the administration has extorted cooperation primarily by threats to act unilaterally, not gained it by persuasion or concessions. Russia was forced to accept a new strategic arms control regime on take-it-or-leave-it American terms. EU member states were similarly compelled to accept an exemption for U.S. officials from prosecution by the International Criminal Court. Germany was snubbed for resisting the war against Iraq. Multilateral initiatives on the environment were summarily rejected. Secretary Rumsfeld, in his personal jottings on strategy, has raised to the level of principle the dictum that the United States should "avoid trying so hard to persuade others to join a coalition that we compromise on our goals."[11] Either the administration believes allies are dispensable, or a powerful faction within it adheres to the Kaiser Wilhelm theory of diplomacy.

Falling Dominoes

Another common myth of empire is the famous domino theory. According to this conception, small setbacks at the periphery of the empire will tend to snowball into an unstoppable chain of defeats that will ultimately threaten the imperial core. Consequently, empires must fight hard to prevent even the most trivial setbacks. Various causal mechanisms are imagined that might trigger such cascades: The opponent will seize ever more strategic resources from these victories, tipping the balance of forces and making further conquests easier. Vulnerable defenders will lose heart. Allies and enemies alike will come to doubt the empire's resolve to fight for its commitments. An empire's domestic political support will be undermined. Above all, lost credibility is the ultimate domino.

Such reasoning has been nearly universal among overstretched empires.[12] For example, in 1898 the British and the French both believed that if a French scouting party could claim a tributary of the Upper Nile—at a place called Fashoda—France could build a dam there, block the flow of the Nile, trigger chaos in Egypt that would force Britain out of the Suez Canal, cut Britain's strategic lifeline to India, and thus topple the empire that depended on India's wealth and manpower. Britain and France, both democracies, nearly went to war because of this chimera. Similarly, Cold War America believed that if Vietnam fell to communism, then the credibility of its commitment to defend Taiwan, Japan and Berlin would be debased. Arguably, the peripheral setback in Vietnam tarnished American deterrent credibility only because we so often and so insistenly said it would.

Similar arguments, especially ones that hinge on lost credibility, have informed Secretary Rumsfeld's brief for preventive war against Iraq. In a nice rhetorical move, he quoted former President Clinton to the effect that if "we fail to act" against Saddam's non-compliance with inspections,

> he will conclude that the international community has lost its will. He will conclude that he can go right on and do more to rebuild an arsenal of devastating destruction. . . . Some day, some way, I guarantee you he will use that arsenal.[13]

Rumsfeld could have added (but didn't) that the Clinton Administration made the same argument even more strongly about the dire precedent that would be set by permitting the further expansion of North Korea's nuclear weapons capability. Ironically, the credibility of the United States is on the line in such cases mainly because of its own rhetoric.

And yet it may be that the threat of an American attack is all *too* credible. The main motivation for North Korea to break out of the 1994 agreement constraining its nuclear program was apparently its perceived need, in light of the Bush Administration's preventive war doctrine and reluctance to negotiate, for more powerful weapons to deter the United States.

A ubiquitous corollary of the domino theory holds that it is cheap and easy to stop aggressors if it is done early on. Secretary Rumsfeld has made this kind of argument to justify a preventive attack on Iraq. Between 35 and 60 million people died needlessly, he claimed, because the world didn't attack Hitler preventively: "He might have been stopped early—at minimal cost in lives—had the vast majority of the world's leaders not decided at the time that the risks of acting were greater than the risks of not acting." Apart from its questionable relevance to the case of Iraq, the historical point is itself debatable: Britain and France were militarily ill-prepared to launch a preventive attack at the time of the Munich crisis, and if they had, they probably would have had to fight Germany without the Soviet Union and the United States as allies. As Bismarck had understood, preventive war is bad strategy in part because it often leads to diplomatic isolation.

El Dorado and Manifest Destiny

Most of the central myths of empire focus on a comparison of the alleged costs of offensive versus defensive strategies. In addition, myths that exaggerate the benefits of imperial expansion sometimes play an important role in strategic debates. For example, German imperialism before World War I was fueled in part by the false idea that Central Africa would be an El Dorado of resources that would strengthen Germany's strategic position in the same way that India had supposedly strengthened Britain's. In debates about preventive war in Iraq, some commentators have portrayed an anticipated oil windfall as a comparable El Dorado. Astutely, the Bush Administration has refrained from rhetoric about this potential boon, realizing that it would be counterproductive and unnecessary to dwell on it. Such a windfall could turn out to be a curse in any event, since pumping massive amounts of oil to pay for an occupation of Iraq could undercut Saudi oil revenues and destabilize the political system there.

Sometimes the promised benefits of imperial expansion are also ideological—for example, France's civilizing mission or America's mission to make the world safe for democracy. In a surprising moment of candor, John Foster Dulles, a decade before he became Dwight Eisenhower's Secretary of State, wrote that all empires had been "imbued with and radiated great faiths [like] Manifest Destiny [and] The White Man's Burden." We Americans "need a faith", said Dulles, "that will make us strong, a faith so pronounced that we, too, will feel that we have a mission to spread throughout the world."[14] An idealistic goal is patently invoked here for its instrumental value in mobilizing support for the imperial enterprise.

The idealistic notes that grace the Bush Administration's strategy paper have the same hollow ring. The document is chock full of high-sounding prose about the goal of spreading democracy to Iraq and other countries living under the yoke of repression. President Bush's preface to the strategy document asserts that "the United States enjoys a position of unparalleled military strength", which creates "a moment of opportunity to extend the benefits of freedom across the globe. We will actively work to bring the hope of democracy, development, free markets, and free trade to every corner of the world." This sounds like insincere public relations in light of candidate Bush's warnings against the temptations of nation-building abroad. The theme of promoting democracy is rare in Secretary Rumsfeld's statements, which may turn out to be a better index of the administration's underlying views.

No Tradeoffs

A final myth of empire is that in strategy there are no tradeoffs. Proponents of imperial expansion tend to pile on every argument from the whole list of myths of empire. It is not enough to argue that the opponent is a paper tiger, or that dominoes tend to fall, or that big stick diplomacy will make friends, or that a preventive attack will help to civilize the natives. Rather, proponents of offensive self-defense inhabit a rhetorical world in which *all* of these things are simultaneously true, and thus all considerations point in the same direction.

The Bush Administration's strategic rhetoric about Iraq in late 2002 did not disappoint in this regard. Saddam was portrayed as undeterrable, as getting nuclear weapons unless deposed and giving them to terrorists, the war against him would be cheap and easy, grumbling allies would jump on our bandwagon, Iraq would become a democracy, and the Arab street would thank the United States for liberating it. In real life, as opposed to the world of imperial rhetoric, it is surprising when every conceivable consideration supports the preferred strategy. As is so often the case with the myths of empire, this piling on of reinforcing claims smacks of *ex post facto* justification rather than serious strategic assessment.

During the 2000 presidential campaign, Condoleezza Rice wrote of Iraq that "the first line of defense should be a clear and classical statement of deterrence—if they do acquire WMD, their weapons will be unusable because any attempt to use them will bring national obliteration."[15] Two years later, however, the possibility of deterrence has become unthinkable as administration rhetoric regarding Iraq has been piled higher and higher. "Given the goals of rogue states [and] the inability to deter a potential attacker" of this kind, says the *NSS*, "we cannot let our enemies strike first." Administration dogma left no room for any assessment of Iraq that did not reinforce the logic of the prevailing preventive strategy.

Why Are Myths of Empire So Prevalent?

In America today, strategic experts abound. Many are self-styled realists, people who pride themselves on accepting the hard reality that the use of force is often necessary in the defense of national interests. It is striking that many of these realists consider the Bush Administration's strategic justifications for preventive war against Iraq to be unconvincing. Indeed, 32 prominent international relations scholars, most of them realists, bought an ad in the *New York Times* to make their case against the Bush strategy. Included among them was the leading proponent of the "offensive realism" school of thought, John Mearsheimer, a professor at the University of Chicago.[16]

Proponents of the new preventive strategy charge that such realists are out of touch with a world in which forming alliances to balance against overwhelming U.S. power has simply become impossible. It is true that small rogue states and their ilk cannot on their own offset American power in the traditional sense. It is also true that their potential greatpower backers, Russia and China, have so far been wary of overtly opposing U.S. military interventions. But even if America's unprecedented power reduces the likelihood of traditional balancing alliances arising against it, the United States could find that its own offensive actions create their functional equivalents. Some earlier expansionist empires found themselves overstretched and surrounded by enemies even though balancing alliances were slow to oppose them. For example, although the prospective victims of Napoleon and Hitler found it difficult to form effective balancing coalitions, these empires attacked so many opponents simultaneously that substantial *de facto* alliances eventually did form against them. Today, an analogous form of self-imposed overstretch—political as well as military—could occur if the need for military operations to prevent nuclear proliferation risks were deemed urgent on several fronts at the same time, or if an attempt to impose democracy by force of arms on a score or more of Muslim countries were seriously undertaken.

Even in the absence of highly coordinated balancing alliances, simultaneous resistance by several troublemaking states and terrorist groups would be a daunting challenge for a strategy of universal preventive action. Highly motivated small powers or rebel movements defending their home ground have often prevailed against vastly superior states that lacked the sustained motivation to dominate them at extremely high cost, as in Vietnam and Algeria. Even when they do not prevail, as on the West Bank, they may fight on, imposing high costs over long periods.

Precisely because America is so strong, weak states on America's hit list may increasingly conclude that weapons of mass destruction joined to terror tactics are the only feasible equalizer to its power. Despite America's aggregate power advantages, weaker opponents can get access to outside resources to sustain this kind of cost-imposing resistance. Even a state as weak and isolated as North Korea has been able to mount a credible deterrent, in part by engaging in mutually valuable strategic trade with Pakistan and other Middle Eastern states. The Bush Administration itself stresses that Iraq bought components for the production of weapons of mass destruction on the commercial market and fears that no embargo can stop this. Iran is buying a nuclear reactor from Russia that the United States views as posing risks of nuclear proliferation. Palestinian suicide bombers successfully impose severe costs with minimal resources. In the September 11 attack, Al-Qaeda famously used its enemy's own resources.

In short, both historically and today, it seems hard to explain the prevalence of the myths of empire in terms of objective strategic analysis. So what, then, explains it?

In some historical cases, narrow interest groups that profited from imperial expansion or military preparations hijacked strategic debates by controlling the media or bankrolling imperial pressure groups. In imperial Japan, for example, when a civilian strategic planning board pointed out the implausibilities and contradictions in the militarists' worldview, its experts were thanked for their trenchant analysis and then summarily fired. In pre-World War I Germany, internal documents showing the gaping holes in the offensive strategic plans of the army and navy were kept secret, and civilians lacked the information or expertise to criticize the military's public reasoning. The directors of Krupp Steelworks subsidized the belligerent German Navy League before 1914, and then in the 1920s monopolized the wire services that brought nationalist-slanted news to Germany's smaller cities and towns. These were precisely the constituencies that later voted most heavily for Hitler.

In other cases, myths of empire were propounded by hard-pressed leaders seeking to rally support by pointing a finger at real or imagined enemies. For example, in the aftermath of the French Revolution, a series of unstable regimes found that they could increase their short-run popularity by exaggerating the threat from monarchical neighboring states and from aristocratic traitors to the Revolution. Napoleon perfected this strategy of rule, transforming the republic of the Rights of Man into an ever-expanding empire of popular nationalism.

Once the myths of empire gain widespread currency in a society, their origins in political expediency are often forgotten. Members of the second generation become true believers in the domino theory, big stick diplomacy and the civilizing mission. Kaiser Wilhelm's ministers were self-aware manipulators, but their audiences, including the generation that formed the Nazi movement, believed in German nationalist ideology with utmost conviction. In a process that Stephen Van Evera has called "blowback", the myths of empire may become ingrained in the psyche of the people and the institutions of their state.

Many skeptics about attacking Iraq suspect that similar domestic political dynamics are at the root of the Bush doctrine of preventive war. In particular, they think that the Iraq project echoes the plot of recent fictions in which a foreign war is trumped up to win an election. Some suggested that the day after the November 2002 election, the drumbeat of war would miraculously slacken and then disappear. Such rank cynicism deserved to be disappointed, and it was. Some members of Bush's inner circle have been spoiling for a rematch with Iraq for years, so clearly the convergence of its timing with the mid-term congressional election was a coincidence. Nonetheless, it probably did not hurt the hawks' cause in White House deliberations that the Iraq issue succeeded in pushing the parlous state of the economy off the front pages at a convenient moment.

A deeper reason for the prevalence of the myths of empire in contemporary debates is the legacy of Cold War rhetoric in the tropes of American strategic discourse. The Rumsfeld generation grew to political maturity inculcated with the Munich analogy and the domino theory. It is true that an opposite metaphor, the quagmire, is readily available for skeptics to invoke as a result of the Vietnam experience. But after the September 11 attack and the easy victory over the Taliban, the American political audience is primed for Munich analogies and preventive war, not for quagmire theories. Indeed, it is striking how many Senate speeches on the resolution authorizing the use of force in Iraq began with references to the effect of September 11 on the American psyche. They did not necessarily argue that the Iraqi government is a terrorist organization like Al-Qaeda. They simply noted the emotional reality that the attacks on the World Trade Center and the Pentagon had left Americans fearful and ready to fight back forcefully against threats of many sorts. In this sense, America is psychologically primed to accept the myths of empire. They "feel right"; but this is no way to run a grand strategy.

A final reason why America is primed to accept the myths of empire is simply the temptation of great power. As the German realist historian Ludwig Dehio wrote about Germany's bid for a hegemonic position in Europe, "since the supreme power stands in the solitude of its supremacy, it must face daemonic temptations of a special kind."[17] More recently, Christopher Layne has chronicled the tendency of unipolar hegemonic states since the Spain of Philip II to succumb to the temptations of overstretch and thereby to provoke the enmity of an opposing coalition.[18] Today, the United States is so strong compared to everyone else that almost any imaginable military objective may seem achievable. This circumstance, supercharged by the rhetoric of the myths of empire, makes the temptation of preventive war almost irresistible.

The historical record warrants a skeptical attitude toward arguments that security can be achieved through imperial expansion and preventive war. Moving beyond mere skepticism, we may consider a general prescription, one that might resonate with both liberals and realists alike.

Liberals might want to review a recent book by G. John Ikenberry, *After Victory*, which tells the story of attempts by the victors in global power contests to establish a stable post-conflict international order.[19] Ikenberry shows that democracies are particularly well suited to succeed in this because the transparency of their political institutions makes them trustworthy bargaining partners in the eyes of weaker states. As a result, strong and weak states are able to commit themselves to an international constitution that serves the interests of both. Realists should study this book, too, because it explains why even the strongest of powers has an incentive to lead through consensus rather than raw coercion.

President Bush's National Security Advisor, former Stanford political science professor and provost Condoleezza Rice, has recently advanced a much different view of the interplay of power-political realism and democratic idealism.

OF EMPIRE, POWER BALANCES AND PREVENTIVE WAR

To speak now of the true temper of empire, it is a thing rare and hard to keep; for both temper, and distemper, consist of contraries. . . . The difficulties in princes' business are many and great; but the greatest difficulty, is often in their own mind. For it is common with princes (saith Tacitus) to will contradictories, *Sunt plerumque regum voluntates vehementes, et inter se contrariae.* For it is the solecism of power, to think to command the end, and yet not to endure the mean. . . .

For their neighbors; there can no general rule be given (for occasions are so variable), save one, which ever holdeth, which is, that princes do keep due sentinel, that none of their neighbors do ever grow so (by increase of territory, by embracing of trade, by approaches, or the like), as they become more able to annoy them, than they were. And this is generally the work of standing counsels, to foresee and to hinder it. During that triumvirate of kings, King Henry the Eighth of England, Francis the First King of France, and Charles the Fifth Emperor, there was such a watch kept, that none of the three could win a palm of ground, but the other two would straightways balance it, either by confederation, or, if need were, by a war; and would not in any wise take up peace at interest. . . .

Neither is the opinion of some of the Schoolmen, to be received, *that a war cannot justly be made, but upon a precedent injury or provocation.* For there is no question, but a just fear of an imminent danger, though there be no blow given, is a lawful cause of a war. . . .

—Francis Bacon

(Once you have been a professor of international relations, it is evidently hard to get these debates out of your blood.) She argues that realism and idealism should not be seen as alternatives: a realistic sense of power politics should be used in the service of ideals. Who could possibly disagree? But contrary to what she and Bush once argued on the campaign trail about humility and a judicious sense of limits, Rice now believes that America's vast military power should be used preventively to spread democratic ideals. She has also said, speaking in New York this past October, that the aim of the Bush strategy is "to dissuade any potential adversary from pursuing a military build-up in the hope of surpassing, or equaling, the power of the United States and our allies." Today, no combination of adversaries can hope to equal America's power under any circumstances. However, if they fear the unbridled use of America's power, they may perceive overwhelming incentives to wield weapons of terror and mass destruction to deter America's offensive tactics of self-defense. Indeed, the history of the myths of empire suggests that a general strategy of preventive war is likely to bring about precisely the outcome that Bush and Rice wish to avert.

Notes

1. Office of the President, *National Security Strategy of the United States* [hereafter *NSS*], September 2002.

2. Office of the President, *National Strategy to Combat Weapons of Mass Destruction,* December 2002.

3. See my *Myths of Empire: Domestic Politics and International Ambition* (Ithaca, NY: Cornell University Press, 1991). I used the term "empire" in the general sense of a powerful state that uses force to expand its influence abroad beyond the point at which the costs of expansion begin to rise sharply.

4. Quoted in my *Ideology of the Offensive: Military Decision Making and the Disasters of 1914* (Ithaca, NY: Cornell University Press, 1984), p. 113.

5. Dale C. Copeland, *The Origins of Major War* (Ithaca, NY: Cornell University Press, 2000).

6. Gordon Craig, *Germany: 1866–1945* (New York: Oxford University Press, 1978), pp. 24–25; and Gerhard Ritter, *The Sword and the Scepter: The Problem of Militarism in Germany,* vol. 1 (Coral Gables, FL: University of Miami Press, 1969), p. 245, quoting Bismarck's Reichstag speech of February 6, 1888.

7. Quoted in Otto Pflanze, *Bismarck and the Development of Germany: The Period of Unification, 1815–1871* (Princeton, NJ: Princeton University Press, 1963), p. 90.

8. Testimony before the House Armed Services Committee, September 18–9, 2002.

9. Speech at the Massachusetts Institute of Technology, March 31, 1949.

10. Testimony before the House Armed Services Committee, September 18–9, 2002.

11. Rumsfeld quoted in the *New York Times,* October 4, 2002.

12. See Charles Kupchan, *The Vulnerability of Empire* (Ithaca, NY: Cornell University Press, 1994).

13. Clinton quoted by Rumsfeld, Testimony before the House Armed Services Committee, September 18–9, 2002.

14. "A Righteous Faith for a Just and Durable Peace," October 1942, Dulles Papers, quoted in Ronald Pruessen, *John Foster Dulles: The Road to Power* (New York: Free Press, 1982), p. 200.

15. Rice, "Promoting the National Interest," *Foreign Affairs* (January/February 2000), p. 61.

16. *New York Times,* September 26, 2002. See also John J. Mearsheimer, "Hearts and Minds," *The National Interest* (Fall 2002), p. 15.

17. Dehio, *Germany and World Politics in the Twentieth Century* (New York: W.W. Norton, 1967 [1959]), p. 15.

18. Layne, "The Unipolar Illusion: Why New Powers Will Rise," *International Security* (Spring 1993).

19. See Ikenberry, *After Victory: Institutions, Strategic Restraint, and the Rebuilding of Order After Major Wars* (Princeton, NJ: Princeton University Press, 2000); and Ikenberry, "Getting Hegemony Right," *The National Interest* (Spring 2001).

POSTSCRIPT

Is American Hegemony Good for the United States and the World?

Many scholars have engaged in the debate over how the United States should exercise its preponderance of power. For more on Mandelbaum's views, see his book *The Case for Goliath: How America Acts as the World's Government in the Twenty-First Century* (Public Affairs, 2005). For other views on how the assertive use of American power can be good for both the United States and the world, see Robert J. Lieber, *The American Era: Power and Strategy for the 21st Century* (Cambridge, 2005) and Robert Kagan, "The Benevolent Empire," *Foreign Policy* (Summer 1998).

For a view that the United States is so powerful that even coalitions of other states are unlikely to balance against it, see William Wohlforth, "The Stability of a Unipolar World," *International Security* (Summer 1999). For a contrasting view that emphasizes balancing against the United States and eventual U.S. decline, see Charles Kupchan, *The End of the American Era: U.S. Foreign Policy and the Geopolitics of the Twenty-First Century* (Vintage, 2003).

For critiques of America's informal "empire," see Andrew Bacevich, *American Empire: The Realities and Consequences of U.S. Diplomacy* (Harvard University Press, 2002), Niall Fergusson, *The Price of Empire* (Penguin, 2004), and Robert W. Merry, *Sands of Empire: Missionary Zeal, American Foreign Policy, and the Hazards of Global Ambition* (Simon and Schuster, 2005).

For recommendations on how the United States can build institutions and use "soft power" (the appeal of American ideas and values) to better achieve its goals, see Joseph S. Nye, Jr., *Soft Power: The Means to Success in World Politics* (Public Affairs, 2004) and Richard Haass, *The Opportunity: America's Moment to Alter History's Course* (Public Affairs, 2005). For a discussion of the role of institutions and "self-binding," see G. John Ikenberry, *After Victory* (Princeton, 2000).

ISSUE 2

Is the United States in Decline?

YES: Richard N. Haass, from "The Age of Nonpolarity: What Will Follow U.S. Dominance," *Foreign Affairs* (May/June 2008)

NO: Robert J. Lieber, from "Falling Upwards: Declinism, the Box Set," *World Affairs Journal* (Summer 2008)

ISSUE SUMMARY

YES: Richard N. Haass, president of the Council on Foreign Relations, maintains that the world is entering a period of "nonpolarity" due to the relative decline of the United States and the dispersal of power to both other states and nonstate actors. No single rival can match U.S. power, but the general dispersal of power will make it more difficult for the United States to achieve international cooperation on security, environmental, and economic issues.

NO: Robert J. Lieber, professor of government at Georgetown University, points out that forecasts of American decline in the 1970s and 1980s proved to be inaccurate. The United States retains a preponderance of power and America's potential rivals face problems of their own that will prevent them from matching U.S. power.

In the late 1970s and early 1980s, many analysts argued that the United States was in a period of long-term decline relative to the rest of the world due. "Declinists" pointed to numerous reasons for why in their view the United States, even though it continued to grow and develop, was falling behind in comparison to other countries that were growing even faster. These included the "oil shocks" of the 1970s, when oil prices rose dramatically and the United States increasingly relied on oil imports as its domestic stocks failed to keep pace with demand; the aftermath of the Vietnam war, which had stretched U.S. military capabilities thin; the growing military power of the Soviet Union; the rising economic clout of Japan; the high inflation and unemployment of the late 1970s; the weakening power of the dollar as the international reserve currency of choice; and the burdens of high defense spending and U.S. security commitments overseas. Indeed, the U.S. economy as a proportion of global economic production, which was at an artificially high level after World War II due to the devastation of the world's other leading economies, was in a period of long-term decline into the early 1980s.

The worst case predictions of America's relative decline proved unfounded by the late 1980s and the 1990s, however. Instead, the Warsaw Pact and the Soviet Union itself dissolved, Japan's economy stagnated, oil prices stabilized, U.S. defense spending as a share of U.S. GDP declined as a result of the end of the Cold War, and the U.S. economy enjoyed a prolonged period of relative stability and growth as international trade rose. In fact, the U.S. economy ended the 1990s with an annual production rate of about 30% of global GDP, a higher proportion than at the start of the decade.

Nonetheless, the fact that the declinists were wrong regarding the last two decades does not mean that the United States cannot decline relative to other countries in the future, and a confluence of events is bringing declinist concerns back onto the agenda. U.S. defense spending has once again risen dramatically in the aftermath of the September 11, 2001, attacks on New York and Washington, and is projected to be $650 billion in fiscal 2009, not including what is likely to be well over $100 billion more in supplemental spending on operations in Iraq and Afghanistan. U.S. military operations in Iraq and Afghanistan have proved more difficult than many expected, and have stretched U.S. ground forces thin. Other countries, most notably China and to a lesser extent India, have enjoyed prolonged periods of double-digit economic growth, while U.S. growth rates have hovered around 2–3%. Many countries in the European Union, which has a combined GDP greater than that of the United States, have criticized U.S. policies in Iraq and refused to contribute to U.S. military efforts there as they did in the 1991 Gulf War. Domestic and demographic trends, including rising health care costs and a growing population of retirees relative to workers as the "baby boom" generation retires, have constrained the U.S. government's ability to commit to ambitious long-term projects. Finally and most dramatically, the world financial crisis, the end of the real-estate boom and the free-spending and low-savings consumer habits that it fueled, has sent the U.S. economy into what is expected to be the deepest recession in over seventy years, renewed concerns about the role of the dollar as a reserve currency in the face of huge U.S. budget deficits, and led other countries to question America's leadership of the world economy.

Despite these challenges, the United States remains far ahead of any potential competitor by almost any measure. It is a world leader in science and technology, its university educational system is the envy of the world, the U.S. government is making large long-term investments in clean domestic sources of energy and transportation as part of the economic stimulus package passed in early 2009, the U.S. economy is still by far the largest in the world, and the United States has global military capabilities and a clear advantage in its technological ability to acquire, integrate, and use tactical military intelligence information. Time will tell whether the United States is able to rise to a new set of security, environmental, and economic challenges as successfully as it rose to the challenges of the Great Depression in the 1930s, the rise of fascism in World War II, and the long, costly, and dangerous competition of the Cold War.

YES ↵

Richard N. Haass

The Age of Nonpolarity: What Will Follow U.S. Dominance

The principal characteristic of twenty-first-century international relations is turning out to be nonpolarity: a world dominated not by one or two or even several states but rather by dozens of actors possessing and exercising various kinds of power. This represents a tectonic shift from the past.

The twentieth century started out distinctly multipolar. But after almost 50 years, two world wars, and many smaller conflicts, a bipolar system emerged. Then, with the end of the Cold War and the demise of the Soviet Union, bipolarity gave way to unipolarity—an international system dominated by one power, in this case the United States. But today power is diffuse, and the onset of nonpolarity raises a number of important questions. How does nonpolarity differ from other forms of international order? How and why did it materialize? What are its likely consequences? And how should the United States respond?

Newer World Order

In contrast to multipolarity—which involves several distinct poles or concentrations of power—a nonpolar international system is characterized by numerous centers with meaningful power.

In a multipolar system, no power dominates, or the system will become unipolar. Nor do concentrations of power revolve around two positions, or the system will become bipolar. Multipolar systems can be cooperative, even assuming the form of a concert of powers, in which a few major powers work together on setting the rules of the game and disciplining those who violate them. They can also be more competitive, revolving around a balance of power, or conflictual, when the balance breaks down.

At first glance, the world today may appear to be multipolar. The major powers—China, the European Union (EU), India, Japan, Russia, and the United States—contain just over half the world's people and account for 75 percent of global GDP and 80 percent of global defense spending. Appearances, however, can be deceiving. Today's world differs in a fundamental way from one of classic multipolarity: there are many more power centers, and quite a few of these poles are not nation-states. Indeed, one of the cardinal features of the contemporary international system is that nation-states have lost their

Reprinted by permission of *Foreign Affairs*, May/June 2008, pp. 44–56. Copyright © 2008 by the Council on Foreign Relations, Inc. www.ForeignAffairs.org

monopoly on power and in some domains their preeminence as well. States are being challenged from above, by regional and global organizations; from below, by militias; and from the side, by a variety of nongovernmental organizations (NGOs) and corporations. Power is now found in many hands and in many places.

In addition to the six major world powers, there are numerous regional powers: Brazil and, arguably, Argentina, Chile, Mexico, and Venezuela in Latin America; Nigeria and South Africa in Africa; Egypt, Iran, Israel, and Saudi Arabia in the Middle East; Pakistan in South Asia; Australia, Indonesia, and South Korea in East Asia and Oceania. A good many organizations would be on the list of power centers, including those that are global (the International Monetary Fund, the United Nations, the World Bank), those that are regional (the African Union, the Arab League, the Association of Southeast Asian Nations, the EU, the Organization of American States, the South Asian Association for Regional Cooperation), and those that are functional (the International Energy Agency, OPEC, the Shanghai Cooperation Organization, the World Health Organization). So, too, would states within nation-states, such as California and India's Uttar Pradesh, and cities, such as New York, São Paulo, and Shanghai. Then there are the large global companies, including those that dominate the worlds of energy, finance, and manufacturing. Other entities deserving inclusion would be global media outlets (al Jazeera, the BBC, CNN), militias (Hamas, Hezbollah, the Mahdi Army, the Taliban), political parties, religious institutions and movements, terrorist organizations (al Qaeda), drug cartels, and NGOs of a more benign sort (the Bill and Melinda Gates Foundation, Doctors Without Borders, Greenpeace). Today's world is increasingly one of distributed, rather than concentrated, power.

In this world, the United States is and will long remain the largest single aggregation of power. It spends more than $500 billion annually on its military—and more than $700 billion if the operations in Afghanistan and Iraq are included—and boasts land, air, and naval forces that are the world's most capable. Its economy, with a GDP of some $14 trillion, is the world's largest. The United States is also a major source of culture (through films and television), information, and innovation. But the reality of American strength should not mask the relative decline of the United States' position in the world—and with this relative decline in power an absolute decline in influence and independence. The U.S. share of global imports is already down to 15 percent. Although U.S. GDP accounts for over 25 percent of the world's total, this percentage is sure to decline over time given the actual and projected differential between the United States' growth rate and those of the Asian giants and many other countries, a large number of which are growing at more than two or three times the rate of the United States.

GDP growth is hardly the only indication of a move away from U.S. economic dominance. The rise of sovereign wealth funds—in countries such as China, Kuwait, Russia, Saudi Arabia, and the United Arab Emirates—is another. These government-controlled pools of wealth, mostly the result of oil and gas exports, now total some $3 trillion. They are growing at a projected rate of $1 trillion a year and are an increasingly important source of liquidity for U.S.

firms. High energy prices, fueled mostly by the surge in Chinese and Indian demand, are here to stay for some time, meaning that the size and significance of these funds will continue to grow. Alternative stock exchanges are springing up and drawing away companies from the U.S. exchanges and even launching initial public offerings (IPOs). London, in particular, is competing with New York as the world's financial center and has already surpassed it in terms of the number of IPOs it hosts. The dollar has weakened against the euro and the British pound, and it is likely to decline in value relative to Asian currencies as well. A majority of the world's foreign exchange holdings are now in currencies other than the dollar, and a move to denominate oil in euros or a basket of currencies is possible, a step that would only leave the U.S. economy more vulnerable to inflation as well as currency crises.

U.S. primacy is also being challenged in other realms, such as military effectiveness and diplomacy. Measures of military spending are not the same as measures of military capacity. September 11 showed how a small investment by terrorists could cause extraordinary levels of human and physical damage. Many of the most costly pieces of modern weaponry are not particularly useful in modern conflicts in which traditional battlefields are replaced by urban combat zones. In such environments, large numbers of lightly armed soldiers can prove to be more than a match for smaller numbers of highly trained and better-armed U.S. troops.

Power and influence are less and less linked in an era of nonpolarity. U.S. calls for others to reform will tend to fall on deaf ears, U.S. assistance programs will buy less, and U.S.-led sanctions will accomplish less. After all, China proved to be the country best able to influence North Korea's nuclear program. Washington's ability to pressure Tehran has been strengthened by the participation of several western European countries—and weakened by the reluctance of China and Russia to sanction Iran. Both Beijing and Moscow have diluted international efforts to pressure the government in Sudan to end its war in Darfur. Pakistan, meanwhile, has repeatedly demonstrated an ability to resist U.S. entreaties, as have Iran, North Korea, Venezuela, and Zimbabwe.

The trend also extends to the worlds of culture and information. Bollywood produces more films every year than Hollywood. Alternatives to U.S.-produced and disseminated television are multiplying. Web sites and blogs from other countries provide further competition for U.S.-produced news and commentary. The proliferation of information is as much a cause of nonpolarity as is the proliferation of weaponry.

Farewell to Unipolarity

Charles Krauthammer was more correct than he realized when he wrote in these pages nearly two decades ago about what he termed "the unipolar moment." At the time, U.S. dominance was real. But it lasted for only 15 or 20 years. In historical terms, it was a moment. Traditional realist theory would have predicted the end of unipolarity and the dawn of a multipolar world. According to this line of reasoning, great powers, when they act as great powers are wont to do, stimulate competition from others that fear or resent them.

Krauthammer, subscribing to just this theory, wrote, "No doubt, multipolarity will come in time. In perhaps another generation or so there will be great powers coequal with the United States, and the world will, in structure, resemble the pre–World War I era."

But this has not happened. Although anti-Americanism is widespread, no great-power rival or set of rivals has emerged to challenge the United States. In part, this is because the disparity between the power of the United States and that of any potential rivals is too great. Over time, countries such as China may come to possess GDPs comparable to that of the United States. But in the case of China, much of that wealth will necessarily be absorbed by providing for the country's enormous population (much of which remains poor) and will not be available to fund military development or external undertakings. Maintaining political stability during a period of such dynamic but uneven growth will be no easy feat. India faces many of the same demographic challenges and is further hampered by too much bureaucracy and too little infrastructure. The EU's GDP is now greater than that of the United States, but the EU does not act in the unified fashion of a nation-state, nor is it able or inclined to act in the assertive fashion of historic great powers. Japan, for its part, has a shrinking and aging population and lacks the political culture to play the role of a great power. Russia may be more inclined, but it still has a largely cash-crop economy and is saddled by a declining population and internal challenges to its cohesion.

The fact that classic great-power rivalry has not come to pass and is unlikely to arise anytime soon is also partly a result of the United States' behavior, which has not stimulated such a response. This is not to say that the United States under the leadership of George W. Bush has not alienated other nations; it surely has. But it has not, for the most part, acted in a manner that has led other states to conclude that the United States constitutes a threat to their vital national interests. Doubts about the wisdom and legitimacy of U.S. foreign policy are pervasive, but this has tended to lead more to denunciations (and an absence of cooperation) than outright resistance.

A further constraint on the emergence of great-power rivals is that many of the other major powers are dependent on the international system for their economic welfare and political stability. They do not, accordingly, want to disrupt an order that serves their national interests. Those interests are closely tied to cross-border flows of goods, services, people, energy, investment, and technology—flows in which the United States plays a critical role. Integration into the modern world dampens great-power competition and conflict.

But even if great-power rivals have not emerged, unipolarity has ended. Three explanations for its demise stand out. The first is historical. States develop; they get better at generating and piecing together the human, financial, and technological resources that lead to productivity and prosperity. The same holds for corporations and other organizations. The rise of these new powers cannot be stopped. The result is an ever larger number of actors able to exert influence regionally or globally.

A second cause is U.S. policy. To paraphrase Walt Kelly's Pogo, the post–World War II comic hero, we have met the explanation and it is us. By both what it has done and what it has failed to do, the United States has accelerated the emergence of alternative power centers in the world and has weakened its own position relative to them. U.S. energy policy (or the lack thereof) is a driving force behind the end of unipolarity. Since the first oil shocks of the 1970s, U.S. consumption of oil has grown by approximately 20 percent, and, more important, U.S. imports of petroleum products have more than doubled in volume and nearly doubled as a percentage of consumption. This growth in demand for foreign oil has helped drive up the world price of oil from just over $20 a barrel to over $100 a barrel in less than a decade. The result is an enormous transfer of wealth and leverage to those states with energy reserves. In short, U.S. energy policy has helped bring about the emergence of oil and gas producers as major power centers.

U.S. economic policy has played a role as well. President Lyndon Johnson was widely criticized for simultaneously fighting a war in Vietnam and increasing domestic spending. President Bush has fought costly wars in Afghanistan and Iraq, allowed discretionary spending to increase by an annual rate of eight percent, and cut taxes. As a result, the United States' fiscal position declined from a surplus of over $100 billion in 2001 to an estimated deficit of approximately $250 billion in 2007. Perhaps more relevant is the ballooning current account deficit, which is now more than six percent of GDP. This places downward pressure on the dollar, stimulates inflation, and contributes to the accumulation of wealth and power elsewhere in the world. Poor regulation of the U.S. mortgage market and the credit crisis it has spawned have exacerbated these problems.

The war in Iraq has also contributed to the dilution of the United States' position in the world. The war in Iraq has proved to be an expensive war of choice—militarily, economically, and diplomatically as well as in human terms. Years ago, the historian Paul Kennedy outlined his thesis about "imperial overstretch," which posited that the United States would eventually decline by overreaching, just as other great powers had in the past. Kennedy's theory turned out to apply most immediately to the Soviet Union, but the United States—for all its corrective mechanisms and dynamism—has not proved to be immune. It is not simply that the U.S. military will take a generation to recover from Iraq; it is also that the United States lacks sufficient military assets to continue doing what it is doing in Iraq, much less assume new burdens of any scale elsewhere.

Finally, today's nonpolar world is not simply a result of the rise of other states and organizations or of the failures and follies of U.S. policy. It is also an inevitable consequence of globalization. Globalization has increased the volume, velocity, and importance of cross-border flows of just about everything, from drugs, e-mails, greenhouse gases, manufactured goods, and people to television and radio signals, viruses (virtual and real), and weapons.

Globalization reinforces nonpolarity in two fundamental ways. First, many cross-border flows take place outside the control of governments and without their knowledge. As a result, globalization dilutes the influence of the major powers. Second, these same flows often strengthen the capacities of non-state actors, such as energy exporters (who are experiencing a dramatic increase in wealth owing to transfers from importers), terrorists (who use the Internet to recruit and train, the international banking system to move resources, and the global transport system to move people), rogue states (who can exploit black and gray markets), and Fortune 500 firms (who quickly move personnel and investments). It is increasingly apparent that being the strongest state no longer means having a near monopoly on power. It is easier than ever before for individuals and groups to accumulate and project substantial power.

Nonpolar Disorder

The increasingly nonpolar world will have mostly negative consequences for the United States—and for much of the rest of the world as well. It will make it more difficult for Washington to lead on those occasions when it seeks to pro-mote collective responses to regional and global challenges. One reason has to do with simple arithmetic. With so many more actors possessing meaningful power and trying to assert influence, it will be more difficult to build collective responses and make institutions work. Herding dozens is harder than herding a few. The inability to reach agreement in the Doha Round of global trade talks is a telling example.

Nonpolarity will also increase the number of threats and vulnerabilities facing a country such as the United States. These threats can take the form of rogue states, terrorist groups, energy producers that choose to reduce their out-put, or central banks whose action or inaction can create conditions that affect the role and strength of the U.S. dollar. The Federal Reserve might want to think twice before continuing to lower interest rates, lest it precipitate a further move away from the dollar. There can be worse things than a recession.

Iran is a case in point. Its effort to become a nuclear power is a result of nonpolarity. Thanks more than anything to the surge in oil prices, it has become another meaningful concentration of power, one able to exert influ-ence in Iraq, Lebanon, Syria, the Palestinian territories, and beyond, as well as within OPEC. It has many sources of technology and finance and numer-ous markets for its energy exports. And due to nonpolarity, the United States cannot manage Iran alone. Rather, Washington is dependent on others to support political and economic sanctions or block Tehran's access to nuclear technology and materials. Nonpolarity begets nonpolarity.

Still, even if nonpolarity was inevitable, its character is not. To paraphrase the international relations theorist Hedley Bull, global politics at any point is a mixture of anarchy and society. The question is the balance and the trend. A great deal can and should be done to shape a nonpolar world. Order will not just emerge. To the contrary, left to its own devices, a nonpolar world will become messier over time. Entropy dictates that systems consisting of a large number of actors tend toward greater randomness and disorder in the absence of external intervention.

The United States can and should take steps to reduce the chances that a nonpolar world will become a cauldron of instability. This is not a call for unilateralism; it is a call for the United States to get its own house in order. Unipolarity is a thing of the past, but the United States still retains more capacity than any other actor to improve the quality of the international system. The question is whether it will continue to possess such capacity.

Energy is the most important issue. Current levels of U.S. consumption and imports (in addition to their adverse impact on the global climate) fuel nonpolarity by funneling vast financial resources to oil and gas producers. Reducing consumption would lessen the pressure on world prices, decrease U.S. vulnerability to market manipulation by oil suppliers, and slow the pace of climate change. The good news is that this can be done without hurting the U.S. economy.

Strengthening homeland security is also crucial. Terrorism, like disease, cannot be eradicated. There will always be people who cannot be integrated into societies and who pursue goals that cannot be realized through traditional politics. And sometimes, despite the best efforts of those entrusted with homeland security, terrorists will succeed. What is needed, then, are steps to make society more resilient, something that requires adequate funding and training of emergency responders and more flexible and durable infrastructure. The goal should be to reduce the impact of even successful attacks.

Resisting the further spread of nuclear weapons and unguarded nuclear materials, given their destructive potential, may be as important as any other set of undertakings. By establishing internationally managed enriched-uranium or spent-fuel banks that give countries access to sensitive nuclear materials, the international community could help countries use nuclear power to produce electricity rather than bombs. Security assurances and defensive systems can be provided to states that might otherwise feel compelled to develop nuclear programs of their own to counter those of their neighbors. Robust sanctions—on occasion backed by armed force—can also be introduced to influence the behavior of would-be nuclear states.

Even so, the question of using military force to destroy nuclear or biological weapons capabilities remains. Preemptive strikes—attacks that aim to stop an imminent threat—are widely accepted as a form of self-defense. Preventive strikes—attacks on capabilities when there is no indication of imminent use—are something else altogether. They should not be ruled out as a matter of principle, but nor should they be depended on. Beyond questions of feasibility, preventive strikes run the risk of making a nonpolar world less stable, both because they might actually encourage proliferation (governments could see developing or acquiring nuclear weapons as a deterrent) and because they would weaken the long-standing norm against the use of force for purposes other than self-defense.

Combating terrorism is also essential if the nonpolar era is not to turn into a modern Dark Ages. There are many ways to weaken existing terrorist organizations by using intelligence and law enforcement resources and military capabilities. But this is a loser's game unless something can be done to reduce recruitment. Parents, religious figures, and political leaders must delegitimize terrorism by shaming those who choose to embrace it. And more important, governments must find ways of integrating alienated young men and women into their societies, something that cannot occur in the absence of political and economic opportunity.

Trade can be a powerful tool of integration. It gives states a stake in avoiding conflict because instability interrupts beneficial commercial arrangements that provide greater wealth and strengthen the foundations of domestic political order. Trade also facilitates development, thereby decreasing the chance of state failure and alienation among citizens. The scope of the World Trade Organization must be extended through the negotiation of future global arrangements that further reduce subsidies and both tariff and nontariff barriers. Building domestic political support for such negotiations in developed countries will likely require the expansion of various safety nets, including portable health care and retirement accounts, education and training assistance, and wage insurance. These social policy reforms are costly and in some cases unwarranted (the cause of job loss is far more likely to be technological innovation than foreign competition), but they are worth providing nonetheless given the overall economic and political value of expanding the global trade regime.

A similar level of effort might be needed to ensure the continued flow of investment. The goal should be to create a World Investment Organization that would encourage capital flows across borders so as to minimize the chances that "investment protectionism" gets in the way of activities that, like trade, are economically beneficial and build political bulwarks against instability. A WIO could encourage transparency on the part of investors, determine when national security is a legitimate reason for prohibiting or limiting foreign investment, and establish a mechanism for resolving disputes.

Finally, the United States needs to enhance its capacity to prevent state failure and deal with its consequences. This will require building and maintaining a larger military, one with greater capacity to deal with the sort of threats faced in Afghanistan and Iraq. In addition, it will mean establishing a civilian counterpart to the military reserves that would provide a pool of human talent to assist with basic nation-building tasks. Continuing economic and military assistance will be vital in helping weak states meet their responsibilities to their citizens and their neighbors.

The Not-So-Lonely Superpower

Multilateralism will be essential in dealing with a nonpolar world. To succeed, though, it must be recast to include actors other than the great powers. The UN Security Council and the G-8 (the group of highly industrialized states) need to be reconstituted to reflect the world of today and not the post–World War II era. A recent meeting at the United Nations on how best to coordinate global responses to public health challenges provided a model. Representatives of governments, UN agencies, NGOs, pharmaceutical companies, foundations, think tanks, and universities were all in attendance. A similar range of participants attended the December 2007 Bali meeting on climate change. Multilateralism may have to be less formal and less comprehensive, at least in its initial phases. Networks will be needed alongside organizations. Getting everyone to agree on everything will be increasingly difficult; instead, the United States should consider signing accords with fewer parties and narrower goals. Trade is something of a model here, in that bilateral and regional accords are filling the vacuum created by a failure to conclude a global trade round. The same approach could work for climate change, where agreement on aspects of the problem (say, deforestation) or arrangements involving only some countries (the major carbon emitters, for example) may prove feasible, whereas an accord that involves every country and tries to resolve every issue may not. Multilateralism à la carte is likely to be the order of the day.

Nonpolarity complicates diplomacy. A nonpolar world not only involves more actors but also lacks the more predictable fixed structures and relationships that tend to define worlds of unipolarity, bipolarity, or multipolarity. Alliances, in particular, will lose much of their importance, if only because alliances require predictable threats, outlooks, and obligations, all of which are likely to be in short supply in a nonpolar world. Relationships will instead become more selective and situational. It will become harder to classify other countries as either allies or adversaries; they will cooperate on some issues and resist on others. There will be a premium on consultation and coalition building and on a diplomacy that encourages cooperation when possible and shields such cooperation from the fallout of inevitable disagreements. The United States will no longer have the luxury of a "You're either with us or against us" foreign policy.

Nonpolarity will be difficult and dangerous. But encouraging a greater degree of global integration will help promote stability. Establishing a core group of governments and others committed to cooperative multilateralism would be a great step forward. Call it "concerted nonpolarity." It would not eliminate nonpolarity, but it would help manage it and increase the odds that the international system will not deteriorate or disintegrate.

Robert J. Lieber   → **NO**

Falling Upwards:
Declinism, The Box Set

Is America finished? Respected public intellectuals, think tank theorists, and members of the media elite seem to think so. The scare headline in a recent *New York Times Magazine* cover story by Parag Khanna titled "Waving Goodbye to Hegemony" asks, "Who Shrunk the Superpower?" Almost daily, learned authors proclaim *The End of the American Era*, as the title of a 2002 book by Charles Kupchan put it, and instruct us that the rise of China and India, the reawakening of Putin's Russia, and the expansion of the European Union signal a profound shift in geopolitical power that will retire once and for all the burden of American Exceptionalism. America has become an "enfeebled" superpower, according to Fareed Zakaria in his book, *The Post-American World*, which concedes that, while the U.S. will not recede from the world stage anytime soon, "Just as the rest of the world is opening up, America is closing down." With barely contained satisfaction, a French foreign minister says of America's standing, "The magic is over . . . It will never be as it was before."

The United States does contend with serious problems at home and abroad, but these prophecies of doom, which spread like a computer virus, hardly reflect a rational appraisal of where we stand. Moreover, it is not too difficult to see the ghosts of declinism past in the current rush to pen America's epitaph. Gloomsayers have been with us, after all, since this country's founding. Late eighteenth- and early nineteenth-century European observers, especially royalists and reactionaries, commonly disparaged and discounted the prospects of the new American enterprise. (As the French author Phillip Roger has written in his insightful history of anti-Americanism, influential Parisian authors deprecated not only the new country, but also its animals and plants.) In the 1920s and 1930s, communist and fascist critics alike offered sweeping condemnations of the U.S. as a degenerate nation. "The last century [the 19th] was the winter of the West, the victory of materialism and skepticism, of socialism, parliamentarianism, and money," proto-declinist Oswald Spengler famously wrote. "But in this century blood and instinct will regain their rights against the power of money and intellect. The era of individualism, liberalism and democracy, of humanitarianism and freedom, is nearing its end."

From *World Affairs*, Vol. 12, no. 2, Summer 2008. Reprinted by permission of the Helen Dwight Reid Educational Foundation. Published by Heldref Publications, 1319 Eighteenth St., NW, Washington, DC 20036-1802. Copyright © 2008. www.heldref.org

It was in the 1970s that declinism began to take on its modern features, following America's buffeting by oil shocks and deep recessions, a humiliating withdrawal from Vietnam, victories by Soviet-backed regimes or insurgent movements in Africa, Central America, and Southeast Asia, and revolution in Iran along with the seizure of the U.S. embassy there. A 1970 book by Andrew Hacker also announced *The End of the American Era*. At the end of the decade, Jimmy Carter seemed to give a presidential stamp of approval to Hacker's diagnosis when he used concerns about a flagging American economy, inflation, recession, and unemployment as talking points in his famous "malaise" speech calling for diminished national expectations.

By the early 1980s, declinism had become a form of historical chic. In 1987, David Calleo's *Beyond American Hegemony* summoned the U.S. to come to terms with a more pluralistic world. In the same year, Paul Kennedy published what at the time was greeted as the *summa theologica* of the declinist movement—*The Rise and Fall of the Great Powers*, in which the author implied that the cycle of rise and decline experienced in the past by the empires of Spain and Great Britain could now be discerned in the "imperial overstretch" of the United States. But Kennedy had bought in at the top: within two years of his pessimistic prediction, the Cold War ended with the Soviet Union in collapse, the Japanese economic miracle entering a trough of its own, and U.S. competitiveness and job creation far outpacing its European and Asian competitors.

Theories of America's obsolescence aspire to the status of science. But cycles of declinism tend to have a political subtext and, however impeccable the historical methodology that generates them seems to be, they often function as ideology by other means. During the 1980s, for instance, these critiques mostly emanated from the left and focused on Reaganomics and the defense buildup. By contrast, in the Clinton era, right-of-center and realist warnings were directed against the notion of America as an "indispensable nation" whose writ required it to nation-build and spread human rights. Likewise, much of today's resurgent declinism is propelled not only by arguments over real-world events, but also by a fierce reaction against the Bush presidency—a reaction tainted by partisanship, hyperbole, ahistoricism, and a misunderstanding of the fundamentals that underpin the robustness and staying power of the United States.

What is new in the new declinism? A typical variation stipulates that slow-motion shifts in the distribution of global power make it impossible for this country to continue to play the dominating role it has since the end of the Cold War. Yet we have heard this argument, made most recently in *Foreign Affairs* by Council on Foreign Relations President Richard Haass, many times before. As far back as 1972, President Richard Nixon depicted an emerging balance among five major powers: the U.S., Russia, China, Europe, and Japan. In recent years, some commentators have detected an analogous dilution of U.S. influence in the rise of the "BRICs" (Brazil, Russia, India, China), coupled with an expanded and increasingly unified European Union and a flourishing East Asia. In this telling, not only has global power become more widely diffused, but other powers have started to "balance" against the United States, seeking to minimize Washington's role and thwart its global ambitions.

The new declinists usually pin the blame (or credit) on the Bush administration's grand strategy (the Bush Doctrine)—a crudely unilateralist assertion of American power that disregards both the views of other countries and international law. This conduct is said to have provoked a global backlash against the United States, evidenced both in rising anti-Americanism and in the "balancing" policies of many foreign governments. In his *New York Times* article, Khanna rehearses the orthodoxy: "America's unipolar moment has inspired diplomatic and financial countermovements to block American bullying and construct an alternate world order."

Declinists cannot help but acknowledge that the U.S. still possesses the world's most formidable military power, but they view America's armed forces as gravely overextended and trapped in a costly misadventure. The immediate problem is the Bush administration's decision to invade Iraq without formal UN authorization; beyond that there are doubts about America's moral credibility in projecting force anywhere at all.

The declinists also see the U.S. reeling economically. A massive inflow of manufactured goods from East Asia coupled with huge trade and payment deficits has severely weakened the dollar and created an enormous buildup of financial reserves in countries like China, Japan, Taiwan, and South Korea. This, in turn, raises the possibility of a crippling financial crisis were these countries suddenly to unload their U.S. Treasury securities. Making matters worse, a spike in world oil prices has accelerated financial outflows and piled up dollar reserves in the OPEC countries and in Russia. Foreign sovereign wealth funds have used these funds to acquire American assets at basement prices and, with them, the capacity to wield economic and political leverage against Washington. The run-up in oil prices has also boosted the fortunes of hostile regimes, including those of Mahmoud Ahmadinejad in Iran and Hugo Chavez in Venezuela.

With impressive detail and more than a hint of condescension, the new declinists mine this data to make the case for an America in jeopardy—watching helplessly as its global power crumbles away. The solution: a more "realistic" America that lowers its sights and shifts course at home and abroad in line with the new realities.

In a time of war, televised terror threats, and economic and political pessimism, declinism has some of the qualities of a universal solvent: it explains everything. But while it may harmonize with current tremors of fear and uncertainty, declinism succeeds less well as a "new paradigm." In contrast to the declinists' arguments and analyses, America boasts a position of unmatched preponderance. No single country or even grouping of countries has emerged as a plausible counterpart or peer competitor, and apart from the very long-term possibility of China, none is likely to do so.

Consider the frequently cited alternatives. With its twenty-seven member states, 500 million people, and the sum of its aggregate economies, the European Union is always mentioned by those who predict an imminent counterbalancing to the United States. But Europe faces steep obstacles in achieving anything resembling a common foreign and security policy. Its cumbersome institutions, public demands for enormous rates of domestic expenditure, hamstrung attempts at political integration, as well as its Hamlet-like uncertainties about the use of force and military spending, give Europe a global impact far less than its size and wealth would otherwise dictate. An additional reason why it punches far below its weight is that, rather than fielding a true pan-European military, its member states continue to maintain separate (and barely funded) defense establishments. Another is that, with limited exceptions, European countries can deploy only modest forces in the field and, lacking critical mass, render themselves far less effective than even their aggregate numbers might suggest.

For these reasons and more, when national leaders attempt to galvanize opposition to American policies, they seldom prove successful. As a conspicuous case in point, during the months prior to the Iraq War, French, German, and Belgian leaders launched a campaign to gin up opposition to the Bush strategy. Though they gained Russian backing in the UN, they largely failed to do so at home within the EU, where some two-thirds of member governments (including, most significantly, those of "New" Europe) ended up endorsing the American-led war. With the passage of time as well as the coming to power of Atlanticist leaders in Germany (Merkel), France (Sarkozy), and Italy (Berlusconi), there appears to be, if anything, even less inclination to stand in America's way.

Farther East, and despite its economic recovery and the restoration of central power under Putin, Russia remains overwhelmingly dependent on the current boom in energy and commodity prices—and correspondingly vulnerable in the event of their decline. The country suffers from pervasive corruption, with a ranking from Transparency International that puts it at 121 among 163 countries in this category. Its population, already less than half that of the U.S. and plagued with alcoholism, chronic violence, a decrepit health-care system, and a male life expectancy of fewer than 60 years of age (lower than that of Bangladesh), shrinks by some half a million people per year. And its army, while bidding for attention and resources, remains weak and in disarray. As *The Economist* recently summarized Putin's Russia, it has become one of the most "criminalized, corrupt and bureaucratized countries in the world."

True, the Putin regime plays to its domestic base with strident nationalism and xenophobia. In doing so, it has actively opposed and occasionally subverted American policies on some issues while providing a degree of cooperation on others. Instances of the former include opposition to NATO enlargement and to the stationing of anti-missile systems in Poland and the Czech Republic, the use of oil and gas resources as leverage against neighboring countries, overt and covert pressure against former Soviet Republics, and arms sales to Syria and Iran. Yet Moscow grudgingly collaborates where it has shared concerns, as with North Korea and combating terrorism. Russia presents a problem for the United States, but its erratic behavior, its priorities at home, and its own internal decline put it well short of being a major power challenger.

As to Japan, having been touted in the 1980s as *the* emergent world power (and the primary justification of the declinist theories of twenty years ago), it only recently recovered from the effects of its economic collapse in the early 1990s. Moreover, as a result of China's newfound economic weight and military power, Japan has moved into a closer embrace with the United States than ever before. This has meant greater cooperation from military logistics through to the strategic realm, and it has even included logistical and personnel support in Iraq. The Japanese case offers a basic reminder of something declinists too often forget: When assessing a rising power such as China, one ought to consider the near-historical certainty that the rising power will provoke a counterbalancing of its own.

India, too, has adopted a far more positive and intimate commercial, political, and security relationship with Washington than at any time since its independence in 1947. During the Cold War, India, although formally nonaligned, had tilted toward the Soviet Union. India's substantial shift toward the United States, made partly in response to China's awakening, offers another example of "bandwagoning" with us rather than balancing against us.

Finally, there is China—America's most serious, and in many respects only true, competitor. It projects greater influence in Asia by the day, and it has been a problematic actor in other regions as well, where it has bolstered and sustained repressive regimes that the U.S. and Europe have sought to isolate, as in Sudan, Zimbabwe, Burma, and to some extent Iran. Its ability to do so, needless to say, rests on economic growth. A huge trade surplus with the United States has spurred the accumulation of $1.5 *trillion* in foreign exchange reserves, the bulk of it invested in U.S. government securities. In theory, this could allow Beijing to undo the American economy in one fell swoop. However, in triggering a run on the dollar China would subvert its own national interest, boosting its own currency against America's and thereby undercutting its own competitiveness as well as its ability to export to the U.S. market.

Still, Beijing now plays an outsized role in global affairs. But, again, as China has become the dominant power in East Asia, its muscle flexing has pushed not only Japan but also Vietnam, Singapore, Australia, and others farther into the U.S. orbit. In any case, China's priorities for the immediate future center mostly on internal development and the absorption of hundreds of millions of workers from its lagging rural and agricultural sectors. The quickening pace of China's military buildup seems intended primarily to deter the United States from intervening in support of Taiwan and, beyond that, to establish regional rather than global power. Over the very long term China may indeed emerge as a great power rival to the United States. But this seems very, very unlikely in the near or medium term.

Not only is there no superpower challenge visible on the horizon, but some regions, particularly much of Africa and Asia, have been either largely untouched by post-Iraq reactions against the United States or, as with Vietnam, Singapore, and Australia, have even adopted a more pro-American stance. Anti-Americanism exists, but it always has, waxing and waning since the end of World War II and becoming especially virulent during the Vietnam, Reagan, and Bush eras. Viewing the malady as acute rather than a chronic staple of the international arena hugely overstates its impact. In fact, the truly new element in the mix is globalization, which, far from being a source of decline, tends to work in favor of the United States. As authors such as Francis Fukuyama and Walter Russell Mead have demonstrated, the more globally integrated developing countries tend to be the least anti-American, placing a premium on liberalism, the rule of law, and other traditions that have come to be seen as U.S. exports.

Not surprisingly, the declinist outlook carries with it policy prescriptions—yearnings, really—that a fading superpower will exit center stage gracefully. Earnest liberal internationalists such as Anne-Marie Slaughter and John Ikenberry admonish Washington to show far more deference and even subservience to world opinion and to work in concert with, and on behalf of, the global community. Indeed, for some declinists, the U.S. has become a sort of genteel version of a rogue nation.

The portrait is often tinged with partisan politics. Merely as a result of a change in administration, two former National Security Council staffers, Nina Hachigian and Mona Sutphen, write in *The Next American Century*, a solipsistic recounting of the Clinton years, their halcyon days in government bureaucracy were exchanged for a condition of "America on one side, the rest of the world on the other." A broader critique assigns responsibility for America's overstretch to the entire post–Cold War era. On this count, authors and public intellectuals loosely associated with the realist tradition, such as Christopher Layne and Dimitri Simes, indict not only neoconservatives, who are said to have engineered the Bush Doctrine, but also liberal internationalists, whom they depict as emboldening neoconservatives with their own enthusiasms for humanitarian intervention, nation-building, and democracy promotion. Still others look inward for the cause of America's demise. Former Secretary of Defense James Schlesinger has complained about the effect of ethnic groups on U.S. foreign policy and questioned whether the Constitution itself contains the seeds of America's decline. Similarly, James Kurth has pointed to multiculturalism and the pollution of pop culture as the culprits, while Samuel Huntington, who writes that "Cultural America is under siege," sees America's fabric frayed by racial, ethnic, and cultural diversity.

Much of the case, however, wilts under close analysis, relying as it does overwhelmingly on transient or reversible indicators. (Comparing America's share of the global economy in the late 1940s with its share today, for example, gives a skewed result for the simple reason that much of the rest of the world was in ruins sixty years ago.) Declinism gains much of its power from cherry-picking among daily reports of bad news and from the assumption that those who defend this country's basic strength have blinkered themselves to the Hegelian logic behind America's weakening. As with the pessimistic intellectual troughs that followed the Depression, Vietnam, and the stagflation of the late 1970s and early 1980s, there is a tendency among declinists to over-extrapolate from a momentous but singular event—in this case, the Iraq War, whose wake propels many of their gloomy forecasts.

On the economic front, without minimizing the impact of today's challenges, they will likely prove less daunting than those that plagued the U.S. in the 1970s and early 1980s. The overall size and dynamism of the economy remains unmatched, and America continues to lead the rest of the world in measures of competitiveness, technology, and innovation. Here, higher education and science count as an enormous asset. America's major research universities lead the world in stature and rankings, occupying seventeen of the top twenty slots. Broad demographic trends also favor the United States, whereas countries typically mentioned as peer competitors sag under the weight of aging populations. This is not only true for Russia, Europe, and Japan, but also for China, whose long-standing one-child policy has had an anticipated effect.

In the realm of "hard power," while the army and Marines have been stretched by the wars in Iraq and Afghanistan, the fact is that no other country possesses anything like the capacity of the United States to project power around the globe. American military technology and sheer might remain unmatched—no other country can compete in the arenas of land, sea, or air warfare. China claims that it spends $45 billion annually on defense, but the truth comes closer to three times that figure. Still, America's $625 billion defense budget dwarfs even that. The latter amounts to just 4.2 percent of GDP. This contrasts with 6.6 percent at the height of the Reagan buildup and double-digit percentages during the early and middle years of the Cold War.

Not surprisingly, given all this, few global problems can be solved, let alone managed, absent a significant American commitment. The United States, as Michael Mandelbaum has put it, remains the world's principal provider of public goods. This can mean, variously, leadership, political backing, financial or diplomatic assistance, logistics, intelligence, or the use of military assets for tasks ranging from disaster relief to combat support. In many instances, and particularly in urgent and dire cases such as the Balkan crises, the choice boils down to this: either the United States will act or no one will.

Other countries understand the unique nature of American power—if not wholly selfless, not entirely selfish, either—and its role in underpinning global stability and maintaining a decent world order. This helps to explain why Europe, India, Japan and much of East Asia, and important countries of the Middle East, Africa, and Latin America have no use for schemes to balance against the United States. Most would rather do business with America or be shielded by it.

In the end, then, this country's structural advantages matter much more than economic cycles, trade imbalances, or surging and receding tides of anti-Americanism. These advantages include America's size, wealth, human and material resources, military strength, competitiveness, and liberal political and economic traditions, but also a remarkable flexibility, dynamism, and capacity for reinvention. Neither the rise of important regional powers, nor a globalized world economy, nor "imperial overstretch," nor domestic weaknesses seem likely to negate these advantages in ways the declinists anticipate, often with a fervor that makes their diagnoses and prescriptions resemble a species of wish fulfillment.

Over the years, America's staying power has been regularly and chronically underestimated—by condescending French and British statesmen in the nineteenth century, by German, Japanese, and Soviet militarists in the twentieth, and by homegrown prophets of doom today. The critiques come and go. The object of their contempt never does.

POSTSCRIPT

Is the United States in Decline?

For an argument that the United States was in a situation of relative decline in the 1980s, see Paul Kennedy, *The Rise and Fall of the Great Powers* (Vintage, 1989). For a contrasting view of U.S. power in this period, see Joseph S. Nye, Jr., *Bound to Lead: The Changing Nature of American Power* (Basic Books, 1991).

For more recent arguments that the United States is currently in a period of relative decline, see Charles Kupchan, *The End of the American Era: U.S. Foreign Policy and the Geopolitics of the Twenty-First Century* (Vintage, 2003), and Fareed Zakaria, *The Post-American World* (W.W. Norton, 2009).

For data on U.S. and global military expenditures, see the information compiled by GlobalSecurity.org at: http://www.globalsecurity.org/military/world/spending.htm.

For figures on U.S. and world GDP, see the data from NationMaster.com at: http://www.nationmaster.com/graph/eco_gro_nat_inc-economy-gross-national-income.

ISSUE 3

Should Promoting Democracy Abroad Be a Top U.S. Priority?

YES: Joseph Siegle, from "Developing Democracy: Democratizers' Surprisingly Bright Development Record," *Harvard International Review* (Summer 2004)

NO: Tamara Cofman Wittes, from "Arab Democracy, American Ambivalence," *The Weekly Standard* (February 23, 2004)

ISSUE SUMMARY

YES: Joseph Siegle, Douglas Dillon Fellow at the Council on Foreign Relations, argues that large numbers of countries are continuing to democratize and, because of the increase in accountability associated with democratization, they tend to experience economic growth as fast as, if not faster than, other countries in the same region.

NO: Tamara Cofman Wittes, research fellow in the Saban Center for Middle East Policy at the Brookings Institution, argues that U.S. efforts to promote democracy in Iraq and the Arab Middle East are likely to fail unless the U.S. government matches its rhetoric with a credible commitment to promote policies institutionalizing the forward movement of liberalism in Iraq and the region at large.

President George H. W. Bush responded to the dramatic increase in the number of countries pursuing democracy in the early 1990s by calling for a "a new world order" in which "nations recognize the shared responsibility for freedom and justice." Since then over 80 previously non-democratic countries have made progress toward democratization. As a result, over two-thirds of the countries in the world practice some form of democratic rule today.

Promoting democracy became a central component of U.S. foreign policy under President Bill Clinton, and it remained so under President George W. Bush. It is not yet clear how central promoting democracy will be to President Obama's foreign policy. The core motivation for this rests on the "Democratic Peace proposition" that democracies tend not to fight with one another and instead are generally highly integrated economically and politically with one another. While some vocal dissenters exist, a large amount of political science research in the 1990s suggests that democracies have historically been less likely to fight wars with other democracies. Promoting democracy is, therefore, seen as a means of increasing stability, peace, and economic prosperity in the international system.

Arguments for why this pattern exists generally emphasize the pacifying effect of constraints that democratic institutions impose on their leaders; the legal, social, and political norms shared by democratic states; and the relatively high level of interdependence among democratic states. Democratic institutions—including open public debate as well as legal and constitutional constraints on the executive—help promote peace by limiting the ability of the executive to act rashly or without consultation. Furthermore, the desire to get reelected is presumed to make politicians less willing to engage in risky foreign policies. Shared norms further decrease the likelihood of conflict by providing a common basis of understanding that enhances trust and reduces the likelihood of misinterpreting one another's actions to be aggressive. Finally, market-based economic systems tend to be more prevalent in—though not exclusive to—democracies, and the interdependence they generate creates incentives to maintain peaceful and mutually beneficial international relationships.

The process of democratization is not always smooth. When, for example, elections take place before legal systems are solidified or before realistic plans for sustained economic growth are established, public expectations can outpace the newly elected government's ability to deliver positive changes. The result may be a political backlash against democracy, the rise of corruption, or other forms of political or economic instability. Research in international relations has demonstrated that while established democracies are less prone to engage in risky behavior, states undergoing the process of democratization are more prone than others to do so. Thus, while a world populated by democracies is likely to be more peaceful than others, a world of countries going through the process of democratization may be more unstable and conflict-prone.

Given these risks, many scholars and politicians have argued that perhaps economic liberalization should take place before political liberalization (as in Singapore or the People's Republic of China) or that political elections in the absence of a strong independent judiciary will simply empower former elites and promote corruption (as in Russia following the fall of the Soviet Union). Joseph Siegle argues that despite these concerns, countries that are truly democratizing have developed faster than their non-democratic counterparts. Tamara Cofman Wittes argues that the transition to democracy is difficult and likely to fail in the Arab Middle East unless the United States dedicates itself to creating the institutions necessary to make it work over the long haul.

YES

Joseph Siegle

Developing Democracy: Democratizers' Surprisingly Bright Development Record

The past 25 years have seen an astonishing advance in the number of democracies around the world. Some 87 previously nondemocratic countries have made discernible advances towards democracy during this time. Of these democratizers, 70 have per capita incomes below US$4,000, making this a largely developing country phenomenon. Today, two-thirds of all countries live under some form of self-governance—a reversal from just 15 years ago.

Despite this tectonic shift in global governance patterns, the sentiment that a poor country must first develop economically before it can democratize persists. The stellar growth of autocratic Singapore, China, and Vietnam as well as the experiences of South Korea, Taiwan, and Chile are trotted out as justification for this seemingly hard but true reality. Low income countries that do start down a democratic path are bound to fail or at least take a sharp economic hit in the process, according to this view. Indeed, authoritarian governments throughout the Middle East, the former Soviet Union, and elsewhere are quick to cite this concern when deflecting growing pressure to democratize.

A closer look at the development track record tells a different story, however. Most of the 87 contemporary democratizers have realized economic growth as fast as, if not faster than, the norm for their respective regions over the past five years. That is, democratizers such as Poland, Hungary, Bulgaria, the Baltic states, Mexico, Senegal, and Mozambique are typically growing more rapidly than countries with autocratic governments such as Syria, Saudi Arabia, Uzbekistan, North Korea, Cuba, Zimbabwe, Togo, and Gabon. The pattern holds up for the entire 25-year period of the contemporary democratization era. This is so despite the fact that a full quarter of (typically underperforming) autocratic governments do not publicly report their economic data and therefore are not even factored into these comparisons.

The differences are even more striking when we consider indicators of well-being such as life expectancy, illiteracy, and access to clean drinking water. Low-income democratizers enjoy demonstrably better living standards than autocracies. Consider infant mortality rates, an indicator many development experts consider the best all around measure of social welfare progress. Autocratic countries with per capita incomes below US$2,000 averaged

79 infant deaths per 1,000 live births during the 1990s. Democratizers in the same income category and time period typically experienced 62 infant deaths. Given that many of these countries still rely on their agricultural sectors for the bulk of their employment and income, democratizers' track record of posting agricultural yields that are on average 25 percent superior to those of developing country autocracies is similarly noteworthy.

Simply put, democratic governance is good for development. This is not to say there are not exceptions; clearly, there are. However, the pattern of superior developmental performance among countries that are on a democratic path is robust. The traditional view that political liberalization inevitably precipitates populist economic policies and economic contraction has not been demonstrated in practice when compared to autocratic countries in the same regions or income groups.

In many ways, this is intuitive—what is government but a mechanism by which a society orders its priorities? The more representative, transparent, and accountable this process, the more balanced the outcomes will be compared to a system that is narrowly based and lacking incentives for responsiveness to citizen interests.

Why Do Some Democratizers Do So Much Better?

Given that democratizers more than hold their own when it comes to development, the more interesting question is why some democratizers do so much better than others in their development efforts? That is, if democracy is a plus for development, why aren't all democratizers thriving?

A significant degree of this difference can be explained by the extent to which democratizers have established institutional mechanisms of shared power, or what I refer to as "accountability institutions." These include checks on the chief executive (for example, a legislature that can initiate legislation and block egregious policies pursued by the executive branch), the separation of political party influence from state structures (evidenced by a merit-based civil service), the separation of economic opportunity from political authority as seen through an autonomous private sector, an independent judiciary, and a free press.

Democratizing states that move to establish and strengthen these institutions of shared power tend to develop more rapidly. Specifically, looking at the experience of democratizers over the last 25 years, it is apparent that annual per capita growth rates for democratizers in the top quartile of a composite measure of these accountability institutions grew, on average, more than a full percentage point faster than democratizers in the bottom quartile of these accountability rankings—2.2 percent versus 1.0 percent. So, democratizers as diverse as Botswana, South Africa, Senegal, Slovenia, Estonia, Czech Republic, Chile, Dominican Republic, and Thailand that have established comparatively stronger institutional mechanisms protecting against the arbitrary use of power have realized substantially more economic growth than other democratizers such as Algeria, Cameroon, Burkina Faso, Guinea, Tajikistan,

Kazakhstan, and Georgia, where restraints on political monopolization have been weak. Analogous growth differences hold across income levels.

Similar differentials are apparent on measures of social progress. Democratizers with stronger institutions of accountability score, on average, 15 to 25 percent higher on indicators of life expectancy, access to medical service, and primary school enrollment among others. Countries in the top quartile of accountability scores for all low income (that is, below US$2,000 per capita) democratizers typically have had infant mortality rates of 37 per 1,000 live births in the 1990s compared to a 79 per 1,000 mortality rate for democratizers in the lower quartile of the accountability rankings. The disparities only widen when the under US$1,000 income category is considered. Understanding the development advantage of democratizers thus involves assessing the extensiveness of their checks and balances on power—as distinguished from those that may solely adopt some of the symbols of democracy, such as elections. Countries that democratize in deed and not just name tend to develop more rapidly.

Progress on any of the individual accountability dimensions tends to improve development outcomes. Thus, strengthening the independence of the judiciary, the civil service, or the private sector each has positive effects for development. In practical terms, however, it is rare for a country to distinguish itself on a sole accountability element. A society commonly makes progress across a number of fronts simultaneously. This suggests that a shift in norms and expectations regarding the limits of political power occurs. A "culture of accountability" begins to take root. And it is the cumulative effect of these enhanced norms that is most important for transferring political change into development improvements. Such a shift occurred in Kenya following the election of President Mwai Kibaki in late 2002, representing the first transfer of power between political parties in Kenyan history. Having campaigned on an anti-corruption platform, upon taking office Kibaki instituted new standards of transparency and disclosure for conflicts of interest among senior government officials. Acting on this cue, ordinary Kenyans began refusing to pay the ubiquitous bribes demanded by Kenyan police. In some cases, incensed crowds would chase bribe-seeking police officers straight off their beats. Government contracts awarded under questionable circumstances, previously accepted as the norm, were increasingly challenged in the courts by the general public. Corrupt judges have been forced to resign. While Kenya still has a way to go, the indirect benefits to the Kenyan economy, in terms of reduced transaction costs, time saved, and improved economic efficiency resulting from the higher level of accountability, are surely substantial.

To the extent that any single accountability factor determines development progress, an independent media stands out. Of all 87 democratizers considered, only Cambodia and Angola have realized economic development in the late 1990s at a rate faster than their regional norm without also establishing at least an intermediate degree of press freedoms. Therefore, while a free press is often invoked for its importance in strengthening democracy, its contribution to material progress may be equally relevant.

More informed deliberation prior to the adoption of a policy, heightened scrutiny and pressure to rectify policies producing poor results, and strengthened market confidence created by the greater transparency fostered by a free press all contribute to this phenomenon. In other words, an independent media creates an environment in which democracy's self-correcting mechanisms can come into play. The end result of this is a more pragmatic set of development policies.

A free press may also be indispensable to the realization of the other accountability structures. Consider the rule of law. Without the transparency and scrutiny fostered by independent media, the scope for misuse of public monies by government officials is substantially greater. This, in turn, affects the prospects for a competitive private sector. The recent experience of the petroleum industry in India is indicative of this phenomenon. Only after an investigation by the newspaper *Indian Express* was it discovered that in state after state, the bulk of licenses for gas stations were going to members of the governing Bharatiya Janata Party and their friends and relatives. The scandal forced Indian Prime Minister Atal Bihari Vajpayee to cancel the allotments for more than 3,000 gas stations, resulting in greater economic competition and lower prices for consumers. In short, it was the transparency generated by the independent media that invigorated the rule of law.

Accordingly, Vladimir Putin's systematic efforts to disembowel an independent media in Russia will likely be self-defeating. His effort to control the flow of information diminishes the rule of law, the autonomy of the private sector, and checks on the executive branch. While he certainly enjoys additional maneuverability under a state-owned media, this advantage is destined to be fleeting. In the process, he is inexorably undermining his stated priority of establishing a strong foundation for Russia's sustained economic growth. As tales of government extortion and intimidation of entrepreneurs increase, foreign direct investment will dwindle further.

Pseudo-Democratizers

The realization that democratizers with relatively stronger institutions of shared power tend to grow more rapidly raises important issues over how we categorize democratizers. The classic litmus test—holding multi-party elections—is increasingly unsatisfactory. With the evolving international norm of according legitimacy only to those leaders that have been democratically elected, heads of authoritarian states have craftily attempted to co-opt the language and trappings of democracy so as to make the grade without ever seriously intending to share power. President Hosni Mubarak's Egypt is the prototypical case. Presidential elections are held every six years and opposition parties, a civil society, and a free press are ostensibly allowed. However, these democratic processes are heavily circumscribed. Political opponents are frequently harassed, licenses of civil society organizations critical of the government are regularly rescinded, and strict self-censorship is imposed. Political power comfortably remains within the hands of Mubarak. Similarly, Rwanda went through an electoral charade late last year in order to anoint Paul Kagame as president. Opposition parties were allowed but were frequently prevented from holding rallies or appearing on state-sponsored television. Not only were supporters afraid to show up at opposition rallies but, intimidated by government threats, opposition candidates themselves would at times preemptively cancel planned gatherings. Some recent examples of autocrats trying to masquerade as democrats in order to attain a degree of international credibility include Azerbaijan's transition of power from father to son in the guise of elections, Robert Mugabe's manipulation of democratic procedures in Zimbabwe, Iran's Guardian Council (representing the unelected clerical hierarchy) barring of 2,400 moderate candidates from running in parliamentary elections, and General Pervez Musharraf's elaborately staged national referenda in Pakistan, to name a few.

This more sophisticated class of "pseudo-democratizers" has learned that they can often avoid international scrutiny so long as they maintain some of the more visible rituals of democratic governance. And to a large extent, they are right. In addition to setting fuzzy and embarrassingly low standards, the international community has yet to figure out how to deal with authoritarian states dressed up in democratic regalia. Arguments for constructive engagement, patience for the slow pace, and a misguided focus on the "glass half-full" argument continue to be convincingly made. The neo-authoritarians have played on this ambiguity to suggest real change is taking place, when all the while, they are, in fact, tightening their grip on power. Unsurprisingly, the democratizer-growth relationship for electoral democracies is only one quarter as strong as when the extent of a democratizer's accountability structures is taken into consideration.

Including this collection of pseudo-democratizers in the broader class of countries undergoing genuine political change, predictably obscures our understanding of the democratizers' development track record. The challenge to the international community is to match the sophistication of the democratic charlatans by devising methods to better discriminate which states are making real, if incremental, progress towards greater political participation and power sharing. Assessing the extent to which accountability institutions have been created provides a potential lens to do so.

Democracy and Accountability

As one would expect, democracies and countries on the road to democracy generally have stronger systems of accountability in place than autocratic states. This creates the self-correcting processes that allow political institutions to moderate and facilitate positive economic and social welfare outcomes. Those democracies and democratizers with relatively stronger accountability institutions within their respective income or regional cohort have typically excelled in their developmental outcomes. Interestingly enough, the same principle applies when we look at groupings of authoritarian countries. Those authoritarian regimes with relatively stronger accountability structures have realized more rapid growth. In other words, the pattern of strong accountability institutions and steady economic development is consistent regardless of whether a country is democratic, democratizing, or authoritarian. It is just that democracies have a considerably higher likelihood of creating such accountability structures.

Understanding the relationship between accountability and development thus sheds light on a couple of missing pieces in the democracy-development puzzle. First, it is widely recognized that almost all of the world's prosperous states are democracies. The real debate has always been about how poor countries get there from where they are starting. That is, how do we reconcile the outstanding record of the industrialized democracies with the checkered results generated by democratizers? Focusing on the depth of accountability institutions, a common trait of both the industrialized democracies and democratizers that have grown more rapidly, provides at least part of the answer. Poor countries that started down the democratization path and established strong accountability structures have generally grown rapidly; democracy and development do go together. The prescription of a prolonged period of authoritarian purgatory before enjoying democratic redemption is unwarranted. For that matter, formerly low-income countries like Malta, Mauritius, Botswana, and post-Pinochet Chile have grown so rapidly and steadily that they have made considerable headway in closing the prosperity gap with the industrialized democracies. While at varying stages in the process, Thailand, Poland, Hungary, the Baltic countries, Mozambique, and the Dominican Republic are recent democratizers also on a development fast track. Democratizers that have moved less cogently to establish institutions that constrain political and economic monopolization have generally grown less quickly.

Second, one of the perplexities to the democracy-development debate has been the stellar economic performance of a selected number of authoritarian countries, most notably in East Asia. How have these exceptional autocratic growers bucked the trend? Their strength of accountability institutions has something to do with it. This category of rapidly-growing autocrats, controlling for income, scores 20 to 40 percent better on the various categories of accountability compared to other authoritarian countries. In short, economically vibrant autocracies are clear-cut outliers.

This helps us to understand the anomalous nature of the fast-growing authoritarians. Yes, they do exist but they are far from representative and therefore a poor basis on which to guide development policy. Specifically, over the past 25 years there have been eight authoritarian countries that have enjoyed rapid economic growth for over a decade: Bhutan, China, Egypt, South Korea, Singapore, Taiwan, Tunisia, and Vietnam. This compares to the roughly 60 other authoritarian governments that experienced stagnant growth during this time period. In other words, it is not the authoritarian character of the fast-growing states that explains their remarkable development. The wait for development in low accountability states such as Turkmenistan, Azerbaijan, Belarus, Sudan, Cameroon, Burma, Haiti, and Syria before the promotion of democracy will be a long wait indeed.

Policy Implications

At present, development funding to low-income democracies, as a share of GDP, is no greater than that to authoritarian states. To better reduce poverty and propel economic growth, this should change. International investors and development agencies should instead identify countries undertaking genuine political reform and target resource flows to them with the aim of accelerating their economic growth and material development. The track record suggests that the impact and returns from such investment will be maximized. Directing capital flows to these countries, coupled with the enhanced economic progress these democratizers would experience, accentuates incentives for other developing countries to initiate democratic political reform in earnest.

The United States' recently inaugurated Millennium Challenge Account is a potentially important instrument for such a democracy-focused development strategy. While substantially scaled-back from US President George Bush's original proposal, this US$1 billion annual fund for countries deemed to be ruling democratically, investing in their populations, and to be establishing basic economic rights could facilitate a marked shift in development outlays towards democratizers. To be effective and to ensure that the incentive structure of this program clearly resounds throughout the developing world, however, robust democratic governance standards should be maintained in selecting eligible countries. This would signal to non-democratic countries that hope to participate in the program that the prospect of gaining access to increased development funding is linked to their pursuit of genuine democratic reforms. The humanitarian instinct to loosen the standards, thereby allowing more countries to qualify for this new pot of resources, would inadvertently undercut the distinctive purpose of this program and should therefore be resisted.

Pursuing a democracy-centered development strategy recognizes that political orientation is a central feature to development, not just one other desirable objective. Such a perspective requires better integration into the foreign policies of the industrialized democracies. It is not a matter that can be solely relegated to their development agencies. In the United States, for example, it requires greater harmonization of the policies of the State, Treasury, and Commerce Departments—and in an age of shifting security threats, the Defense Department and Central Intelligence Agency. What is required is no less than a coherent foreign policy toward the developing world—something that has not existed in the United States for decades. Within agencies whose primary mission is development, such as the US Agency for International Development, better integration of experts dealing with democracy and development issues is needed. Despite their evident complementarities, there remains substantial stove-piping among specialists in these fields. Given the close relationship between democratic governance and positive development outcomes, this compartmentalization is a handicap.

Recognizing the central role that accountability institutions play in development also provides a framework for more effectively targeting development resources. While moving towards a "culture of accountability" and the adoption of political institutions that facilitate shared power and ensure checks and balances are ultimately up to the society in question, certain external efforts can assist this process. Perhaps most important is holding countries claiming to be democracies to international standards of openness, shared power, and political participation. By enforcing a high bar for international democratic legitimacy—with the diplomatic and capital market benefits this branding entails—the international community is ensuring that an incentive structure is in place to propel international reforms, which in turn have a better chance of being sustained. Meanwhile, internal efforts should focus on enhancing the capacity of democratizing countries' institutions of accountability: strengthening the caliber of the civil service, the judiciary, the oversight of the executive branch, and the autonomy of the private sector from political influences. Particular attention should be paid to the establishment of independent media. A free press augments the ability of other institutions, including civil society, to exert the checks and balances against centralized control so critical for sustained development. Mechanisms by which the general public can become better informed of policy debates, actions of public officials, management of public finances, and the functioning of markets will enhance transparency, efficiency, and pressure for corrective action. International efforts can help develop a cadre of trained journalists and media institutions with a clear understanding of their roles and responsibilities. Technical support for the management and marketing skills needed to run regional and national newspapers, television, and radio stations can also better ensure the financial and technological independence of these ventures over time. Notably, these efforts should not be limited to the public sector. Mobilizing private investment into media enterprises, most viably with local partners, further enhances prospects for their sustainability.

There is a compelling case for encouraging democratization in the developing world. Most countries that pursue political reform do economically better. They are not destined to political instability and economic stagnation as established thinking would have us believe. This, of course, is on top of the many moral and justice-based advantages of democracy. However, the policy indecisiveness bred by the conventional view risks unnecessarily propping up dictatorial or neo-authoritarian governments to the detriment of their populations and the world at large. Waiting for a country to develop economically before promoting democratic reform is a *non sequitur* in nearly all cases. Rather, what is needed is an increasingly sophisticated strategy on the part of the world's leading democracies to delineate genuine democratizers from those that are simply going through the motions—and then to ensure that adequate levels of financial and political support are available to foster their success.

Countries undertaking the difficult steps of political liberalization are engaged in one of the most challenging and important political processes of our time. In aggregate, they are shaping global political norms for the 21st century. It is incumbent on the established democracies to better understand this process so as to effect a more decisive and consistent influence.

Tamara Cofman Wittes ➡ **NO**

Arab Democracy, American Ambivalence

Over the past year, the goal of democratizing the Arab Middle East has been elevated from wooly-headed ideal to national security imperative and a key part of the war on terrorism. The Bush administration judged that political dysfunction and failing, corrupt autocracies were making Muslims, and particularly Arabs, especially vulnerable to the appeal of radical Islamist ideologies. America's longtime rationale for supporting Arab autocrats was their promise of stability. But as the president recognized in his landmark speech at the National Endowment for Democracy in November, the price was high and the stability was deceptive. Hence the new "generational commitment" to promote democracy in the Arab world.

In pursuit of this commitment (and other worthy goals), the administration has already taken one enormously large and costly action: It has launched regime change in Iraq, an endeavor on which the U.S. government has lavished considerable blood and treasure, and in which it cannot afford to fail (though fail it might).

It has also done smaller things—and promised in the loftiest rhetoric to do a great many more such things in the decades ahead—to spur democratic development across the entire Middle East. In what the president calls a "forward strategy of freedom," the administration has vowed to reorient U.S. diplomacy and U.S. aid so as to lend moral and material support to pro-democracy forces throughout the Arab world. Its instruments to this end include the Middle East Partnership Initiative, just over one year old; a Middle East Free Trade Area; and a proposed doubling of the budget of the National Endowment for Democracy, a bipartisan grant-giving organization funded by the U.S. government to support the growth of democracy. In addition, at a series of summits this year with the G-8, NATO, and the European Union, Washington reportedly plans to enlist other advanced democracies to endorse reform principles for the Greater Middle East.

Where does this ambitious venture stand at the end of its first year? It is too early, of course, to offer any verdict as to outcomes. But this is clear: For the endeavor to succeed, many within the U.S. government must overcome their own misgivings about it. Only then will Washington convince the Arab world's lonely liberals of the seriousness of its commitment to the goal of "a democratic peace—a peace founded upon the dignity and rights of every man and woman." What's more, given the complexity and scope of the endeavor, its announced centrality to our national security, and its inevitable consequences for our standing in the world, it is none too soon to clarify underlying assumptions, question priorities, and point out pitfalls.

Why, after all, should Arab democrats believe us? Both "anti-imperialist" Arab intellectuals and American analysts note the credibility gap we confront in preaching democracy to the Middle East. Acknowledging our past support for autocrats, as President Bush did in November, is a start. But actually overcoming the credibility gap and building an effective democratization program requires a firmness of purpose the Bush administration has thus far not displayed. Whether it can and will do this remains to be seen.

To be sure, the administration has taken an irrevocable step with the invasion of Iraq. Having committed many billions of dollars to the democratization program there, America must make its success our first priority. One obvious reason is that if democracy takes hold in Iraq, it really might provide a powerful demonstration effect to the neighborhood.

Less obvious is the fact that America's current problems in Iraq—especially the insistence in Washington on a timetable and procedure for transferring sovereignty driven more by our own needs than Iraqis'—are right now providing a powerful *negative* demonstration effect to the neighborhood. The more repressive governments in the region are tightening their domestic controls, confident that we are distracted. Skeptical Arab commentators point out that American liberation has seemingly brought Iraqis nothing but chaos and death. Because President Bush linked the American democracy project in Iraq to reform in other Arab countries, the fate of democracy activists elsewhere in the Arab world now hangs on the success of the new Iraq. If the United States leaves Iraq's political reconstruction half-finished, Washington will have hung Arab democrats out to dry.

Some Arabs doubt President Bush's staying power on behalf of Iraqi democracy, but even more, they doubt that was ever his goal. This deeper skepticism is, sadly, justified by America's historical ambivalence about Arab democracy, an ambivalence that undermines even the new initiatives that are part of the forward strategy. America's error of "excusing and accommodating the lack of freedom in the Middle East," as the president put it, was compounded in 1992, when the U.S. government acquiesced in a military coup in Algeria designed to forestall a victory by the radical Islamic Salvation Front in the country's first free parliamentary elections. The "Algeria problem"—famously defined by veteran diplomat Edward Djerejian as "one man, one vote, one time"—still haunts American policymakers: the fear that free elections in the Arab world will bring to power Islamist governments that can claim democratic legitimacy but are anti-American and ultimately anti-democratic.

Add to this Washington's worry that assertive democracy-promotion in the Arab world will exacerbate tensions with Arab states whose cooperation on other issues is highly valued in the State Department and the Pentagon. The United States has little to lose by calling for a democratic transformation in states like Libya and Syria, but the Middle East is full of regimes America has worked closely with for years, and whose cooperation it desires on a variety of security and economic matters, not least the war on terrorism. In the past, the U.S. government has typically subordinated its concerns about governance and human rights to cooperation on defense, the Arab-Israeli peace process, and other core issues.

Because of these longstanding concerns, American democratization efforts in the Arab world have traditionally been modest, undertaken in consultation with the region's governments, and aimed at delivering technical assistance rather than altering the distribution of political power. Despite the new imperative driving the president's strategy, the policies devised to implement it so far—setting aside the unique case of Iraq—have not escaped these constraints.

In effect, the Bush administration has embraced the Arab regimes' own survival strategy of *controlled liberalization*. Most of the 22 Arab states themselves recognize their systemic failures, and seek to reform in ways that improve government and economic performance without changing the distribution of political power. While a few forward-leaning regimes have placed some power in the hands of their peoples through constitutional and electoral reforms, many others are trying to create just enough sense of forward motion and participation without power to alleviate the building public pressure for change at the top.

The premise underlying America's embrace of this gradual approach is that we can avoid the risk of Islamist victories and minimize bilateral tensions if we help existing governments reform, even if they resist opening up political competition and sharing power. In theory, our new assistance under the Middle East Partnership Initiative and the National Endowment for Democracy is also supposed to identify liberal forces within civil society, give them funding and training, and help them grow to the point where they can bring about velvet revolutions. This gradualist strategy assumes that, over time, liberalization will take on such momentum that the regimes will no longer be able to avoid devolution of power.

But that is an uncertain assumption: If existing regimes do lose control and chaos ensues, there is no guarantee that long-repressed liberals will win out. Indeed, the top-down "liberalization" underway in many Arab states has not relaxed state controls sufficiently to enable any third political force to organize, beyond the state and the Islamist opposition. The Islamists have the mosque as their forum for organizing, but freedom to organize outside the mosque—to talk politics and form parties—is still heavily restricted. So the regimes maintain control, and the Islamists remain the only alternative—as well as the excuse the regimes give Washington for deeming truly free politics too dangerous.

The larger the Algeria scenario looms in American policymakers' minds as the nightmare to be avoided at all costs, the more our policy is paralyzed; recalcitrant Arab leaders are quick to see this. But that's not the worst of it. The longer the U.S. government rewards regimes that "liberalize" without allowing new political forces to develop, the more the Islamists benefit from such limited political openings as exist. The more entrenched the Islamists become as the political alternative to the status quo, the more the language of Islamism becomes *the* language of protest politics, and other voices are marginalized. As an Arab official told me recently, "The only institution expressing freedom [to criticize the government] in the Arab world today is the mosque. That's why they're popular." The net effect of gradual "liberalization," then, may be not to drain the swamp of extremism, but to expand it.

For liberalization to have real meaning, the regimes themselves must change. No matter how many small-bore grants the U.S. government gives to improve parliamentary effectiveness, judicial independence, or the rule of law, the legislature and judiciary in most Arab countries will remain subordinated to their executives—until those executives give up emergency laws and restrain security forces. And no matter how much training the National Endowment for Democracy sponsors for women candidates or liberal politicians, they will not be able to compete in the political marketplace until their governments allow freedom of expression and association.

America can constrain the power of Arab autocrats and help create space for the emergence of liberal alternatives only by putting political pressure on the regimes and, at the same time, developing partnerships with indigenous reformers both in and out of government. To succeed, America must dovetail its assistance with the needs of Arab activists on the ground. This requires American officials to get outside their embassies and cultivate Arab allies. It also requires U.S. assistance programs to abandon familiar but ineffective approaches such as relying on international "trainers" and placing our funds at the service of governments with a different agenda.

This hasn't happened yet. In its first fiscal year, the Middle East Partnership Initiative spent just under $28 million. Only about $2 million of it went directly to local Arab nongovernmental organizations to help them expand their work, all of it in less controversial areas such as family law, literacy, and anticorruption campaigns. This meager involvement of the nongovernmental sector is largely the result of the Americans' working within, and not pushing, the bounds set by Arab governments: Nongovernmental organizations are tightly controlled in most Arab countries, and in many they are barred from receiving foreign funding. As a result, roughly one-quarter of the money for political, educational, and economic reform is spent through Arab governments or on training for government officials.

What did the reform programs do? In the political area, they trained the newly elected members of Morocco's feeble parliament ($600,000); assisted the elections commission in Yemen's de facto one-party state ($325,000); convened a group of Arab judges, whose courts are plagued by corruption and government interference, to discuss "judicial procedure, independence, ethics, appointments, and training" ($1,425,000); and so on. Economic reform projects include funding the translation of government documents, under the rubric of helping Arab states join the World Trade Organization and negotiate free-trade agreements with the United States. Education programs include "English in a Box" for Jordanian and Moroccan teachers ($400,000), Internet connections for Yemeni high schools ($1.5 million), and a "child-centered education program" for North Africa and the Gulf ($1.1 million). None of these programs is intrinsically bad. But as catalysts for tangible political change, they don't stand a chance.

Yet even as American aid programs fail to challenge autocratic regimes from below by supporting local activists, the administration—despite the president's fine words—is failing to challenge the regimes from above. Yet surely the United States must press Arab regimes to reform their politics, not just their political process. The United States should press a consistent message in the region: that controlled "liberalization" that creates quasi-democratic institutions with no power is not democratization. Elections are important, of course, but as Algeria taught us, they are not the primary need. Even more basic are the protections that enable a variety of citizens and groups to speak and organize and operate effectively in politics: freedom of the press, freedom of association, the right to peaceably assemble, and the legalization of political parties and advocacy groups. Some or all of these are absent in most Arab states.

Forcing governments to withdraw their control over the public square and give power to participatory institutions is necessary if non-Islamist political forces are to organize, formulate agendas, and press their case against the state in competition with the Islamists. In Kuwait—where the emir loosened controls under American prodding after the Iraqi occupation of the country in 1991—a decade of freedom of expression, the abolition of state security courts, and the election of parliaments with meaningful oversight over executive policy-making have enabled the emergence of a liberal political movement, with representatives in parliament, as a real alternative to the Islamists and the monarchy. While the Islamists are still the principal opposition, the liberals are viable competitors in the political arena. Even more significant, liberals in Kuwait occasionally ally themselves with Islamists to argue for political freedoms, just as they ally themselves with liberal factions within the royal family to try to contain Islamist initiatives. This embryonic coalition politics is the first evidence that a healthy political pluralism can develop in an Arab society and may be able to prevent liberalization from leading to "one man, one vote, one time." With these ingredients of democracy in place, it seems inevitable that those advocating the vote for women will soon succeed.

But in other states where political expression and the ability to organize are still severely restricted, non-Islamist social groups have a large gap to overcome before they can mount an effective challenge in the marketplace of ideas, much less in the political arena. In Saudi Arabia, for example, there is a group of intellectuals who are essentially liberal reformers. But since political parties and political meetings are outlawed and the press is controlled, they have no means of organizing themselves, no way of demonstrating their base of support within society, and no way to lobby the government beyond open letters to the crown prince.

The U.S. government must also do a better job of coordinating its assistance programs for civil society with its diplomatic agenda. To give one example, funds from the Middle East Partnership Initiative are currently flowing to Internews, an international nonprofit organization, to train journalists across the region—but this program is not accompanied by any noticeable pressure on regimes to relax their controls on the media. Saudi journalists are participating in the Internews program, but abstract discussions of journalistic independence are less relevant to their daily reality than the fact that several Saudi journalists lost their jobs or their columns last year after they questioned the influence of extremist clerics in politics and the exclusion of women from public life. When the United States fails to speak up for those who challenge the system, others have little incentive to try, and activists who would like to take President Bush's words seriously and look to America for support feel betrayed.

In order to build credibility with Arab democrats, American foreign policy must communicate to Arab governments that states that are actually changing the distribution of political power will enjoy better relations with the United States than those that talk about reform but fail to implement it. America has powerful carrots to offer. If we cared to work at devising targeted incentives for real reform we would discover a panoply of underused tools at our disposal. The president's proposal for a Middle East Free Trade Area, in particular, was conceived mainly as a means of integrating Arab economies into world markets and creating wealth, on the general assumption that economic liberalization over time encourages democracy. But opening trade negotiations could be made conditional on political progress. While the United States does not typically insert human rights clauses into trade agreements, it could certainly use trade talks with Arab nations to promote liberal change (notably in such areas as transparency and rule of law). What the United States must *not* do is direct even more money to Arab governments as a reward for limited reform. This, unfortunately, appears to be part of the "Helsinki" plan currently being discussed with the Europeans.

Finally, the United States must trust that shared interests with its Arab interlocutors will mediate the tensions that an effective democratization effort is bound to create. Many in the diplomatic establishment argue that a more aggressive approach to democratization will necessarily cost Arab cooperation with America's other regional goals. A broader perspective is essential.

America's relations with key states are grounded in a web of longstanding mutual interests and benefits. Such relationships can withstand tensions. Riyadh and Washington share interests in the strategic defense of the Gulf and stability in the price of oil, and they still would, even if the United States were to push Saudi Arabia harder on political reform. And in 2002, when Washington threatened to withhold additional aid to Egypt over the imprisonment of democracy activist (and dual U.S. citizen) Saad Eddin Ibrahim, it sent a strong message to the Egyptian government, and did no significant damage to bilateral relations. Although Ibrahim was released by a court ruling, local activists fear he received special treatment because of his dual nationality. The United States should make clear that its handling of his case is to be seen not as an outlier but as a precedent for U.S. policy toward our Arab friends.

If the administration means it when it calls Arab democracy necessary to American security, then we must build a policy to match and back it with political will. We cannot shrink from the tradeoffs required to achieve success, but must accept them and develop ways to manage both the costs for bilateral relations and the risks of undesired outcomes. It must be a policy that combines the assistance to indigenous liberals that the Middle East Partnership

Initiative is supposed to provide but is not now structured to succeed at, with consistent, high-profile diplomatic and economic pressure and incentives to induce states to allow political freedom and to shift power away from the central executive.

America cannot promote democracy in the Arab world unless its strategy is credible. That requires staying the course in Iraq. Equally, it requires a carefully calibrated and robustly supported set of policies institutionalizing the forward strategy of freedom for the long haul. Otherwise, President Bush's powerful rhetoric on the universality of liberal values will prove to be a dead letter, and the cost to the United States, and to the peoples of the Arab world, will be immense.

POSTSCRIPT

Should Promoting Democracy Abroad Be a Top U.S. Priority?

Promoting democracy abroad was a cornerstone of foreign policy under both President Clinton and President George W. Bush. The means by which they pursued this objective, however, varied dramatically. While President Clinton sought to promote democratization through the bolstering of existing international agreements and institutions, President Bush has done so in a more unilateral fashion, often bypassing existing institutions and reinterpreting existing international agreements and practices. Thus, while President Clinton sought to promote political liberalism through politically liberal and institutional means, President Bush sought to promote political liberalism through more politically realist means unconstrained by existing norms. For a useful debate on U.S. policy and the prospects for democracy in the Middle East, see Marina Ottaway and Thomas Carothers, "Middle East Democracy," *Foreign Policy* (November/December 2004).

The theory of democratic peace dates back to the work of Immanual Kant in the eighteenth century, but gained prominence in political science and the policy arena in the 1990s. For a summary of the contemporary debate, see Michael Brown, Sean Lynn-Jones, and Steve Miller, eds., *Debating the Democratic Peace* (Cambridge University Press, 1996). For a discussion of the dangers associated with countries undergoing shifts to democracy, see Edward Mansfield and Jack Snyder, "Democratization and the Danger of War," *International Security* (Summer 1995) and Patricia Weitsman and George Shambaugh, "International Systems, Domestic Structures and Risk," *Journal of Peace Research* (2003).

Additional evidence on the link between democratization and economic development is available in Joseph Siegle's book, *The Democracy Advantage: How Democracies Promote Prosperity and Peace* (Routledge, 2004). Representing another dimension to this debate, the Center for Democracy and the Third Sector (CDATS) at Georgetown University provides training, research, and outreach on the relationship between democratic governance and those parts of civil society that are neither government nor business, including associations, non-governmental organizations, non-profit organizations, advocacy groups, citizen groups, and social movements, as well as the cultures, norms, and social values that enable these social phenomena. Links to this information is available on the Web site at http://www.georgetown.edu/centers/cdats/.

Internet References . . .

War, Peace, and Security Guide

An invaluable resource for general inquiries into global national security—the context within which American defense issues must be set—is this Web site maintained by the Information Resource Centre, Canadian Forces College.

http://wps.cfc.dnd.ca

DefenseLINK

The Department of Defense (DoD) provides an impressive array of information about virtually all aspects of the U.S. military establishment.

http://www.defenselink.mil

Center for Strategic and International Studies

Like all the other agencies and policy analysis centers that relate to defense, the Center for Strategic and International Studies (CSIS) has added extensively to its information on terrorism in the aftermath of the attacks on the United Sates in September 2001.

http://www.csis.org

The Homeland Security Institute

The Homeland Security Institute was involved in collecting and disseminating information and opinions about terrorist threats to the United States before the attacks in September 2001. This site contains links, suggested readings, and other valuable information.

http://www.homelandsecurity.org

U.S. National Security Issues

*F*or nearly a half-century, extending from the end of World War II into the early 1990s, the Cold War provided a context within which a great deal of American foreign policy was formulated. The primary policy goal was to guard against the dual dangers of communist ideology and the military might of the Soviet Union, China, and other communist countries. Now the Soviet Union is gone, and China, while still politically communist, has become a major player in the global market economy. In the aftermath of attacks by foreign terrorists on 9/11/2001, U.S. foreign policy has been dominated by concerns about terrorism, weapons of mass destruction, and interventions in Afghanistan and Iraq that were justified in part as a means of reducing these threats.

- Should the United States Withdraw from Iraq Expeditiously?
- Should the United States Preemptively Attack Iran's Emerging Nuclear Weapons Capability?
- Should the United States Negotiate with the Taliban?
- Should the United States Allow Russia More Leeway in Eurasia in Exchange for Russian Help in Stopping Iran's Nuclear Program?

ISSUE 4

Should the United States Withdraw from Iraq Expeditiously?

YES: **Marc Lynch**, from "How to Get Out of Iraq," *Foreign Policy* (January 2009)

NO: **David H. Petraeus**, from "Testimony to the House Committee on Foreign Affairs and the Committee on Armed Services" (September 10, 2007)

ISSUE SUMMARY

YES: Marc Lynch, associate professor of political science and international affairs at George Washington University, argues that the situation in Iraq remains fragile, but that the failure to withdraw U.S. troops on the schedule President Barack Obama proposed on the campaign trail would cause renewed instability in Iraq.

NO: Gen. David Petraeus, commander of U.S. Central Command and former commander of the Multi-National Force in Iraq, notes that the "surge" policy of increasing U.S. troops in Iraq and changing U.S. strategy and tactics has succeeded in greatly reducing violence in Iraq. This will allow reductions in the level of U.S. troops in Iraq, but further reductions must be contingent on whether Iraq remains stable.

In early 2007, after a series of studies and reports concluded that the conflict in Iraq was becoming more violent and Iraq's political and economic progress were limited, President George W. Bush, working with the top U.S. military commander in Iraq, Gen. David H. Petraeus, decided to carry out a "surge" of U.S. forces in Iraq, adding 20,000 additional U.S. troops to the 142,000 already deployed in Iraq at that time. In addition, U.S. forces in Iraq shifted their strategy and tactics, putting greater emphasis on achieving security for Iraqi civilians and continuing to shift responsibility to Iraq's growing military and police forces. Perhaps most important, U.S. military leaders negotiated with Sunni leaders and their militias to get these groups, collectively known as the "Awakening" movement, to shift their focus from attacks on U.S. forces and the largely Shiite Iraqi army and police force toward attacks on al-Qaeda in Iraq operatives, whose extreme violence had made them unpopular even among Sunnis in Iraq. In addition, by early 2007, over two million Iraqis out of a population of about 28 million had fled to neighboring countries and a nearly equal number left their homes for other areas within Iraq. This imposed an immense humanitarian toll on Iraqis, but by early 2007 "ethnic cleansing" in Iraq had largely run its course, leaving the country divided into devastated but more homogenous and defensible neighborhood enclaves dominated by one ethnic group or another and protected in many cases by concrete or other walls installed by U.S. and Iraqi forces and guarded by U.S. and Iraqi checkpoints. As a result of these developments and changes in U.S. policies, sectarian violence between Iraq's Sunnis and Shiites decreased sharply through 2007 and 2008. Similarly, U.S. military casualties in Iraq, which totaled over 4,000 Americans killed and over 20,000 wounded by 2008, fell from a peak of over 100 soldiers killed per month in 2007 to fewer than 20 Americans killed per month through late 2008 and early 2009.

The diminishing violence in Iraq in 2008 allowed the U.S. military to turn more responsibility over to Iraqi military and police forces. In the spring of 2008, Iraq's Shiite Prime Minister Nouri al-Maliki assertively used Iraqi troops to re-establish government control over areas dominated by the militant Shiite leader Moqtada al-Sadr, greatly reducing Sadr's power and military capabilities. By late spring, the government had reestablished control of the major southern city of Basra and of the "Sadr City" neighborhood of Baghdad, strengthening public support of the government.

In late 2008, the newly strengthened Maliki government negotiated a new "Status of Forces" (SOFA) agreement with the Bush administration, establishing new terms for U.S. military deployments in Iraq. The new SOFA agreement, finalized in December 2008, set a deadline of the end of 2011 for the withdrawal of U.S. troops from Iraq, although the agreement allowed for the possibility that some U.S. troops could stay beyond that date at the invitation of the Iraqi government. This agreement brought the outgoing Bush administration and the Iraqi government close to the 16-month withdrawal schedule that Barack Obama, president-elect at the time of the agreement, had pledged on the campaign trail in the 2008 elections, although Obama cautioned that whether this schedule could be achieved depended on still-evolving circumstances in Iraq. In late January 2009, provincial council elections in Iraq further strengthened the Maliki government.

As of early 2009, experts on all sides of the controversy over U.S. policies in Iraq agreed that violence in that country was down markedly from its peak in 2007, but arguments continued over whether this should lead to a swift withdrawal of most or all of U.S. forces from Iraq. Some, like Marc Lynch, argue that the drop in violence and the strengthening of the Maliki government and its military and police forces have created the conditions for the U.S. to withdraw its forces quickly. Others, echoing General Petraeus, maintain that the situation in Iraq is still fragile and that U.S. troops will be needed for a long transitional period to prevent a return to sectarian violence.

YES

Marc Lynch

Briefing Book: How to Get Out of Iraq

Throughout the campaign, Barack Obama vowed that one of his first actions as president would be to issue a new order to military to end the war in Iraq. Since his resounding electoral victory, however, there has been a quiet campaign among the foreign-policy establishment and parts of the military to roll back those promises. This would be a mistake. The argument for a significant, early withdrawal of U.S. combat forces remains overwhelming. Indeed, a failure to deliver on the promise of early U.S. withdrawals is the most likely thing to cause a rapid deterioration in conditions in Iraq.

Those who warn that security gains in Iraq are fragile and reversible are correct, even if they argued the contrary before the election. We should be under no illusions that Iraq will be stable or peaceful, or that its political divides have been overcome. As Brian Katulis of the Center for American Progress and I argued in September, beneath the superficial veneer of improved security upon which most Americans have focused, Iraq continues to be torn apart by deep divides over ethnicity and religion and by escalating battles between political insiders and popular forces. Despite some promising developments, little political reconciliation has taken place since the "surge" began.

There are some promising developments, and great hopes that the fragile security gains will hold and that the coming rounds of elections will produce a more stable Iraqi political order. But we should not count on best case scenarios coming to pass. It is absolutely essential for the administration to be prepared for a series of challenges that will likely arise. It should anticipate these contingencies and be prepared to respond appropriately, so that they are less likely to disrupt withdrawal plans and destabilize Iraq. To that end, this memo lays out a series of likely challenges in the first six months after the inauguration and a number of plausible contingencies for which the United States must be prepared. It then makes the case for the need to stick to a withdrawal schedule in line with the one presented by President-elect Obama during the campaign— one that does not contradict the Status of Forces Agreement (SOFA), is not irresponsible, and does not threaten Iraq's fragile gains. The new administration will get only one chance to demonstrate the credibility of its commitments, and indefinitely leaving troops at current levels will only postpone rather than solve the problems.

Part I: Implementing the SOFA

Implementing the SOFA (which Iraqis tellingly call the "Withdrawal Agreement") will be the overwhelming priority in U.S.-Iraqi relations over the coming six months, leading up to the all-important referendum on its ratification scheduled for July 31. Iraqis will be watching carefully to see whether the United States honors its commitments, and will likely test the limits of the agreement. Elements within the U.S. military will also likely wish to test those limits, judging by comments made by Gen. Raymond Odierno, the top U.S. commander in Iraq, and others.

Iraqis (and many Americans) are perplexed at the president-elect's real intentions. Addressing these concerns head-on and publicly early in the administration is crucial. The new administration should do everything it can to adhere to the SOFA/WA and to build support inside of Iraq ahead of the referendum. This should not be problematic, since there is no contradiction between Obama's timetable and that of the SOFA/WA. Clarity and consistency is key. He should say clearly that all combat troops could be withdrawn within 16 months, as promised, while the residual force envisioned in the campaign platform could then legally remain in Iraq to carry out training and counterterrorism functions through the end of 2011, at which point their role could be jointly negotiated with the Iraqi government.

Among the major challenges likely to arise:

- **Troops return to bases (June 30).** The first major deadline in the SOFA/WA will pose a significant challenge. The requirement that U.S. troops return to their bases contradicts core elements of U.S. counterinsurgency doctrine, and would represent a significant change to operations particularly in the cities. U.S. military officials have suggested that little will change in practice, but Iraqis clearly expect that they will. Managing the perceptions and the operational realities of this new legal situation will be a serious challenge—particularly given the proximity to the SOFA/WA referendum.
- **Detainee release.** Also related to the SOFA is the question of detainee release, a major Iraqi (and particularly Sunni) demand. But if some 10,000–15,000 detainees rapidly return to their communities, violence and instability could follow. Slow-rolling the detainee releases, on the other hand, could undermine support for the SOFA referendum and trigger a legal challenge, while transferring large numbers of detainees to an Iraqi system seen as sectarian could spark sectarian tensions.
- **Referendum (July 31).** This referendum will hang over all Iraqi politics and U.S.-Iraqi relations for the first half-year of the administration. Should the SOFA/WA fail to pass, U.S. forces will need either to begin withdrawing at an uncomfortably rapid rate or else find some other formal authorization to remain. Neither will be an attractive proposition. The government wants the agreement to pass, and will likely establish rules and a format conducive to success. But opposition forces will attempt to mobilize outrage at every opportunity to portray the United States as violating the terms of the SOFA/WA and not actually intending to withdraw. The referendum will almost certainly

become a major issue in intra-Shia (and to a lesser extent intra-Sunni) political competition. U.S. policy needs to be extremely careful to not feed these flames.

Upcoming Events and Contingencies

- **Provincial elections (January 31).** The fact that these elections are scheduled for less than two weeks after the inauguration is both a gift and a curse. Fortunately, these particular elections have no relevance to the debate over troop withdrawals, since they will be held so soon after the inauguration that no drawdown would begin until well after provincial election day. Still, extraordinary hopes have been invested in them, from creating more representative institutions to empowering friendly Sunni tribal forces. . . .
- **After the provincial elections.** Although the elections may be an attractive target for spoiler violence, the greater risk probably comes afterwards as disgruntled losers defect from the political process and newly elected leaders attempt to take the reins of power. Many groups have exaggerated expectations of these elections, and some disappointment is quite likely—particularly along ethnic and sectarian fault lines in Baghdad and Ninewa province, but also between competing Sunni and Shia groupings who have for years been fiercely struggling over intra-communal power. The United States should be prepared to engage with such dissatisfied groups to prevent their relapse into violence. After the elections, the Provincial Powers Law is due to come into effect, which will have far-reaching effects on the balance of power between Baghdad and the provinces and could trigger clashes between the new provincial governments and the centralizing efforts of Prime Minister Nuri al-Maliki.
- **Basra referendum (possibly April).** The province of Basra is midway through a bid to create an autonomous region. If its backers collect enough signatures by the deadline (recently extended to Jan. 19), the referendum must take place within 60 to 90 days of certification. Its success would have major consequences for the decentralization of the Iraqi state and for possible compromises over oil. It would also frustrate the long-nurtured hopes of ISCI (the powerful Shia party the Islamic Supreme Council of Iraq) for a Shia "super-region" of the center-south, but likely embolden other provinces to bid for similar status. This should be closely monitored. At last count, the pro-referendum forces were far short of the number of required signatures, and the timing and outcome of a referendum are uncertain. But Basra's autonomy bid could emerge as a major issue suddenly, with little time to prepare, should the signature gathering succeed.
- **Kirkuk and disputed territories (March).** The tortuously negotiated annex to the provincial elections law calls for the resolution of power-sharing and elections in Kirkuk by March. Given the ongoing, intense battles between Maliki and the Kurds over a wide range of issues, this will likely not go smoothly and could well become a focal point for wider Arab–Kurdish tensions. Conflicts between Kurds and Arabs have multiplied in recent months: from the armed showdown between the Iraqi army and Kurdish forces at Khanaqin, to the political stalemate

over provincial elections in Kirkuk, to the cross-pressures over oil contracts, to Maliki's attempts to stand up tribal support councils in mixed
areas, to the incendiary language increasingly being exchanged between
the prime minister and Kurdish leaders. While over the long haul the
United States should support the efforts of UNAMI to strike a grand
bargain—probably along the lines of the International Crisis Group's
"Oil for Soil" proposals—in the short term the administration should
be prepared for a flare-up of tensions in Kirkuk, Mosul or elsewhere.

- **Iranian presidential elections (June 12).** Although they are outside
  Iraq, these elections could have a significant effect on the U.S.–Iran–
  Iraq triangle. Should Mahmoud Ahmedinejad lose to a reformist candidate, it would facilitate an American–Iranian dialogue that could well
  entail a changed Iranian role in Iraq. But conservative forces within
  the Iranian state skeptical of such a dialogue may well see an interest
  in stirring up trouble in Iraq to scuttle such talks.
- **Refugee Return.** The estimated 5 million Iraqis displaced from their
  homes inside and outside Iraq will continue to reshape Iraq and the
  region. It would be a mistake to push for early solutions to this problem, since few refugees wish to return to an uncertain Iraq and few
  preparations have been made to deal with the flood of property disputes and local tensions that would accompany significant returns.
  But Prime Minister Maliki has been aggressively encouraging such
  returns, while making few efforts to deal with the implications. The
  Obama team should focus on support for the refugees abroad and on
  building the institutional capacity of the relevant Iraqi state ministries
  to eventually reabsorb them.
- **National elections (December).** National elections will be very much
  on the minds of all political actors as the year progresses. Although
  advocates of slower withdrawals cite these elections as a reason to
  retain high troop levels through 2009, it is worth noting that the elections may not happen on schedule (Iraqi officials have recently been
  suggesting March 2010 as a more likely date) and that continuing high
  U.S. troop levels might help anti-U.S. forces at the polls.

Contingency planning

- **Contingency #1: Testing the SOFA/WA.** In the first few months after
  the SOFA/WA comes into effect, there will likely be a politically significant test of the new Iraqi powers of jurisdiction such as the arrest of an
  American contractor. Given the realities of Iraqi politics ahead of the
  provincial elections and SOFA/WA referendum, such an arrest and trial
  would likely be extremely popular and exploited for political advantage. The United States will find itself caught between the imperative
  of respecting the SOFA/WA and the imperative of protecting its own. A
  plan needs to be ready to go to defuse this test, preferably one rooted
  in joint understandings with the Iraqis.
- **Contingency #2: Resurgence of violence in areas of drawdown.** The
  United States should resist the pressure to re-intervene whenever security conditions deteriorate. Although U.S. troops may need to act in
  the face of genuinely catastrophic developments—whether directly or
  in a support role—they should not be allowed to play the role of safety

net for the Iraqi government indefinitely, especially if it fails to implement key political accommodation initiatives and reforms. Doing so
would remove the incentives to reform that the withdrawal is supposed to trigger. Helping Iraq to find a stable equilibrium that does
not require the presence of U.S. troops at high levels throughout the
country should be a higher imperative than putting out every fire.

- **Contingency #3: Radical political upheaval.** A number of plausible scenarios could unfold: a parliamentary vote of no-confidence in
Maliki (already threatened by major parties); Maliki dissolving Parliament or canceling elections in anticipation of such a move against
him; a military coup against Maliki (less likely but much discussed in
Baghdad); or the assassination or death of a major figure such as Maliki
or Grand Ayatollah Ali al-Sistani. Any of these developments would
test the commitments of the administration to its multiple, competing
interests in Iraq. Whether Obama prioritizes democratic institutions
or stable leadership is a first-order question that he should consider in
advance, not when the crisis hits.

Part II: The Case for Redeployment and Other Difficult Steps

Upon taking office, Obama will likely face great pressure from various parties—
military, Iraqi, and partisan—to relax his plans to begin withdrawing troops
from Iraq. There will likely be coordinated arguments about the fragility of
the current situation, the risk of squandering the gains of the "surge," and the
need to maintain troop strength through the provincial and national elections. These arguments should be resisted. The catalog of political frailties and
security risks are real, but there is little reason to believe they will be any less
real in six months or in a year. Postponing withdrawals would continue to
freeze the current situation in place, while squandering the best opportunity
the United States will ever have to reshape its commitments to Iraq.

There is only one chance to make a first impression. The transition to
a new administration represents a unique—and short-lived—opportunity to
establish a new relationship with the Iraqi government and the Iraqi people. It
is absolutely essential that upon taking office, Obama clearly affirms, publicly
and privately, his commitment to his timetable for withdrawing U.S. troops. At
the same time, the president should assure the Iraqis that he intends to jointly
coordinate and manage the drawdown of U.S. troops. Any uncertainty about
American intentions in this regard should be corrected. Front-loading withdrawals would help significantly with the July referendum on the SOFA/WA.

Several broad recommendations should guide the administration's policy:

- **Make a significant "down payment" on troop withdrawals.** There
will be tremendous pressure to postpone the initial withdrawals
because of the intense calendar of Iraqi events detailed above. This
would be a mistake. A visible, significant early withdrawal would help
significantly with the SOFA/WA referendum, would send an important
message to Iraqi leaders, and would break the institutional inertia that
threatens to lock in the current strategy. Only the certainty of a U.S.

withdrawal will shift the incentives of Iraqi politicians to move quickly towards a minimally acceptable political accommodation. Many Iraqis are deeply concerned about alleged secret annexes to the SOFA/WA and that the United States does not really intend to leave. The more clearly the commitment to withdrawal can be articulated, the better— for both Iraqi and American political purposes. The military is already prepared for such an initial withdrawal, and should have little problem implementing such early cuts—and would welcome the freeing up of resources for Afghanistan and other challenges. Critics will argue that this is not the right time to begin withdrawals, but it never will be.

- **Lower expectations about U.S. ability to micro-manage or shape Iraqi politics.** The United States' goals and expectations in terms of shaping Iraqi domestic politics should reflect its diminishing commitments and presence. One way to operationalize this would be to focus U.S. efforts on the political front on encouraging the implementation of the Iraqi Parliament's Political Reform Document—the comprehensive set of political reform and power-sharing commitments adopted as part of Iraqi negotiations over the SOFA/WA. This ambitious document, drafted and agreed upon by Iraqi politicians rather than by American observers, would address most of the pressing issues undermining stability in Iraq . . . if implemented.

- **Establish a new relationship with the Iraqi government.** The Iraqi leadership has a deep, well-established relationship with Bush administration officials, not to mention a significant set of private understandings. The Iraqis are uncertain about the Obama administration, and likely hope to resume business as usual with the new team. It is important to make clear that relations will change. The withdrawal of combat brigades and defining the mission of residual forces should be jointly managed with the Iraqis, but at the same time it should be made clear that the age of the blank check and permanent commitments has come to an end. This does not mean creating a hostile relationship or negative dynamic. The emphasis should be on partnering to manage the drawdown of U.S. forces and the building of a new, constructive relationship. But it does mean *doing something early on to demonstrate the new approach*—to show that conditionality is real, and that the Bush blank check has ended.

- **Shape the debate on the SOFA/WA.** U.S. policy and public statements should be highly attuned to the urgency of shaping the debate over the SOFA/WA. Deep suspicions about American intentions and a pervasive mood of hostility toward the United States are currently shaping the Iraqi political debate. If left unattended, these suspicions—fanned by opponents of the agreement—could well lead to a deeply undesirable outcome in the July referendum. Obama should move early and aggressively to reassure the Iraqi public about its commitment to the SOFA and to the withdrawal, as well as to the territorial integrity of the Iraqi state. And it is vital that the United States speak with one voice to avoid such confusion: Military commanders should refrain from making statements that throw into question American commitments to the SOFA/WA.

- **Restate commitment to Iraqi territorial unity.** Many Iraqis believe that Vice President-elect Joseph Biden's old proposal to partition Iraq is the administration's "secret" policy. Such concerns should be addressed with clear statements of commitment to Iraq's territorial, federal unity in order to remove one potential and unnecessary irritant in U.S.–Iraqi relations.

Conclusion

President-elect Obama will have an initial window of opportunity to establish credibility at home, in Iraq, and in the wider regional and international arena. An overly cautious approach to the withdrawal of combat forces would quickly squander this opportunity. Muddying the U.S. commitment to withdrawal could well endanger the prospects for the SOFA/WA referendum in Iraq and may trigger, rather than prevent, the feared deterioration in security and political conditions. Obama must therefore move quickly and aggressively to define his new policy, and not allow the impressive catalog of challenges facing Iraq this year to paralyze U.S. policy. The new president should honor his campaign promises and begin his administration by announcing a significant "down payment" on troop withdrawals and presenting a clear vision for the future of the American role in Iraq. Only then will the incentives be aligned to push Iraq towards a stable future and to shape a sustainable U.S.–Iraqi relationship.

David H. Petraeus ➡ **NO**

Testimony to the House Committee on Foreign Affairs and the Committee on Armed Services

Mr. Chairmen, Ranking Members, Members of the Committees, thank you for the opportunity to provide my assessment of the security situation in Iraq and to discuss the recommendations I recently provided to my chain of command for the way forward.

At the outset, I would like to note that this is my testimony. Although I have briefed my assessment and recommendations to my chain of command, I wrote this testimony myself. It has not been cleared by, nor shared with, anyone in the Pentagon, the White House, or Congress.

As a bottom line upfront, the military objectives of the surge are, in large measure, being met. In recent months, in the face of tough enemies and the brutal summer heat of Iraq, Coalition and Iraqi Security Forces have achieved progress in the security arena. Though the improvements have been uneven across Iraq, the overall number of security incidents in Iraq has declined in 8 of the past 12 weeks, with the numbers of incidents in the last two weeks at the lowest levels seen since June 2006.

One reason for the decline in incidents is that Coalition and Iraqi forces have dealt significant blows to Al Qaeda-Iraq. Though Al Qaeda and its affiliates in Iraq remain dangerous, we have taken away a number of their sanctuaries and gained the initiative in many areas.

We have also disrupted Shia militia extremists, capturing the head and numerous other leaders of the Iranian-supported Special Groups, along with a senior Lebanese Hezbollah operative supporting Iran's activities in Iraq.

Coalition and Iraqi operations have helped reduce ethno-sectarian violence, as well, bringing down the number of ethno-sectarian deaths substantially in Baghdad and across Iraq since the height of the sectarian violence last December. The number of overall civilian deaths has also declined during this period, although the numbers in each area are still at troubling levels.

Iraqi Security Forces have also continued to grow and to shoulder more of the load, albeit slowly and amid continuing concerns about the sectarian tendencies of some elements in their ranks. In general, however, Iraqi elements have been standing and fighting and sustaining tough losses, and they have taken the lead in operations in many areas.

U.S. House of Representatives, September 10, 2007.

73

Additionally, in what may be the most significant development of the past 8 months, the tribal rejection of Al Qaeda that started in Anbar Province and helped produce such significant change there has now spread to a number of other locations as well.

Based on all this and on the further progress we believe we can achieve over the next few months, I believe that we will be able to reduce our forces to the pre-surge level of brigade combat teams by next summer without jeopardizing the security gains that we have fought so hard to achieve.

Beyond that, while noting that the situation in Iraq remains complex, difficult, and sometimes downright frustrating, I also believe that it is possible to achieve our objectives in Iraq over time, though doing so will be neither quick nor easy.

Having provided that summary, I would like to review the nature of the conflict in Iraq, recall the situation before the surge, describe the current situation, and explain the recommendations I have provided to my chain of command for the way ahead in Iraq.

The Nature of the Conflict

The fundamental source of the conflict in Iraq is competition among ethnic and sectarian communities for power and resources. This competition will take place, and its resolution is key to producing long-term stability in the new Iraq. The question is whether the competition takes place more—or less—violently. . . . Foreign and homegrown terrorists, insurgents, militia extremists, and criminals all push the ethno-sectarian competition toward violence. Malign actions by Syria and, especially, by Iran fuel that violence. Lack of adequate governmental capacity, lingering sectarian mistrust, and various forms of corruption add to Iraq's challenges.

The Situation in December 2006 and the Surge

In our recent efforts to look to the future, we found it useful to revisit the past. In December 2006, during the height of the ethno-sectarian violence that escalated in the wake of the bombing of the Golden Dome Mosque in Samarra, the leaders in Iraq at that time—General George Casey and Ambassador Zalmay Khalilzad—concluded that the coalition was failing to achieve its objectives. Their review underscored the need to protect the population and reduce sectarian violence, especially in Baghdad. As a result, General Casey requested additional forces to enable the Coalition to accomplish these tasks, and those forces began to flow in January.

In the ensuing months, our forces and our Iraqi counterparts have focused on improving security, especially in Baghdad and the areas around it, wresting sanctuaries from Al Qaeda control, and disrupting the efforts of the Iranian-supported militia extremists. We have employed counterinsurgency practices that underscore the importance of units living among the people they are securing, and accordingly, our forces have established dozens of joint security stations and patrol bases manned by Coalition and Iraqi forces in Baghdad and in other areas across Iraq.

In mid-June, with all the surge brigades in place, we launched a series of offensive operations focused on: expanding the gains achieved in the preceding months in Anbar Province; clearing Baqubah, several key Baghdad neighborhoods, the remaining sanctuaries in Anbar Province, and important areas in the so-called "belts" around Baghdad; and pursuing Al Qaeda in the Diyala River Valley and several other areas.

Throughout this period, as well, we engaged in dialogue with insurgent groups and tribes, and this led to additional elements standing up to oppose Al Qaeda and other extremists. We also continued to emphasize the development of the Iraqi Security Forces and we employed non-kinetic means to exploit the opportunities provided by the conduct of our kinetic operations—aided in this effort by the arrival of additional Provincial Reconstruction Teams.

Current Situation and Trends

The progress our forces have achieved with our Iraqi counterparts has, as I noted at the outset, been substantial. While there have been setbacks as well as successes and tough losses along the way, overall, our tactical commanders and I see improvements in the security environment. We do not, however, just rely on gut feel or personal observations; we also conduct considerable data collection and analysis to gauge progress and determine trends. We do this by gathering and refining data from coalition and Iraqi operations centers, using a methodology that has been in place for well over a year and that has benefited over the past seven months from the increased presence of our forces living among the Iraqi people. We endeavor to ensure our analysis of that data is conducted with rigor and consistency, as our ability to achieve a nuanced understanding of the security environment is dependent on collecting and analyzing data in a consistent way over time. Two US intelligence agencies recently reviewed our methodology, and they concluded that the data we produce is the most accurate and authoritative in Iraq.

As I mentioned upfront . . . the level of security incidents has decreased significantly since the start of the surge of offensive operations in mid-June, declining in 8 of the past 12 weeks, with the level of incidents in the past two weeks the lowest since June 2006 and with the number of attacks this past week the lowest since April 2006.

Civilian deaths of all categories, less natural causes, have also declined considerably, by over 45% Iraq-wide since the height of the sectarian violence in December. . . . Periodic mass casualty attacks by Al Qaeda have tragically added to the numbers outside Baghdad, in particular. Even without the sensational attacks, however, the level of civilian deaths is clearly still too high and continues to be of serious concern.

[The] number of ethno-sectarian deaths, an important subset of the overall civilian casualty figures, has also declined significantly since the height of the sectarian violence in December. Iraq-wide . . . the number of ethno-sectarian deaths has come down by over 55%, and it would have come down much further were it not for the casualties inflicted by barbaric Al Qaeda bombings attempting to reignite sectarian violence. In Baghdad, as the bottom line shows, the number of ethno-sectarian deaths has come down by some 80% since December. [There is a] density of sectarian incidents in various Baghdad neighborhoods and it both reflects the progress made in reducing ethno-sectarian violence in the Iraqi capital and identifies the areas that remain the most challenging.

As we have gone on the offensive in former Al Qaeda and insurgent sanctuaries, and as locals have increasingly supported our efforts, we have found a substantially increased number of arms, ammunition, and explosives caches. [We] have, so far this year, already found and cleared over 4,400 caches, nearly 1,700 more than we discovered in all of last year. This may be a factor in the reduction in the number of overall improvised explosive device attacks in recent months . . . has declined sharply, by about one-third, since June.

The change in the security situation in Anbar Province has, of course, been particularly dramatic. [Monthly] attack levels in Anbar have declined from some 1,350 in October 2006 to a bit over 200 in August of this year. This dramatic decrease reflects the significance of the local rejection of Al Qaeda and the newfound willingness of local Anbaris to volunteer to serve in the Iraqi Army and Iraqi Police Service. As I noted earlier, we are seeing similar actions in other locations, as well.

To be sure, trends have not been uniformly positive across Iraq . . . .. The trend in Ninevah Province, for example, has been much more up and down, until a recent decline, and the same is true in Sala ad Din Province, though recent trends there and in Baghdad have been in the right direction. In any event, the overall trajectory in Iraq—a steady decline of incidents in the past three months—is still quite significant.

The number of car bombings and suicide attacks has also declined in each of the past 5 months, from a high of some 175 in March . . . to about 90 this past month. While this trend in recent months has been heartening, the number of high profile attacks is still too high, and we continue to work hard to destroy the networks that carry out these barbaric attacks.

Our operations have, in fact, produced substantial progress against Al Qaeda and its affiliates in Iraq. [In] the past 8 months, we have also neutralized 5 media cells, detained the senior Iraqi leader of Al Qaeda-Iraq, and killed or captured nearly 100 other key leaders and some 2,500 rank-and-file fighters. Al Qaeda is certainly not defeated; however, it is off balance and we are pursuing its leaders and operators aggressively. Of note, as the recent National Intelligence Estimate on Iraq explained, these gains against Al Qaeda are a result of the synergy of actions by: conventional forces to deny the terrorists sanctuary; intelligence, surveillance, and reconnaissance assets to find the enemy; and special operations elements to conduct targeted raids. A combination of these assets is necessary to prevent the creation of a terrorist safe haven in Iraq.

In the past six months we have also targeted Shia militia extremists, capturing a number of senior leaders and fighters, as well as the deputy commander of Lebanese Hezbollah Department 2800, the organization created to support the training, arming, funding, and, in some cases, direction of the militia extremists by the Iranian Republican Guard Corps' Qods Force. These elements have assassinated and kidnapped Iraqi governmental leaders, killed and wounded our soldiers with advanced explosive devices provided by Iran, and indiscriminately rocketed civilians in the International Zone and elsewhere. It is increasingly apparent to both Coalition and Iraqi leaders that Iran, through the use of the Qods Force, seeks to turn the Iraqi Special Groups into a Hezbollah-like force to serve its interests and fight a proxy war against the Iraqi state and coalition forces in Iraq.

The most significant development in the past six months likely has been the increasing emergence of tribes and local citizens rejecting Al Qaeda and other extremists. This has, of course, been most visible in Anbar Province. A year ago the province was assessed as "lost" politically. Today, it is a model of what happens when local leaders and citizens decide to oppose Al Qaeda and reject its Taliban-like ideology. While Anbar is unique and the model it provides cannot be replicated everywhere in Iraq, it does demonstrate the dramatic change in security that is possible with the support and participation of local citizens. [Other] tribes have been inspired by the actions of those in Anbar and have volunteered to fight extremists as well. We have, in coordination with the Iraqi government's National Reconciliation Committee, been engaging these tribes and groups of local citizens who want to oppose extremists and to contribute to local security. Some 20,000 such individuals are already being hired for the Iraqi Police, thousands of others are being assimilated into the Iraqi Army, and thousands more are vying for a spot in Iraq's Security Forces.

Iraqi Security Forces

As I noted earlier, Iraqi Security Forces have continued to grow, to develop their capabilities, and to shoulder more of the burden of providing security for their country. Despite concerns about sectarian influence, inadequate logistics and supporting institutions, and an insufficient number of qualified commissioned and non-commissioned officers, Iraqi units are engaged around the country.

[There] are now nearly 140 Iraqi Army, National Police, and Special Operations Forces Battalions in the fight, with about 95 of those capable of taking the lead in operations, albeit with some coalition support. Beyond that, all of Iraq's battalions have been heavily involved in combat operations that often result in the loss of leaders, soldiers, and equipment. These losses are among the shortcomings identified by operational readiness assessments, but we should not take from these assessments the impression that Iraqi forces are not in the fight and contributing. Indeed, despite their shortages, many Iraqi units across Iraq now operate with minimal coalition assistance.

As counterinsurgency operations require substantial numbers of boots on the ground, we are helping the Iraqis expand the size of their security forces. Currently, there are some 445,000 individuals on the payrolls of Iraq's Interior and Defense Ministries. Based on recent decisions by Prime Minister Maliki, the number of Iraq's security forces will grow further by the end of this year, possibly by as much as 40,000. Given the security challenges Iraq faces, we support this decision, and we will work with the two security ministries as they continue their efforts to expand their basic training capacity, leader development programs, logistical structures and elements, and various other institutional capabilities to support the substantial growth in Iraqi forces.

Significantly, in 2007, Iraq will, as in 2006, spend more on its security forces than it will receive in security assistance from the United States. In fact, Iraq is becoming one of the United States' larger foreign military sales [FMS] customers, committing some $1.6 billion to FMS already, with the possibility of up to $1.8 billion more being committed before the end of this year. And I appreciate the attention that some members of Congress have recently given to speeding up the FMS process for Iraq.

To summarize, the security situation in Iraq is improving, and Iraqis elements are slowly taking on more of the responsibility for protecting their citizens. Innumerable challenges lie ahead; however, Coalition and Iraqi Security Forces have made progress toward achieving sustainable security. As a result, the United States will be in a position to reduce its forces in Iraq in the months ahead.

Recommendations

Two weeks ago I provided recommendations for the way ahead in Iraq to the members of my chain of command and the Joint Chiefs of Staff. The essence of the approach I recommended is captured in its title: "Security While Transitioning: From Leading to Partnering to Overwatch." This approach seeks to build on the security improvements our troopers and our Iraqi counterparts have fought so hard to achieve in recent months. It reflects recognition of the importance of securing the population and the imperative of transitioning responsibilities to Iraqi institutions and Iraqi forces as quickly as possible, but without rushing to failure. It includes substantial support for the continuing development of Iraqi Security Forces. It also stresses the need to continue the counterinsurgency strategy that we have been employing, but with Iraqis gradually shouldering more of the load. And it highlights the importance of regional and global diplomatic approaches. Finally, in recognition of the fact that this war is not only being fought on the ground in Iraq but also in cyberspace, it also notes the need to contest the enemy's growing use of that important medium to spread extremism.

The recommendations I provided were informed by operational and strategic considerations. The operational considerations include recognition that:

- military aspects of the surge have achieved progress and generated momentum;
- Iraqi Security Forces have continued to grow and have slowly been shouldering more of the security burden in Iraq;
- a mission focus on either population security or transition alone will not be adequate to achieve our objectives;
- success against Al Qaeda-Iraq and Iranian-supported militia extremists requires conventional forces as well as special operations forces; and
- the security and local political situations will enable us to draw down the surge forces.

My recommendations also took into account a number of strategic considerations:

- political progress will take place only if sufficient security exists;
- long-term US ground force viability will benefit from force reductions as the surge runs its course;
- regional, global, and cyberspace initiatives are critical to success; and

Iraqi leaders understandably want to assume greater sovereignty in their country, although, as they recently announced, they do desire continued presence of coalition forces in Iraq in 2008 under a new UN Security Council Resolution and, following that, they want to negotiate a long-term security agreement with the United States and other nations.

Based on these considerations, and having worked the battlefield geometry with Lieutenant General Ray Odierno to ensure that we retain and build on the gains for which our troopers have fought, I have recommended a drawdown of the surge forces from Iraq. In fact, later this month, the Marine Expeditionary Unit deployed as part of the surge will depart Iraq. Beyond that, if my recommendations are approved, that unit's departure will be followed by the withdrawal of a brigade combat team without replacement in mid-December and the further redeployment without replacement of four other brigade combat teams and the two surge Marine battalions in the first 7 months of 2008, until we reach the pre-surge level of 15 brigade combat teams by mid-July 2008.

I would also like to discuss the period beyond next summer. Force reductions will continue beyond the pre-surge levels of brigade combat teams that we will reach by mid-July 2008; however, in my professional judgment, it would be premature to make recommendations on the pace of such reductions at this time. In fact, our experience in Iraq has repeatedly shown that projecting too far into the future is not just difficult, it can be misleading and even hazardous. The events of the past six months underscore that point. When I testified in January, for example, no one would have dared to forecast that Anbar Province would have been transformed the way it has in the past 6 months. Nor would anyone have predicted that volunteers in one-time Al Qaeda strongholds like Ghazaliyah in western Baghdad or in Adamiya in eastern Baghdad would seek to join the fight against Al Qaeda. Nor would we have anticipated that a Shia-led government would accept significant numbers of Sunni volunteers into the ranks of the local police force in Abu Ghraib. Beyond that, on a less encouraging note, none of us earlier this year appreciated the extent of Iranian involvement in Iraq, something about which we and Iraq's leaders all now have greater concern.

In view of this, I do not believe it is reasonable to have an adequate appreciation for the pace of further reductions and mission adjustments beyond the summer of 2008 until about mid-March of next year. We will, no later than that time, consider factors similar to those on which I based the current recommendations, having by then, of course, a better feel for the security situation, the improvements in the capabilities of our Iraqi counterparts, and the enemy situation. I will then, as I did in developing the recommendations I have explained here today, also take into consideration the demands on our Nation's ground forces, although I believe that that consideration should once again inform, not drive, the recommendations I make. . . .

One may argue that the best way to speed the process in Iraq is to change the MNF-I mission from one that emphasizes population security, counterterrorism, and transition, to one that is strictly focused on transition and counter-terrorism. Making that change now would, in our view, be premature. We have learned before that there is a real danger in handing over tasks to the Iraqi Security Forces before their capacity and local conditions warrant. In fact, the drafters of the recently released National Intelligence Estimate on Iraq recognized this danger when they wrote, and I quote, "We assess that changing the mission of Coalition forces from a primarily counterinsurgency and stabilization role to a primary combat support role for Iraqi forces and counterterrorist operations to prevent AQI from establishing a safe haven would erode security gains achieved thus far."

In describing the recommendations I have made, I should note again that, like Ambassador Crocker, I believe Iraq's problems will require a long-term effort. There are no easy answers or quick solutions. And though we both believe this effort can succeed, it will take time. Our assessments underscore, in fact, the importance of recognizing that a premature drawdown of our forces would likely have devastating consequences.

That assessment is supported by the findings of a 16 August Defense Intelligence Agency report on the implications of a rapid withdrawal of US forces from Iraq. Summarizing it in an unclassified fashion, it concludes that a rapid withdrawal would result in the further release of the strong centrifugal forces in Iraq and produce a number of dangerous results, including a high risk of disintegration of the Iraqi Security Forces; rapid deterioration of local security initiatives; Al Qaeda-Iraq regaining lost ground and freedom of maneuver; a marked increase in violence and further ethno-sectarian displacement and refugee flows; alliances of convenience by Iraqi groups with internal and external forces to gain advantages over their rivals; and exacerbation of already challenging regional dynamics, especially with respect to Iran.

Lieutenant General Odierno and I share this assessment and believe that the best way to secure our national interests and avoid an unfavorable outcome in Iraq is to continue to focus our operations on securing the Iraqi people while targeting terrorist groups and militia extremists and, as quickly as conditions are met, transitioning security tasks to Iraqi elements.

Closing Comments

Before closing, I want to thank you and your colleagues for your support of our men and women in uniform in Iraq. The Soldiers, Sailors, Airmen, Marines, and Coast Guardsmen with whom I'm honored to serve are the best equipped and, very likely, the most professional force in our nation's history. Impressively, despite all that has been asked of them in recent years, they continue to raise their right hands and volunteer to stay in uniform. With three weeks to go in this fiscal year, in fact, the Army elements in Iraq, for example, have achieved well over 130% of the reenlistment goals in the initial term and careerist categories and nearly 115% in the mid-career category. All of us appreciate what you have done to ensure that these great troopers have had what they've needed to accomplish their mission, just as we appreciate what you have done to take care of their families, as they, too, have made significant sacrifices in recent years.

The advances you have underwritten in weapons systems and individual equipment; in munitions; in command, control, and communications systems; in intelligence, surveillance, and reconnaissance capabilities; in vehicles and counter-IED systems and programs; and in manned and unmanned aircraft have proven invaluable in Iraq. The capabilities that you have funded most recently—especially the vehicles that will provide greater protection against improvised explosive devices—are also of enormous importance. Additionally, your funding of the Commander's Emergency Response Program has given our leaders a critical tool with which to prosecute the counterinsurgency campaign. Finally, we appreciate as well your funding of our new detention programs and rule of law initiatives in Iraq.

In closing, it remains an enormous privilege to soldier again in Iraq with America's new "Greatest Generation." Our country's men and women in uniform have done a magnificent job in the most complex and challenging environment imaginable. All Americans should be very proud of their sons and daughters serving in Iraq today.

Thank you very much.

POSTSCRIPT

Should the United States Withdraw from Iraq Expeditiously?

It is hard to imagine any developments in Iraq that will definitively end debates over U.S. policies in the next year or more. Most experts agree that the situation in Iraq remains unsettled. Renewed civil conflict could flare up between Sunnis and Shiites as millions of Iraqi refugees attempt to return to their homes. Conflict continues between the Kurds, who have established a great deal of autonomy in Northern Iraq where they constitute the most populous group, and Arabs and other ethnic groups, especially in and around the oil-rich cities of Kirkuk and Mosul. The distribution of national oil revenues among groups and regions in Iraq remains highly contentious as well, especially at a time of low oil prices and falling Iraqi revenues. Finally, Iran might be tempted to become more involved in Iraq on behalf of some of its Shiite allies, while Saudi Arabia may work to protect the interests of the Sunnis, and Turkey could once again send troops across the border into the Kurdish region in pursuit of fighters who are seeking autonomy for Kurds in Turkey.

Whatever developments arise along these fronts, arguments can (and likely will) be made on behalf of either withdrawing U.S. troops or leaving a large contingent in Iraq. If violence remains low, some will argue this indicates U.S. forces are no longer needed, and others will warn that the low levels of violence reduce the costs and risks of the U.S. presence but that a U.S. withdrawal could lead to a renewal of sectarian conflict. If violence once again increases, some will argue a U.S. presence is needed to prevent the situation from getting even worse, and others will emphasize the high and continuing human and economic costs of U.S. deployments and argue that the still-elusive chances of success of what is already one of America's longest conflicts do not justify those costs.

For a few of the more recent of many books on U.S. policy in Iraq, see Thomas Ricks, *Fiasco: The American Military Adventure in Iraq, 2003 to 2005* (Penguin, 2007) and *The Gamble: General David Petraeus and the American Military Adventure in Iraq, 2006–2008* (Penguin, 2009); Bob Woodward, *The War Within: A Secret White House History, 2006–2008* (Simon and Schuster, 2009); Bing West, *The Strongest Tribe: War, Politics, and the Endgame in Iraq* (Random House, 2008); and Linda Robinson, *Tell Me How This Ends: General David Petraeus and the Search for a Way Out of Iraq* (Public Affairs, 2008).

For recent articles on Iraq, see John A. Nagl and Brian M. Burton, "Striking the Balance: The Way Forward in Iraq," *World Policy Journal* (Winter 2008/2009); Daniel Byman, "An Autopsy of the Iraq Debacle: Policy Failure or Bridge Too Far?" *Security Studies* (October 2008); Colin H. Kahl and William E. Odom debating "When to Leave Iraq: Today, Tomorrow, or Yesterday?" *Foreign Affairs* (July/August 2008); Steven Simon, "The Price of the Surge: How U.S. Strategy Is Hastening Iraq's Demise," *Foreign Affairs* (May/June 2008); James Dobbins, "Who Lost Iraq? Lessons From the Debacle," *Foreign Affairs* (September/October 2007); James Fearon, "Iraq's Civil War," *Foreign Affairs* (March/April 2007); and Christopher Fettweis, "On the Consequences of Failure in Iraq," *Survival* (Winter 2007/2008).

ISSUE 5

Should the United States Preemptively Attack Iran's Emerging Nuclear Weapons Capability?

YES: **Norman Podhoretz**, from "Stopping Iran: Why the Case for Military Action Still Stands," *Commentary* (February 2008)

NO: **Scott D. Sagan**, from "How to Keep the Bomb from Iran," *Foreign Affairs* (September/October 2006)

ISSUE SUMMARY

YES: **Norman Podhoretz**, editor-at-large for *Commentary* magazine, asserts that Iran is continuing to pursue the acquisition of nuclear weapons, that carrots and sticks brandished by the United States and others have failed to slow this effort, and that the United States will soon have no alternative but military force if it is to prevent Iran from attaining nuclear weapons.

NO: **Scott D. Sagan**, professor of political science and director of the Center for International Security and Cooperation at Stanford University, argues that other states have been dissuaded from acquiring or keeping nuclear weapons, and that Iran can be as well if the United States gives up the threat of changing the Iranian regime by force.

Iran has been sending mixed signals about its nuclear program for the last six years, and the United States has had a difficult time getting other states to agree on a united and coherent policy toward Iran. In 2003, Iran pledged to stop uranium enrichment, which is an essential step in developing an independent nuclear weapons capability, but provided no means for others to verify this pledge. In November 2004, Iran agreed once again in talks with European Union states that it would halt all enrichment activities, but it reserved the right to resume these efforts in the future. These European states argued at the time that this progress showed that diplomacy, rather than the sanctions that the U.S. favored, was the proper approach toward Iran. The Bush administration thus sought to firm up commitments from Europe and

Russia that they would agree to impose sanctions in the future if diplomacy failed and Iran proceeded with enrichment. Russia, in particular, has been a key player on this issue as it has at times provided technical assistance to Iran's nuclear program and it is a permanent member of the U.N. Security Council with the ability to veto any effort to impose sanctions through the U.N.

Diplomacy alone quickly proved inadequate, as in April 2005, Iran announced that it planned to resume enrichment. By September 2005, the International Atomic Energy Agency (IAEA), the international watchdog on such issues, confirmed that Iran was enriching uranium. This led the IAEA to report Iran's activities to the U.N. Security Council, and in retaliation Iran suspended the IAEA's ability to conduct short-notice nuclear inspections in Iran. The U.N. Security Council then voted unanimously in December 2006 to impose sanctions on Iran over its uranium enrichment program, and to add further sanctions in March of 2007. Meanwhile, a U.S. intelligence report in late 2007 concluded that Iran had put its nuclear weapons program on hold in 2003, even though it continued to enrich uranium. In March 2008, the U.N. Security Council approved a third resolution on sanctions against Iran. In August 2008, Iran failed to respond to a U.N. deadline calling for a halt of Iran's nuclear activities in exchange for a freeze on further sanctions. Experts generally agree that Iran has little use for uranium enrichment other than nuclear weapons that could justify the expense of this process, and that Iran can probably develop a nuclear weapon within a few years, but they remain divided on whether and for how long air strikes, like those which Israel carried out against Iraq's Osirak reactor in 1983, could disable Iran's enrichment capabilities.

YES

Norman Podhoretz

Stopping Iran: Why the Case for Military Action Still Stands

Up until a fairly short time ago, scarcely anyone dissented from the assessment offered with "high confidence" by the National Intelligence Estimate of 2005 that Iran was "determined to develop nuclear weapons." Correlatively, no one believed the protestations of the mullahs ruling Iran that their nuclear program was designed strictly for peaceful uses.

The reason for this near-universal consensus was that Iran, with its vast reserves of oil and natural gas, had no need for nuclear energy, and that in any case, the very nature of its program contradicted the protestations.

Here is how *Time* magazine put it as early as March 2003—long before, be it noted, the radical Mahmoud Ahmadinejad had replaced the putatively moderate Mohamed Khatami as president:

> On a visit last month to Tehran, International Atomic Energy Agency director Mohamed ElBaradei announced he had discovered that Iran was constructing a facility to enrich uranium—a key component of advanced nuclear weapons—near Natanz. But diplomatic sources tell *Time* the plant is much further along than previously revealed. The sources say work on the plant is "extremely advanced" and involves "hundreds" of gas centrifuges ready to produce enriched uranium and "the parts for a thousand others ready to be assembled."

So, too, the Federation of American Scientists about a year later:

> It is generally believed that Iran's efforts are focused on uranium enrichment, though there are some indications of work on a parallel plutonium effort. Iran claims it is trying to establish a complete nuclear-fuel cycle to support a civilian energy program, but this same fuel cycle would be applicable to a nuclear-weapons development program. Iran appears to have spread their nuclear activities around a number of sites to reduce the risk of detection or attack.

And just as everyone agreed with the American intelligence community that Iran was "determined to develop nuclear weapons," everyone also agreed with President Bush that it must not be permitted to succeed. Here, the reasons were many and various.

To begin with, Iran was (as certified even by the doves of the State Department) the leading sponsor of terrorism in the world, and it was therefore reasonable to fear that it would transfer nuclear technology to terrorists who would be only too happy to use it against us. Moreover, since Iran evidently aspired to become the hegemon of the Middle East, its drive for a nuclear capability could result (as, according to the *New York Times,* no fewer than 21 governments in and around the region were warning) in "a grave and destructive nuclear-arms race." This meant a nightmarish increase in the chances of a nuclear war. An even greater increase in those chances would result from the power that nuclear weapons—and the missiles capable of delivering them, which Iran was also developing and/or buying—would give the mullahs to realize their evil dream of (in the words of Mr. Ahmadinejad) "wiping Israel off the map."

Nor, as almost everyone also agreed, were the dangers of a nuclear Iran confined to the Middle East. Dedicated as the mullahs clearly were to furthering the transformation of Europe into a continent where Muslim law and practice would more and more prevail, they were bound to use nuclear intimidation and blackmail in pursuit of this goal as well. Beyond that, nuclear weapons would even serve the purposes of a far more ambitious aim: the creation of what Mr. Ahmadinejad called "a world without America." Although, to be sure, no one imagined that Iran would acquire the capability to destroy the United States, it was easy to imagine that the United States would be deterred from standing in Iran's way by the fear of triggering a nuclear war.

Running alongside the near-universal consensus on Iran's nuclear intentions was a commensurately broad agreement that the regime could be stopped from realizing those intentions by a judicious combination of carrots and sticks. The carrots, offered through diplomacy, consisted of promises that if Iran were (in the words of the Security Council) to "suspend all enrichment-related and reprocessing activities, including research and development, to be verified by the IAEA," it would find itself on the receiving end of many benefits. If, however, Iran remained obdurate in refusing to comply with these demands, sticks would come into play in the form of sanctions.

And indeed, in response to continued Iranian defiance, a round of sanctions was approved by the Security Council in December 2006. When these (watered down to buy the support of the Russians and the Chinese) predictably failed to bite, a tougher round was unanimously authorized three months later, in March 2007. When these in turn failed, the United States, realizing that the Russians and the Chinese would veto stronger medicine, unilaterally imposed a new series of economic sanctions—which fared no better than the multilateral measures that had preceded them.

≈❀≈

What then to do? President Bush kept declaring that Iran must not be permitted to get the bomb, and he kept warning that the "military option"—by which he meant air strikes, not an invasion on the ground—was still on the table as a last resort. On this issue our Western European allies were divided. To the surprise of many who had ceased thinking of France as an ally because of Jacques Chirac's relentless opposition to the policies of the Bush administration, Nicholas Sarkozy, Mr. Chirac's successor as president, echoed Mr. Bush's warning in equally unequivocal terms. If, Mr. Sarkozy announced, the Iranians pressed on with their nuclear program, the world would be left with a choice between "an Iranian bomb and bombing Iran"—and he left no doubt as to where his own choice would fall. On the other hand, Gordon Brown, who had followed Tony Blair as prime minister of the U.K., seemed less willing than Mr. Sarkozy to contemplate military action against Iran's nuclear installations, even as a last resort. Like the new chancellor of Germany, Angela Merkel, Mr. Brown remained—or professed to remain—persuaded that more diplomacy and tougher sanctions would eventually work.

This left a great question hanging in the air: when, if ever, would Mr. Bush (and/or Mr. Sarkozy) conclude that the time had come to resort to the last resort?

Obviously the answer to that question depended on how long it would take for Iran itself to reach the point of no return. According to the NIE of 2005, it was "unlikely . . . that Iran would be able to make a nuclear weapon . . . before early-to-mid next decade"—that is, between 2010 and 2015. If that assessment, offered with "moderate confidence," was correct, Mr. Bush would be off the hook, since he would be out of office for two years at the very least by the time the decision on whether or not to order air strikes would have to be made. That being the case, for the remainder of his term he could continue along the carrot-and-stick path, while striving to ratchet up the pressure on Iran with stronger and stronger measures that he could hope against hope might finally do the trick. If he could get these through the Security Council, so much the better; if not, the United States could try to assemble a coalition outside the U.N. that would be willing to impose really tough sanctions.

Under these circumstances, there would also be enough time to add another arrow to this nonmilitary quiver: a serious program of covert aid to dissident Iranians who dreamed of overthrowing the mullocracy and replacing it with a democratic regime. Those who had been urging Mr. Bush to launch such a program, and who were confident that it would succeed, pointed to polls showing great dissatisfaction with the mullocracy among the Iranian young, and to the demonstrations against it that kept breaking out all over the country. They also contended that even if a new democratic regime were to be as intent as the old one on developing nuclear weapons, neither it nor they would pose anything like the same kind of threat.

All well and good. The trouble was this: only by relying on the accuracy of the 2005 NIE would Mr. Bush be able in all good conscience to pass on to his successor the decision of whether or when to bomb the Iranian nuclear facilities. But that estimate, as he could hardly help knowing from the CIA's not exactly brilliant track record, might easily be too optimistic.

To start with the most spectacular recent instance, the CIA had failed to anticipate 9/11. It then turned out to be wrong in 2002 about Saddam Hussein's possession of weapons of mass destruction, very likely because it was bending over backward to compensate for having been wrong in exactly the opposite direction in 1991, when at the end of the first Gulf war the IAEA discovered that the Iraqi nuclear program was far more advanced than the CIA had estimated. Regarding that by now notorious lapse, Jeffrey T. Richelson, a leading (and devoutly nonpartisan) authority on the American intelligence community, writes in "Spying on the Bomb":

> The extent that the United States and its allies underestimated and misunderstood the Iraqi program [before 1991] constituted a "colossal international intelligence failure," according to one Israeli expert. [IAEA's chief weapons inspector] Hans Blix acknowledged "that there was suspicion certainly," but "to see the enormity of it is a shock."

And these were only the most recent cases. Gabriel Schoenfeld, a close student of the intelligence community, offers a partial list of earlier mistakes and failures:

> The CIA was established in 1947 in large measure to avoid another surprise attack like the one the U.S. had suffered on December 7, 1941 at Pearl Harbor. But only three years after its founding, the fledgling agency missed the outbreak of the Korean war. It then failed to understand that the Chinese would come to the aid of the North Koreans if American forces crossed the Yalu river. It missed the outbreak of the Suez war in 1956. In September 1962, the CIA issued an NIE which stated that the "Soviets would not introduce offensive missiles in Cuba"; in short order, the USSR did precisely that. In 1968 it failed to foresee the Warsaw Pact invasion of Czechoslovakia. . . . It did not inform Jimmy Carter that the Soviet Union would invade Afghanistan in 1979.

Mr. Richelson adds a few more examples of hotly debated issues during the cold war that were wrongly resolved, including "the existence of a missile gap, the capabilities of the Soviet SS-9 intercontinental ballistic missile, [and] Soviet compliance with the test-ban and antiballistic missile treaties." This is not to mention perhaps the most notorious case of all: the fiasco, known as the Bay of Pigs, produced by the CIA's wildly misplaced confidence that an invasion of Cuba by the army of exiles it had assembled and trained would set off a popular uprising against the Castro regime.

On Mr. Bush's part, then, deep skepticism was warranted concerning the CIA's estimate of how much time we had before Iran reached the point of no return. As we have seen, Mohamed ElBaradei, the head of the IAEA, had "discovered" in 2003 that the Iranians were constructing facilities to enrich uranium. Still, as late as April 2007 the same Mr. ElBaradei was pooh-poohing the claims made by Mr. Ahmadinejad that Iran already had 3,000 centrifuges in operation. A month later, we learn from Mr. Richelson, Mr. ElBaradei changed his mind after a few spot inspections. "We believe," Mr. ElBaradei now said, that the Iranians "pretty much have the knowledge about how to enrich. From now on, it is simply a question of perfecting that knowledge."

We also learn from Mr. Richelson that another expert, Matthew Bunn of Harvard's Center for Science and International Affairs, interpreted the new information the IAEA came up with in April 2007 as meaning that "whether they're six months or a year away, one can debate. But it's not 10 years." This chilling estimate of how little time we had to prevent Iran from getting the bomb was similar to the conclusion reached by several Israeli experts (though the official Israeli estimate put the point of no return in 2009).

◦◦◦

Then, in a trice, everything changed. Even as Mr. Bush must surely have been wrestling with the question of whether it would be on his watch that the decision on bombing the Iranian nuclear facilities would have to be made, the world was hit with a different kind of bomb. This took the form of an unclassified summary of a new NIE, published early last December. Entitled "Iran: Nuclear Intentions and Capabilities," this new document was obviously designed to blow up the near-universal consensus that had flowed from the conclusions reached by the intelligence community in its 2005 NIE. In brief, whereas the NIE of 2005 had assessed "with high confidence that Iran currently is determined to develop nuclear weapons," the new NIE of 2007 did "not know whether [Iran] currently intends to develop nuclear weapons."

This startling 180-degree turn was arrived at from new intelligence, offered by the new NIE with "high confidence": namely, that "in fall 2003 Tehran halted its nuclear-weapons program." The new NIE was also confident—though only moderately so—that "Tehran had not restarted its nuclear-weapons program as of mid-2007." And in the most sweeping of its new conclusions, it was even "moderately confident" that "the halt to those activities represents a halt to Iran's entire nuclear-weapons program."

Whatever else one might say about the new NIE, one point can be made with "high confidence": that by leading with the sensational news that Iran had suspended its nuclear-weapons program in 2003, its authors ensured that their entire document would be interpreted as meaning that there was no longer anything to worry about. Of course, being experienced bureaucrats, they took care to protect themselves from this very accusation. For example, after dropping their own bomb on the fear that Iran was hell-bent on getting the bomb, they immediately added "with moderate-to-high confidence that Tehran at a minimum is keeping open the option to develop nuclear weapons." But as they must have expected, scarcely anyone paid attention to this caveat. And as they must also have expected, even less attention was paid to another self-protective caveat, which—making doubly sure it would pass unnoticed—they relegated to a footnote appended to the lead sentence about the halt:

> For the purposes of this Estimate, by "nuclear-weapons program" we mean Iran's nuclear-weapon design and weaponization work and covert uranium conversion-related and uranium enrichment-related work; we do not mean Iran's declared civil work related to uranium conversion and enrichment.

Since only an expert could grasp the significance of this cunning little masterpiece of incomprehensible jargon, the damage had been done by the time its dishonesty was exposed.

The first such exposure came from John Bolton, who before becoming our ambassador to the U.N. had served as undersecretary of state for arms control and international security, with a special responsibility for preventing the proliferation of weapons of mass destruction. Donning this hat once again, Mr. Bolton charged that the dishonesty of the footnote lay most egregiously in the sharp distinction it drew between military and civilian programs. For, he said, "the enrichment of uranium, which all agree Iran is continuing, is critical to civilian and military uses. Indeed, it has always been Iran's 'civilian' program that posed the main risk of a nuclear 'breakout.'"

Two other experts, Valerie Lincy, the editor of Iranwatch.org, and Gary Milhollin, the director of the Wisconsin Project on Nuclear Arms Control, followed up with an explanation of why the halt of 2003 was much less significant than a layman would inevitably be led to think:

> The new report defines "nuclear-weapons program" in a ludicrously narrow way: it confines it to enriching uranium at secret sites or working on a nuclear-weapon design. But the halting of its secret enrichment and weapon-design efforts in 2003 proves only that Iran made a tactical move. It suspended work that, if discovered, would unambiguously reveal intent to build a weapon. It has continued other work, crucial to the ability to make a bomb, that it can pass off as having civilian applications.

Thus, as Ms. Lincy and Mr. Milhollin went on to write, the main point obfuscated by the footnote was that once Iran accumulated a stockpile of the kind of uranium fit for civilian use, it would "in a matter of months" be able "to convert that uranium . . . to weapons grade."

<<◎>>

Yet, in spite of these efforts to demonstrate that the new NIE did not prove that Iran had given up its pursuit of nuclear weapons, just about everyone in the world immediately concluded otherwise, and further concluded that this meant the military option was off the table. George Bush may or may not have been planning to order air strikes before leaving office, but now that the justification for doing so had been discredited by his own intelligence agencies, it would be politically impossible for him to go on threatening military action, let alone to take it.

But what about sanctions? In the weeks and months before the new NIE was made public, Mr. Bush had been working very hard to get a third and tougher round of sanctions approved by the Security Council. In trying to persuade the Russians and the Chinese to sign on, Mr. Bush argued that the failure to enact such sanctions would leave war as the only alternative. Yet if war was now out of the question, and if in any case Iran had for all practical purposes given up its pursuit of nuclear weapons for the foreseeable future, what need was there of sanctions?

Anticipating that this objection would be raised, the White House desperately set out to interpret the new NIE as, precisely, offering "grounds for hope that the problem can be solved diplomatically—without the use of force." These words by Stephen Hadley, Mr. Bush's national security adviser, represented the very first comment on the new NIE to emanate from the White House, and some version of them would be endlessly repeated in the days to come.

Joining this campaign of damage control, Messrs. Sarkozy and Brown issued similar statements, and even Ms. Merkel (who had been very reluctant to go along with Mr. Bush's push for another round of sanctions) now declared that it was "dangerous and still grounds for great concern that Iran, in the face of the UN Security Council's resolutions, continues to refuse to suspend uranium enrichment. . . . The Iranian president's intolerable agitation against Israel also speaks volumes. . . . It remains a vital interest of the whole world community to prevent a nuclear-armed Iran."

As it happened, Mr. Hadley was right about the new NIE, which executed another 180-degree turn—this one, away from the judgment of the 2005 NIE concerning the ineffectiveness of international pressure. Flatly contradicting its "high confidence" in 2005 that Iran was forging ahead "despite its international obligations and international pressure," the new NIE concluded that the nuclear-weapons program had been halted in 2003 "primarily in response to international pressure." This indicated that "Tehran's decisions are guided by a cost-benefit approach rather than a rush to a weapon irrespective of the political, economic, and military costs."

Never mind that no international pressure to speak of was being exerted on Iran in 2003, and that at that point the mullahs were more likely acting out of fear that the Americans, having just invaded Iraq, might come after them next. Never mind, too, that religious and/or ideological passions, which the new NIE pointedly neglected to mention, have over and over again throughout history proved themselves a more powerful driving force than any "cost-benefit approach." Blithely sweeping aside such considerations, the new NIE was confident that just as the carrot-and-stick approach had allegedly sufficed in the past, so it would suffice in the future to "prompt Tehran to extend the current halt to its nuclear-weapons program."

The worldview implicit here has been described by Mr. Richelson (mainly with North Korea in mind) as the idea that "moral suasion and sustained bargaining are the proven mechanisms of nuclear restraint." Such a worldview "may be ill-equipped," he observes delicately, "to accept the idea that certain regimes are incorrigible and negotiate only as a stalling tactic until they have attained a nuclear capability against the United States and other nations that might act against their nuclear programs."

True, the new NIE did at least acknowledge that it would not be easy to induce Iran to extend the halt, "given the linkage many within the leadership probably see between nuclear-weapons development and Iran's key national-security and foreign-policy objectives." But it still put its money on a "combination of threats of intensified international scrutiny and pressures, along with opportunities for Iran to achieve its security, prestige, and goals for regional influence in other ways."

It was this pronouncement, and a few others like it, that gave Stephen Hadley "grounds for hope that the problem can be solved diplomatically." But that it was a false hope was demonstrated by the NIE itself. For if Iran was pursuing nuclear weapons in order to achieve its "key national-security and foreign-policy objectives," and if those objectives explicitly included (for a start) hegemony in the Middle East and the destruction of the state of Israel, what possible "opportunities" could Tehran be offered to achieve them "in other ways"?

⋅◉⋅

So much for the carrot. As for the stick, it was no longer big enough to matter, what with the threat of military action ruled out, and what with the case for a third round of sanctions undermined by the impression stemming from the NIE's main finding that there was nothing left to worry about. Why worry when it was four years since Iran had done any work toward developing the bomb, when the moratorium remained in effect, and when there was no reason to believe that the program would be resumed in the near future?

What is more, in continuing to insist that the Iranians must be stopped from developing the bomb and that this could be done by nonmilitary means, the Bush administration and its European allies were lagging behind a new consensus within the American foreign-policy establishment that had already been forming even before the publication of the new NIE. Whereas the old consensus was based on the proposition that (in Sen. John McCain's pungent formulation) "the only thing worse than bombing Iran was letting Iran get the bomb," the emerging new consensus held the opposite—that the only thing worse than letting Iran get the bomb was bombing Iran.

What led to this reversal was a gradual loss of faith in the carrot-and-stick approach. As one who had long since rejected this faith and who had been excoriated for my apostasy by more than one member of the foreign-policy elites, I never thought I would live to see the day when these very elites would come to admit that diplomacy and sanctions had been given a fair chance and that they had accomplished nothing but to buy Iran more time. The lesson drawn from this new revelation was, however, a different matter.

It was in the course of a public debate with one of the younger members of the foreign-policy establishment that I first chanced upon the change in view. Knowing that he never deviated by so much as an inch from the conventional wisdom of the moment within places like the Council on Foreign Relations and the Brookings Institution, I had expected him to defend the carrot-and-stick approach and to attack me as a warmonger for contending that bombing was the only way to stop the mullahs from getting the bomb. Instead, to my great surprise, he took the position that there was really no need to stop them in the first place, since even if they had the bomb they could be deterred from using it, just as effectively as the Soviets and the Chinese had been deterred during the cold war.

Without saying so in so many words, then, my opponent was acknowledging that diplomacy and sanctions had proved to be a failure, and that there was no point in pursuing them any further. But so as to avoid drawing the logical conclusion—namely, that military action had now become necessary—he simply abandoned the old establishment assumption that Iran must at all costs be prevented from developing nuclear weapons, adopting in its place the complacent idea that we could learn to live with an Iranian bomb.

In response, I argued that deterrence could not be relied upon with a regime ruled by Islamo-fascist revolutionaries who not only were ready to die for their beliefs but cared less about protecting their people than about the spread of their ideology and their power. If the mullahs got the bomb, I said, it was not they who would be deterred, but we.

So little did any of this shake my opponent that I came away from our debate with the grim realization that the president's continued insistence on the dangers posed by an Iranian bomb would more and more fall on deaf ears—ears that would soon be made even deafer by the new NIE's assurance that Iran was no longer hell-bent on acquiring nuclear weapons after all. There might be two different ideas competing here—one, that we could live with an Iranian bomb; the other, that there would be no Iranian bomb to live with—but the widespread acceptance of either would not only preclude the military option but would sooner or later put an end even to the effort to stop the mullahs by nonmilitary means.

ᴇᴬᴏʸᴇ

And yet there remained something else, or rather someone else, to factor into the equation: the perennially "misunderestimated" George W. Bush, a man who knew evil when he saw it and who had the courage and the determination to do battle against it. This was also a man who, far more than most politicians, said what he meant and meant what he said. And what he had said at least twice before was that if we permitted Iran to build a nuclear arsenal, people 50 years from now would look back and wonder how we of this generation could have allowed such a thing to happen, and they would rightly judge us as harshly as we today judge the British and the French for what they did at Munich in 1938. It was because I had found it hard to understand why Mr. Bush would put himself so squarely in the dock of history on this issue if he were resigned to an Iran in possession of nuclear weapons, or even of the ability to build them, that I predicted in the pages of *Commentary,* and went on predicting elsewhere, that he would not retire from office before resorting to the military option.

But then came the new NIE. To me it seemed obvious that it represented another ambush by an intelligence community that had consistently tried to sabotage Mr. Bush's policies through a series of damaging leaks and was now trying to prevent him from ever taking military action against Iran. To others, however, it seemed equally obvious that Mr. Bush, far from being ambushed, had welcomed the new NIE precisely because it provided him with a perfect opportunity to begin distancing himself from the military option.

But I could not for the life of me believe that Mr. Bush intended to fly in the face of the solemn promise he had made in his 2002 State of the Union address:

> We'll be deliberate, yet time is not on our side. I will not wait on events, while dangers gather. I will not stand by, as peril draws closer and closer. The United States of America will not permit the world's most dangerous regimes to threaten us with the world's most destructive weapons.

To which he had added shortly afterward in a speech at West Point: "If we wait for threats to fully materialize, we will have waited too long."

How, I wondered, could Mr. Bush not know that in the case of Iran he was running a very great risk of waiting too long? And if he was truly ready to run that risk, why, in a press conference the day after the new NIE came out, did he put himself in the historical dock yet again by repeating what he had said several times before about the judgment that would be passed on this generation in the future if Iran were to acquire a nuclear weapon?

> If Iran shows up with a nuclear weapon at some point in time, the world is going to say, what happened to them in 2007? How come they couldn't see the impending danger? What caused them not to understand that a country that once had a weapons program could reconstitute the weapons program? How come they couldn't see that the important first step in developing a weapon is the capacity to be able to enrich uranium? How come they didn't know that with that capacity, that knowledge could be passed on to a covert program? What blinded them to the realities of the world? And it's not going to happen on my watch.

❦

"It's not going to happen on my watch." What else could this mean if not that Mr. Bush was preparing to meet "the impending danger" in what he must by now have concluded was the only way it could be averted?

The only alternative that seemed even remotely plausible to me was that he might be fixing to outsource the job to the Israelis. After all, even if, by now, it might have become politically impossible for us to take military action, the Israelis could not afford to sit by while a regime pledged to wipe them off the map was equipping itself with nuclear weapons and the missiles to deliver them. For unless Iran could be stopped before acquiring a nuclear capability, the Israelis would be faced with only two choices: either strike first, or pray that the fear of retaliation would deter the Iranians from beating them to the punch. Yet a former president of Iran, Hashemi Rafsanjani, had served notice that his country would not be deterred by the fear of retaliation:

> If a day comes when the world of Islam is duly equipped with the arms Israel has in its possession, . . . application of an atomic bomb would not leave anything in Israel, but the same thing would just produce damages in the Muslim world.

If this was the view of even a supposed moderate like Mr. Rafsanjani, how could the Israelis depend upon the mullahs to refrain from launching a first strike? The answer was that they could not. Bernard Lewis, the leading contemporary authority on the culture of the Islamic world, has explained why:

> MAD, mutual assured destruction, [was effective] right through the cold war. Both sides had nuclear weapons. Neither side used them, because both sides knew the other would retaliate in kind. This will not work with a religious fanatic [like Mr. Ahmadinejad]. For him, mutual assured destruction is not a deterrent, it is an inducement. We know already that [the mullahs ruling Iran] do not give a damn about killing their own people in great numbers. We have seen it again and again. In the final scenario, and this applies all the more strongly if they kill large numbers of their own people, they are doing them a favor. They are giving them a quick free pass to heaven and all its delights.

Under the aegis of such an attitude, even in the less extreme variant that may have been held by some of Mr. Ahmadinejad's colleagues among the regime's rulers, mutual assured destruction would turn into a very weak reed. Understanding that, the Israelis would be presented with an irresistible incentive to preempt—and so, too, would the Iranians. Either way, a nuclear exchange would become inevitable.

What would happen then? In a recently released study, Anthony Cordesman of the Center for Strategic and International Studies argues that Mr. Rafsanjani had it wrong. In the grisly scenario Mr. Cordesman draws, tens of millions would indeed die, but Israel—despite the decimation of its civilian population and the destruction of its major cities—would survive, even if just barely, as a functioning society. Not so Iran, and not its "key Arab neighbors," particularly Egypt and Syria, which Mr. Cordesman thinks Israel would also have to target in order "to ensure that no other power can capitalize on an Iranian strike." Furthermore, Israel might be driven in desperation to go after the oil wells, refineries, and ports in the Gulf.

"Being contained within the region," writes Martin Walker of UPI in his summary of Mr. Cordesman's study, "such a nuclear exchange might not be Armageddon for the human race." To me it seems doubtful that it could be confined to the Middle East. But even if it were, the resulting horrors would still be far greater than even the direst consequences that might follow from bombing Iran before it reaches the point of no return.

In the worst case of this latter scenario, Iran would retaliate by increasing the trouble it is already making for us in Iraq and by attacking Israel with missiles armed with non-nuclear warheads but possibly containing biological and/or chemical weapons. There would also be a vast increase in the price of oil, with catastrophic consequences for every economy in the world, very much including our own. And there would be a deafening outcry from one end of the earth to the other against the inescapable civilian casualties. Yet, bad as all this would be, it does not begin to compare with the gruesome consequences of a nuclear exchange between Israel and Iran, even if those consequences were to be far less extensive than Mr. Cordesman anticipates.

Which is to say that, as between bombing Iran to prevent it from getting the bomb and letting Iran get the bomb, there is simply no contest.

꧁꧂

But this still does not answer the question of who should do the bombing. Tempting as it must be for George Bush to sit back and let the Israelis do the job, there are considerations that should give him pause. One is that no matter what he would say, the whole world would regard the Israelis as a surrogate for the United States, and we would become as much the target of the ensuing recriminations both at home and abroad as we would if we had done the job ourselves.

To make matters worse, the indications are that it would be very hard for the Israeli air force, superb though it is, to pull the mission off. Thus, an analysis by two members of the Security Studies Program at MIT concluded that while "the Israeli air force now possesses the capability to destroy even well-hardened targets in Iran with some degree of confidence," the problem is that for the mission to succeed, all of the many contingencies involved would have to go right. Hence an Israeli attempt could end with the worst of all possible outcomes: retaliatory measures by the Iranians even as their nuclear program remained unscathed. We, on the other hand, would have a much bigger margin of error and a much better chance of setting their program back by a minimum of five or 10 years and at best wiping it out altogether.

The upshot is that if Iran is to be prevented from becoming a nuclear power, it is the United States that will have to do the preventing, to do it by means of a bombing campaign, and (because "if we wait for threats to fully materialize, we will have waited too long") to do it soon.

When I first predicted a year or so ago that Mr. Bush would bomb Iran's nuclear facilities once he had played out the futile diplomatic string, the obstacles that stood in his way were great but they did not strike me as insurmountable. Now, thanks in large part to the new NIE, they have grown so formidable that I can only stick by my prediction with what the NIE itself would describe as "low-to-moderate confidence." For Mr. Bush is right about the resemblance between 2008 and 1938. In 1938, as Winston Churchill later said, Hitler could still have been stopped at a relatively low price and many millions of lives could have been saved if England and France had not deceived themselves about the realities of their situation. *Mutatis mutandis,* it is the same in 2008, when Iran can still be stopped from getting the bomb and even more millions of lives can be saved—but only provided that we summon up the courage to see what is staring us in the face and then act on what we see.

Unless we do, the forces that are blindly working to ensure that Iran will get the bomb are likely to prevail even against the clear-sighted determination of George W. Bush, just as the forces of appeasement did against Churchill in 1938. In which case, we had all better pray that there will be enough time for the next President to discharge the responsibility that Mr. Bush will have been forced to pass on, and that this successor will also have the clarity and the courage to discharge it. If not—God help us all—the stage will have been set for the outbreak of a nuclear war that will become as inescapable then as it is avoidable now.

Scott D. Sagan

NO

How to Keep the Bomb from Iran

Preventing the Unthinkable

The ongoing crisis with Tehran is not the first time Washington has had to face a hostile government attempting to develop nuclear weapons. Nor is it likely to be the last. Yet the reasoning of U.S. officials now struggling to deal with Iran's nuclear ambitions is clouded by a kind of historical amnesia, which leads to both creeping fatalism about the United States' ability to keep Iran from getting the bomb and excessive optimism about the United States' ability to contain Iran if it does become a nuclear power. Proliferation fatalism and deterrence optimism reinforce each other in a disturbing way. As nuclear proliferation comes to be seen as inevitable, wishful thinking can make its consequences seem less severe, and if faith in deterrence grows, incentives to combat proliferation diminish.

A U.S. official in the executive branch anonymously told *The New York Times* in March 2006, "The reality is that most of us think the Iranians are probably going to get a weapon, or the technology to make one, sooner or later." Such proliferation fatalists argue that over the long term, it may be impossible to stop Iran—or other states for that matter—from getting the bomb. Given the spread of nuclear technology and know-how, and the right of parties to the Nuclear Nonproliferation Treaty (NPT) to enrich uranium and separate plutonium, the argument goes, any foreign government determined to acquire nuclear weapons will eventually do so. Moreover, the 1981 Israeli attack on the Osirak nuclear reactor in Iraq may have delayed Iraq's progress, but similar air strikes are unlikely to disable Iran's capacities, since its uranium-enrichment facilities can be hidden underground or widely dispersed. Imposing economic sanctions through the UN Security Council is clearly a preferable option. But as Washington learned with India and Pakistan in the 1980s and 1990s, sanctions only increase the costs of going nuclear; they do not reduce the ability of a determined government to get the bomb.

Faced with only unattractive options to stem proliferation, some Bush administration officials are reluctantly preparing to live with a nuclear Iran. Military planners and intelligence officers have reportedly been tasked with developing strategies to deter Tehran if negotiations fail. Washington officials cry that the sky is falling whenever they face the prospect of a hostile state's getting the bomb, yet they seem to find solace in the recollection that deterrence and containment did work to maintain the peace during the Cold War.

So why worry that the latest crop of rogue regimes might prove less deterrable than the Soviet Union and China? The Bush administration already appears to have adopted this logic with respect to North Korea. According to *The New York Times,* administration officials privately predict that deterrence will work against Pyongyang: "The North Koreans know that a missile attack on the United States would result in the vaporization of Pyongyang," the paper quoted an official as saying. And if deterrence can work with Kim Jong II, why not with Ayatollah Ali Khamenei? "Iran is just one instance of the [proliferation] problem, and in Iran's case, containment might work," argues Brent Scowcroft, who was national security adviser to President George H. W. Bush.

But both deterrence optimism and proliferation fatalism are wrong-headed. Deterrence optimism is based on mistaken nostalgia and a faulty analogy. Although deterrence did work with the Soviet Union and China, there were many close calls; maintaining nuclear peace during the Cold War was far more difficult and uncertain than U.S. officials and the American public seem to remember today. Furthermore, a nuclear Iran would look a lot less like the totalitarian Soviet Union and the People's Republic of China and a lot more like Pakistan, Iran's unstable neighbor—a far more frightening prospect. Fatalism about nuclear proliferation is equally unwarranted. Although the United States did fail to prevent its major Cold War rivals from developing nuclear arsenals, many other countries curbed their own nuclear ambitions. After flirting with nuclear programs in the 1960s, West Germany and Japan decided that following the NPT and relying on the protection of the U.S. nuclear umbrella would bring them greater security in the future; South Korea and Taiwan gave up covert nuclear programs when the United States threatened to sever security relations with them; North Korea froze its plutonium production in the 1990s; and Libya dismantled its nascent nuclear program in 2003.

Given these facts, Washington should work harder to prevent the unthinkable rather than accept what falsely appears to be inevitable. The lesson to be drawn from the history of nonproliferation is not that all states eyeing the bomb eventually get it but that nonproliferation efforts succeed when the United States and other global actors help satisfy whatever concerns drove a state to want nuclear weapons in the first place. Governments typically pursue nuclear power for one of three reasons: to protect themselves against an external security threat, to satisfy the parochial interests of domestic actors, or to acquire an important status symbol. Iran is, mostly, a classic case of a state that wants nuclear weapons to dissuade an attack. It sits in a perennially unstable region, has long faced a belligerent Iraq, and now wants to stand up to Washington's calls for regime change in Tehran. Any viable solution to Tehran's appetite for nuclear weapons will therefore require that Washington learn to coexist peacefully with Iran's deeply problematic government. U.S. officials should not assume that Iran will go nuclear no matter what and draw up plans for containing it when it does. Nor should Washington rely exclusively on UN sanctions, which might not work. Instead, the U.S. government must dig into its diplomatic toolbox and offer—in conjunction with China, Russia, and the EU-3 (France, Germany, and the United Kingdom)—contingent security guarantees to Tehran.

Delusions of Deterrence

The nuclear monopoly the United States enjoyed at the end of World War II did not last long. Nonproliferation discussions in the United Nations soon after the war came to naught because the Soviet Union understandably distrusted any plan that gave the United States a monopoly on the scientific knowledge and engineering experience needed to build a nuclear weapon. As Cold War hostilities grew, first President Harry Truman and then President Dwight Eisenhower considered launching attacks against the Soviet Union to prevent it from developing a nuclear arsenal. Moscow had tested its first atomic bomb in 1949, but it was the prospect of the Soviets' amassing a large H-bomb arsenal that particularly alarmed Eisenhower. In 1953, he asked Secretary of State John Foster Dulles if "our duty to future generations did not require us to initiate war at the most propitious time that we could designate." Eisenhower eventually rejected the idea, however, because he feared the Red Army would respond by invading U.S. allies in Europe. Even if the United States did emerge victorious from such a conflict, Eisenhower told his advisers in 1954, "the colossal job of occupying the territories of a defeated enemy would be far beyond the resources of the United States at the conclusion of this war."

As the Soviet nuclear arsenal expanded, it triggered a chain reaction. The United Kingdom and France raced to develop their own nuclear weapons (which they first detonated in 1952 and 1960, respectively), partly as an independent deterrent to Soviet aggression in Europe but also as a symbol of their continuing great-power status. That U.S. allies developed such capacities did not much concern Washington, but the U.S. government became deeply worried that China under Mao Zedong might acquire its own bomb. Still, the Kennedy administration rejected plans to launch a preventive air strike on Chinese nuclear facilities in 1963 for fear that it would spark a major war and because the Soviets had rejected Washington's secret request for their assistance.

It is common today to look back nostalgically on those years as "the long peace." But this oversimplifies the challenges of the Cold War. Nuclear weapons did seem to have a sobering influence on the great powers, but that effect was neither automatic nor foolproof. Both the Soviet and the Chinese governments originally hoped that having the bomb would allow them to engage in more aggressive policies with impunity. Moscow repeatedly threatened West Berlin in the late 1950s and early 1960s, for example, confident that its growing arsenal would dissuade the United States from coming to West Germany's defense. Soviet Premier Nikita Khrushchev also believed that if the Soviet Union could place nuclear weapons in Cuba, the United States, once faced with the fait accompli, would be deterred by the Soviet arsenal from attacking Fidel Castro's regime.

What could be called dangerous learning by "trial and terror" also characterized relations with China. Mao appears to have genuinely believed that nuclear weapons were "paper tigers" and that China could survive any large-scale nuclear war. Beijing's foreign policy certainly did not turn moderate after its 1964 nuclear tests. Mao ordered military ambushes of Soviet armed forces on the disputed Chinese-Soviet border in March 1969, instructing Chinese generals not to worry about Moscow's response because "we, too, have atomic bombs." Soviet leaders retaliated against Chinese units along the border and threatened a preventive nuclear strike against China's nuclear facilities. Mao eventually accepted a negotiated settlement of the territorial dispute, but only after evacuating the Chinese leadership to the countryside and putting China's nuclear arsenal on alert.

A Regime Is Born

The frightening crises of the 1960s led U.S. and Soviet leaders to understand that nuclear weapons guaranteed only a precarious peace. Increasingly, the two superpowers pursued bilateral arms control measures—such as the Strategic Arms Limitation Talks and the Anti-Ballistic Missile Treaty—to try to manage their nuclear relationship. They also recognized that a new multilateral approach was needed to stop the spread of nuclear weapons.

In March 1963, President John F. Kennedy told the press that he was "haunted" by the fear that by the 1970s the United States would "face a world in which 15 or 20 or 25 nations" possessed nuclear weapons. Five years of negotiations later, the United States, the Soviet Union, the United Kingdom, and 59 non-nuclear-weapons states signed the NPT. Under the terms of the treaty, states possessing nuclear weapons agreed not to transfer weapons or knowledge about how to build them to their friends and allies. (This commitment effectively ended Washington's hope of supplying West Germany and other NATO powers with "a multilateral force" of nuclear weapons, a prospect that had deeply troubled Moscow.) They also undertook "to work in good faith" toward the eventual elimination of nuclear weapons. The non-nuclear-weapons states, for their part, agreed not to seek nuclear weapons and to cooperate with inspectors from the International Atomic Energy Agency (IAEA) to allow monitoring of their peaceful nuclear research and energy facilities. The idea behind this "I won't if you won't" provision was to reduce the security threats, potential or real, that non-nuclear-weapons states posed to one another. The treaty also guaranteed that non-nuclear-weapons states in good standing would gain the full benefits of peaceful nuclear energy production, creating a "sovereign right," Iran has since argued, for any such state to develop a full nuclear-fuel production cycle of its own. The broad ambition behind the NPT was to slow down proliferation by reducing the demand for nuclear weapons. By both providing some assurance that states subscribing to the treaty would not develop nuclear bombs and creating, through the IAEA, a system to detect their efforts if they did, the NPT assuaged the security concerns of many states. It also reduced the bomb's appeal as a status symbol by creating an international norm according to which "responsible" states followed NPT commitments and only "rogue" states did not. And by offering hope that the nuclear states would take significant steps toward eventual disarmament, the treaty made it easier for nonnuclear governments to justify their own self-restraint to their domestic constituencies.

The NPT system proved reasonably successful for quite a long while. Although they are less discussed than the failures, the nonproliferation successes—the nuclear dogs that did not bark—are more numerous. Many non-nuclear-weapons states did continue to develop nuclear energy facilities after the NPT was signed, and some—such as Japan, with its massive pluto-nium stockpile—kept nuclear materials and continued their nuclear research in case the NPT regime fell apart. (Uncertainty about the treaty was so strong at first that Japan and other nonnuclear states insisted that they be allowed to review and renew their membership every five years.) But the NPT and U.S. security guarantees eventually reduced those countries' interest in prolifera-tion. Other U.S. allies were caught cheating—most notably South Korea in the 1970s and Taiwan in the 1980s—but they ended suspected military-related activities when Washington confronted them and threatened to withdraw its security assistance. Egypt sought nuclear weapons in the early 1960s, but it signed the NPT in 1968 and ratified it in 1979 after striking a peace deal with Israel that reduced its national security concerns. Belarus, Kazakhstan, and Ukraine were nuclear powers from the moment of their independence, having inherited arsenals when the Soviet Union collapsed in 1991. But they soon handed over the weapons to Russia in exchange for economic assistance, highly limited security assurances from the United States, and a chance to join the NPT in good standing. The NPT has been enough of a success that at the 1995 NPT Review Conference, all 178 states that had ratified it agreed to extend it permanently.

Perils of Proliferation

A few outliers have bucked the system, however, and it is their actions that have bred the fatalism about proliferation that now dominates in Washington. Israel has never officially admitted to possessing nuclear weapons, but it is widely known to have constructed (with France's help) a small arsenal in the 1970s. South Africa secretly built seven nuclear devices under the apartheid regime in the 1980s (but unilaterally destroyed them well before a black-majority-rule government took over in 1994). India and Pakistan developed nuclear capabilities in the late 1980s and came out of the closet with them in May 1998. Iraq had been inching along, too, and after the 1981 Israeli air strike on its Osirak reactor, it started an underground gaseous diffusion facility to produce bomb-grade uranium, which was belatedly discovered and destroyed by UN inspectors after the 1991 Gulf War.

A number of political and military developments since the 1990s have further weakened the nonproliferation regime. The Pakistani scientist A. Q. Khan, among others, began secretly selling uranium-enrichment capabilities and even bomb designs to potential proliferators. The emergence of new nuclear states has threatened those states' neighbors, and the United States itself is increasingly seen as a security threat by some potential proliferators. Some states—Iran in particular—insist that they have a "right" to develop nuclear-fuel-production capabilities, which would get them uncomfort-ably close to developing nuclear bombs if they were subsequently to quit the treaty. In 1999, the U.S. Senate also dealt the regime a blow by voting against ratification of the Comprehensive Test Ban Treaty despite the Clinton administration's promise to ratify it during the 1995 NPT conference as proof of the U.S. commitment to eventual disarmament.

Most important, some new nuclear states have proved to be particularly risky actors. Consider the unsettling case of Pakistan. Islamabad has been dangerously lax since its 1998 nuclear tests, exercising weak control over its military personnel, intelligence officials, and scientists who have access to nuclear weapons, materials, and technology. Soon after the 1998 tests, Pakistani military planners developed more belligerent strategies against India. Dusting off an old plan, in the winter of 1999, Pakistani infantry units disguised as mujahideen snuck into Indian-held Kashmir. The incursion sparked the 1999 Kargil War, in which over 1,000 soldiers were killed on both sides before Pakistani forces reluctantly withdrew. According to U.S. and Indian intelligence, before the fighting ended, the Pakistani military had started to ready its nuclear-capable missiles for potential use. But when President Bill Clinton raised the possibility that this had happened with Pakistani Prime Minister Nawaz Sharif, he displayed a disturbing lack of knowledge about what his own military was doing. Similarly, Pakistani leaders gave important nuclear command-and-control responsibilities to the notorious Inter-Services Intelligence (ISI), which has intimate ties to both the Taliban and jihadist groups fighting in Kashmir. Doing so was a recipe for trouble, raising the risks that a rogue faction could steal a weapon or give it to terrorists. According to credible reports, during the Kargil War, Pakistani military planners and the ISI considered hiding Pakistan's nuclear weapons in western Afghanistan to protect them from a potential preemptive attack by India; they even contacted Taliban officials to explore the option. Islamabad has also exercised incredibly loose control over Pakistani nuclear scientists. After the 9/11 attacks, it was discovered that a number of individual scientists—including Sultan Bashiruddin Mahmood, a senior official of the Pakistan Atomic Energy Commission (PAEC)—had met with Osama bin Laden in Afghanistan and discussed techniques for developing nuclear weapons and other weapons of mass destruction. In April 2002, Pakistani President Pervez Musharraf admitted that PAEC scientists had been in contact with al Qaeda but claimed that "the scientists involved had only very superficial knowledge." Most proliferation experts also believe that senior Pakistani military officers were involved in many, if not all, of the deals in which A. Q. Khan and his associates sold nuclear centrifuge components to Iran and Libya, offered to help Saddam Hussein build a bomb just before the 1991 Gulf War, and provided North Korea with uranium-enrichment technology.

The Most Dangerous Game

Dealing with a nuclear Iran in the near future would be more like dealing with Pakistan than with nuclearized democracies such as Israel and India or even nuclear totalitarian states such as the Soviet Union and China. Not only does Iranian President Mahmoud Ahmadinejad spew belligerent anti-Israel and Holocaust-denying statements, but the Iranian government as a whole continues to nurture revolutionary ambitions toward Iran's conservative Sunni neighbors and to support Hezbollah and other terrorist organizations. Tehran, like

Islamabad, would be unlikely to maintain centralized control over its nuclear weapons or materials. In order to deter Tehran from giving nuclear weapons to terrorists, in January 2006 the French government announced that it would respond to nuclear terrorism with a nuclear strike of its own against any state that had served as the terrorists' accomplice. But this "attribution deterrence" posture glosses over the difficult question of what do if the source of nuclear materials for a terrorist bomb is uncertain. It also ignores the possibility that Tehran, once in possession of nuclear weapons, would feel emboldened to engage in aggressive naval actions against tankers in the Persian Gulf or to assist terrorist attacks as it did with the Hezbollah bombing of the U.S. barracks at the Khobar Towers in Saudi Arabia in 1996.

There is no reason to assume that, even if they wanted to, central political authorities in Tehran could completely control the details of nuclear operations by the Islamic Revolutionary Guard Corps. The IRGC recruits young "true believers" to join its ranks, subjects them to ideological indoctrination (but not psychological-stability testing), and—as the IAEA discovered when it inspected Iran's centrifuge facilities in 2003—gives IRGC units responsibility for securing production sites for nuclear materials. The IRGC is known to have ties to terrorist organizations, which means that Iran's nuclear facilities, like its chemical weapons programs, are under the ostensible control of the organization that manages Tehran's contacts with foreign terrorists. It is misguided simply to hope that eventual regime change in Tehran would end the nuclear danger because, in the words of one Bush administration official, who spoke to *The New York Times* anonymously, Washington would then "have a different relationship with a different Iranian government." This wish assumes that another Iranian revolution would end gently, with an orderly transfer of power, rather than in chaos and with the control of nuclear weapons left unclear.

The Reasons Why

If Iran must not be allowed to go nuclear, what then can be done to stop it? A U.S. military strike on Iran today should be avoided for the same prudent reasons that led Eisenhower and Kennedy to choose diplomacy and arms control over preventive war in their dealings with the Soviet Union and China. Even if U.S. intelligence services were confident that they had identified all major nuclear-related sites in Iran (they are not) and the Pentagon could hit all the targets, the United States would expose itself (especially its bases in the Middle East and U.S troops in Afghanistan and Iraq), and its allies, to the possibility of severe retaliation. When asked about possible U.S. air strikes in August 2004, Iranian Defense Minister Ali Shamkhani said, "You may be surprised to know that the U.S. military presence near us is not power for the United States because this power may under certain circumstances become a hostage in our hands. . . . The United States is not the only power present in the region. We are also present from Khost to Kandahar in Afghanistan and we are present in the Gulf and can be present in Iraq." Iran might also support attacks by terrorist groups in Europe or the United States. Bush administration officials have sought to give some teeth to the threat of a military attack by hinting that Israel might strike on Washington's behalf. The Pentagon notified Congress in April 2005 of its intention to sell conventional GBU-28 "bunker-buster" bombs to Israel, and President George W. Bush reasserted Washington's commitment to "support Israel if her security is threatened." But an Israeli air strike on Iran's nuclear facilities would do no more good than a U.S. one: it could not destroy all the facilities and thus would leave Tehran to resume its uranium-enrichment program at surviving sites and would give Iran strong incentives to retaliate against U.S. forces in the Middle East. Muslim sentiment throughout the world would be all the more inflamed, encouraging terrorist responses against the West.

With no viable military option at hand, the only way for Washington to move forward is to give Tehran good reason to relinquish its pursuit of nuclear weapons. That, in turn, requires understanding why Tehran wants them in the first place. Iran's nuclear energy program began in the 1960s under the shah, but even he wanted to create a breakout option to get the bomb quickly if necessary. One of his senior energy advisers once recalled, "The shah told me that he does not want the bomb yet, but if anyone in the neighborhood has it, we must be ready to have it." At first, Ayatollah Ruhollah Khomeini objected to nuclear weapons and other weapons of mass destruction on religious grounds, but the mullahs abandoned such restraint after Saddam ordered chemical attacks on Iranian forces during the Iran-Iraq War. As former Iranian President Hashemi Rafsanjani, then the speaker of Iran's Parliament, noted in 1988, the conflict with Saddam showed that "the moral teachings of the world are not very effective when war reaches a serious stage," and so Iranians must "fully equip ourselves in the defensive and offensive use of chemical, bacteriological, and radiological weapons." Tehran began purchasing centrifuge components from A. Q. Khan's network in 1987 and received, according to the IAEA, documents on how to cast enriched uranium into the form needed for nuclear weapons. Iran's nuclear-development efforts were further accelerated when, after the 1991 Gulf War, UN inspectors discovered and disclosed that Iraq had been just one or two years away from developing nuclear weapons of its own.

The end of Saddam's rule in 2003 significantly reduced the security threat to Tehran. But by then the United States had already taken Iraq's place, Washington having made it clear that it wanted regime change in Iran, too. In his January 2002 State of the Union address, President Bush had denounced the governments of Iran, Iraq, and North Korea as members of an "axis of evil" with ties to international terrorism. Increasingly, Bush administration spokespeople were advocating "preemption" to counter proliferation. After the fall of Baghdad, an unidentified senior U.S. official told a *Los Angeles Times* reporter that Tehran should "take a number," hinting that it was next in line for regime change. It did not help that the 2002 Nuclear Posture Review, which was leaked to the press, listed Iran as one of the states to be considered as a potential target by U.S. nuclear war planners. When asked, in April 2006, whether the Pentagon was considering a potential preventive nuclear strike against Iranian nuclear facilities, President Bush pointedly replied, "All options are on the table."

In the meantime, Iran's program has advanced. The last official U.S. intelligence estimate given to Congress, in February 2006, vaguely stated that if Iran "continues on its current path [it] will likely have the capacity to produce a nuclear weapon within the next decade"—an estimate that has since been widely interpreted to mean five to ten years. Last April, Tehran began operating a cascade of 164 uranium-enrichment centrifuges at Natanz. According to the State Department, it will take over 13 years for an experimental cascade of this size to produce enough highly enriched uranium for even a single nuclear weapon. But without an arms control agreement, Iran is free to construct more centrifuge cascades at Natanz, and without intrusive IAEA inspections in place, Iran could build a covert enrichment facility elsewhere. What was once a proliferation problem is now a proliferation crisis.

Agreed Framework in Farsi

The depth of Tehran's security concerns is precisely the reason that, despite the Bush administration's hopes, Libya cannot be a model for how to deal with Iran now. Libyan President Muammar al-Qaddafi finally relinquished the pursuit of nuclear weapons in 2003 in exchange for both an end to trade sanctions and positive economic incentives. But Tripoli was always a very different foe from Tehran. For one thing, the Libyans turned out to be the gang that could not proliferate straight. For years, Qaddafi reportedly tried but failed to purchase complete nuclear weapons directly from China, India, and Pakistan. When he did purchase 20 centrifuges and components for another 200 from A. Q. Khan in 1997, he could not get enough of the machines assembled in the right way. In the late 1990s, moreover, as Qaddafi's regime was becoming more concerned with domestic threats—economic stagnation and the rise of jihadist insurgents—than it was with external ones, its nuclear program began to turn into a liability. Tehran today is in a very different position: it is much closer to being able to develop weapons, and it continues to have serious external security reasons for wanting them.

A better source of inspiration for handling Iran would be the 1994 Agreed Framework that the United States struck with North Korea. The Bush administration has severely criticized the deal, but it contained several elements that could prove useful for solving the Iranian nuclear crisis.

After the North Koreans were caught violating their NPT commitments in early 1993 (they were covertly removing nuclear materials from the Yongbyon reactor), they threatened to withdraw from the treaty. Declaring that "North Korea cannot be allowed to develop a nuclear bomb," President Clinton threatened an air strike on the Yongbyon reactor site if the North Koreans took further steps to reprocess plutonium. In June 1994, as the Pentagon was reinforcing military units on the Korean Peninsula and briefing Clinton on war preparations, Pyongyang froze its plutonium production, agreed to let IAEA inspectors monitor the reactor site, and entered into bilateral negotiations with a view to eventually eliminating its nuclear capability. It is unclear whether North Korea blinked out of fear of military intervention, because of concerns about economic sanctions, or because Washington's proposal held out the promise of security guarantees and normalized relations. But the talks produced the October 1994 Agreed Framework, under which North Korea agreed to eventually dismantle its reactors, remain in the NPT, and implement full IAEA safeguards. In exchange, the United States promised to provide it with limited oil supplies, construct two peaceful light-water reactors for energy production, "move toward full normalization of political and economic relations," and extend "formal assurances to [North Korea] against the threat or use of nuclear weapons by the U.S."

By 2002, however, the Agreed Framework had broken down, not only because Pyongyang was suspected of cheating but also because it believed that the United States, by delaying construction of the light-water reactors and failing to start normalizing relations, had not honored its side of the bargain. When confronted with evidence of its secret uranium program, in November 2002, Pyongyang took advantage of the fact that the U.S. military was tied down in preparations for the invasion of Iraq and withdrew from the NPT, kicked out the inspectors, and started reprocessing plutonium. Pyongyang is now thought to have six to eight nuclear weapons, to be producing more plutonium in the Yongbyon reactor, and to be constructing a larger one.

President Bush famously promised, in his 2002 State of the Union address, that the United States "will not permit the world's most dangerous regimes to threaten us with the world's most destructive weapons." Yet when North Korea kicked out the IAEA inspectors, Secretary of State Colin Powell proclaimed that the situation was "not a crisis," and Bush repeatedly declared that the United States had "no intention of invading North Korea." Deputy Secretary of State Richard Armitage quickly underscored the position: "The president has no hostile intentions and no plans to invade. That's an indication that North Korea can have the regime that [it] want[s] to have." The point was not lost on Tehran.

The 1994 Agreed Framework thus serves as a reminder of what to do, and its failure as a warning about what to avoid. If Washington is to offer security assurances to Tehran, it would be wise to do so soon (making the assurances contingent on Tehran's not developing nuclear weapons), rather than offering them too late, as it did with North Korea (and thus making them contingent on Tehran's getting rid of any existing nuclear weapons). As with North Korea, any deal with Iran must be structured in a series of steps, each offering a package of economic benefits (light-water reactors, aircraft parts, or status at the World Trade Organization) in exchange for constraints placed on Iran's future nuclear development.

Both Washington and Tehran will need to make major compromises. The Bush administration has said that a condition of any deal must be that "not a single centrifuge can spin" in Iran. But it might have to soften its stance. Allowing Tehran to maintain its experimental 164-centrifuge cascade, which poses no immediate danger and yet is an important status symbol for the Iranian regime, could help Tehran save face and sell a deal with Washington to its domestic constituencies by allowing it to claim that the arrangement protects Iran's "sovereign right" to have a full nuclear fuel cycle. One way to do this would be to draw a line between research on uranium enrichment (which would be allowed) and significant production of enriched uranium (which would be prohibited). In exchange, Tehran would have to accept verifiable safeguards on all its enrichment operations, permit throughout the country the more intrusive type of inspections required by the Additional Protocol of the IAEA, supply the IAEA with full documentation about suspected past violations, and freeze the construction of more centrifuges and heavy-water reactors that could produce plutonium.

History, particularly that of U.S.-North Korean relations, suggests that such agreements are just the start of serious negotiations. Even if a deal is struck, delays and backsliding should be expected. To limit their impact and keep them from leading to the agreement's dissolution, it would be necessary for Washington to both keep its promises and maintain credible threats that it would impose sanctions or even use limited force against Iran if Tehran violated its commitments.

Most important, however, would be a reduction in the security threat that the United States poses to Iran. Given the need for Washington to have a credible deterrent against, say, terrorist attacks sponsored by Iran, it would be ill advised to offer Tehran a blanket security guarantee. But more limited guarantees, such as a commitment not to use nuclear weapons and other commitments of the type offered North Korea under the Agreed Framework, could be effective today. They would reassure Tehran and pave the way toward the eventual normalization of U.S.-Iranian relations while signaling to other states that nuclear weapons are not the be all and end all of security. None of this will happen, however, if U.S. officials keep threatening to topple the Iranian government. In any final settlement, Tehran will need to agree to freeze its nuclear program and end its support for terrorism, and Washington—along with China, Russia, and the EU-3—must issue a joint security guarantee that respects Iran's political sovereignty, thus committing the United States to promote democracy only by peaceful means. Peaceful coexistence does not require friendly relations, but it does mean exercising mutual restraint. Relinquishing the threat of regime change by force is a necessary and acceptable price for the United States to pay to stop Tehran from getting the bomb.

POSTSCRIPT

Should the United States Preemptively Attack Iran's Emerging Nuclear Weapons Capability?

There are conflicting reports on whether Israel sought U.S. agreement for an Israeli air strike on Iran's nuclear facilities, and whether the United States restrained Israel on this issue. The British newspaper *The Guardian*, citing anonymous diplomatic sources, reported that Israeli Prime Minister Ehud Olmert asked President Bush in May 2008 whether he would support Israeli air strikes on Iran, and Bush urged Olmert not to take such an action (Jonathon Steele, "Israel Asked U.S. for Green Light to Bomb Nuclear Sites in Iran," *The Guardian*, September 25, 2008). Olmert has denied this, however (Haaretz News Service, "Olmert: U.S. never advised Israel to use restraint against Iran," November 25, 2008).

President Obama has pledged to engage in higher level and more direct diplomacy with Iran than his predecessors, but as of early 2009 the form that this diplomacy would take remains unclear. One complication here is that Iranian President Mahmoud Ahmadinejad, who has engaged in harsh rhetoric regarding the United States and made bold claims on Iran's nuclear programs, faces an election in June 2009. Thus, if the United States engages in diplomatic contacts before the June elections, Ahmadinejad might portray this as evidence that his hard-line approach is working, and if the United States holds off on talks, he may present this as evidence that a hard line policy is justified.

For books on Iran and its relations with the United States, see Shahram Chubin, *Iran's Nuclear Ambitions* (Carnegie Endowment for International Peace, 2006); Ray Takeyh, *Hidden Iran: Paradox and Power in the Islamic Republic* (Holt Paperbacks, 2007); Sas Fayazmanesh, *The United States and Iran: Sanctions, Wars and the Policy of Dual Containment* (Routledge, 2008); and Ali Ansari, *Confronting Iran: The Failure of American Foreign Policy and the Next Great Crisis in the Middle East* (Basic Books, 2006).

For articles on these subjects, see William E. Odom, "The Problem: The Nuclear Option," *Foreign Policy* (May/June 2007); Richard Haass and Martin Indyk, "Beyond Iraq: A New U.S. Strategy for the Middle East," *Foreign Affairs* (January/February 2009); Ray Takeyh, "Time for Detente with Iran," *Foreign Affairs* (March/April 2007); Steven Simon, "Bitter Friends, Bosom Enemies: Iran, the U.S., and the Twisted Path to Confrontation," *Survival* (August/September 2008); and Robert Litwak, "Living with Ambiguity: Nuclear Deals with Iran and North Korea," *Survival* (February/March 2008).

ISSUE 6

Should the United States Negotiate with the Taliban?

YES: Barnett R. Rubin and Ahmed Rashid, from "From Great Game to Grand Bargain: Ending Chaos in Afghanistan and Pakistan," *Foreign Affairs* (November/December 2008)

NO: Joseph J. Collins, from "To Further Afghan Reconciliation: Fight Harder," *Small Wars Journal* (October 31, 2008)

ISSUE SUMMARY

YES: Barnett R. Rubin, director of studies and senior fellow at the Center on International Cooperation at New York University, and Ahmed Rashid, a Pakistani journalist and fellow at the Pacific Council on International Policy, propose that the U.S. should pursue negotiations with Taliban insurgents in Afghanistan and Pakistan to establish stability in the region.

NO: Joseph J. Collins, a retired army colonel who teaches at the National War College, asserts that many of the diverse groups fighting against the United States in Afghanistan are irrevocably opposed to U.S. goals and that the United States must achieve greater military successes in Afghanistan before pursuing any negotiations with the opposition so that it can bargain from a position of strength.

After the Soviet Union withdrew its troops from Afghanistan in 1989 and gave up on its decade-long effort to establish socialism in Afghanistan, the country descended into a period of lawlessness and chaotic conflict among rival ethnic factions and warlords. By the mid-1990s, the Afghan people, exhausted by ten years of military occupation and five more years of civil strife, were open to leadership by any group that could establish order. This provided an opening for the Taliban, a fundamentalist Islamic group comprised predominantly of Pashtun peoples of southern Afghanistan and western Pakistan, and by Pakistan's intelligence service (the ISI), which sought to establish influence over Pakistan's neighbor. The Taliban, led by Mullah Mohammed Omar, managed to establish control over the capital of Kabul and much of the rest of the country by 1996, although it continued to fight with Tajik groups known as the Northern Alliance, who controlled territory in northern Afghanistan under the leadership of Ahmad Shah Massoud, one of the most capable military leaders in the fight against the Soviet Union.

Mullah Omar imposed draconian fundamentalist constraints on all aspects of Afghan social life, and by 2001 the Taliban were unpopular in much of Afghanistan but retained rule by force of arms. Omar also openly provided a safe haven for Osama Bin Laden and other al-Qaeda leaders. After al-Qaeda launched its terrorist attacks on the United States in September 2001, the United States issued an ultimatum to Mullah Omar to capture and turn over Bin Laden and other al-Qaeda leaders or face invasion from the United States. Omar refused to comply, and although al-Qaeda leaders had taken the precaution of assassinating Massoud before the September 11 attacks to make U.S. intervention in Aftghanistan more difficult, within a few weeks the United States and its NATO allies, working together with Northern Alliance forces, was able to take control of Afghanistan and force both Taliban and al-Qaeda leaders to flee to Pakistan.

In the eight years that have followed, however, the Taliban and al-Qaeda have waged an increasingly violent insurgent campaign against U.S. forces in Afghanistan and the government of President Hamid Karzai, elected in 2004. In 2008, the rate of U.S. casualties in Afghanistan rivaled that of U.S. casualties in Iraq on an absolute basis and surpassed the casualty rate in Afghanistan in terms of the proportion of deployed soldiers killed or wounded. Approximately 65,000 U.S. and allied troops were deployed in Afghanistan in 2008, a number that proved insufficient to establish control over much of Afghanstan's mountainous territory or security for its population of nearly 33 million people.

YES

**Barnett R. Rubin
and Rashid Ahmed**

From Great Game to Grand Bargain: Ending Chaos in Afghanistan and Pakistan

The Great Game is no fun anymore. The term "Great Game" was used by nineteenth-century British imperialists to describe the British–Russian struggle for position on the chessboard of Afghanistan and Central Asia—a contest with a few players, mostly limited to intelligence forays and short wars fought on horseback with rifles, and with those living on the chessboard largely bystanders or victims. More than a century later, the game continues. But now, the number of players has exploded, those living on the chessboard have become involved, and the intensity of the violence and the threats it produces affect the entire globe. The Great Game can no longer be treated as a sporting event for distant spectators. It is time to agree on some new rules.

Seven years after the U.S.-led coalition and the Afghan commanders it supported pushed the leaderships of the Taliban and al Qaeda out of Afghanistan and into Pakistan, an insurgency that includes these and other groups is gaining ground on both the Afghan and the Pakistani sides of the border. Four years after Afghanistan's first-ever presidential election, the increasingly besieged government of Hamid Karzai is losing credibility at home and abroad. Al Qaeda has established a new safe haven in the tribal agencies of Pakistan, where it is defended by a new organization, the Taliban Movement of Pakistan. The government of Pakistan, beset by one political crisis after another and split between a traditionally autonomous military and assertive but fractious elected leaders, has been unable to retain control of its own territory and population. Its intelligence agency stands accused of supporting terrorism in Afghanistan, which in many ways has replaced Kashmir as the main arena of the still-unresolved struggle between Pakistan and India.

For years, critics of U.S. and NATO strategies have been warning that the region was headed in this direction. Many of the policies such critics have long proposed are now being widely embraced. The Bush administration and both presidential campaigns are proposing to send more troops to Afghanistan and to undertake other policies to sustain the military gains made there. These include accelerating training of the Afghan National Army and the Afghan National Police; disbursing more money, more effectively for reconstruction and development and to support better governance; increasing pressure on

Reprinted by permission of *Foreign Affairs*, November/December 2008, pp. 30–44. Copyright © 2008 by the Council on Foreign Relations, Inc. www.ForeignAffairs.org

and cooperation with Pakistan, and launching cross-border attacks without Pakistani agreement to eliminate cross-border safe havens for insurgents and to uproot al Qaeda; supporting democracy in Pakistan and bringing its Inter-Services Intelligence (ISI) under civilian political control; and implementing more effective policies to curb Afghanistan's drug industry, which produces opiates equal in export value to half of the rest of the Afghan economy.

Cross-border attacks into Pakistan may produce an "October surprise" or provide material for apologists hoping to salvage George W. Bush's legacy, but they will not provide security. Advancing reconstruction, development, good governance, and counternarcotics efforts and building effective police and justice systems in Afghanistan will require many years of relative peace and security. Neither neglecting these tasks, as the Bush administration did initially, nor rushing them on a timetable determined by political objectives, can succeed. Afghanistan requires far larger and more effective security forces, international or national, but support for U.S. and NATO deployments is plummeting in troop-contributing countries, in the wider region, and in Afghanistan itself. Afghanistan, the poorest country in the world but for a handful in Africa and with the weakest government in the world (except Somalia, which has no government), will never be able to sustain national security forces sufficient to confront current—let alone escalating—threats, yet permanent foreign subsidies for Afghanistan's security forces cannot be guaranteed and will have destabilizing consequences. Moreover, measures aimed at Afghanistan will not address the deteriorating situation in Pakistan or the escalation of international conflicts connected to the Afghan–Pakistani war. More aid to Pakistan—military or civilian—will not diminish the perception among Pakistan's national security elite that the country is surrounded by enemies determined to dismember it, especially as cross-border raids into areas long claimed by Afghanistan intensify that perception. Until that sense of siege is gone, it will be difficult to strengthen civilian institutions in Pakistan.

U.S. diplomacy has been paralyzed by the rhetoric of "the war on terror"—a struggle against "evil," in which other actors are "with us or with the terrorists." Such rhetoric thwarts sound strategic thinking by assimilating opponents into a homogenous "terrorist" enemy. Only a political and diplomatic initiative that distinguishes political opponents of the United States—including violent ones—from global terrorists such as al Qaeda can reduce the threat faced by the Afghan and Pakistani states and secure the rest of the international community from the international terrorist groups based there. Such an initiative would have two elements. It would seek a political solution with as much of the Afghan and Pakistani insurgencies as possible, offering political inclusion, the integration of Pakistan's indirectly ruled Federally Administered Tribal Areas (FATA) into the mainstream political and administrative institutions of Pakistan, and an end to hostile action by international troops in return for cooperation against al Qaeda. And it would include a major diplomatic and development initiative addressing the vast array of regional and global issues that have become intertwined with the crisis—and that serve to stimulate, intensify, and prolong conflict in both Afghanistan and Pakistan.

Afghanistan has been at war for three decades—a period longer than the one that started with World War I and ended with the Normandy landings on D-Day in World War II—and now that war is spreading to Pakistan and beyond. This war and the attendant terrorism could well continue and spread, even to other continents—as on 9/11—or lead to the collapse of a nuclear-armed state. The regional crisis is of that magnitude, and yet so far there is no international framework to address it other than the underresourced and poorly coordinated operations in Afghanistan and some attacks in the FATA. The next U.S. administration should launch an effort, initially based on a contact group authorized by the UN Security Council, to put an end to the increasingly destructive dynamics of the Great Game in the region. The game has become too deadly and has attracted too many players; it now resembles less a chess match than the Afghan game of buzkashi, with Afghanistan playing the role of the goat carcass fought over by innumerable teams. Washington must seize the opportunity now to replace this Great Game with a new grand bargain for the region.

The Security Gap

The Afghan and Pakistani security forces lack the numbers, skills, equipment, and motivation to confront the growing insurgencies in the two countries or to uproot al Qaeda from its new base in the FATA, along the Afghan–Pakistani border. Proposals for improving the security situation focus on sending additional international forces, building larger national security forces in Afghanistan, and training and equipping Pakistan's security forces, which are organized for conflict with India, for domestic counterinsurgency. But none of these proposals is sufficient to meet the current, let alone future, threats.

Some additional troops in Afghanistan could protect local populations while the police and the administration develop. They also might enable U.S. and NATO forces to reduce or eliminate their reliance on the use of air strikes, which cause civilian casualties that recruit fighters and supporters to the insurgency. U.S. General Barry McCaffrey, among others, has therefore supported a "generational commitment" to Afghanistan, such as the United States made to Germany and South Korea. Unfortunately, no government in the region around Afghanistan supports a long-term U.S. or NATO presence there. Pakistan sees even the current deployment as strengthening an India-allied regime in Kabul; Iran is concerned that the United States will use Afghanistan as a base for launching "regime change" in Tehran; and China, India, and Russia all have reservations about a NATO base within their spheres of influence and believe they must balance the threats from al Qaeda and the Taliban against those posed by the United States and NATO. Securing Afghanistan and its region will require an international presence for many years, but only a regional diplomatic initiative that creates a consensus to place stabilizing Afghanistan ahead of other objectives could make a long-term international deployment possible.

Afghanistan needs larger and more effective security forces, but it also needs to be able to sustain those security forces. A decree signed by President Karzai in December 2002 would have capped the Afghan National Army at 70,000 troops (it had reached 66,000 by mid-2008). U.S. Secretary of Defense

Robert Gates has since announced a plan to increase that number to 122,000, as well as add 82,000 police, for a total of 204,000 in the Afghan National Security Forces (ANSF). Such increases, however, would require additional international trainers and mentors—which are, quite simply, not available in the foreseeable future—and maintaining such a force would far exceed the means of such a destitute country. Current estimates of the annual cost are around $2.5 billion for the army and $1 billion for the police. Last year, the Afghan government collected about 7 percent of a licit GDP estimated at $9.6 billion in revenue—about $670 million. Thus, even if Afghanistan's economy experienced uninterrupted real growth of 9 percent per year, and if revenue extraction nearly doubled, to 12 percent (both unrealistic forecasts), in ten years the total domestic revenue of the Afghan government would be about $2.5 billion a year. Projected pipelines and mines might add $500 million toward the end of this period. In short, the army and the police alone would cost significantly more than Afghanistan's total revenue.

Many have therefore proposed long-term international financing of the ANSF; after all, even $5 billion a year is much less than the cost of an international force deployment. But sustaining, as opposed to training or equipping, security forces through foreign grants would pose political problems. It would be impossible to build Afghan institutions on the basis of U.S. supplemental appropriations, which is how the training and equipping of the ANSF are mostly funded. Sustaining a national army or national police force requires multiyear planning, impossible without a recurrent appropriation—which would mean integrating ANSF planning into that of the United States' and other NATO members' budgets, even if the funds were disbursed through a single trust fund. And an ANSF funded from those budgets would have to meet international or other national, rather than Afghan, legal requirements. Decisions on funding would be taken by the U.S. Congress and other foreign bodies, not the Afghan National Assembly. The ANSF would take actions that foreign taxpayers might be reluctant to fund. Such long-term international involvement is simply not tenable.

If Afghanistan cannot support its security forces at the currently proposed levels on its own, even under the most optimistic economic scenario, and long-term international support or a long-term international presence is not viable, there is only one way that the ANSF can approach sustainability: the conditions in the region must be changed so that Afghanistan no longer needs such large and expensive security forces. Changing those conditions, however, will require changing the behavior of actors not only inside but also outside of the country—and that has led many observers to embrace putting pressure on, and even launching attacks into, Pakistan as another deus ex machina for the increasingly dire situation within Afghanistan.

Borderline Insecurity Disorder

After the first phase of the war in Afghanistan ended with the overthrow of the Taliban in 2001 (and as the United States prepared to invade Iraq), Washington's limited agenda in the region was to press the Pakistani military to go after al Qaeda; meanwhile, Washington largely ignored the broader insurgency, which remained marginal until 2005. This suited the Pakistani military's strategy, which was to assist the United States against al Qaeda but to retain the Afghan Taliban as a potential source of pressure on Afghanistan. But the summer of 2006 saw a major escalation of the insurgency, as Pakistan and the Taliban interpreted the United States' decision to transfer command of coalition forces to NATO (plus U.S. Secretary of Defense Donald Rumsfeld's announcement of a troop drawdown, which in fact never took place) as a sign of its intention to withdraw. They also saw non-U.S. troop contributors as more vulnerable to political pressure generated by casualties.

The Pakistani military does not control the insurgency, but it can affect its intensity. Putting pressure on Pakistan to curb the militants will likely remain ineffective, however, without a strategic realignment by the United States. The region is rife with conspiracy theories trying to find a rational explanation for the United States' apparently irrational strategic posture of supporting a "major non-NATO ally" that is doing more to undermine the U.S. position in Afghanistan than any other state. Many Afghans believe that Washington secretly supports the Taliban as a way to keep a war going to justify a troop presence that is actually aimed at securing the energy resources of Central Asia and countering China. Many in Pakistan believe that the United States has deceived Pakistan into conniving with Washington to bring about its own destruction: India and U.S.-supported Afghanistan will form a pincer around Pakistan to dismember the world's only Muslim nuclear power. And some Iranians speculate that in preparation for the coming of the Mahdi, God has blinded the Great Satan to its own interests so that it would eliminate both of Iran's Sunni-ruled regional rivals, Afghanistan and Iraq, thus unwittingly paving the way for the long-awaited Shiite restoration.

The true answer is much simpler: the Bush administration never reevaluated its strategic priorities in the region after September 11. Institutional inertia and ideology jointly assured that Pakistan would be treated as an ally, Iran as an enemy, and Iraq as the main threat, thereby granting Pakistan a monopoly on U.S. logistics and, to a significant extent, on the intelligence the United States has on Afghanistan. Eighty-four percent of the materiel for U.S. forces in Afghanistan goes through Pakistan, and the ISI remains nearly the sole source of intelligence about international terrorist acts prepared by al Qaeda and its affiliates in Pakistan.

More fundamentally, the concept of "pressuring" Pakistan is flawed. No state can be successfully pressured into acts it considers suicidal. The Pakistani security establishment believes that it faces both a U.S.–Indian–Afghan alliance and a separate Iranian–Russian alliance, each aimed at undermining Pakistani influence in Afghanistan and even dismembering the Pakistani state. Some (but not all) in the establishment see armed militants within Pakistan as a threat—but they largely consider it one that is ultimately controllable, and in any case secondary to the threat posed by their nuclear-armed enemies.

Pakistan's military command, which makes and implements the country's national security policies, shares a commitment to a vision of Pakistan as the homeland for South Asian Muslims and therefore to the incorporation of

Kashmir into Pakistan. It considers Afghanistan as within Pakistan's security perimeter. Add to this that Pakistan does not have border agreements with either India, into which Islamabad contests the incorporation of Kashmir, or Afghanistan, which has never explicitly recognized the Durand Line, which separates the two countries, as an interstate border.

That border is more than a line. The frontier between Pakistan and Afghanistan was structured as part of the defenses of British India. On the Pakistani side of the Durand Line, the British and their Pakistani successors turned the difficulty of governing the tribes to their advantage by establishing what are now the FATA. Within the FATA, these tribes, not the government, are responsible for security. The area is kept underdeveloped and overarmed as a barrier against invaders. (That is also why any ground intervention there by the United States or NATO will fail.) Now, the Pakistani military has turned the FATA into a staging area for militants who can be used to conduct asymmetric warfare in both Afghanistan and Kashmir, since the region's special status provides for (decreasingly) plausible deniability. This use of the FATA has eroded state control, especially in Pakistan's Northwest Frontier Province, which abuts the FATA. The Swat Valley, where Pakistani Taliban fighters have been battling the government for several years, links Afghanistan and the FATA to Kashmir. Pakistan's strategy for external security has thus undermined its internal security.

On September 19, 2001, when then Pakistani President Pervez Musharraf announced to the nation his decision to support the U.S.-led intervention against the Taliban in Afghanistan, he stated that the overriding reason was to save Pakistan by preventing the United States from allying with India. In return, he wanted concessions to Pakistan on its security interests.

Subsequent events, however, have only exacerbated Pakistan's sense of insecurity. Musharraf asked for time to form a "moderate Taliban" government in Afghanistan but failed to produce one. When that failed, he asked that the United States prevent the Northern Alliance (part of the anti-Taliban resistance in Afghanistan), which had been supported by India, Iran, and Russia, from occupying Kabul; that appeal failed. Now, Pakistan claims that the Northern Alliance is working with India from inside Afghanistan's security services. Meanwhile, India has reestablished its consulates in Afghan cities, including some near the Pakistani border. India has genuine consular interests there (Hindu and Sikh populations, commercial travel, aid programs), but it may also in fact be using the consulates against Pakistan, as Islamabad claims. India has also, in cooperation with Iran, completed a highway linking Afghanistan's ring road (which connects its major cities) to Iranian ports on the Persian Gulf, potentially eliminating Afghanistan's dependence on Pakistan for access to the sea and marginalizing Pakistan's new Arabian Sea port of Gwadar, which was built with hundreds of millions of dollars of Chinese aid. And the new U.S.-Indian nuclear deal effectively recognizes New Delhi's legitimacy as a nuclear power while continuing to treat Islamabad, with its record of proliferation, as a pariah. In this context, pressuring or giving aid to Pakistan, without any effort to address the sources of its insecurity, cannot yield a sustainable positive outcome.

Big Hat, No Cattle

Rethinking U.S. and global objectives in the region will require acknowledging two distinctions: first, between ultimate goals and reasons to fight a war; and, second, among the time frames for different objectives. Preventing al Qaeda from regrouping so that it can organize terrorist attacks is an immediate goal that can justify war, to the extent that such war is proportionate and effective. Strengthening the state and the economy of Afghanistan is a medium- to long-term objective that cannot justify war except insofar as Afghanistan's weakness provides a haven for security threats.

This medium- to long-term objective would require reducing the level of armed conflict, including by seeking a political settlement with current insurgents. In discussions about the terms of such a settlement, leaders linked to both the Taliban and other parts of the insurgency have asked, What are the goals for which the United States and the international community are waging war in Afghanistan? Do they want to guarantee that Afghanistan's territory will not be used to attack them, impose a particular government in Kabul, or use the conflict to establish permanent military bases? These interlocutors oppose many U.S. policies toward the Muslim world, but they acknowledge that the United States and others have a legitimate interest in preventing Afghan territory from being used to launch attacks against them. They claim to be willing to support an Afghan government that would guarantee that its territory would not be used to launch terrorist attacks in the future—in return, they say, for the withdrawal of foreign troops.

The guarantees these interlocutors now envisage are far from those required, and Afghanistan will need international forces for security assistance even if the current war subsides. But such questions can provide a framework for discussion. To make such discussions credible, the United States must redefine its counterterrorist goals. It should seek to separate those Islamist movements with local or national objectives from those that, like al Qaeda, seek to attack the United States or its allies directly—instead of lumping them all together. Two Taliban spokespeople separately told *The New York Times* that their movement had broken with al Qaeda since 9/11. (Others linked to the insurgency have told us the same thing.) Such statements cannot simply be taken at face value, but that does not mean that they should not be explored further. An agreement in principle to prohibit the use of Afghan (or Pakistani) territory for international terrorism, plus an agreement from the United States and NATO that such a guarantee could be sufficient to end their hostile military action, could constitute a framework for negotiation. Any agreement in which the Taliban or other insurgents disavowed al Qaeda would constitute a strategic defeat for al Qaeda.

Political negotiations are the responsibility of the Afghan government, but to make such negotiations possible, the United States would have to alter its detention policy. Senior officials of the Afghan government say that at least through 2004 they repeatedly received overtures from senior Taliban leaders but that they could never guarantee that these leaders would not be captured by U.S. forces and detained at Guantánamo Bay or the U.S. air base at Bagram, in Afghanistan. Talking with Taliban fighters or other insurgents does not mean replacing Afghanistan's constitution with the Taliban's Islamic Emirate of Afghanistan, closing girls' schools, or accepting other retrograde social policies. Whatever weaknesses the Afghan government and security forces may have, Afghan society—which has gone through two Loya Jirgas and two elections, possesses over five million cell phones, and has access to an explosion of new media—is incomparably stronger than it was seven years ago, and the Taliban know it. These potential interlocutors are most concerned with the presence of foreign troops, and some have advocated strengthening the current ANSF as a way to facilitate those troops' departure. In November 2006, one of the Taliban's leading supporters in Pakistan, Maulana Fazlur Rahman, publicly stated in Peshawar that the Taliban could participate as a party in elections in Afghanistan, just as his party did in Pakistan (where it recently lost overwhelmingly), so long as they were not labeled as terrorists.

The End of the Game

There is no more a political solution in Afghanistan alone than there is a military solution in Afghanistan alone. Unless the decisionmakers in Pakistan decide to make stabilizing the Afghan government a higher priority than countering the Indian threat, the insurgency conducted from bases in Pakistan will continue. Pakistan's strategic goals in Afghanistan place Pakistan at odds not just with Afghanistan and India, and with U.S. objectives in the region, but with the entire international community. Yet there is no multilateral framework for confronting this challenge, and the U.S.–Afghan bilateral framework has relied excessively on the military-supply relationship. NATO, whose troops in Afghanistan are daily losing their lives to Pakistan-based insurgents, has no Pakistan policy. The UN Security Council has hardly discussed Pakistan's role in Afghanistan, even though three of the permanent members (France, the United Kingdom, and the United States) have troops in Afghanistan, the other two are threatened by movements (in the North Caucasus and in Xinjiang) with links to the FATA, and China, Pakistan's largest investor, is poised to become the largest investor in Afghanistan as well, with a $3.5 billion stake in the Aynak copper mine, south of Kabul.

The alternative is not to place Pakistan in a revised "axis of evil." It is to pursue a high-level diplomatic initiative designed to build a genuine consensus on the goal of achieving Afghan stability by addressing the legitimate sources of Pakistan's insecurity while increasing the opposition to its disruptive actions. China, both an ally of Pakistan and potentially the largest investor in both Afghanistan and Pakistan, could play a particularly significant role, as could Saudi Arabia, a serious investor in and ally of Pakistan, former supporter of the Taliban, and custodian of the two holiest Islamic shrines.

A first step could be the establishment of a contact group on the region authorized by the UN Security Council. This contact group, including the five permanent members and perhaps others (NATO, Saudi Arabia), could promote dialogue between India and Pakistan about their respective interests in Afghanistan and about finding a solution to the Kashmir dispute; seek a long-term political vision for the future of the FATA from the Pakistani government, perhaps one involving integrating the FATA into Pakistan's provinces, as proposed by several Pakistani political parties; move Afghanistan and Pakistan toward discussions on the Durand Line and other frontier issues; involve Moscow in the region's stabilization so that Afghanistan does not become a test of wills between the United States and Russia, as Georgia has become; provide guarantees to Tehran that the U.S.–NATO commitment to Afghanistan is not a threat to Iran; and ensure that China's interests and role are brought to bear in international discussions on Afghanistan. Such a dialogue would have to be backed by the pledge of a multiyear international development aid package for regional economic integration, including aid to the most affected regions in Afghanistan, Pakistan, and Central Asia, particularly the border regions. (At present, the United States is proposing to provide $750 million in aid to the FATA but without having any political framework to deliver the aid.)

A central purpose of the contact group would be to assure Pakistan that the international community is committed to its territorial integrity—and to help resolve the Afghan and Kashmir border issues so as to better define Pakistan's territory. The international community would have to provide transparent reassurances and aid to Pakistan, pledge that no state is interested in its dismemberment, and guarantee open borders between Pakistan and both Afghanistan and India. The United States and the European Union would have to open up their markets to Pakistan's critical exports, especially textiles, and to Afghan products. And the United States would need to offer a road map to Pakistan to achieving the same kind of nuclear deal that was reached with India, once Pakistan has transparent and internationally monitored guarantees about the nonproliferation of its nuclear weapons technology.

Reassurances by the contact group that addressed Pakistan's security concerns might encourage Pakistan to promote, rather than hinder, an internationally and nationally acceptable political settlement in Afghanistan. Backing up the contact group's influence and clout must be the threat that any breaking of agreements or support for terrorism originating in the FATA would be taken to the UN Security Council. Pakistan, the largest troop contributor to UN peacekeeping operations, sees itself as a legitimate international power, rather than a spoiler; confronted with the potential loss of that status, it would compromise.

India would also need to become more transparent about its activities in Afghanistan, especially regarding the role of its intelligence agency, the Research and Analysis Wing. Perhaps the ISI and the RAW could be persuaded to enter a dialogue to explore whether the covert war they have waged against each other for the past 60 years could spare the territory of Afghanistan. The contact group could help establish a permanent Indian–Pakistani body at the intelligence and military levels, where complaints could be lodged and discussed. The World Bank and the Asian Development Bank could also help set up joint reconstruction programs in Afghanistan. A series of regional conferences on economic cooperation for the reconstruction of Afghanistan have already created a partial framework for such programs.

Then there is Iran. The Bush administration responded to Iranian cooperation in Afghanistan in 2001 by placing Tehran in the "axis of evil" and by promising to keep "all options on the table," which is understood as a code for not ruling out a military attack. Iran has reacted in part by aiding insurgents in Afghanistan to signal how much damage it could do in response. Some Iranian officials, however, continue to seek cooperation with the United States against al Qaeda and the Taliban. The next U.S. administration can and should open direct dialogue with Tehran around the two countries' common concerns in Afghanistan. An opening to Iran would show that the United States need not depend solely on Pakistan for access to Afghanistan. And in fact, Washington and Tehran had such a dialogue until around 2004. In May 2005, when the United States and Afghanistan signed a "declaration of strategic partnership," Iran signaled that it would not object as long as the partnership was not directed against Iran. Iran would have to be reassured by the contact group that Afghan territory would not be used as a staging area for activities meant to undermine Iran and that all U.S. covert activities taking place from there would be stopped.

Russia's main concern—that the United States and NATO are seeking a permanent U.S.–NATO military presence in Afghanistan and Central Asia—will also need to be assuaged. Russia should be assured that U.S. and NATO forces can help defend, rather than threaten, legitimate Russian interests in Central Asia, including through cooperation with the Shanghai Cooperation Organization. Russia and the Central Asian states should be informed of the results of legitimate interrogations of militants who came from the former Soviet space and were captured in Afghanistan or Pakistan.

To overcome the zero-sum competition taking place between states, ethnic groups, and factions, the region needs to discover a source of mutual benefit derived from cooperation. China—with its development of mineral resources and access roads in Afghanistan and Pakistan, the financial support it gave to build the port of Gwadar, and its expansion of the Karakoram Highway, which links China to northern Pakistan—may be that source. China is also a major supplier of arms and nuclear equipment to Pakistan. China has a major interest in peace and development in the region because it desires a north–south energy and trade corridor so that its goods can travel from Xinjiang to the Arabian Sea ports of Pakistan and so that oil and gas pipelines can carry energy from the Persian Gulf and Iran to western China. In return for such a corridor, China could help deliver much-needed electricity and even water to both countries. Such a corridor would also help revive the economies of both Afghanistan and Pakistan.

More Than Troops

Both U.S. presidential candidates are committed to sending more troops to Afghanistan, but this would be insufficient to reverse the collapse of security there. A major diplomatic initiative involving all the regional stakeholders in problem-solving talks and setting out road maps for local stabilization efforts is more important. Such an initiative would serve to reaffirm that the West is indeed committed to the long-term rehabilitation of Afghanistan and the region. A contact group, meanwhile, would reassure Afghanistan's neighbors that the West is determined to address not just extremism in the region but also economic development, job creation, the drug trade, and border disputes.

Lowering the level of violence in the region and moving the global community toward genuine agreement on the long-term goals there would provide the space for Afghan leaders to create jobs and markets, provide better governance, do more to curb corruption and drug trafficking, and overcome their countries' widening ethnic divisions. Lowering regional tensions would allow the Afghan government to have a more meaningful dialogue with those insurgents who are willing to disavow al Qaeda and take part in the political process. The key to this would be the series of security measures the contact group should offer Pakistan, thereby encouraging the Pakistani army to press—or at least allow—Taliban and other insurgent leaders on their soil to talk to Kabul.

The goal of the next U.S. president must be to put aside the past, Washington's keenness for "victory" as the solution to all problems, and the United States' reluctance to involve competitors, opponents, or enemies in diplomacy. A successful initiative will require exploratory talks and an evolving road map. Today, such suggestions may seem audacious, naive, or impossible, but without such audacity there is little hope for Afghanistan, for Pakistan, or for the region as a whole.

Joseph J. Collins

NO

To Further Afghan Reconciliation: Fight Harder

It's official. Everyone from the Pentagon to Saudi Arabia thinks that reconciliation between the Taliban and the Karzai government is a good idea and a step toward settling the conflict in Afghanistan. A few deluded analysts even see dealing with the Taliban as the Afghan equivalent of the Sunni Awakening in Iraq. One wonders whether war weariness, success with reconciliation in Iraq, and a lack of familiarity with the Afghan context may not be pushing us toward a tactical error or worse, an endless round of talking with an illegitimate adversary that believes it has the upper hand.

Reconciliation in Afghanistan is fraught with complications. For one, there is no Taliban per se. In the south we have Mullah Omar's "old" Taliban, but in the East, the toughest fighters come from the Haqqani network and Gulbuddin Hekmatyar's Hezbi Islami, both of which work closely with Al Qaeda. Complicating the issue even more, there is now a multi-branch Pakistani Taliban, some of whom operate in both countries. Ironically, the Afghan Taliban and its friends seem to be well tolerated by Pakistani authorities who are now in conflict with their own Taliban.

Second, the Taliban have never been anyone's model combatants. They have tried to win hearts and minds through terror tactics and extreme repression. Even today, the Taliban's support in polls does not approach 20 percent across Afghanistan. When the Taliban ruled, it conducted numerous crimes against humanity for which there has never been an accounting. In addition to the extreme repression of its citizenry—no kites, no music, no female education, executions at soccer matches etc.—thousands of non-Pashtun Afghans were killed for sport by the Taliban.

Anyone wanting to reconcile with the Taliban will also have to figure out how to deal with the guys who have been planting IEDs, kidnapping civilians, and destroying reconstruction projects in the countryside. How will it sit with the U.S. public when and if the democratically elected government of Afghanistan and the Coalition sit down to negotiate with people whose signature tactics are burning girls' schools and cutting off the heads of non-combatants?

Third, all politics in Afghanistan is ethnic and tribal. Right now Father Karzai holds together a loose coalition of moderate modernizers from all groups, but Tajiks, Uzbeks, and especially the Hazara, Shiite Muslims, remember well the lash of the Taliban. While Karzai may see some of the Taliban as wayward brothers, his non-Pashtun allies do not. Reconciliation with mass murderers will be difficult, especially as we approach 2009, an election year in Afghanistan.

Fourth, reconciliation talks with the Taliban come at a time of increasing Taliban battlefield successes. Taliban attacks through the end of September 2008 have already exceeded the total for 2007. This year already ranks as the worst year for fighting since the capture of Kabul in 2001. The Taliban have also fought pitched battles to control Lashkargah, a provincial capital in the south. They are so cocky that their "official" position has been that they will never negotiate with Karzai, only with the Americans. If the Afghan government sits down with the Taliban now, it does so from a position of increasing weakness, and diminished strength. To increase the prospects for Kabul's success in negotiation, we will have to reverse that condition. How should we proceed?

To create favorable conditions for reconciliation and later negotiations, we must first step up our military efforts. General Petraeus is right: we cannot kill our way to victory in Afghanistan. We can, however, create a more pliable enemy, one eager to negotiate, if we defeat Taliban offensive operations and threaten their sanctuaries. While wizards may imagine ways to do more militarily with less, in the short run, more Afghan and NATO troops, as well as more aid money will be essential.

In the long run, we need to continue to build Afghan police and military capacity to stand alone. We have done better at this in Iraq than in Afghanistan, but Iraq had much more human capital. Building across-the-board Afghan capacity for governance and management must be the top long-term priority.

Stepping up anti-Taliban activities in Pakistan will be essential but tricky. Cross border operations are a limited tool. Moreover, the Pakistani government—both in its military and prior civilian versions—have been Taliban sponsors. We should demand that they reassess their support and, as a minimum, exert extreme pressure on the Haqqani network and the Hezbi Islami, both of which are Al Qaeda allies. As Pakistan wrestles with its own Taliban, they may well realize that the key to success will come in a united front with NATO and the United States. Again, more aid—military and economic—for Pakistan must be part of the program.

We also need to ask the Gulf states to crack down on charity toward Taliban-affiliated groups. Charity, drug money, and other protection payments are paying Taliban bills. We need to dry up their funds as much as we can to weaken Taliban military efforts.

Finally, reconciliation is an issue on which the Afghan government must lead. We cannot navigate the maze of Afghanistan's ethnic politics. Only the Afghan leadership can do that. Even public suggestions by Western officials about the desirability of reconciliation are risky. But inside this challenge, Kabul may find an opportunity to go over the heads of Omar, Haqqani, and Hekmatyar and encourage the rank and file of the resistance to come home as individuals.

For their part, the Taliban are looking for an opportunity to drive another wedge between the Kabul government and the West. The unfortunate civilian casualties and collateral damage that come with NATO military operations have already given the Taliban a chance to divide and conquer. We cannot let these 21st century barbarians play us off against our Afghan allies on the issue of reconciliation. In the meantime, we must all fight harder.

POSTSCRIPT

Should the United States Negotiate with the Taliban?

In early 2009, President Obama approved the deployment of 17,000 additional U.S. troops to Afghanistan, bringing the U.S. total there to 55,000 soldiers and the allied troop total to approximately 80,000 troops. At the same time, U.S. Central Command Commander Gen. David Petraeus, who as the top U.S. officer in Iraq in 2007 and 2008 was successful in decreasing violence in that country, has made it clear that any resolution to the conflict in Afghanistan must rely on a successful political and economic-aid strategy as much as it does on a military/security strategy. In this context, President Obama has appointed Richard Holbrooke, an experienced diplomat credited with helping to resolve the conflicts in the former Yugoslavia in the 1990s, as a special envoy to address the problems of both Afghanistan and Pakistan.

In this context, the United States faces numerous challenges in Afghanistan, including attacks by Taliban and al-Qaeda forces on vital supply lines that run through Pakistan, rampant corruption in the Afghan government, an Afghan economy that is highly dependent on the production of heroin-producing poppies (which are also a source of Taliban revenue), and the growing unpopularity of the Karzai government in Afghanistan in view of its failure to establish security or stop corruption. Meanwhile, U.S. air strikes on al-Qaeda and Taliban leaders in Pakistan and Afghanistan, which have continued under the Obama Administration, are creating strong public opposition in both countries due to the civilian casualties that they sometimes create. Afghan President Karzai, facing a presidential election in August 2009, has increasingly criticized U.S. air strikes and offered to negotiate with the Taliban, but so far despite low-level contacts in third countries, no prominent Taliban leaders have taken up this offer.

For recent books and articles on the Taliban, Afghanistan, and U.S. policies, see Ahmed Rashid, *Descent into Chaos: The United States and the Failure of Nation Building in Pakistan, Afghanistan, and Central Asia,* (Viking, 2008); James Dobbins, *After the Taliban: Nation-Building in Afghanistan* (Potomac Books, 2008); Robert Crews and Amin Tarzi, eds., *The Taliban and the Crisis of Afghanistan* (Harvard, 2008); Barnett Rubin, *Afghanistan's Uncertain Transition from Turmoil to Normalcy* (Council on Foreign Relations 2007); Robert Rotberg, ed., *Building a New Afghanistan* (Brookings, 2007); Steve Coll, *Ghost Wars: The Secret History of the CIA, Afghanistan, and Bin Laden, from the Soviet Invasion to September 10, 2001* (Penguin, 2004); and Nathaniel Fick and John Nagl, "Counterinsurgency Field Manual: Afghanistan Edition," *Foreign Policy* (January/February 2009).

ISSUE 7

Should the United States Allow Russia More Leeway in Eurasia in Exchange for Russian Help in Stopping Iran's Nuclear Program?

YES: Nikolas Gvosdev, from "Parting with Illusions: Developing a Realistic Approach to Relations with Russia," CATO Institute, Policy Analysis No. 611 (February 29, 2008)

NO: Stephen Sestanovich, from "What Has Moscow Done? Rebuilding U.S.-Russian Relations" *Foreign Affairs* (November/December 2008)

ISSUE SUMMARY

YES: Nikolas Gvosdev, senior editor of *The National Interest* and adjunct senior fellow at the Nixon Center, suggests that Russia is unlikely to be integrated into the Euro-Atlantic community and cannot be coerced into acquiescing in U.S. policies. The United States must prioritize its core interests vis-à-vis Russia, particularly the need for cooperation on non-proliferation and counterterrorism, and allow Russia greater flexibility in policy issues that are more important to Russia than to the United States.

NO: Stephen Sestanovich, professor of international diplomacy at Columbia University and senior fellow at the Council on Foreign Relations, rejects calls for a grand bargain with Russia, which in his view would not achieve greater Russian cooperation on Iran and other issues. Instead, the United States should pursue more modest and incremental steps to integrate Russia into a European security framework.

U.S.-Russian relations have gone through several phases since the end of the Cold War. In the early 1990s, Russia cooperated with the United States on issues like the U.N. vote to authorize the use of force to reverse Iraq's August 1990 invasion of Kuwait. By the late 1990s, however, relations between the two countries cooled as Russia's economy cooled and Russia carried out brutal military interventions in Chechnya, a breakaway region of Russia, in 1994 and 1999.

The 1999 intervention proved popular in an increasingly nationalist Russia, however, and contributed to Vladimir Putin's election as President of Russia.

After the terrorist attacks on the United States in September 2001, President Putin was one of the first international leaders to pledge his support in fighting terrorism, once again improving U.S.-Russian relations. This led to intelligence sharing an the issue of terrorism between the two countries, and Russia acquiesced in U.S. efforts to establish air bases in the Central Asia to supply U.S. troops in Afghanistan.

By 2003, however, the U.S. and Russia were at odds over their policies toward missile defenses, Iraq, Iran, the former Soviet republics, and NATO enlargement. The U.S. began preparing to deploy a missile defense system in Poland and a missile defense radar in the Czech Republic, despite Russian objections, as a way of addressing Iran's potential acquisition of nuclear weapons. Meanwhile, Russia continued its technical assistance to Iran's nuclear program and watered down U.S. efforts to impose sanctions on Iran, although Russia did approve some sanctions on Iran through its votes on the U.N. Security Council. In addition, Russia opposed the U.S.'s unsuccessful efforts to get a U.N. Security Council resolution authorizing the use of force against Iraq.

U.S.-Russian relations became even more tense in the summer and fall of 2008 as Russia harshly criticized efforts by the Bush administration to move toward making Ukraine and Georgia members of the NATO alliance. In part as a response, in August 2008 Russia sent its military forces into Ossetia and Abkhazia, regions of Georgia that had exercised de facto autonomy under Russian protection since the early 1990s. Russian forces also moved into and bombed areas of Georgia beyond these two regions before withdrawing back into Ossetia and Abkhazia. This led to strong criticism from Europe and the United States, although Georgia's leaders bore some responsibility for escalating the conflict by carrying out missile attacks on Russian forces in Ossetia prior to Russia's intervention into Georgia.

More recently, in February, 2009, Russia pressured Kyrgystan into closing its Manas air force base to use by U.S. forces, which had used this base for seven years to supply American forces in Afghanistan. Russia allowed the U.S. to begin supply convoys to Afghanistan through Russian territory, but this shift in supply routes could give Russia more leverage over U.S. policies in the region.

Many American analysts view Russia's recent policies as efforts to carve out a renewed "sphere of influence" in the regions formerly controlled by the Soviet Union. These analysts have also criticized moves away from democracy by Russia's leaders, including attacks on journalists and democracy advocates and Putin's decision to become Prime Minister and put in place a hand-picked successor, Dmitry Medvedev, as Russian president. Russian leaders, meanwhile, joined many Europeans in criticizing the Bush administration for its policies in Iraq. It is in this context that experts have begun debating over proposals for a "grand bargain" in which the U.S. would not object to more assertive Russian policies in the former Soviet region in exchange for stronger Russian support for U.S. counterterrorism efforts and greater cooperation in countering nuclear proliferation in Iran and elsewhere.

YES ↩

Nikolas Gvosdev

Parting with Illusions: Developing a Realistic Approach to Relations with Russia

Executive Summary

A review of America's post-Soviet strategy toward Russia is long overdue. The illusions that once guided policy are now at an end. What is needed is a dispassionate approach to Russia, wherein Americans would neither magnify nor excuse the virtues and vices of the Russian Federation but would accept the following realities:

- Russia is unlikely to become integrated into the Euro-Atlantic community and is unwilling to adjust its foreign policy priorities accordingly;
- There is broad-based support within Russia for the direction in which Vladimir Putin has taken the country;
- Russia has undergone a genuine—if limited—recovery from the collapse of the 1990s;
- Washington lacks sufficient leverage to compel Russian acquiescence to its policy preferences; and
- On a number of critical foreign policy issues, there is no clear community of interests that allows for concepts of "selective partnership" to be effective.

Any approach to Russia must be based on realistic expectations about the choices confronting Washington. The United States has two options. It can forgo the possibility of Russian assistance in achieving its key foreign policy priorities in an effort to retain complete freedom of action vis-à-vis Moscow. Or it can prioritize its objectives and negotiate a series of quid pro quos with Russia. The latter choice, however, cannot be indefinitely postponed.

Seeking an accommodation with Russia is more likely to guarantee American success in promoting its core national interests while minimizing costs—but will require U.S. policymakers to accept limits on what can be demanded of Russia.

From *Policy Analysis*, No. 611, February 29, 2008, pp. 1–16. Copyright © 2008 by Cato Institute. Reprinted by permission.

Introduction

Why does the United States find it so difficult to establish and sustain a durable and beneficial relationship with the Russian Federation?

The post-Soviet/post-Cold War U.S.-Russia relationship has been one of the most studied, discussed, and analyzed topics in international affairs. There is certainly no lack of advice and guidance on the matter. Many of the reports that have been written take a "rational actor" approach—that is to say, by laying out common interests and threats, these reports presume that a blueprint for joint action can be created that will serve as the foundation for a renewed relationship.

In contrast, this analysis seeks to examine the factors that have inhibited policymakers from solidifying the U.S.-Russia relationship.

Whereas all bilateral relationships involve a measure of give and take, this report does not seek to provide advice to Russia on what Moscow must do in order to improve the relationship. This is not to suggest that the Russians somehow are faultless. Indeed, one can easily amass a long litany of Moscow's missteps, ill-conceived policy initiatives and needless provocations, ranging from the Kremlin's inability to denounce the 1939 Molotov-Ribbentrop Pact to its clumsy and ham-fisted efforts to use its energy resources to extract concessions from neighboring governments such as Ukraine or foreign companies working on Russian soil.

But U.S. policy toward Russia—or any other major power—should not be solely reactive to events; it must also be based on an honest assessment of U.S. needs, interests, and capabilities. And there are always risks when embarking on such a venture; policies can fail and new approaches do not always ensure success. There is never a guarantee that the other side will accept any U.S. offer; this does not mean that the effort was worthless or that the strategic assessments that served as the foundation for the policy should be discarded outright. Indeed, it is far easier to fine-tune a policy or to discover a new tactical approach if there is clarity about not only America's ultimate goals but also America's willingness to absorb costs.

Regrettably, over the last 15 years, many have clung to illusions that the United States can achieve most of its objectives at little cost and without having to make much accommodation to the interests of others. That point of view was particularly prevalent with respect to Russia, which, having emerged from the wreckage of the Soviet Union, seemed at times to be in no position to thwart U.S. preferences but instead to have to accept any relationship on American terms. Increasingly, that is no longer the case, because of Russia's own recovery from its mid-1990s nadir as well as clear signs of "superpower fatigue" affecting America's ability to sustain power and influence on a variety of issues around the world.

The goal of this report is not to insist on any one particular policy blueprint but instead to focus attention on the need to make choices and to be prepared to live with the outcomes. Any U.S. policy toward Russia is going to require trade-offs. Russia's own economic recovery in recent years, coupled with the emergence of alternate international networks that give other states the ability to bypass the United States altogether, has reduced Washington's maneuvering room. The following piece of advice, by three respected analysts, and meant to apply to U.S. policy in general, perfectly sums up what this report hopes to achieve: "We must face head-on and lean into, rather than away from, the real choices that we confront. Some are gut-wrenching in the sense that they will force us to make truly hard compromises among sets of values, preferences, and expectations that we don't want to trade off. That is no excuse to ignore or hide from those choices."

The Failure to Consummate

Many Americans are tempted to look back with nostalgia at a supposed "better time" whenever there are difficulties in the U.S.-Russia relationship. In his memoir, Strobe Talbott, former deputy secretary of state in the Clinton administration, recorded two such instances in President Clinton's conduct of policy toward Russia. The first, in late 1993, was Clinton's lament, in confronting the complexities of dealing with Boris Yeltsin (as well as the ongoing impact of the Soviet collapse), "Boy, do I ever miss the Cold War." Seven years later, after a particularly grueling session with Yeltsin's successor Vladimir Putin—someone prepared to be far less accommodating to American proposals—Clinton told Talbott, "Let's get this thing over with so we can go see Ol' Boris." Today, as relations between Moscow and Washington continue to deteriorate, and as pundits ominously intone that a new Cold War is looming between the United States and Russia, even Republicans who were extremely critical of the Yeltsin administration during the 1990s look back at that time as preferable to the situation today.

Despite the promise of a new and improved relationship between Russia and the United States in the immediate aftermath of 9/11—when Robert Legvold of Columbia University could write that "Russia and the United States both stand on the verge of fundamental foreign policy choices likely to change dramatically their mutual relationship" with an eye to crafting a true alliance between the two states—the old patterns have reasserted themselves. Today, Legvold declares, "Gone is the talk of 'strategic partnership,' not to mention the fanciful vision of a genuine Russo-American alliance held by some . . . not so long ago."

Has Russia—or the rest of the former Soviet Union, for that matter— changed so dramatically between 2001 and 2008 that an entirely new approach is required? It's true that the Russian economy has begun a dramatic recovery from the aftermath of the collapse of the USSR and the 1998 financial crash and that high energy prices have engendered what some call confidence and others "petro-arrogance" within the Kremlin, but over the last seven years, there has been no whole-scale change in Russia's strategic orientation that would justify a major shift in U.S. policy. Either the opportunities were over-stated or the differences are not so dire.

This narrative of past opportunities lost in U.S.-Russian relations is com-pounded by major and dramatic disagreements within the American foreign policy establishment over how to view Russia. Indeed, one cannot help but wonder whether leading U.S. political figures are looking at the same country when they make pronouncements. In July 2007, following his meeting with President Putin, U.S. President George W. Bush declared, "Russia is a good, solid partner," citing in particular cooperation on a number of strategic issues. Senator Barack Obama, a leading Democratic candidate for president, had a much less positive assessment, telling the Chicago Council on Global Affairs earlier that spring that "Russia is neither our enemy nor close ally right now." But the chairman of the Senate Foreign Relations Committee, Joseph Biden (D-DE), went even further, identifying Russia under the Putin administration as one of the three principal threats to the United States.

Although the United States may have contentious and difficult relations with other important countries—such as China, Pakistan, and Saudi Arabia—it is quite a sign of dissonance for a country like Russia to be described by senior officials and policymakers as both a strategic partner and an adversary at the same time. And such divergent positions make fashioning a coherent policy extremely difficult. Take, for instance, the question of preventing the proliferation of nuclear material. If the United States government is so divided over whether Russia is friend or foe, how can there be meaningful intelligence cooperation between the two countries? In a climate of suspicion, how can either side agree to grant access to sensitive facilities? It would be almost impossible, for example, for the United States to "help Russia obtain and maintain an effective, economic, and reliable space-based early-warning system" if a substantial segment of the U.S. foreign policy establishment was to decry the sharing of sensitive and advanced American technologies with an "enemy" state. Meanwhile, hostile rhetoric has surely stirred Russian suspicions about American intentions, further undermining the prospects for rapprochement. In such an environment of uncertainty, therefore, any policy that emerges is unlikely to be based on a dispassionate analysis of U.S. interests—and certainly not from a genuine strategic dialogue with Moscow.

A final ingredient to throw into the mix is an assumption shared by many that the default setting in any bilateral relationship between the United States and another country must be friendship. Richard Pipes provocatively titled his 1997 *Foreign Affairs* essay "Is Russia Still an Enemy?" but nonetheless began by noting that Russia's pre-Soviet relations with the United States "were exceptionally friendly" and that "seven decades of U.S.-Russia hostility that followed the Bolshevik coup d'état were the result not of a conflict of interests but of the particular needs of Russia's conquerors, the Soviet ruling elite." But what happens if the condition described by Senator Obama—a Russia fated to be neither a close ally nor an outright adversary to the United States—is the best outcome for the United States in terms of fulfilling most of its foreign policy objectives?

The many discussions, commissions, and committees that have advanced meaningful proposals for structuring U.S.-Russia relations since 1991 are remarkably consistent in their recommendations for a durable, "interest-based" relationship—one predicated on stemming nuclear proliferation, combating international terrorism, strengthening the United Nations as a more effective international actor, deepening Russian integration into the global economy, and promoting energy security. Moreover, presidents Bush and Putin have publicly discussed these proposals at their summit meetings—in Moscow; Bratislava; and, most recently, Kennebunkport.

The problem is not the lack of an agenda—it is in getting Moscow and Washington to move to the execution stage, to make commitments and in so doing be prepared to foreclose other options. Both sides are at fault, but as former secretary of state Henry Kissinger noted in February 2001, it should be possible to manage a relationship between Russia and the United States even when their "national interests sometimes are parallel and sometimes do not coincide." However, Kissinger went on to say, this "requires of the United States that it have a clear sense of its own priorities."

The Crucial Questions

On December 31,1991, the United Nations approved the request tendered by Yuli M. Vorontsov, the Soviet Ambassador to the United Nations, for the Russian Federation to be recognized as the sole successor to the Union of Soviet Socialist Republics, in accordance with the protocol that had been negotiated among the republics of the Soviet Union in Alma-Ata (Almaty), Kazakhstan, three days earlier.

Had the collapse of the USSR fulfilled the conditions laid out by the administration of Harry S. Truman in NSC-68—the first formal attempt to define an official U.S. strategy for the Cold War? That document directed American policy "by all means short of war to (1) block further expansion of Soviet power, (2) expose the falsities of Soviet pretensions, (3) induce a retraction of the Kremlin's control and influence, and (4) in general, so foster the seeds of destruction within the Soviet system that the Kremlin is brought at least to the point of modifying its behavior to conform to generally accepted international standards." To the extent that all of these things occurred over the course of the Cold War, it is not clear how much was attributable to U.S. actions. In any case, a new set of questions must be applied to U.S.-Russian policy since the end of the Cold War, although these questions draw on lessons learned during the Cold War and even before.

No U.S. administration can hope to craft a sustainable, enduring policy toward Russia if it cannot provide definitive answers to three questions. Were the forces that drove the Soviet Union to expand its influence and led it into conflict with the Atlantic powers a product largely of its Marxist-Leninist ideology, or were they rooted primarily in earlier, pre-Soviet Russian imperial tendencies? If the latter, does that mean that Russia's national interests will always set it at odds with fundamental U.S. security objectives whether tsar, commissar or democratically elected president sits in the Kremlin? Second, are American interests better served by promoting separatist tendencies across the Eurasian plain, or is the maintenance of a unified Russian state conducive to overall U.S. foreign policy goals? Finally, is the existence of Russia—in its current configuration—necessary for the functioning not only of a regional Eurasian political and economic order but also for a global international system that supports overall U.S. national interests?

Americans have often hedged their bets on these questions. Public Law 86-90, passed in 1959 and still on the books, identified "Russian communism" and its "imperialistic and aggressive policies" as a "dire threat to the security of the United States and of all the free peoples of the world," without clarifying what was particularly Russian and what was particularly communist about the threat. In addition, a number of the "Captive Nations" whose liberation that legislation calls for are still constituent parts of the post-Soviet Russian Federation. An influential text of the early 1960s—Victor S. Mamatey's *Soviet Russian Imperialism*—described imperial expansion as part and parcel of Russia's historic aims and "expressed the aspirations of the great Russian people accurately enough." George Kennan's famous "Long Telegram" of 1946 was more nuanced; while identifying pre-Soviet Russian expansionism as a problem, for Kennan it was in the "new guise of international Marxism, with its honeyed promises to a desperate and war torn outside world" that the threat posed by Moscow was "more dangerous and insidious than ever before."

American expectations have changed over time. When, in 1990, Alexander Solzhenitsyn suggested that Moscow, in addition to relinquishing control over the "outer empire" that was the Soviet bloc in Eastern Europe, should also allow the Soviet republics of the Baltic States, the Caucasus and Central Asia to chart their own destinies, this was considered to be a radical declaration far in excess of stated U.S. objectives at the time. By 2004, the proposal for the creation of a common market (the "Single Economic Space") that would encompass the territories Solzhenitsyn had identified in 1990 as part of a proposed "Russian Union"—Belarus, Ukraine, Kazakhstan and Russia—was denounced in the West as an unacceptable manifestation of Russia's "imperial ambitions" and a plot to bring about a "reconstituted empire."

Dissonance in the U.S. approach to Russia could be managed during the 1990s when a weak Russia was significantly dependent on Western aid and when the Russian leadership was prepared to make major concessions to Washington in the hopes of accelerating Russian integration into the West. In turn, the United States was able to use a series of delaying measures and vague promises to postpone the inevitable day of reckoning—for example, using the "Partnership for Peace" as a hedge on the question of NATO expansion—with the hope being that the states of the former Soviet bloc and the former Soviet Union would never qualify for actual membership or that somehow the "Russia problem" would be solved. But sooner or later, this maneuvering room would run out, as NATO has expanded not simply to encompass the former Soviet satellites of Central Europe but states directly on Russia's own borders, and as countries such as Ukraine and Georgia continue to press for inclusion. Russia's recovery from the trauma of the 1990s has not only lessened American influence over Moscow but has allowed Russia to raise the costs of American indecision.

Russia will never be a perfect partner to the United States; but very few nations are—not even America's close allies among the advanced post-industrial democracies. Either the strategic advantages Russia brings to the table make it worth overlooking Russia's obvious faults or the cost of Russia's help is too high in relation to the benefits.

Washington would much prefer to avoid these hard choices. For example, the U.S. Congress is unwilling to graduate Russia from the provisions of the Jackson-Vanik legislation, which prevents permanent normal trading relations with a state that restricts emigration rights—even though Russia had been found to be in compliance with its requirements since 1994. Meanwhile, the Bush administration continues to express its desire for a closer relationship with Russia, but it is clearly ambivalent about the prospects and not sure about the price it is willing to pay to try to work with the Kremlin. That uncertainty will be passed to the next administration, which will have no better luck in crafting and maintaining an effective, coherent, and credible approach toward Russia unless it is willing to answer basic questions about Russia and to dispense with any remaining illusions that currently inhibit the formulation of a realistic policy.

Dangerous Illusions

Too often, outside observers have first created their image of Russia, and then located the appropriate facts and personalities to support their construction. Too often, hopes and aspirations have been substituted for facts when shaping policy.

Dispensing with the illusions that have guided policy toward Russia is a necessary precondition for moving forward—even if it requires abandoning cherished dreams of the "Russia that might have been."

Illusion No. 1: By Cooperating with the United States, Russia Will Join the West

The first illusion is that Russia is destined to become a full member of the West and assume a position of leadership within the Euro-Atlantic community. That was a dream shared not only by many in the United States but in post-Soviet Russia as well. Alexey Pushkov, a leading Russian commentator who was part of Mikhail Gorbachev's foreign policy team, recalled this:

> Many of us thought the way forward as the Cold War ended would be the emergence of a new Europe, one not defined by blocs, and where the old confrontations and antagonisms would be gone. . . . In the beginning of the 1990s, the idea of a close partnership with the United States, even an alliance, was popular in Moscow. Although the Cold War ended in the fall of the Warsaw Pact and the collapse of the Soviet Union, the new Russian elites were operating from the presumption that democratic Russia should not be treated as a defeated country. On the contrary, we thought, it should be included in the Western community as a new state that had decidedly parted with communism."

Even at the beginning of the Putin administration, then–foreign minister Igor Ivanov was still touting the "development of a constructive partnership between my country, Europe and the United States" that is "united by a common responsibility for maintaining peace and stability in the vast Euro-Atlantic area" and declared that a goal of Russian foreign policy would be the "preserva-tion of a unified Euro-Atlantic community, *with Russia now part of it."*

But were such expectations ever realistic? The likelihood that Russia was going to follow a path of internal development that would bring its domestic institutions into closer conformity with Euro-Atlantic standards was extremely low to begin with. Even if that had occurred, Russia, as a Eurasian-continental power, was going to have different interests and priorities than either the United States or Western Europe. Therefore, there could be no expectations that Russia would automatically support the general Western consensus on any given issue. How to secure Russian cooperation with Western initiatives without giving Russia a share of the decisionmaking authority was the dilemma the United States faced in considering Russian integration into Euro-Atlantic structures.

So the compromise position was to give Russia a "voice but no veto" in the deliberations of the West. This was reflected in the negotiations that led to the Founding Act on Mutual Relations, Cooperation and Security between the North Atlantic Treaty Organization and the Russian Federation, signed on May 27, 1997. Washington hoped that, by giving Russia a formal association with NATO, the path could be cleared for enlarging the alliance by including former Soviet bloc states.

That compromise didn't work. If Russia was not going to join the alliance, Moscow's next preference was for an arrangement that would essentially create a system of joint decision making between Russia and NATO on major issues of European and Eurasian security. Moscow was especially insistent that any military operations outside the territory of the member-states of NATO would require either UN or OSCE sanction. The United States, in contrast, wanted to keep a good deal of European security matters designated as matters "internal" to NATO and not subject to the purview of the NATO-Russia Council.

In analyzing the effectiveness of die Permanent Joint Council, which was supposed to be the principal organ of the NATO-Russia partnership, Peter Trenin-Straussov, in an assessment prepared for the Berlin Information Center for Transatlantic Security, concluded:

> The [two] sides . . . failed to agree on what the PJC would do and—as a result—they got a 'disabled child.' The council lacked a 'home' and a permanent secretariat. It was also hugely asymmetrical in operation—Russia was presented with a joint position of the NATO members, and could deal with NATO only *en bloc.* If the Russians made a bid, its NATO partners needed to go in retreat to discuss it and then present Russia with their joint reply. This was cumbersome, but 'safe', from the NATO point of view. The Russians, for their part, soon discovered that dealing with individual NATO member states outside the PJC was more effec-tive and satisfying. The PJC quickly turned itself into a talking shop for rather stale dialogue.

The creation of the NATO-Russia Council in 2002 to replace the PJC cre-ated a system where Russia could sit at the table with all other NATO members for discussion, but never resolved the fundamental dilemma of what weight

Russia's "voice" should have in alliance deliberations. This has meant that Moscow is not really a stakeholder in the alliance, while making the partnership more effective has not been a major priority for NATO members. Major General Peter Williams, who headed the first NATO Military Liaison Mission in Moscow, made this assessment of the first 10 years of Russia's partnership with NATO: "Political will, structures and projects mean little without resources. . . . The resources committed for the execution of NATO-Russia Council policies and plans have been far below those suggested by the political rhetoric."

Meanwhile, the question of Russian membership in the European Union is also off the table as Russia and the Union attempt to develop their set of "common spaces." That has proved difficult. For example, at an EU-Russia summit meeting in Samara in May 2007, the president of the European Commission Jose Manuel Barroso explained that "Russia is a European country that is close to us [the European Union]," while Putin characterized the Russia-EU summit as a forum for "coordinating our cooperation." Russia may be associated with Europe, but both sides have clearly come to the conclusion that Russia, for the foreseeable future, will remain outside the Union.

All of this should lead U.S. policymakers to the conclusion reached by Cliff Kupchan of the Eurasia Group: "The reality of today's international system is that Russia is rapidly becoming a major non-aligned power more along the lines of China or India than a junior partner or disciple of the West."

Illusion No. 2: A Democratic Russia Is a Pro-American Russia

The second illusion casts the Russian masses as anxious to support a U.S. global agenda, but for the authoritarian tyrants who suppress the will of the people. Those who embrace the "democratic peace" theory maintained that as Russia moved further away from its authoritarian Soviet past, its interests would necessarily converge with those of the United States. Congressman Robert Wexler (D-FL) declared at a 2003 hearing on the U.S.-Russia relationship that "the success of Russia's democratic transformation will largely determine and shape the present and future possibilities of cooperation and engagement" with the United States.

It is a common assertion now in Washington that how Russia governs itself shapes its foreign policy and that continued disagreements between the United States and the Russian Federation over foreign policy issues can be attributed to a growing authoritarian trend in Russia. The implication is that a more democratic Russian government would make fundamentally different choices. It might decide not to object to its neighbors joining the NATO alliance or drop its efforts to export its energy resources directly to Germany and other Western European markets, bypassing the transit countries of Central and Eastern Europe.

Although such views are commonly held, they are badly mistaken. First, it is important to stress the wide support Putin receives among Russians for his policies—something the results of the December 2007 Duma elections confirm. In recent polls, 72 percent of Russians agree with the assessment that

Putin has moved Russia "in the right direction" and identify with his call for a resurgent Russia capable of playing a major role in world affairs. While some might dismiss Putin's strong ratings as the product of a slick propaganda campaign, his popularity is based rather in the public's assessment that his government has improved the quality of life for most ordinary Russians. Some 66 percent believe that Russians in 2007 live better than in the Soviet Union of 1991 (immediately before the economic collapses of the 1990s). And among 18- to 24-year-olds—the demographic that supplied the foot soldiers for the democratic "color revolutions" in Georgia and Ukraine—the Putin administration has a 57 percent approval rating.

Second, one cannot find a strong reservoir of support for U.S. foreign policy among Russians. Some 73 percent of Russians agree with the statement that "the United States cannot be trusted," and 66 percent believe that "U.S. foreign policy does not take Russian interests into account." More than 60 percent of Russians see the United States as having a negative influence in the world; more than half believe that the United States is unfriendly to Russia. Those sentiments are especially true among young Russians aged 16 to 29—the post-Soviet generation. In a 2007 survey, almost 70 percent disagreed with the notion that the United States "does more good than harm"; 64 percent saw the United States either as an "enemy" or at least a "rival" to Russia. (China, in contrast, was viewed by only 27 percent of respondents in the same way.)

Even if President Putin had been inclined in the early years of his relationship with President Bush to join the "coalition of the willing," he would have had to defy the overwhelming majority of Russians to do so, since 89 percent opposed any participation of Russian forces in an American-led coalition in Iraq. With regard to Iran, a 2007 poll indicates that 45 percent of Russians consider Iran a friendly country; only 20 percent agreed that a military strike would be justified if sanctions failed to stop Iran's uranium enrichment. A 2006 poll conducted by the Pew Research Center showed that by a two-to-one margin Russians were more likely to view the U.S. presence in Iraq as a greater threat to global peace than Iran's uranium enrichment program.

Indeed, it is difficult to conceive of any Putin foreign policy decision of the last several years that would have been reversed by a more democratically accountable Russian government.

So, would a more democratic Russia be more inclined to accommodate U.S. preferences? Would it agree to implement punitive sanctions against Iran? Or to restructure its energy industry to meet our needs?

In a word, no. A more democratic Russia would still not see eye to eye with the United States on a number of pressing issues—for the same reasons that the United States and France, despite both being democracies, have fundamental disagreements over foreign policy.

None of this is to deny that a more democratic Russia would benefit the United States in some ways. Governments that are open and transparent, and subject to scrutiny and criticism, are generally more constrained than authoritarian regimes and, in some ways, more predictable. But we should not fall into the trap of believing that if Russia were to become more liberal, have genuinely free and competitive elections and strengthened rule of law, that would automatically translate into a foreign policy more aligned with U.S. priorities. The two countries have different objectives.

Illusion No. 3: Russia Is about to Collapse

The third illusion that must be dispensed with is the assertion that Russia is near collapse and that its recovery is but a house of cards—and that, therefore, there is no need for the United States to take Russia's interests or preferences into account when shaping policy. While such sentiments have receded in the last several years, they were quite pronounced when the Bush administration first took office. Perhaps the most famous example of this thinking was a May 2001 essay in the *Atlantic Monthly* provocatively entitled "Russia Is Finished." Written by Jeffrey Tayler, an American journalist who had lived and worked in Russia during the 1990s, the article chronicled the "unstoppable descent of a once great power into social catastrophe and strategic irrelevance." Tayler described post-Soviet Russia as "Zaire with permafrost." Conservative analyst General William Odom, who headed the National Security Agency during the Reagan administration, picked up this assessment when he characterized Russia as "weak, poor and ambling along [its] own paths headed nowhere in particular" and a "marginal power."

Russia continues to face massive problems—notably in its health care system and in coping with an aging infrastructure. Its greatest challenge is a very low life expectancy for its male population that portends a labor shortage and deprives the economy of decades of potential productivity from the premature demise of its citizens. But the Russia of 2007 is far more capable than the Russia of 1997 in coping with these challenges.

Russia has experienced robust economic growth for the past several years, an average of 6.8 percent per year. Russia is displaying many signs of economic health. The government no longer runs a budget deficit (and for the last two years the federal budget surplus has exceeded 7 percent of GDP), while the state's foreign debt has shrunk dramatically; it was 100 percent of Russia's GDP in 1999, today it stands around 8 percent. By July 2007, Russia had accumulated gold and foreign exchange reserves of $413.1 billion—the largest in its history. On August 1, 2007, the Finance Ministry announced that there was $127 billion in its Stabilization Fund—and it set up that same month a reserve fund that, over time, would be expected to total 10 percent of Russia's GDP and would exist solely for the purpose of cushioning the federal budget in the event of an oil price plunge.

One cannot rule out the possibility of some major disaster that could reverse Russia's recovery—but American policy seems based on the belief that Russia will forever remain in the debilitating condition of the 1990s and will have no choice but to accept Washington's diktat. Any policy that assumes that Russia will accept a status quo in Eurasia and the world, or that is predicated on an assumption of perpetual Russian weakness, is foolhardy and dangerous.

Russia will never return as a superpower to rival the United States. And Lehigh University's professor Rajan Menon, a leading expert on Eurasian affairs, is absolutely correct to counsel Americans not to overreact to Russia's recovery.

But Russia is resuming its position as a major regional power with some ability to influence the overall global agenda—especially to raise costs for the United States to act. That is multiplied if Russia can act in concert with other major powers, especially China.

Illusion No. 4: The U.S. (and Europe) Can Fundamentally Transform Eurasia at Little Cost

The fourth illusion is that the United States, in partnership with the European Union, is capable of fundamentally transforming the geopolitical and geoeconomic realities of Eurasia. A related conceit is of building a network of stable, prosperous, pro-Western states all along Russia's periphery that will give Moscow no choice but to accept these new realities.

For starters, the pace of European Union and NATO expansion has slowed considerably. Absorbing Central and Eastern Europe placed great strains on both the Atlantic alliance and the EU; continuing with further expansion is highly unlikely, especially in the near term. Romano Prodi, when he was president of the European Commission, made this perfectly clear at the close of 2002, when he declared, "The integration of the Balkans into the European Union will complete the unification of the continent." While Prodi conceded that the process of EU enlargement "has worked very well," he went on: "We cannot go on enlarging forever. We cannot water down the European political project and turn the European Union into just a free trade area on a continental scale."

Expansion fatigue contributed to the rejection of the European constitution in France and the Netherlands and led then-German Chancellor Gerhard Schroeder to vehemently oppose any increases in the EU budget (and in Germany's contributions) for 2007–2013. And there is no sign that new leadership in Europe is prepared to resume eastward expansion of the European Union.

But even if full membership in Euro-Atlantic organizations is not forthcoming, what about extending a number of the privileges of membership, including free-trade agreements, visa-free travel, and rights to live and work in Western countries? The European Union has been willing to consider the extension of free-trade agreements, but with exceptions in place for agricultural products and some industrial goods (such as steel), which would nullify the benefits of access to European markets for countries such as Ukraine. The U.S. government, meanwhile, has been reluctant to take any such steps, other than support for Ukraine's inclusion into the World Trade Organization.

The bottom line is that neither the United States nor Europe is prepared to undertake the massive effort that would be required to displace Russia as Eurasia's economic and political center of gravity. Fifteen years after the collapse of the Soviet Union, more than 75 percent of the GDP of the states of the former Soviet Union is generated by Russia. Russia remains Ukraine's and Kazakhstan's largest trading partner. The International Monetary Fund estimated that guest workers from post-Soviet states living in Russia send home $12 billion annually. Official remittances from workers in Russia, as recorded by the IMF, make up approximately 16 percent of Moldova's GDP. Grandiose schemes for a new Black Sea Commonwealth that bypasses Russia look wonderful on paper but don't correspond to realities on the ground.

Illusion No. 5: The U.S. Version of "Selective Partnership" Is a Viable Policy Option

In theory, selective partnership is not a bad concept. It was the basis of the "Grand Alliance" in World War II, as well as the anti-Taliban coalition that emerged in the weeks after 9/11 between a disparate group of nations. Indeed, most relationships between states—even those who consider themselves close allies—are often in reality "selective partnerships"; it is extremely rare that interests and priorities between two different countries are aligned 100 percent of the time.

Given the disillusionment of many in both Russia and the United States over the failure to build an effective working relationship as allies or close strategic partners, selective partnership, on paper, seems to be the most feasible alternative. In this vein, the 2006 Council on Foreign Relations task force report on Russia tries to lay out a strategy for "how to make selective cooperation—and in some cases selective opposition—serve important international goals."

Unfortunately, "selective partnership" has been interpreted—both by some in the Congress as well as in the current administration—as meaning that Washington can expect and will receive full Russian cooperation on a whole host of important matters to U.S. national security while being free to ignore Russian concerns that conflict with American preferences.

For selective partnership to work, both sides must have similar perceptions of threats, and of the benefits of cooperation. As we are seeing with Iran, however, this is not the case. U.S. secretary of state Condoleezza Rice staked out the U.S. position, "that Iran constitutes the single most important single-country strategic challenge to the United States and to the kind of Middle East that we want to see." That is certainly not Moscow's perspective. Russia is not in favor of additional countries gaining nuclear weapons, but those in the United States who repeat the mantra that an "Islamist" Iran with nuclear weapons would fundamentally jeopardize Russian security are seemingly unaware that, from Moscow's perspective, Iran has, on the whole, behaved as a "responsible citizen" in Russia's neighborhood—not extending support to Islamist rebels in the North Caucasus, working to achieve a peace settlement in Tajikistan, and cooperating with Russia in aiding the Northern Alliance against the Taliban. Indeed, Russia's attitude toward Iran is not unlike that of India toward Iran—this despite the fact that India is the world's largest democracy and an emerging strategic partner of the United States.

Like India, Russia may be prepared to pay a price to accommodate U.S. concerns, even at the expense of valuable economic ties with Tehran—but achieving a non-nuclear Iran on a U.S. timetable and leaving Washington free to frustrate Russian interests elsewhere in the world is an insufficient reward. This reticence to cooperate grows stronger when, as some U.S. foreign policy commentators have advised, ending the nuclear stand-off with Iran would open up its vast energy reserves to U.S. investment, allow for new energy transport routes to bypass Russia, and enable America to further counter Russia's overall energy ambitions.

Yet many in Washington continue to use the rubric of "selective partnership" to argue that Russian concerns about the expansion of NATO or the increased American presence in Central Asia are unjustified or at least overblown. They further maintain that the security challenges that threaten the United States, including nuclear proliferation and violent Islamic extremism, are also such a threat to Russia that Moscow will have no choice but to cooperate with Washington, and therefore there is no need to accommodate the Kremlin's preferences. But there is a big difference between token cooperation and the sort of active, engaged effort (including more effective intelligence sharing or closer working relationships between armed forces) that could lead to major breakthroughs. General Peter Williams points out, "It will take courage to change this political and military culture of noncooperation," between Russia and the West, but this cannot occur if neither side feels that partnership serves their interests. At present, breaking the diplomatic logjam requires the United States to offer much more if it wants Russian help. In discussing Russian reluctance to embrace the U.S. position on Iran, Graham Allison and Dimitri Simes made this point clear: "Getting what the United States needs . . . will require not only penalties but incentives."

There is still hope for a partnership without illusions in some key areas where both sides have common interests, such as nonproliferation or combating nuclear terrorism. Neither the United States nor Russia, for example, is interested in a nuclear-armed Iran or witnessing a nuclear exchange between India and Pakistan. Russian analyst Alexey Pushkov contends that "Putin has not dropped the idea of partnership with the United States altogether, but he has definitely moved away from some of the more grandiose proposals in favor of a much more limited arrangement." But for Russia this means obtaining clear and tangible benefits, not vague assurances of future goodwill.

Making Choices

When we strip away these five illusions, we discover a series of "inconvenient truths"—the "democracy paradox" of Putin's regime enjoys broad-based public support; Russia, especially now that it is in the midst of a major recovery, remains the dominant Eurasian power; and the United States is no longer in a position to assume or compel Russian acquiescence to its policy preferences. Recognizing these facts forces us into a long-overdue discussion about U.S. foreign-policy priorities and where Russia fits in, taking us away from "having our cake and eating it too" scenarios in favor of assessing whether the costs of partnership with Moscow are worth the benefits.

Reasonable people can disagree in terms of their assessments of Russia and how to best achieve U.S. interests. For example, many Americans are displeased that Russia under Vladimir Putin has moved in an authoritarian direction and is in no way a "reliable" partner for Washington on a variety of issues. Many U.S. interest groups are not happy with the restricted zone of civil and political liberties in Putin's Russia. In the end, the question we need to ask is not whether the Russia that has emerged is a Russia we like—it isn't. The more important question is whether it is a Russia we can do business with, and more importantly, whether or not the United States can achieve some of its most pressing objectives without Russian help.

For the last several years, the Bush administration has tried to compartmentalize the relationship, hoping to preserve cooperation on issues that are central to the United States (such as counterterrorism and nonproliferation) while maintaining that acrimonious exchanges on other matters (such as questions of democracy promotion or Russia's relations with its Eurasian neighbors) need not damage U.S.-Russian relations. But at some point the two countries have to move beyond symbolic declarations and "agreements in principle" if there is to be real progress on any shared U.S.-Russia agenda. President Bush, as well as all the leading candidates who would succeed him in January 2009, have identified the same three foreign policy priorities: protecting the United States from further mass-casualty terrorist attacks; preventing "rogue" states from acquiring nuclear weapons; and stopping the spiraling costs of energy from destabilizing not only die United States but the entire global economy. The record as of February 2008 shows that much work remains to be done: Osama bin Laden and Ayman al-Zawahiri remain at large; Afghanistan and Iraq are in serious trouble; Iran is on the path to becoming a nuclear power; and energy prices are at record levels.

U.S. policymakers have to decide whether a resurgent Russia, the growing authoritarian trend of the Putin administration, and Russia's expanding leverage over energy markets—namely its ability to restrict flows of natural gas to other former Soviet states and to EU members—prevents the United States from achieving its principal foreign policy priorities or otherwise directly threatens core U.S. interests. We may already have one clear answer: Vice President Cheney's Vilnius speech in 2006 implied that he believed, as Russian political analyst and Putin adviser Gleb Pavlovsky concluded, that it was time to eliminate "the vestiges of strategic partnership between Russia and the United States" and that as long as Russia remained under its present government it would be nearly impossible for the two countries to find common ground on key international issues.

If the Bush administration has been committed to a policy of confrontation with Russia, however, then U.S. policy has been extremely deficient in making the arrangements that would be needed for the U.S. to move ahead with its international agenda against more active Russian opposition. One would expect, for instance, a much greater effort to expand NATO eastward coupled with much more generous amounts of aid to construct a true cordon sanitaire against a reviving Russia, certainly much more than the paltry steps undertaken so far to encourage the emergence of an alternative to a Russian-led Eurasia via the creation of the GUAM Organization for Democracy and Economic Development.

On the foreign policy issue of greatest concern to Washington—Iran—moving into a position of greater hostility to Russia would also severely complicate matters. Not only would it effectively torpedo any remaining diplomatic efforts to resolve the problem (including being able to threaten genuinely effective sanctions), it would mean American policymakers will be left with only one real option: a massive military strike. Such an attack would be likely to precipitate a wider war that would require major spending to overhaul and expand the armed forces already severely weakened by the Iraq war.

Finally, a more aggressive posture toward Russia would require the United States to reassess its relationship with China—not only for the financial support Washington would need to gear up for these new challenges but also to impede the development of any sort of Sino-Russian axis designed to counter the U.S. position in the world.

Those who argue that Russia has little of value to offer the United States in coping with its most serious challenges might reach similar conclusions. If the United States were to assume the burden of stabilizing what Brzezinski has called the "Global Balkans"—a geographical "swathe of Eurasia between Europe and the Far East," encompassing primarily the Middle East and Central Asia—and if it were to attempt to do so without Russian support, then Washington has been remiss in taking the necessary steps to ensure it has the necessary resources and capabilities at its disposal.

The reality is that, simply put, Americans are understandably unprepared and unwilling to shoulder the costs that moving to a more confrontational stance with Russia would entail. Meanwhile, many policymakers would agree with the proposition that the United States has bigger problems in the world than focusing on Russia's faults—notably protecting itself against a major mass-casualty attack and safeguarding the economic health of the country. And finally, Russia is indeed in a position to assist the United States in achieving its principal foreign policy objectives. For all of these reasons, a confrontational policy should be rejected.

The problem, however, is that meaningful cooperation is not possible if Russia is seen primarily as an enemy who just happens to be, at this particular time, a less immediate threat. If Senator Biden was sincere in his assessments of threats to the United States, it is difficult to understand why Russia would cooperate closely with Washington in dealing with Iraq, Iran, and North Korea—in essence to remove them as challenges to the United States—so that Russia itself could then become the primary focus of U.S. attention.

The outward show of good personal chemistry between presidents Bush and Putin and their willingness to let this camaraderie define their joint public appearances has counteracted some of the voices in both countries that are arguing against closer relations. An assistant secretary of state or deputy foreign minister who might be inclined toward confrontation does not want to publicly contradict his or her respective chief executives. But there is no guarantee that Bush and Putin's successors will have a similarly cordial relationship. Moreover, forging a climate of mutual comfort—if not real trust—that will allow for greater U.S. access to Russia's sensitive intelligence information and its military and nuclear sites (not to mention closer working relations with Russia's diplomatic and business establishments) cannot be accomplished overnight. Moreover, it is not something Russia can be bullied into for the long haul. So any sort of grandstanding that blocks real cooperation without measurably improving U.S. security could be very costly—and that is not a price worth paying.

But what price is worth paying in exchange for better relations with Russia? Is it worth giving Moscow something beyond vague assurances of goodwill? In particular, what about Russia's demands that its paramount position in the lands of the former Soviet Union be recognized by the United States and that Washington cease what Moscow perceives as attempts to interfere in Russia's domestic affairs?

Russia has consistently maintained that its primary interest is to ensure that no other Eurasian state can obstruct Russian engagement with the outside world and that no foreign troops are based anywhere in Eurasia without Russia's blessing (for example, to combat international terrorism). As a result, Moscow maintains that no Eurasian state should belong to a military bloc or alliance of which Russia is not also a member. Russia has also expressed continued interest in creating a single economic zone so that Russian capital and goods can move more efficiently across borders. Within limits, Russia has no objection to other Eurasian states developing supplemental political and economic ties to other states, as long as Russian vital interests are respected. But Russia wants to create a Eurasian economic and political zone where Moscow sets the overall agenda.

Is acceding to such a vision something Washington should consider? There is broad agreement about what the United States is *not* prepared to concede. No one argues that Russia should have a blank check to use force against its neighbors or to forcibly incorporate them into a new version of the Soviet Union and still have a "business as usual" relationship with Washington. Russia should be held accountable for all obligations (whether in treaties, conventions or contracts) it has voluntarily assumed—especially when Russian interests are being safeguarded by reciprocal arrangements. Nor is the United States inclined to give Moscow a veto if a core U.S. interest is at stake—such as maintaining military bases in Central Asia to sustain the ongoing efforts in Afghanistan. Finally, Washington is under no obligation to pretend that Russia is a democracy (in the Western understanding of the term) or to refrain from criticism of the Russian government's slide toward authoritarianism.

Between Russia's stated preferences and these bedrock American priorities remains a great deal of room for finding consensus positions. Unfortunately, however, such a discussion is not taking place. Consider this: In March 2007, the U.S. Congress decided, by large margins in both houses, that NATO membership was the way for the post-Soviet states to safeguard their independence, when it approved legislation providing support for Ukraine and Georgia's bid to join the Western alliance.

What was amazing was the near-total lack of debate in the United States over what was to be gained by including Ukraine or Georgia in NATO. Few dared to ask whether the continual expansions of the alliance have weakened its ability to function as a collective security organ. Likewise, what the inclusion of those states would contribute to solving the major challenges to U.S. and Western security posed by Iran, Afghanistan, North Korea, and international terrorism was never addressed, nor was the likely impact on U.S.-Russia relations.

A zero-sum mentality for Eurasia—where the United States is confronted by a binary choice that only permits one of two outcomes (Ukraine in NATO or Ukraine "lost" to the West altogether)—flies in the face of America's ability to successfully balance multiple and sometimes conflicting priorities in other parts of the world. In a number of complicated bilateral relationships, Washington has been able to avoid embracing the maximalist positions of either side in order to find acceptable, if imperfect, compromises.

Early last year, Anatol Lieven, a long-standing critic of U.S. policy toward Russia, proposed an arrangement whereby the United States would agree to "abandoning NATO enlargement to [include] Ukraine and Georgia in favour of mutually agreed restraints on western and Russian behaviour on the territory of the former Soviet Union." In practical terms, this might lead to a situation where the United States would drop its opposition to Russian-led multilateral institutions in which other Eurasian countries participate on a voluntary basis (such as the Common Economic Space or the Collective Security Treaty Organization)—in return for Russian guarantees that any Eurasian state is free to seek membership in the European Union. (This would also then put the onus on Brussels to decide when and where to halt EU expansion.)

These sorts of compromises do not satisfy politicians in Georgia, Ukraine and Moldova, who would like nothing better than for the United States to put its full political, military, and economic might into changing their geopolitical position. It is equally unsettling for a number of American politicians who are unprepared to recognize that the unipolar moment has passed. But such an approach seems to have the greatest chance of satisfying the greatest number of U.S. objectives—acquiring some security guarantees for Russia's neighbors, keeping the door in Eurasia at least partly open, and paving the way for closer cooperation with Russia on other issues.

Is There a Way Forward?

Secretary of State Condoleezza Rice has often stressed the "excellent relationship" between Presidents Bush and Putin, noting that the two leaders "feel that they can discuss anything." However, this personal relationship has not been translated into effective cooperation between the bureaucracies of the two countries. It is unlikely that presidents Bush and Putin will bequeath a lasting legacy of cooperation to their successors.

On the Russian side, in fact, officials just one level below Putin have shown little enthusiasm for making the case for renewed cooperation with the United States. The July 2007 resignation of Igor Ivanov, the former foreign minister who then became the secretary of the Security Council, marked the departure of the last high-level Yeltsin-era foreign policymaker as well as someone who was still an advocate for closer ties with the United States. Skepticism toward U.S. intentions is now the norm in the Russian foreign policy establishment. While this view may not be accurate or fair, it nonetheless exists, and it hampers further cooperation. It also suggests that the alternative to a difficult partnership with Putin is not a better relationship with someone else.

On the U.S. side, the Bush administration, from the beginning, found little support for its efforts to engage Russia either in Congress or within the U.S. foreign policy community. There were constant irritants—some of which were caused by the Kremlin's own actions, to be sure—which made it difficult to argue the case that a closer and more cooperative relationship with Russia outweighed the concerns.

By contrast, the United States has managed to design a sound policy toward China, a country which is much less free and could pose a much greater challenge than Putin's Russia to U.S. interests not only in East Asia but around the globe. Serious concerns—about human rights, the environment, Taiwan, and so on—are nonetheless balanced within a cohesive, and what we hope will remain a durable bi-partisan, framework of engagement. The same could be said of U.S. policies toward other undemocratic, yet strategically important, states such as Saudi Arabia, Egypt, and Pakistan.

Moscow isn't waiting for Washington to reconcile these inconsistencies. As the U.S.-Russia relationship has stumbled along, Russia, especially in the last five years, has begun to evolve into a "post-American" country. There are still several critical issues where Moscow and Washington continue to interact—control of nuclear arms, negotiations in the Security Council, and so on—but in terms of many of the day-to-day matters that underwrite any bilateral relationship, including trade, tourism, and other people-to-people exchanges, the Russia-Europe and specifically the Russia-Germany relationships are much more important. Moreover, an increasing percentage of Russia's trade—and not only in weapons systems—is with the largest and richest countries of the developing world, especially China and India. Moscow has also begun to accelerate the development of new international institutions that bypass the United States, such as the Shanghai Cooperation Organization.

The sense that Russia is increasingly moving outside of an American-led system has contributed to a new feeling of self-sufficiency in Moscow. In fact, Russia is now much more likely to see itself evolving into an independent center of global power.

What that means, therefore, is that, at present, there is simply no basis for an alliance or major partnership between Russia and the United States, no matter how many reports stress common interests. In the absence of major linkages—particularly in terms of connecting the two countries' business, military, and intelligence establishments—the U.S.-Russia relationship lacks the ballast to navigate through the tempests that arise over their differences.

What is far more feasible, given the climate in both capitals, is to have a relationship characterized by a pragmatic approach to resolving issues and preventing disagreements from flaring up into full-scale crises.

That might not seem like much, especially in the aftermath of grandiose rhetoric about alliances, a world with no blocs, or the promise of a new global order. And as memories of the Cold War fade, it may not be apparent that the state of affairs today is far preferable to what preceded it—when U.S. policy was focused on dealing with a Soviet state attempting to dominate both Western Europe and East Asia and trying to make inroads in Africa and Latin America with an eye not only to an encirclement of the United States but the very destruction of our way of life.

For the time being, the U.S. government, barring a profound transformation of the Russian state, should be concerned largely with Russia's behavior beyond its borders and be prepared to deal with Moscow on a quid pro quo basis. That will require a change in attitude, away from a post-Cold War American triumphalism back to a more realistic approach. As former senator Gary Hart noted, "Until recent years, when U.S. foreign policy assumed a theological aura, we consistently sought self-interested relations with disagreeable nations." The same holds true today and into the future. "A working relationship is not a favor to the Russians but an advantage to us."

It is difficult to conceive of a solution to any of the most pressing challenges facing the United States where Russia does not have some part to play. That may be galling to those who reveled in the period of the immediate post-Soviet collapse when Russia was a supplicant nation and where the U.S. could move ahead with its own vision for how to structure global affairs without much consideration for Moscow's perspective. But the situation has changed—and nothing makes that clearer than Russia's newfound position as the third-largest holder of dollars in the world (after Japan and China).

The United States has two options. It can forgo the possibility of Russian assistance in achieving its key foreign policy priorities in order to retain complete freedom of action vis-à-vis Moscow. Or it can prioritize its objectives and negotiate a series of quid pro quos with Russia. This choice, however, cannot be indefinitely postponed.

The latter is the better course. Seeking broad accommodation with Russia is more likely to guarantee American success in promoting its core national interests—especially in a changing international environment where the sources of power that sustain American global leadership are weakening—but it will require U.S. policymakers to accept limits not only on what can be demanded of Russia but also on the satisfaction of American preferences. If we are willing to accept this compromise and part with our illusions, we can move forward. If not, then U.S.-Russia relations will continue to deteriorate, and proposals for cooperation will languish.

Stephen Sestanovich ⟶ **NO**

What Has Moscow Done?
Rebuilding U.S.-Russian Relations

This past summer's war in Georgia—and its aftermath—delivered a higher-voltage shock to U.S.-Russian relations than any event since the end of the Cold War. It made Russia an unexpected flashpoint in the U.S. presidential campaign and probably won Russia a place at the top of the next administration's agenda. Yet this is hardly the first time in the last two decades that Washington has buzzed with discussion of ominous events in Russia. Before long, the buzzing has usually subsided. Will this crisis prove different? Has Washington's thinking about Russia really changed, and how much?

At first glance, the change seems fundamental. Five years ago, the U.S. ambassador in Moscow, Alexander Vershbow, said that the main difficulty in U.S.-Russian relations was a "values gap." The two sides were cooperating effectively on practical problems, he argued, but were diverging on issues such as the rule of law and the strengthening of democratic institutions. No U.S. official would make such a statement today—or would have even six months ago. Well before Russian tanks rolled into Georgia in August, the list of issues separating Washington from Moscow had grown long, and, more important, these issues extended well beyond the values gap. Although great powers are widely thought to have stopped viewing security as the core problem in their dealings with one another, that is what most troubles U.S.-Russian relations. Things were bad enough when the U.S. government used to say that then Russian President Vladimir Putin was undermining Russian democracy. Once Putin, now prime minister but apparently still the country's leader, started saying that the United States was undermining Russia's nuclear deterrent, he took tensions to an entirely new level.

Against this backdrop, Russia's invasion of a small neighbor might have seemed to be final confirmation of the view that Russia has become, in the words of the British economist Robert Skidelsky, "the world's foremost revisionist power." And yet, for all the recent references to the Sudetenland and the crushing of the Prague Spring, Western governments have made clear that such parallels will not guide their response. Government officials and pundits alike have been coupling their denunciations of Moscow with assurances that they want to work with it in advancing common interests, whether on nuclear proliferation, terrorism, energy security, drug trafficking, or climate change. The more these issues are invoked, the less one should expect U.S.

Reprinted by permission of *Foreign Affairs*, Vol. 87, no. 6, November/December 2008. Copyright © 2008 by the Council on Foreign Relations, Inc.

policy toward Russia to change. Harry Truman, it might be recalled, did not usually speak of his determination to work with Joseph Stalin.

For two decades, the idea that the United States needs Russia for practical reasons has led Washington, even in moments of shock and confusion over Russia's actions, to want to keep relations with Russia from becoming any worse than necessary. Although U.S. policymakers have considered Moscow a high-maintenance partner with whom getting to yes is extremely frustrating and sometimes almost hopeless, they have never been ready to give up on the effort. Even Russia's war with Georgia has not changed this outlook, and for the foreseeable future probably nothing will.

What the war has done, however, is subject the high-stakes and now disappointing U.S.-Russian relationship to a top-to-bottom reassessment—its first real reconsideration since the Cold War. Suddenly, saying that Washington has to cooperate with Moscow when possible and push back emphatically when necessary no longer seems a fully satisfactory formula. Determining the right balance between cooperating and pushing back—between selective engagement and selective containment—has become the main task of U.S. policy toward Russia. This effort will surely last well into the next U.S. administration, providing a key challenge for the new president and his advisers as they refashion the United States' role in the world.

Is This Realism's Moment?

Whenever U.S. foreign policy faces a major failure, so-called realist commentators come forward to suggest a way out, usually by recalibrating ends and means and rethinking national priorities. Long before the war in Georgia, the souring of U.S.-Russian relations had been the subject of many such analyses. (Examples include Nikolas Gvosdev's February 2008 paper "Parting with Illusions: Developing a Realistic Approach to Relations with Russia," published by the Cato Institute; Robert Blackwill's January/February 2008 National Interest article, "The Three Rs: Rivalry, Russia, 'Ran"; and Dimitri Simes' November/December 2007 Foreign Affairs piece, "Losing Russia.") These realists' argument, which has gained a more respectful hearing since the war, is that Washington has let secondary interests prevent accommodation on issues of overriding importance to U.S. security. If Washington wants Moscow's help on things that really matter, the reasoning goes, then it should back off on policies that provoke Moscow unnecessarily.

For these realists, most of the U.S. moves that have irked Moscow in the past few years—regularly hectoring Moscow about democracy, recklessly encouraging Georgia and Ukraine to seek membership in NATO, attempting to install ballistic missile defenses in eastern Europe, challenging Russia's energy dominance in Central Asia and the Caucasus, recognizing Kosovo's independence—are not worth the bad blood, and now the bloodshed, that they have generated with Russia. Washington would better serve U.S. interests by negotiating a series of quid pro quos that focused on getting from Russia the things that the United States truly needs. The details of such proposed understandings vary, of course, but in the most frequently mentioned one,

Washington would take care not to encroach on Russia's hoped-for sphere of influence in its neighborhood in exchange for Russia's help in preventing Iran from acquiring nuclear weapons.

This "let's make a deal" approach to diplomacy has a tempting simplicity to it. And (because this is the role realism usually plays in U.S. foreign policy debates) it will surely force U.S. decision-makers to think harder about the ends they seek, by what means they should pursue them, and at what cost. Even so, it is not likely to be the strategy that the next U.S. administration adopts. Diplomats are widely thought to be negotiating such deals all the time, but it is in fact very rare that any large problem is solved because representatives of two great powers trade completely unrelated assets. The "grand bargains" favored by amateur diplomats are almost never consummated.

The specific deals that some realists propose rest, moreover, on unexamined assumptions about both the flexibility and the leverage of Russian policy. Moscow is no more likely to support a drastic increase in U.S. pressure against Iran, for example, than it did against Iraq in the lead-up to the 2003 war. (At the time, some analysts thought a mini "grand bargain" might bring the United States and Russia together on this issue, but neither side was interested.) And the suggestion that Russian leaders could get Iran to end its quest for nuclear weapons raises doubts about whether this sort of policy thinking should be called "realism" at all. Some realists claim that Moscow has enormous influence over Tehran, but they rarely explain how. In reality, the United States has far more leverage—military, economic, and diplomatic—with which to influence Iranian policy.

Important as these reasons are, they are not the most significant grounds for questioning the realist prescription for U.S.-Russian relations. Although realists claim that good relations between Washington and Moscow are impossible if one side annoys the other too much, not long ago Putin himself presided over just such good but somewhat fractious relations. As he awaited a visit from his friend U.S. President George W. Bush in the middle of 2002, Putin could look back over a three-year stretch during which the United States had bombed Serbia and occupied Kosovo, accused Russia of war crimes in Chechnya, abrogated the Anti-Ballistic Missile Treaty, established a military presence in Central Asia, begun to train and equip Georgia's armed forces, and completed the largest-ever expansion of NATO, which included three former Soviet states, Estonia, Latvia, and Lithuania. Bush administration officials naturally gushed that U.S.-Russian relations had never been better. What is more, Putin agreed. Some of the U.S. actions that might have seemed to be problems for Russia were nothing of the sort, he said; after all, strengthening the ability of Russia's neighbors to deal with terrorism strengthened Russia's security, too. Yes, the two sides did not see eye to eye on some issues, but these would not threaten their deepening strategic partnership. After an earlier meeting with Putin, Bush himself had captured this outlook in his customary homey language: "You probably don't agree with your mother on every issue. You still love her, though, don't you?"

Now that U.S.-Russian relations have sunk to a new low, it is essential to recall—and understand—their previous high. Why did Putin say things in

2002 that he would never dream of saying in 2008? Was it, as realists might say, weakness? Maybe. But if the Russian economy was less robust six years ago than it is now, it was already on the upswing. And in any event, in the 1990s then Russian President Boris Yeltsin objected far more vocally than Putin did to U.S. policies he disliked, even though during his tenure Russia was far weaker than it was in 2002.

Was Putin expecting a greater payoff from Washington than he actually received, and did he then change course when he did not get it? There is not as much to this explanation as Russian officials and sympathetic Western analysts like to allege. Within a year of the attacks of September 11, 2001, Bush had offered Putin a new strategic arms treaty (which Putin had said he needed for political reasons), shifted U.S. policy on Chechnya from condemnation of Russia to understanding, recognized Russia as a market economy (an important step in easing bilateral trade disputes), supported Russia's accession to the World Trade Organization, agreed to have Russia chair the G-8 (the group of highly industrialized states) for the first time, initiated a multibillion-dollar international version of the Nunn-Lugar program (a U.S. effort launched in 1992 to help dismantle weapons of mass destruction in the former Soviet Union), and upgraded Russia's ties to NATO so that Russia's representatives could participate on a more equal footing in deliberations on European security.

As payoffs go, this was not bad, and at the time both sides emphasized that it represented more than U.S. President Bill Clinton had ever offered Yeltsin. But what really undergirded the U.S.-Russian relationship in its post-9/11 heyday was not any transactional reward. It was the two sides' shared conviction that the two countries saw major goals and major problems in broadly compatible terms—and that, more than ever before, they could deal with each other as equals. Washington and Moscow resolved their disagreements not by exchanging payoffs but by choosing not to see differences as expressions of a deeper conflict. Russian arms sales to China did not block cooperation, nor did the U.S. State Department's human rights report. Henry Kissinger has called this kind of understanding between great powers a "moral consensus." Although the term may seem a little grand, it is a useful reminder that enduring strategic cooperation involves more than trading my quids for your quos.

The U.S.-Russian "moral consensus" of 2002 is now a distant memory, and realists are not wrong to emphasize the disagreements that have marked the relationship's downward path. Yet what changed the relationship far more than any disagreements themselves was a shift in the way Russian leaders understood them. Many events played a part in this transformation—the Iraq war, the Orange Revolution in Ukraine, and soaring energy prices, among others. From them, Putin and his colleagues seem to have drawn very different conclusions from those of 2002—namely, that Russia's relations with the United States (and the West in general) were inherently unequal and conflictual and that Russia would better serve its interests if it followed its own course.

As officials in the next U.S. administration examine the individual pieces of a U.S.-Russian relationship gone bad, they will have many reasons to consider specific changes in policy. On issues ranging from the military balance to democracy promotion to Russia's relations with its neighbors, new U.S. policymakers will review what is working and what is not and try to fashion a new and more productive relationship. The most significant obstacle they will face, however, is not the complexity of the individual issues in dispute—many of those are, actually, exceedingly simple. It is the fact that Russia's leaders have gone a long way toward reconceiving the relationship. In their view, common interests and strategic compatibility are no longer at its core.

The Return of Arms Control

The impact of Russia's new strategic outlook will be particularly evident when the next U.S. administration reviews U.S. arms control policy. The East-West treaties on nuclear and conventional weapons negotiated at the end of the Cold War have caused a more massive and more dramatic reshaping of military forces than is generally recognized. Since 1990, with little fanfare and virtually no opposition on either side, the number of Russian nuclear warheads on intercontinental ballistic missiles—which make up the largest part of Russia's nuclear force—has been cut by almost 70 percent. Also with no controversy, the largest part of the United States' strategic nuclear force—weapons deployed on submarines—has been cut by almost 50 percent. Cuts in conventional forces have been even more dramatic: the number of U.S. tanks in Europe has dropped from over 5,000 to 130; Germany has eliminated more than 5,000 tanks of its own; Russia, over 4,000; and the Czech Republic, Hungary, Poland, and Ukraine, together almost 8,000 tanks. With all this dismantling going on, the U.S.-Russian military balance gradually became the quietest corner of the relationship.

Now, however, arms control is back at center stage. One reason is the calendar: the two treaties on U.S.-Russian strategic arms reductions will expire during the next U.S. president's term. But far more important is Moscow's altered view of what is at stake. The former chief of the Russian general staff, Yuri Baluyevsky, declared earlier this year that U.S. nuclear policies reflect a "drive for strategic domination." Ignoring the ongoing decline in military forces across Europe, Putin has charged that other states are taking advantage of Russia's peaceful nature to wage an "arms race" (and on this basis, in December 2007 he suspended Russia's compliance with the Treaty on Conventional Armed Forces in Europe). Russian officials also insist that the U.S. missile defense system planned for deployment in eastern Europe after 2012 is, despite Washington's denials, designed to neutralize Russia's strategic deterrent. To thwart this, they say, Russia must deploy nuclear forces that restore it to a position of rough equality with the United States. "National security," Putin and his successor as president, Dmitry Medvedev, have taken to saying, "is not based on promises."

Many U.S. foreign policy specialists look at the return of arms control with a mixture of boredom and regret. Most stopped viewing Russia as an interesting security problem years ago. In the U.S. military, Russian issues are no longer where the promotions are. When civilian experts bother with the issue of strategic arms reductions, it is usually not because they think that the U.S.-Russian strategic balance matters but because they want to revive attention to some related issue, such as "loose" nuclear weapons and materials or the need for the United States and Russia to strengthen nonproliferation efforts by making large cuts in their own arsenals. It is telling that the most significant arms control idea of recent years, advanced by the Cold War veterans Kissinger, Sam Nunn, William Perry, and George Shultz, has been nuclear abolition. Mere nuclear parity apparently bores them, too.

Hostility to old-style arms control and inattention to the growing mismatch between U.S. and Russian thinking on national security clearly led the Bush administration to mishandle these issues with Moscow. Merely dismissing Moscow's charges that the U.S. missile defense plans threaten Russia's security has not stopped the Russians from objecting—or from winning the sympathy of some U.S. allies. Washington proposed allowing Russian military monitors at the U.S. missile defense sites in the Czech Republic and Poland, but the Czechs and the Poles opposed this plan, giving Moscow one more reason to complain.

To keep military issues from becoming a continuing source of U.S.-Russian discord, the next U.S. president will want to adopt a different approach. He will surely drop his predecessor's resistance to formal and legally binding arms control agreements. Yet both Washington and Moscow will further benefit by preserving some elements of the Bush administration's outlook—above all, the recognition that the treaties that work best are those that allow each side maximum flexibility in implementation. If both sides can also agree that their military forces do not really threaten each other, they will not have to sweat every detail over limiting them.

On this basis, arms control could once more become the easy part of the U.S.-Russian agenda. Washington and Moscow would face no real obstacles to the quick negotiation of a new strategic arms treaty that preserved the framework of existing treaties while making further (although probably small) cuts. The current impasse over conventional forces might also be resolved, which could result in bringing more states into the treaty, lowering the caps on major weapons systems, and easing the restrictions on deployments within a country's own boundaries (the last a feature that the Russians have long and loudly denounced as "colonial"). On missile defense, an understanding could be easily reached that offered Russia concrete and binding commitments that U.S. deployment plans would not be fully implemented if the threat from Iran did not grow; for its part, Moscow would not try to block them if the threat did grow.

This should not turn out to be a completely fanciful forecast. Putin quietly laid the groundwork for such an agreement on missile defense in the statement that he and Bush issued in the Black Sea port of Sochi last spring. In it, Putin declared that the conditions Washington had offered to place on the deployment and operation of its radars and interceptors in eastern Europe would, if fully and sincerely put into practice, "assuage" Russia's concerns. Although this language will hardly keep Putin from trying to get still better terms from a new U.S. administration, his approach does suggest that Russia's leaders do not necessarily believe the charges they level against Washington.

Resolving outstanding disagreements on nuclear and other security issues would not remove all the contentious issues in U.S.-Russian relations, much less revive the consensus of 2002. But it would achieve what arms control advocates claimed to want in the latter years of the Cold War: a measure of predictability and mutual confidence in the relationship. And for now, that would be progress enough.

Why, then, is it so hard to imagine such a new round of agreements? Many of the major players in Russian domestic politics have benefited from the new atmosphere that Moscow's angry zero-sum rhetoric has created: the military leaders whose budget has grown by almost 500 percent since 2000, the political leaders who have made suspicion of the outside world a kind of ersatz regime ideology, the bureaucrats and businesspeople who say that reviving the defense industry will require continued infusions of state funds. None of these groups will change course except very reluctantly. The balance of power between the United States and Russia may matter to them, but the balance of power within Russian politics matters even more. Until Russia's domestic situation changes, it may be a long time before military issues again become the quiet corner of U.S.-Russian relations.

Democracy After Bush

The next U.S. president will inevitably review a second issue that has been part of the growing contentiousness of U.S.-Russian relations: democratic reform. Like arms control, this issue played a large role in the international transformation that followed the Cold War. At that time, governments across eastern Europe, Moscow included, saw the embrace of Western ideology and institutions as the path to international acceptance and even self-respect. Few questioned the idea that multilateral forums should define democratic norms and practices, such as the criteria for judging whether elections were free and fair. There was simply no other way for a government to show that it had broken with the past.

Both Bush and Putin have fundamentally altered the role of this issue in U.S.-Russian relations. Bush made it all too easy to portray his "freedom agenda" as a hypocritical tool for advancing narrow U.S. interests. And Putin built his popularity in part on the idea that foreigners have no right to judge Russia's political system. His slogan "sovereign democracy" offered a nationalist cover for arbitrary and centralized rule. Western criticism may have strengthened Putin's appeal and helped him tar his domestic opponents as disloyal and subversive.

No matter how much the next U.S. president deplores Putin's success, he cannot ignore it. Making criticism of Russian democracy a strong theme of U.S. foreign policy no longer enhances respect for either democracy or the United States in Russia. In its waning years, the Bush administration has itself retreated to intermittent and perfunctory treatment of the issue, usually through statements by low-ranking officials. A new president who hopes for a fresh start in relations with Moscow will get advice from many directions to avoid tough ideological rhetoric. From his own diplomats and analysts, he will hear that

Medvedev, whatever the limitations on his power, has been a thoughtful and consistent advocate of the rule of law and other liberal reforms—and has on occasion (gently) criticized Putin's record. From members of Russia's democratic opposition, he will hear that it is not the job of Washington—or any other foreign government—to advance democracy in their country. (All they ask is that Americans not undercut them by suggesting—or, worse, believing—that Russia is a democracy.) And from European governments, he will hear that the success of democracy promotion depends on de-Americanizing the brand.

The next U.S. administration, then, will have good reasons to make the issue of democracy a less contentious part of U.S.-Russian relations. There is no surprise in this: the old approach was not working. But will treating Russia more like, say, Kazakhstan—as a nondemocracy ready for practical cooperation—actually improve U.S.-Russian relations? Although removing an irritant ought to help matters, it is worth noting that it was not simply U.S. policy that made the issue difficult. From Putin on down, Russian leaders have actually continued to put heavy emphasis on their ideological estrangement from the West even as Americans and Europeans have started to pay less attention to democracy. The reason is simple. Confrontation on this issue has paid enormous political dividends. Russians who think it can keep doing so will not want to drop it just because a new U.S. administration is tempted to give it a rest.

Whose Sphere of Influence?

When Russian tanks rolled across a neighbor's borders this past summer, they forced new choices on U.S. policymakers: how and how much to support a small Western nation with no chance of resisting a Russian invasion. Yet even if the choices were new, the policy behind them was not. From the moment the Soviet Union collapsed, it was the policy of the United States and its Western allies to give Russia's neighbors, like other postcommunist states, a chance to integrate themselves into the Western world. In the 1990s, states of the former Soviet Union—unlike Hungary and Poland, or even Bulgaria and Romania—were not considered good candidates for the ultimate prize: full membership in the European Union and NATO. But they enjoyed many other forms of support from the West: sponsorship of oil and gas pipelines that provided access to international markets, the encouragement of foreign direct investment, mediation efforts to resolve separatist disputes, technical advice to speed accession to the World Trade Organization, training and equipment to combat drug trafficking and nuclear smuggling, cooperation on intelligence and counterterrorism, and funding for nongovernmental election-monitoring groups. All these were the same tools that the United States employed in its relations with Russia, and their goal was also the same: to encourage the emergence of somewhat modern-looking, somewhat European-looking political and economic systems from the post-Soviet rubble.

At first, this U.S. policy did not threaten U.S.-Russian relations. But then, something unexpected happened: Russia's neighbors began to succeed. In the past five years, the economic growth of many former Soviet states has outstripped Russia's own. While Russia became less democratic, several of its neighbors made important political breakthroughs. All of them began to seek ties with the West that would bring them out of Moscow's shadow, and two—Georgia and Ukraine—have sought to lay claim to membership in the European Union and NATO.

In part because U.S. policy had not really changed over time, Washington probably underestimated the significance of encouraging such aspirations. It surely underrated the single-mindedness of Russia's opposition. With its own economy reviving, Moscow sought to block Western pipeline projects and to close off the West's military access to air bases in Central Asia. It accused Western nongovernmental organizations of trying to destabilize Russia's neighbors. And in April, Putin labeled the further enlargement of NATO "a direct threat to the security of our country."

In all this, the United States and Europe misjudged their ability to help Russia's neighbors slip into the Western orbit without a full-blown international crisis. Now that there has been a test of strength, and Russian strength has prevailed, many of the tools of Western policy are severely damaged. Those NATO members that had endorsed eventual membership for Georgia or Ukraine are now divided on the issue. Those former Soviet states that had viewed closer cooperation with NATO (even without membership in the alliance) as a critical lifeline to the outside world now wonder whether this is still a good idea. Energy producers in Central Asia that were considering new pipelines outside the Russian network may see such projects as too risky. Western mediation efforts are on hold along Russia's entire periphery; in Georgia, they are dead.

Yet whatever else Putin has accomplished in his pummeling of Georgia, he has failed at the most important thing. Even as Russian leaders have begun to speak openly about their desire for a sphere of influence, their actions have made Russia's acquisition of such a sphere less, not more, acceptable to the United States and Europe. It is now necessary to consider whether Russia's invasion marks the beginning of a concerted drive by Moscow to restore its influence over other post-Soviet states. In the past, such a revival might have seemed undesirable in the West for sentimental reasons. Today, the reasons are more serious. There can be no doubt that a Russia that dominated an industrial powerhouse such as Ukraine, an energy storehouse such as Kazakhstan, and the other pieces of the old Soviet Union as well would change the national security calculations of virtually all the world's leading states.

Because the stakes are high, simple prudence will oblige the next U.S. administration to move cautiously. Whatever Washington embarks on now, it must be able to carry through, and that rules out overreaching. To have broader options down the road, U.S. policymakers must offer Georgia, in the short term, effective humanitarian relief; then, support for economic stabilization and reconstruction; and, after that, help in restoring the country's armed forces. As such steps begin to succeed, the question of Georgia's membership in NATO will arise again. Georgia deserves a place in the Western alliance, but nothing will do more harm to Georgia's security than to raise the issue before NATO is ready with an answer.

Rebuilding Georgia—and rebuilding a policy that gives post-Soviet states a place in the Western world—must be the first order of business for the next U.S. administration. There is no other way to deal seriously with the wreckage created by Russian aggression. But in making this effort, the United States and its European allies will have to wrestle with a seeming paradox: in the past, the United States was able to do more for Russia's neighbors when its own relations with Moscow were good (and the neighbors' relations with Moscow were at least civil). For the foreseeable future, U.S.-Russian relations will not be good, and that will impose a serious burden on U.S. policy. There is no way to break cleanly out of this box, but to do so at all, the United States needs to regain the diplomatic initiative. It needs ideas and proposals that can blunt Russia's recent strategy while offering Moscow a different path to international influence.

As it happens, the Russians themselves may have put forward the most readily usable idea of this kind. Before the war against Georgia, in his most substantive foray into foreign policy to date, President Medvedev called for a new conference on European security, explicitly harking back to the diplomacy of the mid-1970s, out of which the Helsinki Final Act emerged. To be sure, his goals seemed a little too much like those of the Soviet leader Leonid Brezhnev, who hoped that a conference on "security and cooperation" would bring Western recognition of the division of Europe. For his part, Medvedev wants recognition of the Commonwealth of Independent States, the Collective Security Treaty Organization, and other arrangements that link Moscow to a number of post-Soviet states. And like Brezhnev, who lived to see Helsinki become a banner for opponents of the Soviet regime, Medvedev might discover that such a forum, whatever its short-term propaganda value, would give other governments a chance to put Russia's conduct in the spotlight and promote principles that would make the realization of its would-be imperium harder to achieve.

With Georgia still bleeding from defeat, the idea of exploring proposals whose clear aim is to consolidate Russia's gains, devalue and constrain NATO, and close off avenues to the outside world for Russia's neighbors may seem untimely, even defeatist. And yet the United States and its allies should not forget that they have permanent advantages in diplomatic enterprises of this kind. It is not easy to imagine a European security conference, now or in the future, in which Russia would not be isolated by its own behavior. Would anyone but Russia oppose the principle that all states are free to join alliances of their own choosing? Which states could Russia count on to object to a reaffirmation of Georgia's sovereignty and territorial integrity? Who would support Russia's idea that having waged war against Georgia, its own forces should now assume the mantle of peacekeepers? Who would agree with Putin's view, expressed openly to Bush, that "Ukraine isn't even a state"?

Policymakers in Moscow claim that Russia simply wants to sit at the high table of global diplomacy, to be a rule maker and norm setter for the international order. They seem to believe that a European security conference, even a European security treaty, would strengthen Russia's sphere of influence. They want to show that when they speak, they get a hearing. Such aims and expectations may produce only stalemate. Yet the process would not be a waste of time if it did nothing more than demonstrate that Russia's ideas and conduct are at odds with the opinions of all the other participants. The next U.S. administration should therefore look carefully at Russia's proposals, consult with its friends and allies, hold exploratory conversations, seek clarifications, bracket ideas it does not like, and so forth. Then it should accept Medvedev's idea with pleasure.

Conflict of Interests

"That's one of the tragedies of this life—that the men who are most in need of a beating up are always enormous," says one of the characters in the 1942 Preston Sturges film *The Palm Beach Story*. The same is true of the new predicament of U.S. foreign policy. Russia seems to be on an increasingly confrontational course, powered by a bristlier conception of its interests than at any time since the end of the Cold War, by domestic political arrangements that appear to feed on international tension, and by an enhanced ability to stand its ground. Neither Russia's power nor Russia's aims should be exaggerated. Its new strength has a narrow, even precarious base, and its new goals may be reconsidered if the cost of pursuing them gets too high. But in the wake of the war in Georgia, a more disturbing outcome seems likely to prevail. Russia's power may actually keep growing, and carry the country's ambitions with it.

As the United States' involvement in Iraq begins to wind down, U.S. policymakers and U.S. commentators alike have started to wonder about the array of problems that Washington will have to deal with next. Will it wrestle with new and deferred difficulties against a backdrop of largely cooperative ties with other major powers, or are such relations turning more conflictual? If conflict becomes the new norm, how hard will it be to manage it in ways that serve U.S. interests? Sooner than expected, Russia has given Americans a feel for the answers.

POSTSCRIPT

Should the United States Allow Russia More Leeway in Eurasia in Exchange for Russian Help in Stopping Iran's Nuclear Program?

In the 2008 presidential campaign and in his administration's early months in office, President Obama has called for hitting the "reset button" and trying to improve U.S.-Russian relations and cooperation on a variety of fronts. At the same time, Obama criticized Russia's intervention in Georgia during the campaign and made clear that U.S. plans for missile defenses in Poland and the Czech Republic would be driven by whether such defenses were technically feasible and whether Iran continued with its evident nuclear weapons program, rather than by Russian objections. Some limited cooperation between the two countries emerged with the first U.S. supply convoy to Afghanistan passing through Russia and other former Soviet republics in March 2009, but whether there is to be any kind of implicit or explicit "grand bargain" between the United States and Russia, and what the terms of such a bargain might be, remains to be seen.

For books on Russia and its relations with the United States, see Edward Lucas, *The New Cold War: Putin's Russia and the Threat to the West* (Palgrave McMillan 2008); Marshall Goldman, *Petrostate: Putin, Power, and the New Russia* (Oxford, 2008); Dmitri Trenin, *Getting Russia Right* (Carnegie Endowment for International Peace, 2007); and James Goldgeier and Michael McFaul, *Power and Purpose: U.S. Policy Toward Russian After the Cold War* (Brookings, 2003). For articles on these subjects, see Ronald Asmus, "Europe's Eastern Promise; Rethinking NATO and EU Enlargement," *Foreign Affairs*, New York (January/February 2008); and Robert Blackwill, "The Three Rs: Rivalry, Russia, 'Ran," *The National Interest* (January/February 2008).

Internet References . . .

The World Factbook

A first step toward better knowledge of the regional and bilateral policy concerns of the United States is to learn more about the other countries and political entities in the world. An excellent source, and one that is updated annually, is *The World Factbook*, which is a product of the Central Intelligence Agency. It can be bought from the commercial publishing house that prints it or it can be found at this site.

https://www.cia.gov/library/publications/the-world-factbook/index.html

International Information Programs

This Web site is operated by the U.S. Department of State's Office of International Information Programs. The site is divided into regional groups, among other things, and it gives a good array of the regional issues that are of current foreign policy concern.

http://www.america.gov/

Editor & Publisher

It is always good advice in diplomacy and other endeavors to try to see yourself as others see you. The publication *Editor & Publisher* has an excellent Web site to sample the foreign media newspapers, magazines, radio, television, and wire services. You can search by region, media types, and other categories.

http://www.editorandpublisher.com

Carnegie Endowment for International Peace

The Carnegie Endowment for International Peace is a good source for research, publications, and conferences regarding the relations among governments, business, international organizations, and civil society across different regions. It focuses on the economic, political, and technological forces driving global change.

http://www.carnegieendowment.org/

Brookings Institution

The Brookings Institution provides nonpartisan perspectives and expertise on issues facing the United States. It has focused on issues including improving the equity of the American democratic process, the performance of the economy, the health of society, the effectiveness of diplomacy and defense, the quality of public discourse, and the workings of institutions—public and private, domestic and international.

http://www.brookings.edu

The United States and the World: Regional and Bilateral Relations

*T*he debates in this section address some of the issues in American foreign policy that relate to various countries in different regions of the world. The range of issues include the difficulties of allying strategically with countries whose practices or policies otherwise run counter to U.S. ideals; determining how and when to act as a broker between groups engaged in ongoing regional struggles; managing relations with countries that have been hostile and could again become antagonistic toward the United States; and developing economic and political relations with countries with whom the United States shares common objectives in some areas and divergent objectives in others.

- Should the United States Challenge a Rising China?

- Should the United States Seek Negotiations and Engagement with North Korea?

- Should the United States Engage Hamas?

- Should the United States Contribute to a NATO Peacekeeping Force to Encourage and Guarantee an Israeli–Palestinian Peace?

- Should the United States Continue Sanctions on Cuba?

- Is Loosening Immigration Regulations Good for the United States?

ISSUE 8

Should the United States Challenge a Rising China?

YES: Aaron L. Friedberg, from "Are We Ready for China?" *Commentary* (October 2007)

NO: Christopher Layne, from "China's Challenge to US Hegemony," *Current History* (January 2008)

ISSUE SUMMARY

YES: Aaron L. Friedberg is a professor of politics and international affairs at Princeton University and director of Princeton's Research Program in International Security. He served in the Office of the Vice President of the United States as deputy assistant for national security affairs and director of policy planning from 2003 to 2005. He argues that the United States should respond to China's rising strength and soft power with a strategy that includes intensified efforts to maintain a favorable balance of power by reinforcing existing alliances and institutions, building bilateral relations with major states in Asia, and maintaining forces sufficient to deter and, if necessary, defeat China militarily.

NO: Christopher Layne is a professor at Texas A&M University's George H. W. Bush School of Government and Public Service. He argues that a U.S.–P.R.C. military conflict is certain if the United States tries to maintain its dominance in Asia, but that such a conflict can be avoided if the United States engages in offshore balancing, relying more on regional powers to counter China, and using force only in the face of direct threats to vital American interests.

T he relationship between the United States and China has been aptly described as one involving constructive ambiguity. The ambiguity derives from the multiple dimensions of American-Chinese interaction. At one level, the relationship involves two dominant powers with high levels of trade and monetary interdependence and increasing societal and cultural ties, who share common interests in a variety of issues ranging from fighting terrorism to maintaining stability in the global economy. On another level, it involves two dominant military and political powers with very different historical backgrounds who were key players occasionally on opposing sides of the bipolar world during the Cold War, the vestiges of which remain and are most visible in their ongoing discussions regarding the status of the people on the island of Taiwan and the divided Korean peninsula. On yet another level, it is the relationship between one country that defines itself in terms of liberal economic and political principles and another that has undergone a dramatically successful economic liberalization but continues to govern itself through a highly centralized political system and harshly repressed demonstrations in Tiananmen Square in 1989 and, more recently, in Hong Kong to counter societal movements toward democratization. It is also a relationship between a superpower with the most advanced military in the world and a growing regional power seeking to modernize its military capabilities, both of whom, despite their capabilities, are cognizant of their vulnerability in the current strategic environment. The ambiguity created by these and other dimensions of the American-Chinese relationship have been constructive to the extent that since the Sino-American rapprochement of 1971–1972, the two countries have managed tensions between themselves and developed a deeper and increasingly complex relationship.

Current dramatic events in the international arena have created new opportunities and risks for U.S.-Chinese relations. These events include the disintegration of the Soviet Union and the Warsaw Treaty Organization, the worldwide recognition of China as a major economic and political power as symbolized by its entry into the World Trade Organization and increasingly active roles in the United Nations the potential nuclear conflict between Pakistan and India, the importance of Pakistan in U.S. actions in Afghanistan and Iraq, the resurgence of U.S. involvement abroad in its fight against global terrorism, ongoing U.S. and regional concerns about North Korea, and increasing calls from the people of Taiwan for political independence. U.S. and Chinese responses to these events are likely to make the ambiguity in their relationship more difficult to maintain. Whether specificity in U.S.-Chinese relations will reveal a relationship that is more cooperative or competitive is a matter of debate.

Aaron L. Friedberg argues that increasing uncertainty about China's future, the success of its soft power, and its growing hard power make it critical for the United States to maintain a strong balance of power position in Asia. In contrast, Christopher Layne argues that such a strategy will lead to a Sino-American war. To avoid such an outcome, the United States should engage in offshore balancing and engage the P.R.C. directly only when vital American interests are at stake.

YES ↵

Aaron L. Friedberg

Are We Ready for China?

Though our leaders are loath to admit it, the United States is almost two decades into what is likely to prove a protracted geopolitical rivalry with the People's Republic of China. The PRC is fast acquiring military capabilities that will allow it to contest America's long-standing preponderance in the Western Pacific. In Asia and beyond, Beijing is working assiduously to enhance its own influence while at the same time seeking quietly to weaken that of the United States. Meanwhile, China continues to run huge trade surpluses with the United States, accumulating vast dollar holdings and advancing rapidly up the technological ladder into ever more sophisticated industries.

In recent years, China has managed to challenge America's preeminence in virtually every domain while at the same time drawing closer to it, establishing warm relations even with administrations that start out suspicious, if not downright hostile. How has Beijing accomplished this feat of diplomatic legerdemain? Part of the answer, of course, is that since 9/11 Washington has been preoccupied with other troubles: fighting terrorism, trying to stem the further spread of nuclear weapons, and attempting to extricate U.S. forces from Iraq. American policymakers have had their hands full in the last six years, and this has dampened whatever impulse they might otherwise have had to respond vigorously to China's initiatives.

But the problem runs deeper than this. Instead of attempting a premature, frontal assault on America's strategic position, Beijing has taken a low-key, indirect approach, using newly acquired instruments to chip away at its foundations. The extent of China's challenge has thus been difficult to assess and easy to ignore. This tendency toward denial has been reinforced by a set of widely held, rosy assumptions about that country's future. At least until recently, the consensus view among experts has been that China's economic growth is leading it rapidly and inexorably toward political reform. In light of this fact, the United States need only maintain cordial relations, trade and invest, and let nature take its course.

But suppose these assumptions are wrong. What if the PRC continues to grow wealthier and stronger without making the transition to liberal democracy? Could a rich, authoritarian China use its newfound power and influence to reshape the world in its own image? Two books by astute China-watching journalists help readers wrestle with these troubling possibilities.

Reprinted from *Commentary*, Vol. 124, no. 3, October 2007, pp. 39–43, by permission of Commentary and Aaron L. Friedberg. Copyright © 2007 by Commentary, Inc. All rights reserved.

Joshua Kurlantzick has spent the better part of the last decade reporting on China's activities in Southeast Asia. *Charm Offensive: How China's Soft Power Is Transforming the World,* his engaging and informative new book, summarizes what he found there as well as noting some similar developments in other regions.

As his title suggests, Kurlantzick believes that China has embarked on a deliberate "charm offensive" aimed at extending its influence while reassuring others about its rise. Instead of trying to intimidate its neighbors into passivity and submission, as it did in the first half of the 90's, Beijing now hopes to woo them to its side.

This shift began during the Asian financial crisis of 1997. While Washington remained aloof, or urged painful reforms, Beijing won points by refusing to devalue its currency, thereby helping to speed a regional recovery. In the wake of the crisis, China shifted its approach to Southeast Asia and to other parts of the developing world. Where the United States was often harsh and judgmental, demanding liberalization of markets and politics, China was studiously neutral, willing to deal with anyone and eager to engage authoritarian holdouts (especially those with oil like Venezuela and Iran) that Washington sought to isolate.

As Kurlantzick describes, in recent years Beijing has deployed a new generation of sophisticated and well-trained diplomats, even to countries that the U.S. treats as backwaters. China has also sought to promote the study of its language and culture by setting up "Confucius Institutes," attracting foreign students to its universities, and building ties with ethnic Chinese business elites across Southeast Asia.

In addition to the "tools of culture," Beijing has also used the "tools of business" to win friends and influence people. Developing nations are eager to trade their minerals, food, and raw materials for China's inexpensive consumer goods. Most also welcome Chinese investment in their industries and infrastructure, and official aid that comes with no "good-governance" strings attached. Some may even look to China as an example. In the 1960's and 70's, Maoist China styled itself a leader of world revolution. At least implicitly, today's China offers a very different model, one that promises embattled autocrats that they, too, can retain their grip on power while enjoying the benefits of rapid economic growth.

To what extent does all of this reflect a deliberate strategy? How well is it working? And what difference does it make to the United States? Kurlantzick wrestles with all of these questions. But perhaps inevitably, given ambiguities in the evidence and uncertainties about the future, his answers are less than definitive.

China's "smile diplomacy" and its deployment of the "tools of culture" are clearly elements in a purposeful, government-directed campaign to reassure, charm, and gain influence. Whether the diverse, far-flung transactions of Chinese firms are also part of a larger plan is less apparent. As Kurlantzick notes, most of these companies are not simply tools of the regime and "may make decisions based on corporate rather than national interests." On the other hand, Kurlantzick maintains that "the government has some significant degree of oversight" over what Chinese businesses are doing, even if it is not directing their every move.

The recent explosion in overseas Chinese business activity is driven, in the first instance, by commercial considerations and, in particular, by the need for resources. Still, Beijing has clearly been quick to recognize and to seek to exploit the new opportunities for political influence presented by its growing global activity. What remains to be seen is whether China, like other great powers of the past, will adopt more interventionist foreign policies to protect and promote its increasingly sprawling commercial interests. Nineteenth-century theorists of empire believed that "trade follows the flag." Today the reverse is more likely to be true.

As to whether China's "charm offensive" has been effective, Kurlantzick reports expressions of enthusiasm for the "Chinese model" from strongmen like Ayatollah Khameini and Raoul Castro. But these are hard to take seriously. Others may wish to mimic China's mix of economic growth and political stasis, but, at least so far, its leaders have been circumspect about urging foreigners to follow in their footsteps. They appear to realize that the preconditions for their own success (including an enormous supply of low-wage workers and vast, efficient internal-security forces) are unusual, if not unique.

Kurlantzick also cites opinion polls that show China's popularity rising in various places, even as America's has declined. But these are notoriously fickle measures of "soft power." China is enjoying a honeymoon of sorts, and its appeal is due almost entirely to its phenomenal economic performance. As Kurlantzick notes, "Any slippage would cost it dearly in soft power." Even now there are signs of a backlash in Africa, where Chinese firms, like their Western predecessors, find themselves accused of exploiting workers and stripping natural resources. As its face becomes more familiar, some of China's "charm" will begin to fade.

Still, on balance, there can be little doubt that China's growth and dynamism have made it far more attractive, and more influential, than it was only a decade ago. Is this a good or a bad thing for America and the world? Kurlantzick says hopefully that "Beijing could wield its soft power responsibly" by resolving international disputes and embracing multilateral institutions. But he notes that China's growing influence could also be used to malign effect, shielding aspiring proliferators like Iran from American pressure, building a sphere of influence in Central Asia, prodding "countries like the Philippines or Thailand . . . to downgrade their close relations with the United States," and seeking at a minimum to complicate America's relations with some of its most important regional allies, including Australia and South Korea.

Unfortunately, at least for the moment, there is far more evidence of exactly these forms of assertive, competitive behavior than there are signs of growing "responsibility." As long as China is ruled by a one-party dictatorship, and threatened therefore by the mere existence of the United States and neighboring Asian democracies, we are likely to see more of the same in the years ahead.

❧

But how long can the current regime last? In *The China Fantasy: How Our Leaders Explain Away Chinese Repression,* James Mann suggests that the answer could be a depressingly long time. Mann is an experienced observer of China and of U.S.-China relations. He served for three years as Beijing bureau chief for the *Los Angeles Times* and is the author of several justly praised books on American foreign policy. To judge from his writing, Mann is no hawk or hard-liner, but his most recent work is a scathing indictment of American China-watchers, U.S. China policy, and China's one-party Communist dictatorship. Precisely because it states some uncomfortable truths, Mann's book will win him few friends, and has no doubt already made him new enemies on both sides of the Pacific.

Mann makes three central claims, each more controversial than the last. First he maintains that American analysts and policymakers have been mesmerized by what he calls the "Soothing Scenario": the belief that "China's economic development will lead inexorably to an opening of China's political system." This assumption has far-reaching implications. It has caused American observers to misinterpret developments like the organization of village elections and recent moves to strengthen the rule of law. Far from being genuine reforms, these steps are actually designed to shore up the regime. They "create the appearance of change, while leaving the fundamentals of China's political system undisturbed."

The assertion that reform is inevitable, and that it will be the direct result of economic growth, has also served to support a policy of essentially unconditional engagement with China. As Mann notes, since the end of the cold war, "virtually every change in U.S. policy toward China has been justified to the American public on the basis that it would help to open up China's political system." The belief that "everything is going to be fine in the long run" has also permitted American Presidents to "avert their gaze from the Chinese Communist party's continuing repression of all organized opposition."

In fact, as Mann correctly points out, there is no meaningful evidence of liberalization and no sign that it is just around the corner. Precisely because it has become so skillful at coopting or crushing potential opponents, the current regime could remain ensconced for some time to come. And it may have support from some surprising quarters. Contrary to what so many have predicted, China's new middle class appears to be more eager to hold onto its recent gains than to push for potentially disruptive political reforms.

In short, 25 or 30 years from now China could be much wealthier and "fully integrated into the world's economy" while at the same time remaining "entirely undemocratic." Mann is not alone in such speculations. Scholars like Minxin Pei and Edward Friedman have warned that the current regime may prove more tenacious and adaptable than many assume. Still, this scenario and its implications deserve far more attention than they have thus far received from analysts and planners, as does the possibility of regime collapse and disorder. Either one is probably more likely than the Soothing Scenario on which so many hopes now ride.

⚜

Mann's second argument is that the prevailing view of China, and the policies that flow from it, are defended by what he aptly terms a "lexicon of dismissal." Those who criticize China's government for its continuing repression, or raise questions about its strategic intentions, find themselves labeled "China bashers" or "ideologues" in the grips of an obsolete "cold-war mentality." Even worse, they are accused of raising the risk of conflict by violating the prime directive of China policy. "Treat China like a threat," goes this bit of conventional wisdom, "and it will become one."

Mann astutely observes that American China specialists tend to see them-selves as the embattled defenders of reason and prudence, struggling to hold back powerful forces—labor unions, human-rights groups, left-wing Demo-crats, and right-wing Republicans—that would otherwise tear the U.S.-China relationship apart. Casting their minds back to the early 1950's and the ugly era of McCarthyism, these China hands fear "the old specter, that Congress and American public opinion might become too aroused about China." They are therefore strongly motivated to squelch debate and head off possible challenges to current policy.

Yet their feelings of vulnerability comport oddly with the fact that, for over 30 years, in both Republican and Democratic administrations, advocates of engagement have held "most, if not all, of the top positions for China policy" and filled almost all of the working-level positions at the White House, State Department, CIA, and even the Pentagon. Moreover, Mann writes, "most of the China scholars at American universities and think tanks also strongly support the idea of engagement, as do the chairmen and chief executives of most Fortune 500 companies." If there is a struggle over China policy, it is clear who occupies the high ground.

All of this leads to Mann's most explosive claim: "The proclivity of American elites to refrain from public criticism of China's repressive system is reinforced all the more by the influence of money." Think tanks get hefty donations from companies doing business in China. High-ranking politicians and government officials know that if they work on China issues and "don't become identified as critics of the regime," they can move on to lucrative careers as advisers and consultants to those same corporations. Even academic China specialists can make money on the side by playing similar roles.

It is neither necessary nor entirely fair to invoke pecuniary motives to explain the views of many of the former diplomats and scholars Mann cites, including Henry Kissinger, Brent Scowcroft, Madeleine Albright, William Cohen, and former Clinton aide and University of Michigan professor Kenneth Lieber-thal. Long before the China trade became so lucrative, most of these people expressed views very similar to those they hold now. And there is no reason to doubt that they are sincere in believing that the policies they prefer are best for their country and most likely to keep the peace.

Still, Mann has put his finger on a real problem. China's growth has increased the country's influence in the developing world, but it has also enhanced Beijing's ability to shape American perceptions and preferences. The hope that China will soon change, and the assurance that, in the meantime, there is a great deal of money to be made, have helped lull many in this country into a state of comfortable complacency.

⚜

But complacency is not something we can afford. China's rising strength and increasing uncertainty about its future make it necessary for the United States to pursue a strategy that mixes engagement (and a continuing search for effective means of encouraging political reform) with intensified efforts to maintain a favorable balance of power. As a first step, Washington needs to reinforce the foundations of its regional position by continuing to tend to existing alliances and quasi-alliances. Among other things, this will mean sustaining the momentum that has been gained in recent years with Japan, India, and Australia, working to improve the strained alliance with South Korea, and, with all due delicacy, restoring trust and communication with Taiwan.

In addition to strengthening bilateral ties, Washington should also do what it can to encourage existing tendencies toward the formation of a largely informal, multilayered network of cooperative ties among various combinations of Asian states: Japan and Australia, Japan and India, India and Australia, and so on. There is no appetite now for a formal "Asian NATO," but closer links among the region's democracies are both desirable and feasible.

Nor should such linkages be limited to Asia. In recent years, European nations have increased their economic engagement in the region and, in particular, with China. As Europe's stakes grow, active efforts will be required to make sure that it is not working at cross purposes to the United States, Japan, and the other Asian democracies. The recent trans-Atlantic tussle over whether the EU should lift its post-Tiananmen arms embargo on China is an indication of possible future tensions over trade and technology-transfer issues.

Last, but by no means least, the United States will need to develop, deploy, and maintain forces that are capable of deterring and if necessary defeating China's growing "anti-access" capabilities, which are designed to push the U.S. military back from the Western Pacific. And it must do so even as it continues to wage a prolonged war against Islamist terrorism and prepares for possible nearer-term conflicts with nuclear (or near-nuclear) rogue states.

Doing all of these things, while at the same time trading and talking with China, will not be easy. The difficulties are partly conceptual: Americans are used to dividing the world neatly into friends (who have been our major trading partners, as well as our military allies) and enemies (with whom we have typically dealt very little). China does not fall cleanly into either category, and, unless it moves sharply toward democracy or open hostility, it will not do so for some time to come.

There will also be practical challenges to maintaining the right mix of engagement and balancing. The former is both pleasurable and profitable, while the latter is difficult and costly. Every one of the steps described above will evoke criticisms and warnings not only from China but from those in this country who make it their business to interpret Beijing's anxieties and intentions. There is a real danger that, as a result of inertia, misplaced optimism, and a desire to avoid being "provocative" or creating "self-fulfilling prophecies," the United States will allow the balancing side of its mixed policy to atrophy.

If China stays on its current path, if it continues to grow richer and stronger while remaining autocratic, it will likely become bolder, more assertive, and possibly more aggressive than it is today. If the United States wishes to preserve its present military, diplomatic, and technological advantages, it will have to compete much more vigorously and deliberately than it has been doing in recent years. We are going to have to run faster just to stay in place. But we are unlikely to do so if we cannot even acknowledge to ourselves that we are in a race.

Christopher Layne

➜ **NO**

China's Challenge to US Hegemony

The Soviet Union's collapse transformed the bipolar cold war international system into a "unipolar" system dominated by the United States. During the 1990s, the US foreign policy community engaged in lively debate about whether America's post–cold war hegemony could be sustained over the long haul or was merely a "unipolar moment." More than 15 years after the cold war's end, it is obvious that American hegemony has been more than momentary. Indeed, the prevailing view among policy makers and foreign policy scholars today is that America's economic, military, and technological advantages are so great that it will be a long time before US dominance can be challenged.

There is mounting evidence, however, that this view is mistaken, and that, in fact, the era of American hegemony is drawing to a close right before our eyes. The rise of China is the biggest reason for this. Notwithstanding Washington's current preoccupation with the Middle East, in the coming decades China's great power emergence will be the paramount issue of grand strategy facing the United States.

Whether China will undergo a "peaceful rise"—as Beijing claims—is doubtful. Historically, the emergence of new poles of power in the international system has been geopolitically destabilizing. For example, the rise of Germany, the United States, and Japan at the end of the nineteenth century contributed to the international political frictions that culminated in two world wars. There is no reason to believe that China's rise will be an exception.

However, while it is certainly true that China's rise will cause geopolitical turmoil, a Sino-American war is not inevitable. Whether such a conflict occurs will hinge more on Washington's strategic choices than on Beijing's.

Rise of a Great Power

From the mid-1980s through the late 1990s China's economy grew at a rate of approximately 10 percent a year. From the late 1990s until 2005 its economy grew at 8 percent to 9 percent annually. In 2006 China's annual growth rate was above 11 percent, as it is projected to be for 2007. China's phenomenal economic growth is driving its emergence as a great power—and this is a familiar pattern in international politics. The economic power of states grows at different rates, which means that some states are always gaining power and some are losing power relative to others. As Paul Kennedy demonstrated in his

From *Current History,* January 2008, pp. 13–18. Copyright © 2008 by Current History, Inc. Reprinted by permission.

1987 book *The Rise and Fall of the Great Powers,* time and again these relative economic shifts have "heralded the rise of new great powers which one day would have a decisive impact on the military/territorial order."

The leadership in Beijing understands the link between economic strength and geopolitical weight. It realizes that, if China can continue to sustain near–double digit growth rates in the early decades of this century, it will surpass the United States as the world's largest economy (measured by gross domestic product). Because of this astonishing economic growth, China is, as journalist James Kynge has put it (with a nod to Napoleon), truly shaking the world both economically *and* geopolitically. Studies by the US Central Intelligence Agency and others have projected that China will be a first-rate military power and will rival America in global power by 2020.

Engage or Contain?

In fact, China's rise has been on the radar screens of US foreign policy experts since the early 1990s. Broadly speaking, the debate about how the United States should respond to China's emergence as a great power has focused on two policy alternatives: engagement and containment.

Engagement assumes that, as China's contacts with the outside world multiply, its exposure to Western (that is, mostly American) political and cultural values will result in evolutionary political change within China. The proponents of engagement believe that the forces of domestic political liberalization and economic globalization will temper Beijing's foreign policy ambitions and lead to a peaceful Sino-American relationship.

On the economic side, the logic of engagement is that, as China becomes increasingly tied to the international economy, its interdependence with others will constrain it from taking political actions that could disrupt its vital access both to foreign markets and capital and to high-technology imports from the United States, Japan, and Western Europe. This was the claim made in the 1990s by the Clinton administration and its supporters during a debate about whether the United States should extend permanent normal trade relations to China and support Beijing's accession to the World Trade Organization.

Proponents of engagement have also argued that the United States can help foster political liberalization in China by integrating the country into the international economy and embedding it in the complex web of international institutional arrangements. A China so engaged, it is said, will have strong interests in cooperation and will not be inclined to pursue security competition with America or with its Asian neighbors.

Engagement is a problematic strategy, however, because it rests on a shaky foundation. The conventional wisdom notwithstanding, there is little support in the historical record for the idea that economic interdependence leads to peace. After all, Europe never was more interdependent (not only economically but also, among the ruling elites, intellectually and culturally) than before World War I. It was famously predicted, on the eve of World War I, that the economic ties among Europe's great powers had ushered in an era in which war among them was unthinkable. Yet, as we know, the prospect of forgoing the economic gains of trade did not stop Europe's great powers from fighting a prolonged and devastating war.

Beijing's actual foreign policy furnishes a concrete reason to be skeptical of the argument that interdependence leads to peace. China's behavior in the 1996 crisis with Taiwan (during which it conducted missile tests in waters surrounding the island in the run-up to Taiwan's presidential election) suggested it was not constrained by fears that its muscular foreign policy would adversely affect its overseas trade.

Of course, during the past decade, China has been mindful of its stake in international trade and investment. But this does not vindicate the US strategy of engagement. China's current policy reflects the fact that, for now, Beijing recognizes its strategic interest in preserving peace in East Asia. Stability in the region, and in Sino-American relations, allows China to become richer and to catch up to the United States in relative power. For a state in China's position vis-à-vis the United States, this is the optimal realpolitik strategy: buying time for its economy to grow so that the nation can openly balance against the United States militarily and establish its own regional hegemony in East Asia. Beijing is pursuing a peaceful policy today in order to strengthen itself to confront the United States tomorrow.

The belief that a democratic—or more liberal—China would be pacific and collaborative in its external policies is similarly dubious. This view rests on the so-called "democratic peace theory" which is near and dear to many US foreign policy experts. In fact, the democratic peace theory is another one of those bits of foreign policy conventional wisdom that is based on flimsy evidence. The historical record demonstrates that when vital national interests have been at risk, democratic states have routinely practiced big-stick diplomacy against other democracies (including threats to use force). In other words, when the stakes are high enough, great powers act like great powers even in their relations with other democracies. Thus, even if China does undergo political liberalization in the future, there is no reason to believe that its foreign policy behavior would be fundamentally affected.

A US containment strategy for China differs from engagement in that it relies mostly on the traditional "hard power" tools of military might and alliance diplomacy to thwart China's great power emergence. Containment calls for the United States to emulate its anti-Soviet cold war strategy by assembling a powerful coalition of states sharing a common interest in curbing rising Chinese power—particularly by tightening the US security relationship with Japan while simultaneously investing that alliance with an overtly anti-Chinese mission. Containment would require the United States to pledge explicitly to defend Taiwan while bolstering Taiwanese military capabilities. Some containment advocates also argue that the United States should engage in covert operations to destabilize China, especially by fomenting unrest among China's ethnic minorities.

To contain China, the United States would maintain both its nuclear and conventional military superiority over China, and would develop a credible first strike option based on a combination of robust offensive nuclear capabilities and effective ballistic missile defenses. Advocates of containment hope that the various measures encompassed by this strategy could halt China's rise and preserve American dominance in East Asia. However, as argued for example by Missouri State University's Bradley A. Thayer, if these steps failed to stop China's great power emergence, the United States would have to consider "harsher measures." In other words, the United States should be prepared to engage in a preventive war against China. Containment, therefore, is a strategy that at best would result in an intense Sino-American security competition. At worst, it could lead to war.

The Actual Strategy

Engagement and containment are "ideal type" grand strategies toward China. In the real world, Washington's actual approach fashions elements of both engagement and containment into a hard-edged grand strategy that requires China to accept US geopolitical and ideological hegemony—or else. In this respect, American policy toward China is the specific manifestation of overall US grand strategy, which rests on both strategic and idealistic pillars.

Strategically, the goal of post–cold war US strategy has been to prevent the emergence of new great powers (or, as the Pentagon calls them, "peer competitors"). This strategy was first articulated in March 1992 in the initial draft of the Pentagon's *Defense Planning Guidance* document for fiscal years 1994–1999. It stated that the goal of US grand strategy henceforth would be to maintain America's preponderance by preventing new great powers from emerging. The United States, it declared, "must maintain the mechanisms for deterring potential competitors from even aspiring to a larger regional or global role."

The Clinton administration similarly was committed to the perpetuation of US preponderance. And the administration of George W. Bush has embraced the hegemonic strategy of its two immediate predecessors. The 2002 *National Security Strategy of the United States* promises that America will act to prevent any other state from building up military capabilities in the hope of "surpassing, or even equaling, the power of the United States."

Ideologically, US grand strategy amounts to "realpolitik-plus," to borrow Brandeis University professor Robert Art's phrase. As such, national interests are defined in terms of both hard power and the promotion of American ideals. As the *National Security Strategy* puts it, US grand strategy is "based on a distinctly American internationalism that reflects the union of our values and our national interests."

Some observers have described this formula as "liberal realism," "national security liberalism," or (as neoconservative pundit Charles Krauthammer puts it) "democratic realism." This sort of liberalism is more muscular and offensive than idealistic. The spread of democracy and economic openness are imbedded in American grand strategic thought because policy makers believe that US power, influence, and security are enhanced in a world comprised of "free market democracies."

America's post–cold war strategy is based firmly on these twin pillars of military superiority and liberal internationalist ideology. And because domestic ideology is the fundamental driver of US grand strategy, America's geopolitical aims transcend those traditionally associated with power politics. Not only does the emergence of a powerful challenger in general threaten America's ability to control its environment, but China in particular is seen as a threat because its politico-economic system challenges America's need for a world compatible with—and safe for—its own liberal ideology. China's rise threatens to close East Asia to US economic and ideological penetration.

Liberalize—or Else

Because of ideology, engagement has a role in US strategy, but it is engagement with (bared) teeth. The United States is willing to give China the opportunity to integrate itself into the US-led international order—on Washington's terms. Thus, as a Pentagon document has put it, the United States wants China to become a "responsible member of the international community." Responsibility, however, is defined as Beijing's willingness to accept Washington's vision of a stable international order. As President Bush declared in a November 2005 speech in Kyoto, responsibility also requires China to achieve political liberalization and develop as a free market economy firmly anchored to the international economy.

Indeed, US policy makers believe that, over the long term, peaceful relations are possible with Beijing *only* if China undergoes domestic political and economic liberalization. As a result, the United States aims to promote China's internal transformation. As the Bush administration's *National Security Strategy* declares: "America will encourage the advancement of democracy and economic openness" in China, "because these are the best foundations for domestic stability and international order." As then–Deputy Secretary of State Robert Zoellick said in 2005, "Closed politics cannot be a permanent feature of Chinese society."

US officials believe that nations such as China that do not adopt American-style political and economic systems, and that do not play by the rules of the American-led international order, are *ipso facto* threats to US interests—threats to which America must be prepared to respond aggressively.

Here is where America's willingness to employ the hard fist of military power against China comes into play. The Bush administration has said it "welcomes a confident, peaceful, and prosperous China that appreciates that its growth and development depend on constructive connections with the rest of the world." At the same time, however, Washington has made crystal clear that it will not countenance a China that emerges as a great power rival and challenges American primacy. The 2002 *National Security Strategy* enjoins Beijing from challenging the United States militarily and warns that, "In pursuing advanced military capabilities that can threaten its neighbors in the Asia-Pacific region, China is following an outdated path that, in the end, will hamper its own pursuit of national greatness. In time, China will find that social and political freedom is the only source of that greatness."

As Washington sees it, China has no justifiable grounds for regarding the US military presence in East Asia as threatening to its interests. Then–Defense Secretary Donald Rumsfeld made this point in 2005 when he stated that any moves by China to enhance its military capabilities necessarily are signals of aggressive Chinese intent. According to Rumsfeld, China's military modernization cannot possibly be defensive because "no nation threatens China." Rumsfeld's view was echoed in the administration's 2005 report on *The Military Power of the People's Republic of China,* which stated that "China's military modernization remains ambitious," and warned that in coming years "China's leaders may be tempted to resort to force or coercion more quickly to press diplomatic advantage, advance security interests, or resolve disputes."

Similarly, at an October 2007 conference on Sino-American relations Admiral Timothy Keating, the commander in chief of the US Pacific Command, made three points with respect to America's China strategy. First, the United States will seek to maintain its present military dominance over China. Second, America will, through arms sales, ensure there is a cross-Strait military balance between Taiwan and China. Third, the United States will not allow China to change the status quo in Taiwan by force. In short, the United States is determined both to make sure that China does not emerge as a peer competitor and to impose itself as an obstacle to China's overriding national goal of reunification with Taiwan.

Strangling the Baby

China's rise affects the United States because of what international relations scholars call the "power transition" effect: Throughout the history of the modern international state system, ascending powers have always challenged the position of the dominant (hegemonic) power in the international system—and these challenges have usually culminated in war. Notwithstanding Beijing's talk about a "peaceful rise," an ascending China inevitably will challenge the geopolitical equilibrium in East Asia. The doctrine of peaceful rise thus is a reassurance strategy employed by Beijing in an attempt to allay others' fears of growing Chinese power and to forestall the United States from acting preventively during the dangerous transition period when China is catching up to the United States.

Does this mean that the United States and China are on a collision course that will lead to a war in the next decade or two? Not necessarily. What happens in Sino-American relations largely depends on what strategy Washington chooses to adopt toward China. If the United States tries to maintain its current dominance in East Asia, Sino-American conflict is virtually certain, because US grand strategy has incorporated the logic of anticipatory violence as an instrument for maintaining American primacy. For a declining hegemon, "strangling the baby in the crib" by attacking a rising challenger preventively—that is, while the hegemon still holds the upper hand militarily—has always been a tempting strategic option.

An Alternative Plan

Washington, however, faces perhaps a last chance to adopt a grand strategy that will serve its interests in ensuring that Chinese power is contained in East Asia but without running the risk of an armed clash with Beijing. This strategy is "offshore balancing," a concept that is finding increasing favor with a group of influential American scholars in the field of security studies. According to this strategy, the United States should deploy military power abroad only in the face of direct threats to vital American interests. The strategy recognizes that Washington need not (and in fact cannot) directly control vast parts of the globe, that it is better off setting priorities based on clear national interests and relying on local actors to uphold regional balances of power. The idea of offshore balancing is to husband national power for maximum effectiveness while minimizing perceptions that this power represents a threat.

As an offshore balancer in East Asia, the United States would embrace a new set of policies regarding Sino-American economic relations, political liberalization in China, the defense of Taiwan, and America's strategic posture in the region.

An offshore balancing strategy would require the United States to approach economic relations with China based on a policy of strategic trade rather than free trade. A strategic trade policy would seek to curtail the flow of high technology and direct investment from the United States to China. It also would require a shift in current US trade policy to drastically reduce the bilateral trade deficit, which is a de facto American subsidy of the very economic growth that is fueling China's great power emergence.

Second, the United States would abandon its efforts to effectuate political liberalization in China. This policy is a form of gratuitous eye-poking. Because the United States lacks sufficient leverage to transform China domestically, the primary effect of trying to force liberalization on China is to inflame Sino-American relations.

An offshore balancing strategy also would require a new US stance on Taiwan, a powder-keg issue because China is committed to national reunification and would regard a Taiwanese declaration of independence as a *casus belli*. If US policy fails to prevent a showdown between China and Taiwan, the odds are that America will be drawn into the conflict because of its current East Asia strategy. There would be strong domestic political pressure in favor of US intervention. Beyond the arguments that Chinese military action against Taiwan would constitute aggression and undermine US interests in a stable world order, powerful incentives for intervention would also arise from ideological antipathy toward China, concerns for maintaining US "credibility," and support for a democratic Taiwan in a conflict with authoritarian China.

Notwithstanding these arguments, which are underpinned by a national security discourse that favors American hegemony, the issues at stake in a possible showdown between China and Taiwan simply would not justify the risks and costs of US intervention. Regardless of the rationale invoked, the contention that the United States should go to war to prevent Beijing from using force to achieve reunification with Taiwan (or in response to a unilateral declaration of independence by Taipei) amounts to nothing more than a veiled argument for fighting a "preventive" war against a rising China.

Sharing the Burden

The final element of a US offshore balancing strategy would be the devolution from the United States to the major powers in Asia of the responsibility for containing China. An offshore balancing strategy would rely on the balance-of-power dynamics of a twenty-first century multipolar global order to prevent China from dominating East Asia. The other major powers in Asia—Japan, Russia, and India—have a much more immediate interest in stopping a rising China in their midst than does the United States.

In a multipolar system, the question is not whether balancing will occur, but which state or states will do the heavy lifting. Because the United States is geographically distant from China—and protected both by the expanse of the Pacific Ocean and by its own formidable military (including nuclear) capabilities—the United States has the option of staying out of East Asian security rivalries (at least initially) and forcing Beijing's neighbors to assume the risks and costs of stopping China from attaining regional hegemony. Because its air and naval power is based on long-range strike capabilities, the United States can keep its forces in an over-the-horizon posture with respect to East Asia and limit itself to a backstopping role in the unlikely event that the regional balance of power falters.

It is hardly surprising—indeed, it parallels in many ways America's own emergence as a great power—that China, the largest and potentially most powerful state in Asia, is seeking a more assertive political, military, and economic role in the region, and even challenging America's present dominance in East Asia. However, this poses no direct threat to US security. Japan, India, and Russia, on the other hand, are worried about the implications of China's rapid ascendance for *their* security. They should bear the responsibility of balancing against Chinese power.

An incipient drift toward multipolarity—which is the prerequisite for the United States to adopt an offshore balancing strategy—is already apparent in East Asia. Driven by fears of US abandonment in a future East Asian crisis, Japan has embarked on a buildup of its military capabilities and has even hinted that it is thinking about acquiring nuclear weapons. Moreover, the past several years have seen a significant escalation in tensions between China and Japan, fueled both by nationalism and by disputes over control of the South China and East China seas (which may contain large energy deposits).

From the standpoint of offshore balancing, Japan's military buildup in response to its fear of China is a good thing if it leads to Japan's reemergence as an independent geopolitical actor. However, Japan's military resurgence is not so good (for the United States) if it takes place under the aegis of the US–Japan security alliance, and if the United States remains in the front lines of the forces containing China. Under those conditions, the United States could find itself ensnared in an Asian conflict; its alliance with Japan risks dragging it into a war with China in which American strategic interests would not be engaged. The idea of an offshore balancing strategy is to get the United States out of China's crosshairs, not to allow it to remain a target because of its present security commitments to allies in the region.

The wisdom of risking war with China to maintain US hegemony in East Asia is all the more doubtful because America's predominance in the region is ebbing in any event. One indication of this is that US economic supremacy in East Asia is waning as China rises. China is emerging as the motor of the region's economic growth.

While the United States has been preoccupied with Iraq, Iran, and the so-called war on terrorism, China has used its burgeoning economic power to extend its political influence throughout East and Southeast Asia. Indeed, most of the smaller states in Southeast Asia are gradually slipping into Beijing's political orbit because their own prosperity is ever more closely tied to their relations with China.

America's strategy of trying to uphold the geopolitical status quo in East Asia clashes with the ambitions of a rising China, which has its own ideas about how East Asia's political and security order should be organized. If the United States puts itself in the forefront of those trying to contain China, the potential for future tension—or worse—in Sino-American relations can only increase. By pulling back from its hegemonic role in East Asia and adopting an offshore balancing strategy, the United States could better preserve its relative power and strategic influence. It could stand on the sidelines while that region's great powers enervate themselves by engaging in security competitions.

The Temptation of Power

If American strategy were determined by the traditional metrics that have governed the grand strategies of great powers—the distribution of power in the international system, geographic proximity of rivals, and military capabilities—China would not be considered much of a threat to the United States. The well-spring of US grand strategy lies elsewhere, however: in Wilsonian ideology. This is why the United States remains wedded to a strategy of upholding its predominance in East Asia, as well as in Europe and the Middle East.

One of the few ironclad lessons of history is that great powers that seek hegemony are always opposed—and defeated—by the counterbalancing efforts of other states. Yet the prevailing belief among the American foreign policy community is that the United States is exempt from the fate of hegemons. This belief, really a form of American exceptionalism, is wrong. If Washington gives in to the temptation of hegemonic power, dangerous times lie ahead.

POSTSCRIPT

Should the United States Challenge a Rising China?

The answer to whether China's economic, political, and military rise is threatening to the United States depends on how their relationship is assessed. The two books cited by Aaron L. Friedberg, Joshua Kurlantzick, *Charm Offensive: How China's Soft Power Is Transforming the World* (Yale University Press, 2007), and James Mann, *The China Fantasy: How Our Leaders Explain Away Chinese Repression* (Viking Penguin, 2007), provide further evidence to support the questions he raised. *Foreign Policy* published a useful exchange between a realist policymaker, Zbigniew Brzezinski, and a realist academic, John Mearsheimer, about China and U.S.-Chinese relations. See "Clash of the Titans," *Foreign Policy* (January/February 2005).

In contrast, Andrew Nathan and Robert Ross support Christopher Layne by arguing that China can be integrated peacefully and productivily into the international system in *The Great Wall and the Empty Fortress: China's Search for Security* (W. W. Norton, 1997). From this viewpoint, conflict is not inevitable, and continued interaction between the two countries may mitigate the potential threats each may perceive from the other. Meanwhile, regional experts have argued that China, in particular, is undergoing dramatic changes and that its behavior must be understood in the context of evolving political, economic, and social processes taking place within the country. (See David Shambaugh, ed. *Power Shift: China and Asia's New Dynamics* [University of California Press, 2005].) This suggests that rather than trying to clarify the precise nature of Sino-American friendship, it may be constructive to recognize that this relationship is multifaceted and multidimensional, and that the resulting ambiguity may enable it to develop and provide mutual gains in some arenas, despite ongoing conflicts in others.

Information about contemporary U.S.-Chinese relations is available at the Department of State Web Bureau of East Asian and Specific Affairs at http://www.state.gov/p/eap/. The State Department also maintains also maintains a Web page with information specifically related to China. See: http://www.state.gov/p/eap/ci/ch.

ISSUE 9

Should the United States Seek Negotiations and Engagement with North Korea?

YES: David C. Kang, from "The Debate over North Korea," *Political Science Quarterly* (vol. 119, no. 2, 2004)

NO: Victor D. Cha, from "The Debate over North Korea," *Political Science Quarterly* (vol. 119, no. 2, 2004)

ISSUE SUMMARY

YES: David C. Kang, associate professor of government at Dartmouth College, contends that the threat posed by North Korea is overblown because North Korea will continue to be deterred from acting aggressively and, consequently, that engagement offers the best strategy promoting economic, political, and military change.

NO: Victor D. Cha, associate professor of government and D. S. Song-Korea Foundation Chair in Asian Studies in the School of Foreign Service at Georgetown University and Asia director in the National Security Council of the U.S. government, argues that North Korea remains hostile and opportunistic. Engagement—if used at all—should be highly conditional, and the United States and its allies should remain prepared to isolate and contain North Korea if engagement fails.

The Korean Peninsula remains the most fortified and potentially the most militarily dangerous area in the world. The Democratic People's Republic of Korea (DPRK, or North Korea) has a 1.1-million-man army facing opposing soldiers representing the United States and the Republic of Korea (ROK, or South Korea). These troops are separated by a narrow demilitarized zone (DMZ) that cuts across the country a very short distance north of the South Korean capital in Seoul. North Korea also produces and tests ballistic missiles, which it has supplied to Iran and Pakistan. Directed by a dictator, Kim Jong Il, it is believed to possess stockpiles of biological and chemical weapons, and is known to possess the technology to produce nuclear weapons.

Politicians in the United States, South Korea, and other countries in the region have long debated how best to manage relations with North Korea, often evaluating the policy choices in partisan terms. In the 1990s, U.S. policy centered around the agreed framework under which the DPRK agreed to freeze and eventually dismantle its graphite-moderated nuclear reactors and related facilities at Yongbyon and Taechon, to reaffirm its member status in the Nuclear Non-Proliferation Regime, to comply with its International Atomic Energy Agency safeguards agreement, and to implement the North-South Denuclearization Agreement. In exchange, the United States agreed to lead an international consortium to oversee and finance the construction of two 1000-megawatt light water reactors, to compensate the DPRK for energy foregone by providing 500,000 metric tons of heavy fuel oil annually, and to take steps to reduce economic and financial restrictions on the DPRK. In parallel, South Korean President Kim Dae Jung instituted a "sunshine" policy of unconditional engagement with North Korea that included some personal family reunions, the exchange of food and other goods, and the building of a railroad and road system that could connect the North and South. When the George W. Bush administration entered office, it did not engage with North Korea. Instead, the president identified North Korea as a member of the "axis of evil" in his 2002 State of the Union Address.

In October 2002, despite the appearance of recently improved relations with the United States and Japan, North Korea announced the existence of a second secret nuclear program using highly enriched uranium and withdrew from the nuclear non-proliferation treaty. Thus, it acknowledged violating the nuclear non-proliferation treaty, the 1994 U.S.-DPRK Agreed Framework agreement, and the 1992 Korean De-Nuclearization Declaration.

The United States responded by demanding that North Korea comply with its non-proliferation agreements and suspended its shipments of heavy fuel oil under the terms of the Agreed Framework. The North Koreans responded by reactivating the Yongbyon nuclear facilities, dismantling the IAEA monitoring cameras, and expelling IAEA inspectors. In April and August 2003, the United States, North Korea, and China met in Beijing but made little progress in resolving their disputes. The North Korean delegation demanded bilateral negotiations with the United States and threatened to test nuclear weapons if the United States did not offer security assurances. The United States refused and demanded multilateral talks.

Most dramatically, North Korea claimed to have carried out a successful nuclear test in October 2006, although the low yield of the North Korean explosion left observers in doubt whether it was an extremely small nuclear device or a larger weapon that only partially exploded.

David Kang argues that provocative behavior by North Korea and the United States is making each state less secure and more suspicious, thereby making the crisis worse. He argues that engagement offers a way to defuse the crisis and promote change in North Korea. In contrast, Victor Cha argues that North Korea blatantly violated its non-proliferation agreements and should not be trusted. Engagement should only be tried if the United States is willing to switch to strategies of isolation and containment if North Korea fails to carry out its promises.

YES

David C. Kang

Getting Back to "Start"

. . . [T]he nuclear revelations of October 2002 and the ensuing crisis intensified an already acute dilemma for both the United States and North Korea. For the United States, the focus on Iraq was now potentially diverted by an unwanted crisis over an "axis of evil" country in Northeast Asia. For North Korea, the slowly intensifying economic and diplomatic moves of the past few years were also potentially thwarted. For both sides, their worst suspicions were confirmed in the worst of ways. North Korea concluded that the United States had never had any intention of normalizing ties or concluding a peace treaty. The United States concluded that North Korea had never had any intention of abandoning its nuclear weapons program.

The North Korean regime is a brutal and morally reprehensible regime. It has enriched itself while allowing hundreds of thousands of its own citizens to die of starvation. That this regime is odious is not in question. Rather, the issue is: what tactics will best ameliorate the problems on the peninsula?

Many Western policy makers and analysts viewed the nuclear revelations with alarm and surprise. However, much of the Western hand-wringing has elements of Kabuki theater to it, and the accusations ring hollow. "Outrage and shock! at North Korean nuclear programs" is not so convincing in view of the fact that the Bush administration has been openly derisive of Kim Jong Il, has been contemptuous of the Agreed Framework, and has known about North Korea's nuclear program since June 2001. An American intelligence official who attended White House meetings in 2002 said that "Bush and Cheney want this guy's head on a platter. Don't be distracted by all this talk about negotiations. . . . They have a plan, and they are going to get this guy after Iraq." A North Korea that feels threatened and perceives the U.S. administration to be actively attempting to increase pressure on it is unlikely to trust the United States.

Does North Korea have legitimate security concerns? If not, then their nuclear program is designed for blackmail or leverage. If the North does have legitimate security concerns, then it is not that surprising that such a program exists, given the open hostility toward the regime that the Bush administration has evidenced. However, despite the furor over the revelation, not much has changed on the peninsula. Deterrence is still robust. North Korea's basic strategy remains the same: simultaneously deter the United States and also find a way to fix the economy. The United States, for its part, faces the same choices

From *Political Science Quarterly,* vol. 119, no. 2, 2004, pp. 229–236 (references omitted). Copyright © 2004 by David Kang and Victor Cha. Reprinted by permission of The Academy of Political Science and the authors.

it did a decade ago: negotiate, or hope that the North collapses without doing too much damage to the region.

Without movement toward resolving the security fears of the North, progress in resolving the nuclear weapons issue will be limited. It is unsurprising that the 1994 Agreed Framework fell apart, because it was a process by which both sides set out to slowly build a sense of trust and both sides began hedging their bets very early on in that process. Because neither the United States nor North Korea fulfilled many of the agreed-upon steps, even during the Clinton administration, the Framework was essentially dead long before the nuclear revelation of October 2002. Neither side acts in a vacuum; the United States and North Korea each react to the other's positions, and this interaction has led to a spiral of mistrust and misunderstanding. Threats and rhetoric from each side impact the other's perceptions and actions, and this interaction can be either a mutually reinforcing positive or a negative spiral.

The accepted wisdom in the United States is that North Korea abrogated the Framework by restarting its nuclear weapons program. The reality is more complicated, however. Both the Clinton and Bush administrations violated the letter and the spirit of the agreement. Admitting that the United States is hostile toward North Korea does not make one an apologist—the United States *is* hostile, and it is unconvincing to pretend that we are not. The Bush administration made clear from the beginning that it had serious doubts about the Agreed Framework and engagement with the North. This began with the inception of the Bush administration—South Korean President Kim Dae Jung's visit to Washington DC in March 2001 was widely viewed as a rebuke to his sunshine policy that engaged the North, with Bush voicing "skepticism" in regard to the policy. By the time of President Bush's now famous "axis of evil" speech, it had long been clear that the Bush administration did not trust the North. For the Framework to have had any hope of being even modestly successful, each side needed to have worked more genuinely toward building confidence in the other.

The 1994 Agreed Framework

The Agreed Framework of 1994 was not a formal treaty; rather, it was a set of guidelines designed to help two countries that were deeply mistrustful of each other find a way to cooperate. But both sides began backing out of the Agreed Framework well before the autumn of 2002. From its inception, the Bush administration made very clear how much it disdained the Framework, and the North had begun its nuclear program as far back as 1998. The core of the Framework was a series of steps that both sides would take that would ultimately lead to North Korea proving it had no nuclear weapons or nuclear weapons program and to the United States normalizing ties with the North and providing it with light-water nuclear reactors that could make energy but not weapons. Table 1 shows the key elements of the Framework.

Neither side fulfilled its obligations under the Framework. The key elements on the U.S. side were a formal statement of nonaggression (article 2.3.1), provision of the light-water reactor (article 1.2), and progress toward normalization of ties (article 2.1). The reactor is now four years behind schedule. The United

Table 1

Key Conditions of the Agreed Framework

Agreed Framework Condition	Implemention and Discussion
The United States agrees to provide two light-water reactor (LWR) power plants by the year 2003 (article 1.2).	Four years behind schedule. There has been no delay in South Korean or Japanese provision of funds. The delay has been U.S. implementation and construction.
The United States agrees to provide formal assurances to the DPRK against the threat or use of nuclear weapons by the United States (article 2.3.1).	No. The United States maintains that military force is an option on the peninsula. The United States continues to target North Korea with nuclear weapons via the "Nuclear Posture Review."
The DPRK agrees to freeze its nuclear reactors and to dismantle them when the LWR project is completed (article 1.3).	Until December 2002.
The DPRK agrees to allow the International Atomic Energy Agency to monitor the freeze with full cooperation (article 1.3).	Until December 2002.
The United States and the DPRK agree to work toward full normalization of political and economic relations, reducing barriers of trade and investment, etc. (article 2.1).	Limited lowering of U.S. restrictions on trade, no other progress toward normalization or peace treaty. The United States continues to list North Korea as a terrorist state.
The United States and the DPRK will each open a liaison office in the each other's capital, aiming at upgrading bilateral relations to the ambassadorial level (articles 2.2, 2.3).	No.

Source: Compiled from KEDO, "Agreed Framework Between the United States of America and the Democratic People's Republic of Korea," Geneva, Switzerland, 21 October 1994.

States also has not opened a liaison office in Pyongyang and has not provided formal written assurances against the use of nuclear weapons. The U.S. "Nuclear Posture Review" still targets North Korea with nuclear weapons. The North did freeze its reactors and allow IAEA monitoring, but in December 2002, it backed out of the agreement and expelled inspectors from North Korea.

It is possible to argue that the uranium enrichment plant is a more serious breach of the Framework than not providing a formal nonaggression pact or not providing a reactor. But this argument will be compelling only to domestic constituencies. Given U.S. reluctance to fulfill its side of the Framework, it was unlikely that the North would continue to honor its side of the agreement in the hope that at some point the Bush administration would begin to fulfill its side. The implicit U.S. policy has demanded that the North abandon its military programs, and only after it does so would the U.S. decide whether to be benevolent. As Wade Huntley and Timothy Savage write:

> The implicit signal sent to Pyongyang was that the Agreed Framework . . . was at its heart an effort to script the abdication of the DPRK regime. Immediate reticence by the United States to implement certain specific steps toward normalization called for in the agreement, such

as lifting economic sanctions, reinforced this perception. . . . [S]uch an underlying attitude could never be the basis for real improvement in relations.

The United States and North Korea are still technically at war—the 1953 armistice was never replaced with a peace treaty. The United States has been unwilling to discuss even a nonaggression pact, much less a peace treaty or normalization of ties. While the United States calls North Korea a terrorist nation and Donald Rumsfeld discusses the possibility of war, it is not surprising that North Korea feels threatened. For the past two years, U.S. policy toward the North has been consistently derisive and confrontational. Table 2 shows a selection of statements by U.S. and North Korean officials.

Table 2

Selected U.S.–North Korean Rhetoric over the Agreed Framework

Date	U.S. Statements	DPRK Statements
9 October 2000	"Neither government will have hostile intent towards the other." (Joint Communique)	
6 June 2001	"The U.S. seeks improved implementation [of the Agreed Framework], prompt inspections of past reprocessing . . . [and] a less threatening conventional military posture." (White House press release)	
11 June 2001		"Washington should implement the provisions of the D.P.R.K.–U.S. Agreed Framework and the D.P.R.K.–U.S. Joint Communique as agreed upon." (DPRK Foreign Ministry spokesman)
3 July 2001	"We need to see some progress in all areas . . . we don't feel any urgency to provide goodies to them. . . ." (senior administration official, on the broadened demands to North Korea)	
29 January 2002	"States like these . . . constitute an axis of evil, arming to threaten the peace of the world." (George W. Bush, State of the Union speech)	
2 February 2002		"His [Bush's] remarks clearly show that the U.S.-proposed 'resumption of dialogue' with the DPRK is intended not for the improvement of the bilateral relations but for the realization of the U.S. aggressive military strategy. It is the steadfast stand and transparent will of the DPRK to counter force with force and confrontation with confrontation." (Korean Central News Agency)
1 June 2002	"We must take the battle to the enemy . . . and confront the worst threats before they emerge." (George W. Bush)	

Table 2 (Continued)

Selected U.S.–North Korean Rhetoric over the Agreed Framework

Date	U.S. Statements	DPRK Statements
10 June 2002	"First, the North must get out of the proliferation business and eliminate long-range missiles that threaten other countries. . . . [T]he North needs to move toward a less threatening conventional military posture . . . and liv[e] up to its past pledges to implement basic confidence-building measures." (Secretary of State Colin Powell)	
29 August 2002	North Korea is "in stark violation of the Biological weapons convention. . . . [M]any doubt that North Korea ever intends to comply fully with its NPT obligations." (Undersecretary of State John Bolton)	
31 August 2002		"The D.P.R.K. clarified more than once that if the U.S. has a willingness to drop its hostile policy toward the D.P.R.K., it will have dialogue with the U.S. to clear the U.S. of its worries over its security." (North Korean Foreign Ministry spokesman)
20 October 2002		"If the United States is willing to drop its hostile policy towards us, we are prepared to deal with various security concerns through dialogue." (Kim Young Nam, Chair of the Supreme People's Assembly)
5 November 2002		"Everything will be negotiable, including inspections of the enrichment program. . . . [O]ur government will resolve all U.S. security concerns through the talks if your government has a will to end its hostile policy." (Han Song Ryol, DPRK ambassador to the UN)
29 December 2002	"We cannot suddenly say 'Gee, we're so scared. Let's have a negotiation because we want to appease your misbehavior.' This kind of action cannot be rewarded." (Secretary of State Colin Powell)	
5 January 2003	"We have no intention of sitting down and bargaining again." (State Department Spokesman Richard Boucher)	

(continued)

Table 2 (Continued)

Selected U.S.–North Korean Rhetoric over the Agreed Framework

Date	U.S. Statements	DPRK Statements
9 January 2003	"We think that they [Russia] could be putting the screws to the North Koreans a little more firmly and at least beginning to raise the specter of economic sanctions." (senior U.S. official)	"[W]e have no intention to produce nuclear weapons. . . . After the appearance of the Bush Administration, the United States listed the DPRK as part of an 'axis of evil,' adopting it as a national policy to oppose its system, and singled it out as a target of pre-emptive nuclear attack. . . . [I]t also answered the DPRK's sincere proposal for conclusion of the DPRK–US non-aggression treaty with such threats as 'blockade' and 'military punishment.' . . ." (DPRK official announcement of withdrawal from the NPT)
23 January 2003	"First is regime change. It need not necessarily be military, but it could lead to that." (senior U.S. official)	

Sources: Jay Solomon, Peter Wonacott, and Chris Cooper, "North Asian Leaders Criticize Bush on North Korea," *Wall Street Journal,* 6 January 2003; Jay Solomon, Peter Wonacott, and Chris Cooper, "South Korea is Optimistic About End to Nuclear Crisis," *Wall Street Journal,* 4 January 2003; Michael Gordon, "Powell Says U.S. Is Willing to Talk with North Korea," *New York Times,* 29 December 2002; "N. Korea pulls out of nuclear pact," MSNBC News Services, 10 January 2003; Leon Sigal, "North Korea Is No Iraq: Pyongyang's Negotiating Strategy," Special Report, Nautilus Organization, 23 December 2002; Susan V. Lawrence, Murray Hiebert, Jay Solomon, and Kim Jung Min, "Time to Talk," *Far Eastern Economic Review,* 23 January 2003: 12–16.

The Bush administration began adding new conditions to the Agreed Framework early on in its tenure. On 6 June 2001, the White House included reduction of conventional forces in the requirements it wanted North Korea to fulfill, saying that "The U.S. seeks improved implementation [of the Agreed Framework], prompt inspections of past reprocessing . . . [and] a less threatening conventional military posture." On 11 June 2001, North Korea replied that "Washington should implement the provisions of the D.P.R.K.–U.S. Agreed Framework and the D.P.R.K.–U.S. Joint Communique as agreed upon." The Bush administration continued its stance. On 3 July 2001, a senior administration official said that "We need to see some progress in all areas . . . we don't feel any urgency to provide goodies to them."

In 2002, Secretary of State Powell added a reduction in the North's missile program to the list of conditions necessary for progress on the Framework. Missiles had originally been excluded from the Agreed Framework, and the Clinton administration had begun working out a separate agreement with the North about them. On 10 June 2002, Colin Powell said that "First, the North must get out of the proliferation business and eliminate long-range missiles that threaten other countries. . . . [T]he North needs to move toward a less threatening conventional military posture . . . and [toward] living up to its past pledges to implement basic confidence-building measures."

The North consistently maintained that it wanted the United States to lower the pressure. On 20 October 2002, Kim Yong Nam, Chair of the Supreme People's Assembly, said that "If the United States is willing to drop its hostile policy towards us, we are prepared to deal with various security concerns through dialogue." On 3 November 2002, Han Song Ryol, DPRK Ambassador to the UN, reiterated that "Everything will be negotiable, including inspections of the enrichment program. . . . [O]ur government will resolve all U.S. security concerns through the talks if your government has a will to end its hostile policy." As the crisis intensified, Colin Powell refused to consider dialogue with the North, remarking that "We cannot suddenly say 'Gee, we're so scared. Let's have a negotiation because we want to appease your misbehavior.' This kind of action cannot be rewarded."

As one North Korean diplomat noted: "The Agreed Framework made American generals confident that the DPRK had become defenseless; the only way to correct this misperception is to develop a credible deterrent against the United States." As of winter 2003, the situation was one of standoff. North Korean statements made clear their fear that the Bush administration would focus on pressuring North Korea once the situation in Iraq was stabilized. The 28 January 2003 statement of the Korean Anti-Nuke Peace Committee in Pyongyang concluded by saying that

> If the U.S. legally commits itself to non-aggression including the non-use of nuclear weapons against the DPRK through the non-aggression pact, the DPRK will be able to rid the U.S. of its security concerns. . . . Although the DPRK has left the NPT, its nuclear activity at present is limited to the peaceful purpose of power generation. . . . If the U.S. gives up its hostile policy toward the DPRK and refrains from posing a nuclear threat to it, it may prove that it does not manufacture nuclear weapons through a special verification between the DPRK and the U.S. . . . It is the consistent stand of the DPRK government to settle the nuclear issue on the Korean peninsula peacefully through fair negotiations for removing the concerns of both sides on an equal footing between the DPRK and the U.S.

Causes and Consequences of the October Revelation

Thus, the Agreed Framework of 1994 is dead. Both North Korea and the United States are now in essentially the same position they were in 1994—threatening war, moving toward confrontation. Given the levels of mistrust on both sides, this comes as no surprise. If North Korea feels threatened, threatening them is unlikely to make them feel less threatened. Gregory Clark pointed out that "Washington's excuse for ignoring the nonaggression treaty proposal has to be the ultimate in irrationality. It said it would not negotiate under duress. So duress consists of being asked to be nonaggressive?"

An intense security dilemma on the Korean peninsula is exacerbated by an almost complete lack of direct interaction between the two sides. Levels of mistrust are so high that both sides hedge their bets. The United States refused to provide formal written assurances of nonaggression to the North. The North thus retains its military and nuclear forces in order to deter the United States from acting too precipitously.

The consequences are fairly clear: the United States can continue a policy of pressure in the hope that the North will buckle and give in to U.S. pressure or collapse from internal weakness, or it can negotiate a bargain of normalization for nuclear weapons. Without resolving North Korea's security fears, the opportunity for any quick resolution of the confrontation on the peninsula will be limited. This is disappointing because North Korea, unlike Iraq, is actively seeking accommodation with the international community. Even while the Bush administration was increasing its pressure on the North, the North continued its voluntary moratorium on missile testing until 2003. The North's tentative moves toward economic openness have also been stymied for the time being. In July 2002, North Korea introduced a free-market system, allowing prices to determine supply and demand for goods and services. In September 2002, it announced a special economic zone in Shinuiju. In the last six months of 2002, work was begun to clear a section of the demilitarized zone to allow the reconnection of the railway between North and South Korea. To cap all of these developments, Kim Jong Il finally admitted in September 2002, after three decades of denials, that the North kidnapped Japanese citizens in the 1970s.

If North Korea really wanted to develop nuclear weapons, it would have done so long ago. Even today, North Korea has still not tested a nuclear device, tested an intercontinental ballistic missile, or deployed a nuclear missile force. Even if North Korea develops and deploys nuclear weapons, it will not use them, because the U.S. deterrent is clear and overwhelming. The North wants a guarantee of security from the United States, and a policy of isolating it will not work. Isolation is better than pressure because pressure would only make it even more insecure. But even isolation is at best a holding measure. And the imposition of economic sanctions or economic engagement is equally unlikely to get North Korea to abandon its weapons program.

Above all, the North Korean regime wants better ties with the United States. The policy that follows from this is clear: the United States should begin negotiating a nonaggression pact with the North. It should let other countries, such as South Korea and Japan, pursue economic diplomacy if they wish. If the North allows UN nuclear inspectors back and dismantles its reactors, the United States could then move forward to actual engagement. But to dismiss the country's security fears is to miss the cause of its actions.

The Bush administration's reluctance to consider dialogue with the North is counterproductive. Even at the height of the Cold War, Ronald Reagan, despite calling the Soviet Union "the Evil Empire," met with Soviet leaders and held dialogue with them. The United States had ambassadorial relations with the Soviets, engaged in trade with the Soviets, and interacted regularly—precisely in order to moderate the situation and keep information moving between the two adversaries and to keep the situation from inadvertently escalating out of control. The United States was in far greater contact with the Soviet Union during the Cold War than it is with North Korea in 2004. By refusing to talk, the United States allows the situation to spiral out of control and harms its own ability to deal with the reality of the situation.

Does the October nuclear revelation provide any insight as to North Korea's foreign policy strategy? Essentially, no: North Korea has always sought to deter the United States and has viewed the United States as belligerent. Thus, the nuclear program is consistent with North Korea's attempts to provide for its own security. It is also important to remember that a nuclear weapons program does not mean that North Korea is any more likely to engage in unprovoked military acts now than it was before. North Korea was deterred before the revelations, and it remains deterred after the revelations. The way to resolve the crisis is by addressing the security concerns of North Korea. If the United States genuinely has no intention of attacking North Korea or pressuring it for regime change, the administration should conclude a nonaggression pact. It is not that surprising that North Korea does not believe the Bush administration's occasional assurances about having no intention of using force when the administration refuses to formalize those assurances.

In terms of U.S. policy toward the North, the revelations are actually an opening. It is impossible to negotiate with a country over an issue whose existence they deny. In the case of the nuclear program, the United States has the opportunity to actually reach a conclusion to this problem. If the Bush administration were to handle negotiations adroitly, it could possibly finally resolve an issue that has plagued Northeast Asia for far too long.

Victor D. Cha   ➔ **NO**

Past the Point of No Return?

Many moderates argued, as David Kang has done, that this new nuclear confession reveals Pyongyang's true intentions. Although of concern, they argue, these actions represent North Korean leader Kim Jong Il's perverse but typical way of creating a crisis to pull a reluctant Bush administration into serious dialogue. By "confessing" to the crime, in other words, Pyongyang is putting its chips on the table, ready to bargain away this clandestine program in exchange for aid and a U.S. pledge of nonaggression. Moderates would, therefore, advocate continued negotiations by the United States and its allies, providing incentives for the North to come clean on its uranium enrichment activities as well as to extend a more comprehensive nonproliferation arrangement to replace the Agreed Framework. In exchange for this, the allies would put forward a package of incentives including economic aid and normalization of political relations.

Before the world accepts this "cry for help" thesis, however, the North's confession must be seen for what it is—admission of a serious violation of a standing agreement that could, in effect, be North Korea's last gambit for peaceful engagement with the United States and its allies. North Korea's actions constitute a blatant breakout from the 1994 U.S.–DPRK Agreed Framework designed to ensure denuclearization of the North. Those who try to make a technical, legalistic argument to the contrary are patently wrong. Although the Agreed Framework dealt specifically with the plutonium-reprocessing facilities at Yongbyon, this document was cross-referenced with the 1991–1992 North–South Korea denuclearization declaration, which banned both North and South Korea from the uranium enrichment facilities now found to be covertly held in the North. Moreover, any legal gymnastics over this issue were rendered moot by North Korea's subsequent withdrawal from the nonproliferation treaty, the first in the NPT's history.

Moreover, the implications of this act extend beyond a mere violation of legal conventions. Arguably, all of the improvements in North–South relations, including the June 2000 summit, breakthroughs in Japan–North Korea relations in 2001, and the wave of engagement with the reclusive regime that spread across Europe, Australia, and Canada in 2000–2001, were made possible by what was perceived to be the North's good-faith intentions to comply with a major nonproliferation commitment with the United States in 1994. The subtext of this commitment was that the North was willing to trade in its

From *Political Science Quarterly,* vol. 119, no. 2, 2004, pp. 237–254. Copyright © 2004 by Victor D. Cha. Reprint by permission of The Academy of Political Science and the author.

rogue proliferation threat for a path of reform and peaceful integration into the world community. The subsequent diplomatic achievements by Pyongyang, therefore, would not have been possible without the Agreed Framework. And now the North has shown it all to be a lie.

Alternative Explanations for North Korean Misbehavior

Many of the justifications offered by either Pyongyang or mediating parties in Seoul (an irony in itself) for the HEU program and the restarting of the plutonium program at Yongbyon are, at best, suspect. North Korea claimed its actions were warranted as responses to American failure to keep to the time-table of the Agreed Framework as well as to Washington's reneging on promises to normalize relations with the North. Moreover, they argued, the aggressive language of the United States and President Bush's "axis of evil" statements made these actions necessary. North Korean pursuit of the HEU program, how-ever, as assistant secretary Kelly noted in the October 2002 meeting with Kang Sok Ju, predated the Bush administration's accession to office in 2001, and indeed, was well under way as Pyongyang was enjoying the benefits of Kim Dae Jung's sunshine policy from 1999 to 2002. There is no denying that the United States and the KEDO fell behind in the implementation of the Agreed Framework, in large part because the signing of the accord in October 1994 was followed by congressional elections that put in control Republicans with strong antipathy to Clinton (and by definition then, the Agreed Framework). The North Koreans were aware of this possibility and, therefore, sought during the negotiations a personal guarantee from President Clinton that the United States would do what it could to keep implementation on schedule. In other words, as far back as October 1994, Pyongyang was cognizant of such poten-tial problems in implementation. To argue otherwise as justification for their illicit nuclear activities is a stretch. Moreover, although the Agreed Framework was not a legally binding document, arguably there is a distinction between negligence in implementing a contract and completely breaking out of one. Washington could certainly be guilty of the former, but that does not warrant the other party's actions to do the latter.

Kim Jong Il's justification that he needs to wield the nuclear threat as a backstop for regime survival and deterrence against U.S. preemption also does not hold water. This is not because anyone should expect Kim to believe Bush's public assurances that he has no intention of attacking North Korea but because any logical reasoning shows that the North already possesses these deterrent capabilities. Its 11,000 artillery tubes along the DMZ hold Seoul hostage, and its Nodong ballistic missile deployments effectively hold Japan hostage. The warning time for a North Korean artillery shell landing in Seoul is measured in seconds (fifty-seven) and for a ballistic missile fired on the Japanese archipelago in minutes (ten). There is no conceivable defense against these threats, which would result in hundreds of thousands, if not millions, of casualties. As long as the United States values the welfare of these two key allies in Northeast Asia (as well as the 100,000-plus American service personnel and expatriate community), the North holds a credible deterrent against any hypothetical contemplation of American preemption.

Finally, the argument that with the latest crisis. North Korea is seeking direct negotiations with the United States rather than a bonafide nuclear weapons capability is both disturbing and logically inconsistent. North Korea seeks a nonaggression pact, these advocates argue, and a new relationship, by using the only leverage it can muster—its military threat. There are three glaring problems with this argument. First, the notion that North Korean proliferation is solely for bargaining purposes runs contrary to the history of why states proliferate. Crossing the nuclear threshold is a national decision of immense consequence and, as numerous studies have shown, is a step rarely taken deliberately for the purpose of negotiating away these capabilities. Second, even if one were to accept these as the true North Korean intentions, the moral hazard issues become obvious. Rather than moving Pyongyang in the direction of more-compliant behavior, indulging the North's brinkmanship is likely only to validate their perceived success of the strategy. Such coercive bargaining strategies in the past by the North might have been met with engagement by the United States, but in the aftermath of the October 2002 nuclear revelations, such behavior is more difficult to countenance. The difference, as I will explain below, largely stems from the gravity of North Korean misbehavior in 2002 and violation of the Agreed Framework.

Third, the "negotiation" thesis for North Korean proliferation, upon closer analysis, actually leads one to the *opposite* logical conclusion—in other words, a North Korean "breakout" strategy of amassing a midsized nuclear weapons arsenal. South Korean advocates of the negotiation thesis maintain that Pyongyang is aware of the antipathy felt by the Bush administration toward the Clinton-era agreements made with it. Therefore, Pyongyang seeks to leverage the proliferation threat to draw the Bush administration into bilateral negotiations, ostensibly to obtain a nonaggression pact, but in practice to obtain *any* agreement with this government. Ideally, this agreement would offer more benefits than the 1994 agreement, but even if this were not the case, the key point, according to these officials, is that the agreement would have the Bush administration's imprimatur rather than that of Clinton and therefore would be more credible in North Korean eyes.

Though plausible, such an argument, however, leads to a compelling counterintuitive conclusion. If North Korea wants a new and improved agreement and knows that this current administration is more "hard-line" than the previous one, then the logical plan of action would not be to negotiate away its potential nuclear capabilities (the modus operandi in 1994) but to *acquire* nuclear weapons and *then* confront the United States from a stronger position than they had in 1994. Indeed, North Korean actions in December 2002 appear to have been more than a bargaining ploy. If coercive bargaining had been the primary objective, then the North Koreans arguably would have needed to undertake only one of several steps to denude the 1994 agreement. On the contrary, their unsealing of buildings, disabling of monitoring cameras, expelling international inspectors, withdrawal from the NPT, restarting the reactor, and reprocessing represented a purposeful drive to develop weapons. As one

U.S. government official observed, "[W]e made a list of all the things the North Koreans might do to ratchet up a crisis for the purpose of negotiation. They went through that list pretty quickly."

What Follows Hawk Engagement?

There is no denying that Bush's "axis of evil" statements exacerbated a downward trend in U.S.–DPRK relations. But actions matter more than semantics. The problem is not what the United States, South Korea, or Japan may have done to irk the North. The problem is North Korea. What is most revealing about the North's actions is that hawkish skepticism vis-a-vis a real change in Kim Jong Il's underlying intentions, despite behavior and rhetoric to the contrary, remains justified.

This skepticism, as I have argued in *Foreign Affairs* (May/June 2002), is what informs the "hawk engagement" approach toward North Korea. Unlike South Korea's "sunshine policy" of unconditional engagement, this version of the strategy is laced with a great deal more pessimism, less trust, and a pragmatic calculation of the steps to follow in case the policy fails. In short, hawks might pursue engagement with North Korea for very different tactical reasons than might doves. Engagement is useful with rogues like North Korea because: first, "carrots" today can serve as "sticks" tomorrow (particularly with a target state that has very few); second, economic and food aid can start a slow process of separating the people of North Korea from its despotic regime; and third, engagement is the best practical way to build a coalition for punishment, demonstrating good-faith efforts at negotiating and thereby putting the ball in the North's court to maintain cooperation.

The 2002–2003 nuclear revelations confirm much of the skepticism that informs the hawk engagement approach. The premise of hawk engagement is that engagement should be pursued for the purpose of testing the North's intentions and genuine capacity to cooperate. If this diplomacy succeeds, then the sunshine policy advocates are correct about North Korea, and honest hawks (as opposed to ideological ones) would be compelled to continue on this path. But if engagement fails, then one has uncovered the North's true intentions and built the consensus for an alternate course of action. The nuclear violations, in this context, have created more transparency about the extent to which the North's reform efforts represent mere tactical changes or a true shift in strategy and preferences. As hawk engagement behevers had always expected, Kim Jong Il has now dropped the cooperation ball. What comes next? The first step is to rally a multilateral coalition for diplomatic pressure among the allies. The fall 2002 Asia Pacific Economic Cooperation (APEC) meetings in Mexico and the U.S.–Japan-Korea trilateral statement at these meetings were important first steps in this direction. Both Seoul and Tokyo decreed that any hopes Pyongyang might have for inter-Korean economic cooperation or a large normalization package of Japanese aid hinge on satisfactory resolution of the North's current violation. (People also have wrongfully discounted the significance of a similar statement made by APEC as a whole—the first of its kind from the multilateral institution to explicitly address a security problem.) A second important step was taken in November 2002, when the three allies, through KEDO, agreed to suspend further shipments of heavy fuel oil to North Korea that had been promised under the 1994 agreement until Pyongyang came back into compliance. A third step effectively "multilateralizing" the problem occurred in August 2003, when China hosted talks involving the United States, the DPRK, South Korea, Japan, China, and Russia. Although unsuccessful in resolving the crisis, these talks were critical to enlisting China and the region in a more proactive role in helping to solve the problem.

Pundits and critics have blasted the United States for its "no-talk, no-negotiation" position until North Korea rolls back its HEU program. Hawk engagement, in contrast, would posit that the Bush administration's relatively low-key response to North Korea's violation (especially when compared with its response to Iraq's), coupled with its withholding negotiations with Pyongyang until it first makes gestures to come back into compliance, is effectively an offer to the North of one last chance to get out of its own mess. In this sense, as Harry Rowen at Stanford University has observed, this *is* the negotiating position. Kim Jong Il needs to unilaterally and verifiably address international concerns by dismantling the HEU program and returning to the status quo ante. If he were to do this, then the possibility of new U.S.–DPRK negotiations involving quid pro quos of economic aid for nonproliferation would lie ahead.

Why Not Hawk Engagement Again?

Prominent figures in the United States, such as former President Carter, Ambassador Robert Gallucci, and others have argued for turning back the engagement clock and entering into new negotiations to gain access to the HEU program and to roll back the 1994 Agreement violations. In a related vein, other commentators and journalists have argued implicitly that the United States should pursue some form of hawk engagement in the aftermath of the HEU revelations to at least "test" whether North Korea is interested in giving up the program. Others have explicitly invoked the hawk engagement argument to criticize the Bush administration's nonengagement with North Korea.

I do not find engagement a feasible option after the HEU revelations for one very critical reason: the initial rationale for hawk engagement was based on some degree of uncertainty with regard to the target regime's intentions. As long as such uncertainty existed, as it did in 1994, and Pyongyang remained somewhat compliant thereafter with the standing agreements that were the fruits of engagement, it would have been difficult for hawks to advocate otherwise. Hence, even when the North Koreans test-fired a ballistic missile over Japan in 1998, conducted submarine incursions into the South, attacked South Korean naval vessels, and undertook other acts of malfeasance, I still believed that engagement, even for hawks, was the appropriate path. However, the current violations by the North are on a scale that removes any uncertainty in regard to its intentions. Its behavior does not represent minor deviations from the landmark agreement, but rather a wholesale and secretive breakout from it. Negotiating under these conditions, for hawks, would be tantamount to appeasement.

If the current impasse is resolved diplomatically, however, and the DPRK takes unilateral steps toward dismantlement of the facilities, then regional diplomatic pressures, allied entreaties, and public opinion would again compel hawks to pursue some form of engagement. Such engagement would not be informed by any newfound trust in North Korea or its intentions. Indeed, hawk engagement in such a scenario would be informed by infinitely more palpable skepticism and distrust than existed prior to the HEU revelations and would perhaps be characterized by an even shorter tolerance for additional misbehavior by the North before switching to an alternate, more coercive path.

Isolation and Containment

If the North Koreans do not take a cooperative path out of the current crisis, then from a hawk engagement perspective, there is no choice but isolation and containment. The strategy's general contours would be to rally interested regional powers to isolate and neglect the regime until it gave up its proliferation threat. Although this would be akin to a policy of benign neglect, it would not be benign. The United States and its allies would maintain vigilant containment of the regime's military threat and would intercept any vessels suspected of carrying nuclear- or missile-related materials in and out of the North. Secondary sanctions would also be levied against firms in Japan and other Asian countries involved in illicit North Korean drug trafficking in an effort to restrict the flow of remittances to the DPRK leadership. The United States and the ROK might also undertake a reorientation of their military posture on the peninsula, focusing more on long-range, deep-strike capabilities, and betting that the DPRK will respond by scaling back forward deployments in defense of Pyongyang.

This strategy of "malign neglect" would also entail more proactive humanitarian measures, including the continuation of food aid, designed to help and engage the North Korean people. The United States would urge China and other countries to allow the United Nations High Commissioner for Refugees to establish North Korean refugee processing camps in neighboring countries around the Peninsula, enabling a regularized procedure for dealing with population outflows from the decaying country. Potentially a more significant watershed in this regard would be passage of a bill clearing the way for the United States to accept any North Korean who meets the definition of "refugee" and desires safe haven in the United States. In this regard, the United States would lead by example in preparing to facilitate passage out of the darkness that is North Korea to those people who have the courage to vote with their feet. . . .

No doubt there are dangers associated with an isolation strategy, not least of which is North Korean retaliation. Pyongyang states clearly that they would consider isolation and sanctions by the United States an act of war. To support isolation, however, is not to crave war on the peninsula. Indeed after engagement has been proven to fail (as it has for hawk engagers after the HEU revelations), then isolation is the *least* likely strategy to provoke war, inasmuch as the remaining options (including preemptive military strikes) are all much more coercive.

There is no denying the gravity of the crisis in 2003–2004. For hawk engagement, the offer to Kim Jong Il to resolve concerns about his dangerous uranium enrichment and plutonium nuclear weapons programs if he wants to get back on the engagement path is, in effect, the last round of diplomacy. Not taking up this offer would mean a path of isolation and containment of the regime and an end to many positive gains Pyongyang has accumulated since the June 2000 inter-Korean summit. Given the high stakes involved, one hopes that Kim Jong Il makes the correct calculation. . . .

POSTSCRIPT

Should the United States Seek Negotiations and Engagement with North Korea?

While it is clear that North Korea poses a significant security threat to southeast Asia, policymakers and academics continue to disagree about how best to manage relations with the DPRK. An expanded discussion of the debate between Kang and Cha is available in their recent book, *Nuclear North Korea: A Debate on Engagement Strategies* (Columbia University Press, 2003). In addition, each has written additional books on North Korea including Victor Cha, *The US-Korea-Japan Security Triangle* (Columbia University Press, 2000). For other recent books and articles on North Korea and its relations with the United States, see Mike Chinoy, *Meltdown: The Inside Story of the North Korean Nuclear Crisis* (St. Martin's, 2008); Charles Pritchard, *Failed Diplomacy: The Tragic Story of How North Korea Got the Bomb* (Brookings, 2007); and Kim Hyun Sik, "The Secret History of Kim Jong Il," *Foreign Policy* (September/October 2008). The Center for International Policy runs an Asia project that provides expert commentary on Korea and other related materials on its Web site at http://www.ciponline.org/asia/index.htm. The federal research division of the Library of Congress provides current information on North Korea on the Web at http://lcweb2.loc.gov/frd/cs/kptoc.html. The Department of State maintains current information about North Korea and U.S. foreign policy regarding South Korea on its Web site for the Bureau of East Asian and Pacific Affairs at http:// www.state.gov/p/eap/ci/ks/ and North Korea at http://www.state.gov/p/eap/ci/kn/.

Debates about engagement versus containment in North Korea are very similar to long-standing debates in international relations about the use of incentives versus sanctions as tools of foreign policy. David Baldwin provides a useful analysis of these strategies in comparison to other tools of foreign policy in *Economic Statecraft* (Princeton University Press, 1985).

ISSUE 10

Should the United States Engage Hamas?

YES: Steven A. Cook and Shibley Telhami, from "Addressing the Arab-Israeli Conflict," in Richard Haass and Martin Indyk, eds., *Restoring the Balance: Middle East Strategy for the Next President* (Saban Center at Brookings and the Council on Foreign Relations, 2009)

NO: David Pollock, from "Conclusions: Next Step Toward Peace," in David Pollock, ed., *Prevent Breakdown, Prepare for Breakthrough: How President Obama Can Promote Israeli-Palestinian Peace*, Washington Institute for Near East Policy, Policy Focus #90 (December 2008)

ISSUE SUMMARY

YES: Steven A. Cook, senior fellow for Middle Eastern studies at the Council on Foreign Relations, and Shibley Telhami, professor of peace and development at the University of Maryland, assert that Hamas has genuine support from a sufficient number of Palestinians that it must be brought into a Palestinian unity government and included in the peace process, if it is not to be a spoiler in any negotiations.

NO: David Pollock, senior fellow at the Washington Institute for Near East Policy, recommends that the United States continue to isolate Hamas unless it first recognizes Israel, renounces violence, and promises to honor past Palestinian agreements with Israel.

Hamas is a Palestinian organization that grew out of the Muslim Brotherhood, a fundamentalist Islamic movement founded in 1928. The Muslim Brotherhood forms the largest opposition group in many Arab states, particularly Egypt, and seeks to establish Islamic governments that would observe Sharia, a strict set of Islamic laws based in the Quran. Although political leaders of the Muslim Brotherhood have disavowed the use of violence to achieve the movement's goals, individuals affiliated with the movement and groups that have grown out of it, including Hamas, have engaged in violence and terrorism.

Hamas was founded in 1987 by Sheikh Ahmed Ismail Yassin and others, and it played a role that year in the start if the "first intifada," a violent uprising of Palestinians against Israeli rule in the territories occupied by Israel since the 1967 war. Since its founding, Hamas has consistently refused to recognize Israel's right to exist. Israel outlawed Hamas in 1989 as a terrorist organization and imprisoned Yassin after attacks on civilians by Hamas operatives.

In 1993 Israel and the Palestinian Liberation Organization agreed in the Oslo Accords on a process of mutual recognition and a path toward eventual statehood for the Palestinians (with territorial boundaries and other important details yet to be determined). Hamas responded with a series of suicide bombings intended to disrupt political support for the Oslo Accords on both sides and to underscore its continuing rejection of Israel's right to exist. In January 1996, Hamas boycotted the first Palestinian elections organized under the Oslo Accords, deepening its split with the transitional Palestinian Authority (PA) that was moving toward governance of Palestinian areas under the Oslo process.

By 1997, the Oslo process essentially ground to a halt, with Israel blaming the PA for its inability or unwillingness to stop Hamas from carrying out terrorist bombings. Meanwhile, Israel released Yassin from prison in exchange for two Israelis held by Jordan, and Yassin vowed to continue Hamas's attacks on Israel. Growing tensions between Israel and the Palestinians, sparked by continuing attacks by Hamas and hard-line responses by the conservative Israeli government of Prime Minister Ariel Sharon, led to a second Palestinian uprising beginning in 2000. Over the next several years, Hamas continued to carry out terrorist suicide bombings, and Israel conducted a campaign of targeted assassinations of Hamas leaders, including the killing of Yassin in 2004.

Hamas once again boycotted the 2005 Palestinian presidential election, in which Mahmoud Abbas was elected as the Fatah party candidate to replace the late Yasir Arafat as head of the PA. Israel withdrew its troops from Gaza in August 2005, leaving it under the control of the PA. Hamas declared this to be a victory for its movement, and sought to build its political power within Gaza while also launching thousands of crude rockets into Israel, causing relatively few casualties but keeping tensions at a high level. In January 2006, Hamas won the majority of the seats in the Palestinian parliamentary elections, defeating the Fatah faction, which Hamas criticized as corrupt and complacent. Tensions between Hamas and Fatah escalated until direct fighting broke out in the summer of 2007, and Hamas was able to sieze control of Gaza and expel Fatah members to the West Bank, where Abbas continued in power. Over the next several years Israel, with U.S. backing, worked to isolate Gaza and Hamas politically and economically, while trying to establish greater security and prosperity in the West Bank as an enticing alternative to Hamas's rule of Gaza. Hamas's continued rocket attacks on Israel prompted Israel to carry out air strikes on Hamas strongholds in Gaza in late December 2008 and send its ground forces into Gaza for three weeks in January 2009, resulting in the deaths of 13 Israelis and over 1000 Palestinians, many of them civilians intermixed with Hamas fighters. The fighting only intensified controversy over Hamas, with some Palestinians blaming it for provoking Israel and others rallying to its side and blaming Israel for the violence.

YES

**Steven A. Cook
and Shibley Telhami**

Addressing the
Arab-Israeli Conflict

Executive Summary—Chapter 5

After seven years on the back burner of American foreign policy, Arab-Israeli peacemaking needs to become a priority for the new president. Recent trends in Israel and the Palestinian territories have created a situation in which the option of a two-state solution may soon no longer be possible. Failure to forge an agreement will present serious complications for other American policies in the Middle East because the Arab-Israeli conflict remains central not only to Israel and its neighbors but also to the way most Arabs view the United States. Failure will also inevitably pose new strategic and moral challenges for American foreign policy. The need for active and sustained American peace diplomacy is therefore urgent.

The Obama administration's agenda in the Middle East will be crowded: the Iraq war, Iran's nuclear program, the war on al Qaeda, and the supply and cost of energy. These immediate issues make it harder to emphasize Arab-Israeli peacemaking since many of the costs of ignoring it are not directly visible (such as the impact on Arab public opinion) or are long term, such as the consequences of the collapse of the two-state solution. While Arab-Israeli diplomacy should be an important goal of the new administration, it can succeed only as part of a regional initiative that frames the Arab-Israeli issue in the context of other American priorities.

Because the way an administration frames its foreign policy objectives is highly consequential for the direction and effectiveness of any particular initiative, very early in the administration, the president should announce a multitrack "framework for security and peace in the Middle East" that connects the Arab-Israeli conflict to the regional and global agenda.

Resolving this conflict is an important American interest. This is not to suggest that settling the Arab-Israeli conflict can resolve all the other challenges Washington confronts in the region. Nevertheless, it is a mistake to underestimate the importance of the conflict, even beyond its psychological role in the political identity of most Arabs: it is certainly central to Israel, the Palestinians, Syria, and Lebanon. It remains important to both Jordan and Egypt, the only two Arab states at peace with Israel, who could be drawn further into the conflict if the two-state solution collapses. The conflict remains the prism through which many Arabs view the United States and the source of much of the Arab public's anger with American foreign policy. It is a primary source of militancy, and it is a source of influence for Iran in the Arab world. Pro-American governments in the region face internal public pressures whenever the conflict escalates. While Arab authoritarians have withstood this pressure through repression and co-optation, the gap between publics and governments in the region is wide. This has been a constant source of empowerment for militant groups posing threats to the regional order and to American interests. The American commitment to Israel and American interests in the Arab world ensure that when conflict escalates, the United States is affected or drawn into the conflict. As the United States seeks to end the Iraq war while minimizing its detrimental consequences, regional cooperation in that effort becomes more likely when the Arab-Israeli conflict is reduced. Arab-Israeli peace could change the regional environment for American foreign policy, open new alliance options, and turn public opinion against al Qaeda, much of whose support appears to be based on the logic of the "enemy of my enemy" rather than on an embrace of its agenda.

In designing a broad framework for security and peace in the Middle East, the new administration should learn from the failures and successes of previous American diplomatic efforts. Of particular note are the lessons drawn in a recent report by a study group of the United States Institute of Peace (of which one of us was a member). Specifically, the Obama administration should undertake a number of steps on the Arab-Israeli front:

—Begin by recognizing that an effective diplomatic initiative aimed at a lasting peace cannot be attained so long as the Palestinians are organizationally divided and without an enforced cease-fire with Israel. These divisions could become even wider if Palestinian presidential elections are not held in January 2009 and Hamas (the Islamic Resistance Movement) no longer recognizes the legitimacy of the presidency. Thus, American diplomacy must begin with the twin aims of encouraging an effective cease-fire and supporting a Palestinian unity government. A unity government negotiating with Israel is not sustainable so long as Hamas carries out violent attacks against its Palestinian competitors and Israel. A central feature of Washington's diplomacy must be to work with its regional allies to induce Hamas into an effective cease-fire coupled with sustained regional efforts to limit the flow of arms into the Palestinian territories.

—Recognize that Hamas's power stems from genuine support among a significant segment of the Palestinian public and that Hamas will likely remain a spoiler as long as it is outside of Palestinian governing institutions. Although there is no guarantee that the organization will play a more constructive role within a national unity government, Washington should support conciliation between Fatah and Hamas as a way to diminish the Islamists' incentive to undermine negotiations, forcing Hamas to either accept a peace agreement that addresses Palestinian rights or lose the support of the Palestinian public. The aim should be less to "reform" Hamas than to put in place political arrangements that are conducive to successful negotiations and that limit Hamas's incentives to be a spoiler.

—Encourage Egypt, Saudi Arabia, and other Arab actors to pressure Hamas to police the cease-fire agreement with Israel and to convince the Hamas leadership to accept the April 2002 Arab League Peace Initiative, especially as Israeli leaders are voicing renewed interest in that plan. In this context, the United States should be willing to drop its insistence that Hamas accept the Quartet's criteria—recognition of Israel, renunciation of armed struggle, and adherence to previous Israel-Palestinian Authority agreements.

—Recognize that no one can predict election outcomes in Palestine, as the Bush administration discovered, that elections are unlikely to resolve the current Palestinian divisions, and that they cannot be a substitute for efforts of political reconciliation, although such elections should be supported.

—Hold Israel to its commitment to freeze new construction of Jewish settlements in the West Bank and in the Jerusalem area. Critically, this freeze should halt the construction of new communities, outposts, and "thickening" of existing settlements, which often entails expropriation of additional Palestinian land. In addition, Washington must urge Israel to allow Palestinians greater freedom of movement throughout the West Bank. In Gaza, provided the cease-fire between Israel and Hamas holds, the Israelis must permit a greater flow of goods in and out of the territory.

—Appoint a special peace envoy to pursue actively a final-status agreement between Israel and the Palestinians, while coordinating with other tracks of negotiations. A special envoy, however, cannot be a substitute for the direct involvement of the president or the secretary of state, who must be engaged to sustain an effective diplomatic effort.

—Put forth American ideas on final status in the Palestinian-Israeli track at the appropriate moment. To keep the hope of a two-state solution alive, this should be done sooner rather than later.

—Work to bolster and train Palestinian forces to police effectively the West Bank and lay the ground for capable unified Palestinian security forces after an agreement is reached.

—Support Turkish mediation in the Syrian-Israeli negotiations and become more actively engaged in these negotiations as both sides have indicated a strong desire for an American role. The United States should also return its ambassador to Damascus.

—Encourage the continuation of a Lebanese national unity government and its participation in negotiations with Israel.

—Activate two new multilateral tracks: one addressing regional economic cooperation, especially in a postpeace environment, the other addressing regional security cooperation.

—Develop a plan for the deployment of international forces in the West Bank and Gaza once a peace agreement is in place; these forces will be essential in the implementation phase for building a unified Palestinian police force and beginning the effective separation of Israelis and Palestinians. Their deployment must commence immediately following an agreement to help coordinate the peaceful withdrawal of Israeli forces.

David Pollock

➔ **NO**

Conclusion: Next Steps Toward Peace

How should soon-to-be President Obama handle the Israeli-Palestinian problem? The preceding essays present diverse points of view. There are clear differences on precisely how, and how urgently, the United States should pursue further peace talks. These differences are linked, at least in part, to divergent individual judgments about how dangerous, or how potentially promising, the status quo in the region really is—and how the several imminent political transitions will most likely alter that status quo, for better or for worse.

Views also differ on how other regional players—Jordan, Syria, the entire Arab League, or even Iran—might or might not fit into a plan of action on the issue. And significant disagreement exists as well about the overall medium-term prospects for reaching new agreements, or for actually implementing any such agreements if they can be put on paper. Although these differences illuminate the judgment calls that Washington will soon need to make on these issues, they are naturally somewhat contradictory. Overall, however, the essays in this anthology collectively point a way forward. This is because most of the authors share a rough consensus, or at least a surprising degree of convergence, on certain key questions.

One common (though not universal) theme is support for continuing some form of Israeli-Palestinian peace talks with high-level U.S. involvement. Even if there is not much hope of quick success or much linkage to other regional issues, many of the authors believe that further talks could help avert even worse short-term outcomes—provided there is no stampede to an unworkable deal.

Another theme is that Hamas is part of the problem, not part of the solution. The authors are understandably less clear about how to handle this very difficult issue. Still, there exists considerable agreement on a general strategy:

- First, maintain Hamas's political isolation, unless the group unexpectedly meets the conditions set forth by the Quartet (the United States, UN, European Union, and Russia) for diplomatic engagement. These conditions include recognizing Israel, renouncing violence, and reaffirming past Israeli-Palestinian agreements.

From *Prevent Breakdown, Prepare for Breakthrough: How President Obama Can Promote Israeli-Palestinian Peace,* David Pollock, ed., Policy Focus #90, December 2008, pp. 58–66. Copyright © 2008 by Washington Institute for Near East Policy. Reprinted by permission.

- Second, try to work around the Hamas obstacle by actively support-ing the internal development of, external support for, and Israeli rapprochement with the Palestinian Authority (PA) under President Mahmoud Abbas.
- Third, keep chipping away at Hamas's popular support, not by aggra-vating the humanitarian problems in Gaza, but rather by improving security and living conditions in the West Bank and demonstrating that Fatah offers Palestinians better economic, political, and peace prospects.

Yet another common theme is that recent experience offers a few hard lessons. For one, unilateral Israeli withdrawals—whether from Lebanon in 2000 or from Gaza in 2005—have tended to backfire. Both sides need the combination of a "political horizon" and a "ground game" of pragmatic security, economic, and humanitarian fixes to keep the peace process moving with sufficient pop-ular support. One without the other breeds cynicism, despair, or both. Small agreements that work are better than grand plans that fall apart. In the long run, a two-state solution probably remains the only outcome with a chance of acceptance by both sides. But it is also probably unachievable for the moment, and in time will likely need to be supplemented by additional elements.

These lessons lead to a final common thread that can be teased out of the diverse presentations in this collection—intrinsically the broadest theme, and probably also the most important and original one. In short, only new and more creative regional input has any chance of breaking the current deadlock between Israelis and Palestinians. This deadlock is deeper than may appear from the good intentions and improved atmospherics among some of their leaders lately, or from the seemingly narrow gaps that separate some of their positions. Instead, it reflects serious underlying problems of political weakness and frag-mentation, persistent security concerns, growing demographic pressures, and an understandable lack of trust on both sides, all compounded by continual cases of incitement or actual violence.

To cope with or perhaps even overcome these hard bilateral realities, the authors offer a variety of regional remedies. Some advocate new variations on the old "Jordanian option" for the West Bank, or Egyptian involvement for Gaza. Others are highly skeptical or dismissive of these proposals. Some sup-port the Arab Peace Initiative endorsed by the Arab League summits in 2002 and 2007 as a valid (albeit conditional) framework for both Palestinian and pan-Arab accord with Israel. Others doubt whether this framework can really function as much more than a symbolic or rhetorical device; they also ques-tion what tangible contributions the Arab states could actually make toward a workable and mutually acceptable Israeli-Palestinian peace settlement.

The latter point raises a deceptively simple but crucial issue: the plausible timeframe for any such regional contribution. Some authors argue that until the regional power constellation realigns in a more favorable manner, con-flict management rather than conflict resolution must remain the only realis-tic approach to the Israeli-Palestinian impasse. Others wonder, perhaps more optimistically, whether today's regional alignment is actually better for peace than is likely to be the case tomorrow; if so, they argue, now may be the time for the United States to push hard for a final deal. In short, while there is some convergence on the necessity for new regional input, there is little agreement on what form that input should take, or when and how it should be injected into the Israeli-Palestinian equation.

This concluding chapter will attempt to sort out the anthology's mix of convergent and divergent analyses and judgments, reviewing the major issues at hand and drawing the appropriate policy prescriptions. These prescriptions are the sole responsibility of the editor, incorporating insights gleaned from all of the authors' contributions but not representing any individual among them. In addition, a few new ideas will be identified along the way. The first two sections to follow outline the most immediately relevant and significant developments, analyzing their short-term implications for U.S. policy.

First Immediate Issue: Israel's Election Season

Above and beyond the usual issues between Israelis and Palestinians, internal political rivalries within each society are rapidly approaching a turning point, preoccupying the public and politicians alike. Israel scheduled an early parliamentary election for February 10, 2009, after Prime Minister Ehud Olmert resigned over corruption charges and his successor as Kadima Party leader, Foreign Minister Tzipi Livni, failed to form a new coalition commanding a majority in the Knesset. In the meantime, Olmert remains as caretaker prime minister, but with his political authority severely restricted as the country's divisive political campaign season gathers momentum.

In their most recent public statements, the three major contenders for Olmert's post have taken noncommittal yet noticeably divergent postures on the Palestinian question. Livni has suggested a focus on continuing the peace talks, in which she has been engaged with Palestinian negotiator Ahmed Qurei (Abu Ala). Defense Minister and Labor Party leader Ehud Barak has indicated some interest in reconsidering the broader Arab Peace Initiative, which would presumably bring Syria and the Golan Heights issue back into the mix. And opposition leader Binyamin Netanyahu of the Likud Party has emphasized what he would not do—namely, "divide Jerusalem" or "risk Israeli security"— while also voicing some support for the idea of a national unity government including more dovish parties. Most recently, Netanyahu has also elaborated a bit on his concept of forging an "economic peace" with the Palestinians, "in parallel to conducting political negotiations."

The latest Israeli opinion polls (which are notoriously volatile) suggest that Netanyahu is running slightly ahead of Livni, each with about a quarter of the likely vote, while Barak trails far behind. As always in Israel, there is virtually no chance of any single party obtaining an outright majority. Consequently, whatever government emerges will almost certainly be a coalition, and one with a necessarily blurry platform reflecting various compromises, an ambiguous policy in practice, and a tendency to fall apart well short of a full term in office.

Even so, the nature and leadership of that coalition will matter greatly for the medium-term prospects of the peace process. This unavoidably raises the delicate but urgent question of whether the United States should try to promote an outcome that serves its own interests, or adopt a truly hands-off approach. In the two most clear-cut cases involving significant influence on Israeli elections, the U.S. record is mixed. In 1992, the Bush administration's refusal to issue loan guarantees for immigrant absorption without a freeze on Jewish settlements in occupied territory helped Labor's Yitzhak Rabin defeat the incumbent Likud's Yitzhak Shamir, partly with votes from the new Russian immigrants themselves.

In contrast, four years later, revulsion against a wave of Palestinian suicide bombings helped Likud's Binyamin Netanyahu eke out a narrow victory over Labor's Shimon Peres, despite the Clinton administration's very visible preference for the latter. This preference was evident at the Sharm al-Sheikh "anti-terrorism" summit of March 1996, which Clinton hastily put together with Peres, Yasser Arafat, and various other Arab leaders; it was also clear in Clinton's election-eve remarks expressing hope that Israelis would vote "for peace." Washington kept a lower profile in 1999, when Netanyahu opposed Labor's new standard-bearer, Ehud Barak, who subsequently emerged the winner. And in the 2001 election, a popular backlash against renewed Palestinian attacks helped Likud's Ariel Sharon win handily while the new Bush administration looked on. A similar U.S. approach pertained in 2005, when Sharon broke with Likud to create the Kadima Party but was felled by a stroke and succeeded by Olmert, who won the most recent Israeli election in March 2006.

This record, while far from conclusive, suggests that considerable U.S. caution is advisable when it comes to Israeli domestic politics. In the two recorded cases of active "cheerleading" from Washington, the second may actually have backfired, making the strategy a very risky proposition. Moreover, any reversion to such attempts today—especially given the absence of any visible U.S. intervention in Israeli elections over the past decade—could provoke a nationalist backlash among at least some segments of the Israeli electorate.

Nevertheless, in the aftermath of Barack Obama's victory, some Israeli politicians are already injecting the issue into their own election campaigns. Livni was relatively circumspect, noting only that "if Israel puts itself in a corner and is seen as rejecting diplomatic processes, we could enter an era that is worse than the current one." By comparison, two senior Labor legislators immediately went on record with the claim that Obama would get along better with someone from their side of the Israeli aisle. Knesset member Ophir Pines-Paz was explicit in this regard:

> It would be a missed opportunity if we elect Netanyahu. Netanyahu's English is fluent, but they still won't understand each other. Obama will try to advance the peace process from day one, and he can do it, because he has more trust from the Arab world than his predecessors. Then Netanyahu would say no to the Saudi peace plan, no to dividing Jerusalem, no to withdrawing from the Golan. That's why it's so important that the center-Left bloc win our election.

Likud spokesmen naturally disputed this assertion. In fact, it is not clear that a Likud-led government would be so at odds with an Obama administration, especially if Israel remained open to incremental but substantive progress with the Palestinians and to the potential for a peace deal with Syria. Moreover, the political impact in Israel, if any, of perceived U.S. preferences will almost certainly pale in comparison with other issues and events on the ground. Given these circumstances, any blatant U.S. attempt to play favorites is probably more likely to fail or even backfire. Although a great deal is at stake for the peace process, extreme discretion must be the better part of valor for Washington bystanders to this complex Israeli political contest.

Second Immediate Issue: Internal Palestinian Politics

Since mid-2007, Palestinian politics has been consumed by the divide between Fatah control in the West Bank and Hamas control in Gaza. These parties continue to talk of unity, but in reality the division is growing sharper and deeper. As if this were not enough, internecine tensions remain acute in the West Bank, whether among opposing personalities such as Prime Minister Salam Fayad and his many old-guard rivals, or among local, generational, or other factions inside the still-dominant but brittle Fatah network. There is a real danger that, without serious extra support, the PA could confront a tough new showdown with Hamas inside the West Bank, or even disintegrate in the face of these internal and external pressures.

Today, the most immediate question centers on how Washington should handle the formal expiration of Mahmoud Abbas's four-year presidential term on January 9, 2009. As explained in the preceding essays, Abbas can make what lawyers might call a "colorable claim" to extend his term automatically for one more year, until the parliamentary elections due in January 2010. Hamas, however, is preparing to contest this claim, and it is unclear what the response on the ground will be. Some have proposed that the United States consider openly supporting Abbas's bid to hold on to the presidency, or perhaps even an offer to run for reelection sooner if Hamas can somehow guarantee a fair vote in Gaza.

There is little historical record of direct American intervention in Palestinian electoral politics, but what precedent exists is not encouraging. In early 2006, Washington made clear its preferences regarding the timing and terms of the planned parliamentary elections, without directly endorsing any particular candidate or party. Yet encouraging this election—at a time when Hamas was poised to participate, the outcome was far from certain, and the election itself was not clearly called for by any legal or practical requirement—turned out to be a disaster for Palestinians, Israelis, the peace process, and U.S. interests. Hamas swept to power, splitting the Palestinian government into two incompatible pieces, renouncing peaceful coexistence with Israel, and presenting Washington with a Hobson's choice between opposing the results of an admittedly democratic election or abandoning all hope of reviving the peace process anytime soon.

Policy Prescriptions for the Year Ahead

The preceding discussion yields an important short-term injunction for the United States: be exceedingly cautious about attempting, or even appearing, to interfere directly in either Israeli or Palestinian elections, while scrupulously avoiding any actions that might inadvertently strengthen Hamas. The following sections present more medium-term guidelines for next steps in the pursuit of Arab-Israeli peace—primarily, but not exclusively, on the Israeli-Palestinian front. These policy recommendations fall under three general categories: preventing collapse, outflanking Hamas, and seeking regional support to end the Israeli-Palestinian impasse.

Recommendations for Preventing Collapse

Rush to restart Israeli-Palestinian peace talks, but not to finish them. This measured and realistic approach offers the best prospect of avoiding two historic pitfalls. One such pitfall swallowed the early Bush administration, which deliberately deferred the Israeli-Palestinian issue for too long, even after Arafat's death in November 2004. This omission unwittingly helped pave the way for Hamas's rise to power. The Clinton administration set the stage for this error, however, by falling into the opposite sort of pitfall. Its last-minute push to wrap up a final-status deal at the July 2000 Camp David summit proved, in retrospect, to be Arafat's main pretext for launching the bloody and protracted second intifada, using popular protests against Ariel Sharon's visit to the Temple Mount two months later as the immediate trigger.

During the long 2008 U.S. presidential campaign, statements from both sides created the impression that other regional issues—Iran, Iraq, Afghanistan, Pakistan, and al-Qaeda—would outrank the Israeli-Palestinian problem in the new list of U.S. policy priorities. On its face, this is a reasonable position, given the higher immediate stakes for the United States in all of those arenas, and the low odds of rapid success in the Arab-Israeli arena. The big drawback, however, is that without sufficient American attention, rejectionists are more likely to provoke a real Arab-Israeli crisis, as in the twin kidnappings of Israeli soldiers by Hamas and Hizballah that sparked the 2006 Lebanon war. Any crisis of this sort would most likely require some kind of emergency diplomatic response, which would both distract from and further complicate U.S. policy dilemmas elsewhere in the neighborhood.

Currently, Washington has two good options for avoiding past pitfalls and maximizing its diplomatic room for maneuver. First, the outgoing Bush administration should refrain from any dramatic diplomatic departures during its last few weeks in office. Second, [President] Obama should signal forcefully and immediately—even before his inauguration—that he intends to make a serious and sustained commitment to seeking Palestinian and wider Arab-Israeli peace. On the campaign trail, he repeatedly stated that he would promote the peace process "from day one" in office. He can fulfill this pledge not only by appointing a senior official and close confidante to oversee the task, but also by inviting Israeli and Palestinian leaders to visit him in the White House.

Make things better on the ground before shooting for the moon. It is imperative that U.S. policymakers understand the importance of concrete support for everyday Israeli-Palestinian coexistence, even if the improvements are painfully slow and fall far short of historic breakthroughs. A final-status agreement is impossible while an unreconstructed Hamas clings to power in Gaza. But this does not mean that the peace process must be held hostage. On the contrary, one way to outflank Hamas is to pursue practical agreements that can actually be implemented in the West Bank, even as Israel and the PA continue negotiating their longer-term future.

In fact, it will be absolutely crucial for the new U.S. policy team to nurture the palpable recent progress in beefing up Palestinian security capabilities and coordination with Israel. This subject is explored in detail in a companion Washington Institute companion paper titled *Security First,* so suffice it to underscore here how vital (if unglamorous) this work really is. There have been some promising signs lately on the West Bank economic front as well, and they should be given equally strenuous support—not only with continued funding, but also with the high-level political backing needed to circumvent all the technical and literal roadblocks. In this regard, the Quartet mission led by former British prime minister Tony Blair could be a very useful mechanism, provided it receives more unstinting U.S. support.

At the rhetorical level, the promise of Israeli cooperation on this front spans most of the political spectrum, at least as far right as the opposition Likud Party. The Palestinians are similarly eager to cooperate. It remains in the interest of all parties to make reality match this promise to the maximum possible extent.

Put the most recent understandings on the agenda, but not on paper. Limited as they may have been, the peace talks that followed the November 2007 Annapolis summit did produce some unwritten understandings of real value, if only in reaffirming previous parameters of peace. First, and most basic, is the very concept of a two-state solution: Israel and Palestine living side by side in peace. This concept has come under attack lately by some Israelis and Palestinians alike, from different perspectives.

At the same time, a Bush administration push to secure an agreed Israeli-Palestinian statement of principles before leaving office is overly ambitious. It runs the risk of turning into yet another vague, impractical, and probably counterproductive paper plan, inflating expectations for a short while only to dash them soon afterward, and giving rival politicians on all sides a convenient target to rail against without conferring any solid offsetting benefits.

Another crucial (and newly established) Israeli-Palestinian peacemaking concept is that of mutually agreed modifications to Israel's 1949–1967 armistice lines. Specifically, in any final peace agreement, Israel will likely get to keep some settlement blocs beyond the 1967 "Green Line," and will likely give the Palestinians some other roughly equivalent land in exchange. This is a very hard-won pragmatic adjustment that is indispensable to peace. The incoming U.S. administration, and the Israeli and Palestinian leaders, could further help matters by reiterating their support for this principle. It would be equally helpful if other Arab governments affirmed it as well (as discussed later in this chapter).

Keep peace hopes alive, but do not look to U.S. initiatives on Arab-Israeli issues for help with other regional problems. The recent record suggests that the reverse is more true: regional successes tend to create openings in the Arab-Israeli arena. For example, successful U.S. moves in the Persian Gulf—in the aftermath of the 1991 war to liberate Kuwait and the 2007 "surge" in Iraq—helped bring Israelis and Arabs together at the peace conference table. In contrast, progress toward Israeli-Palestinian compromise—as in the mid-1990s Oslo peace process—has actually spurred Israeli, Palestinian, Iranian, and other extremists to greater acts of violence.

Nevertheless, a complete collapse of the Arab-Israeli peace process could alienate some U.S. friends or embolden some adversaries. In this negative sense, U.S. support for the process is helpful—if not in solving other regional problems, then at least in averting new ones. But the United States should avoid any statements or signals that it considers progress on Arab-Israeli issues as somehow key to solving other problems, or even to rehabilitating the U.S. reputation in the region. Even if there are some grains of truth in this nostrum, repeating or reinforcing it only puts more cards in the hands of Hamas and other extremists who actually stand in the way of Arab-Israeli peace.

Put peace ahead of democracy. These two objectives are among the highest human values, and in the long term, U.S. policy should strive to foster both. All of the relevant parties have a strong interest in cultivating a stable, legitimate, accountable, and effective Palestinian partner for peace, to match that on the Israeli side. Yet for other Arab governments that have already achieved some or all of these characteristics (e.g., Egypt and Jordan), democracy has not been a precondition for peace with Israel, nor should it be for peace efforts with Syria or other Arab states. Indeed, in certain short-term situations, peace and democracy may actually conflict.

Priorities must therefore be assigned. The first human right, a precondition for all others, is the right to live in peace. People may rightfully choose to fight for their own freedom. But third parties must be especially mindful of this tragic tradeoff; they should not knowingly instigate someone else's war, even on behalf of a noble but abstract ideal like democracy. Therefore, if a sudden move to free elections—in, say, the Palestinian territories, Egypt, Lebanon, Jordan, or even Syria—seems likely to spark an Arab-Israeli war, the United States should avoid pushing any of its partners or even its adversaries to take that chance. Instead, it should concentrate on the critical but gradual task of building the foundations of democracy: the rule of law; accountable, transparent governance; and a culture of tolerance that delegitimizes violence, incitement, and hate-speech. As for the upcoming Israeli election, the United States should make clear that it intends to pursue the peace process regardless of which party wins or what kind of coalition is formed.

Recommendations for Outflanking Hamas

Hold fast to the Quartet conditions for engaging Hamas. Some observers have argued that since it behooves the United States to jumpstart the peace process, Washington had better begin by engaging Hamas, despite the fact that the group is a U.S.-designated terrorist organization. A variant of this argument holds that Washington should encourage Mahmoud Abbas to negotiate with the rival Hamas government in Gaza, or at least resist the temptation to set boundaries on those talks. This could mean another Palestinian attempt at a national unity government (similar to the February 2007 Mecca accord) and/or an agreement to hold early elections. Both are exceedingly risky propositions, however, because they could dilute both Fatah's power in the West Bank and its commitment to peace. Therefore, the United States should resist any Fatah-Hamas agreement that moves in either of these directions.

At the same time, in order to preempt a new Hamas challenge to Abbas when his term runs out in January 2009, the United States should tacitly support the continuation of inconclusive Palestinian "unity" talks. This is probably the best method of playing for time while Abbas and Fatah strengthen their position. Of course, Hamas will be alert to this maneuver, but it is the only tactic available that is not liable to prove self-defeating. Moreover, Hamas may be unwilling or unable to mount a meaningful counter to this approach.

Recently, Dennis Ross, a senior advisor to the president-elect, told a leading Israeli daily that Obama would not deal with Hamas unless it accepts the Quartet's three conditions; as mentioned previously, these include recognizing Israel, renouncing terror, and reaffirming past Israeli-Palestinian agreements. Another Obama advisor, however, asserted that although Washington need not become directly engaged with the group, it should follow Abbas's lead on this issue—in other words, let Abbas decide whether and on what terms to resume some kind of unity deal or other arrangement with Hamas. But the wisdom of that course would be a function of the relative power balance and prospects of the two Palestinian camps. Only if a new intra-Palestinian accord clearly favored Abbas would the United States have an interest in supporting it. And if Abbas uses the next year to strengthen Fatah's position and popular appeal, then the 2010 parliamentary election would be a better calculated risk for U.S. policy this time around.

Accept Arab mediation between Palestinian rivals, but urge pressure on Hamas. Clearly, there is a strong impulse among many Palestinian and other Arab officials, and among some European politicians, to keep chasing the elusive objective of Fatah–Hamas unity despite their increasingly deep divisions. Egypt has taken the lead in this quixotic quest from Saudi Arabia, which brokered the ill-fated and short-lived Mecca accord. As of this writing, these talks have at least averted a complete rupture. For the time being, forestalling such a split is in America's interests as well, if only because it holds some promise of finessing the looming controversy over Abbas retaining his post beyond January 2009.

Nevertheless, the Annapolis conference showed another way to deal with this division: mobilize an Arab consensus that opposes Hamas's rejection of peace while supporting Abbas and the PA in the West Bank. One cardinal virtue of this approach is that, even if it cannot soon unseat Hamas, it resolves a contradiction at the heart of Arab diplomacy in recent years. On the one hand, the Arab Peace Initiative offers Israel recognition under certain conditions. On the other hand, many of the same Arab governments that made this offer also give various forms of material, moral, and political support to Hamas, which is sworn to Israel's destruction and dedicated to supplanting the rival Palestinian government that has formally offered to make peace.

The Obama administration will have an important opportunity in this regard. In return for early engagement on Israeli-Palestinian and broader Arab-Israeli peacemaking, it can ask that all parties, including Arab governments, stop supporting Hamas until the group meets the Quartet's reasonable and required conditions.

Prepare a plan in case the Gaza ceasefire breaks down. The de facto ceasefire (or *tahdiya*) between Israel and Hamas—which has remained in effect for six months despite occasional breaches and retaliatory actions by both sides, but is now about due to expire—allows Hamas to arm and entrench itself in Gaza. Yet it also gives Israel and the PA a breathing spell in which to strengthen their own security posture and coordination with each other. And as its Arabic name indicates, the *tahdiya* also helps to calm the situation, protecting innocent lives on both sides while enabling peace talks to proceed without Hamas obstruction. On balance, then, the ceasefire is a net plus for the United States and its Israeli and Palestinian allies.

Israel and the PA may eventually find a new opportunity to work together if a military confrontation erupts in Gaza. All other things being equal, it would be best if Hamas could somehow be voted peacefully out of power. But at some point, if the ceasefire collapses, Israel may well decide to unleash a large-scale military assault against the group. For the United States and its regional friends, the biggest danger in this scenario would be the absence of a plausible plan for the day after the fighting dies down. This is another reason why it will be so important to enhance Palestinian security capabilities, so that the PA may one day be prepared to help restore order in Gaza—with Hamas's acquiescence if possible, but even without it if necessary.

Recommendations for Seeking Regional Support

Welcome Israeli-Syrian as well as Israeli-Palestinian peace talks. The historical record suggests that it would take a miracle to reach actual agreements on both of these negotiating tracks at once, let alone to implement any such agreements in tandem. Yet from the U.S. standpoint, there is no good reason why these two tracks cannot proceed simultaneously, as they did during the 1990s and again in 2007–2008. Moreover, U.S. acceptance of negotiations with Syria need not signify advance endorsement of any particular terms for a deal, particularly those concerning third parties linked to Syria (e.g., Lebanon, Hizballah, Hamas, Iraq,

Iran). In fact, the United States may be able to use Israeli-Syrian talks to promote a larger common interest in restraining the more radical elements in all of those linked parties, thereby consolidating gains for friendly democratic governments in both Lebanon and Iraq. Reactivating such talks (if necessary with renewed U.S. involvement) would also serve as a sort of diplomatic insurance policy in case Israelis reelect Netanyahu, who has long hinted at greater willingness to make territorial concessions on the Golan than the West Bank.

Seen in this light, U.S. reservations about the recent Turkish-mediated Israeli-Syrian talks seem misplaced. As for the impact of Syrian talks on the Palestinian track, there is little basis to suppose that they would have much effect at all, either positive or negative. An actual Israeli-Syrian agreement, however, would presumably include some restrictions on Syria's support for Hamas and other rejectionists, which could improve the odds of achieving and implementing an accord on the Palestinian track as well.

Intensify the search for Egyptian and Jordanian security support. Talk of a "Jordanian Option" for the West Bank or of "Egyptian responsibility" for Gaza, however well-intentioned, has become more inflammatory than inspiring. But talk of more direct Jordanian assistance to PA security forces, and of more effective Egyptian efforts to prevent Hamas arms smuggling, should be translated into immediate action. Although these are essential steps that serve the interests of all parties except Hamas, even that may not be sufficient incentive. Therefore, the United States should intensify its search for the best combination of carrots (e.g., even greater funding and technical assistance) to push these programs to the next level of operational success.

Supplement the Arab Peace Initiative, perhaps even with a grand gesture. The Arab Peace Initiative of 2002, reaffirmed as recently as 2007, is finally beginning to gain recognition in Israel as a valuable point of departure. The United States should echo this appraisal, without endorsing any details. Yet the initiative appears to neglect the human and emotional dimensions of the problem, and it lacks a step-by-step or even a schematic plan for how to get to the desired end-state of "land for peace." The first step toward filling these gaps is to encourage more specific declarations by all parties. For example, Israel could do the following:

- declare officially that it is ready to negotiate on the basis of the Arab initiative;
- formally announce its willingness to maintain full freedom of access and religious practice for all holy places—Muslim, Christian, and Jewish—in Jerusalem;
- declare a moratorium on settlement activity, at least beyond the relatively small areas near the Green Line that both sides envision swapping as part of a peace deal.

For their part, Arab governments could:

- emphasize that they are prepared to offer practical support for the return of refugees to a new Palestinian state (not to Israel);

- offer to end their formal state of war with Israel as a first step toward full reconciliation and recognition;
- fulfill their periodic promises to end incitement, and cease supporting the anachronistic "boycott offices" (targeting Israeli goods) that still operate in various Arab capitals;
- publicly acquiesce to the increasingly obvious idea, already tacitly accepted by the PA, that minor modifications to Israel's 1967 de facto borders can be negotiated by mutual agreement. This would have significant benefits for peacemaking on both the Palestinian and Syrian tracks;
- announce their willingness, as part of a peace accord, to recognize Israel as a Jewish state, alongside a Palestinian state—precisely the parties specified in the historic UN resolution of November 29, 1947, whose acceptance at the time might conceivably have spared the region generations of war.

Finally, it should be mentioned that in November 2008, Saudi Arabia hosted a UN symposium in New York with senior Israeli officials in attendance. Why not hold another such event in a major Arab city, or accept a return invitation to Israel? Why not encourage Iran to participate as well? Such regionally symbolic initiatives could very usefully supplement—even if they cannot substitute for—the hard work that will surely still be required to resolve the lasting tragedy of Israeli-Palestinian conflict. In fact, without new help from inside the region, that conflict has every prospect of preoccupying U.S. policy for generations to come.

POSTSCRIPT

Should the United States Engage Hamas?

As of early 2009, the Obama administration had pledged money to help rebuild Gaza but continued the Bush administration's policy of refusing to engage Hamas diplomatically until it renounces violence and accepts Israel's right to exist. Some observers hope that Hamas might reconcile its differences with Fatah and form a more united Palestinian political leadership that can deliver on any peace agreements forged with Israel. The consensus among most experts is that dramatic progress in relations between Israel and the Palestinians is unlikely in view of the aftershocks of the fighting in Gaza in early 2009. These include the election of a conservative coalition in Israel under Prime Minister Benjamin Netanyahu in February 2009. Netanyahu is a Likud Party leader who took a hard-line stance toward Hamas in an earlier term as prime minister and opposed Israel's 2005 withdrawal from Gaza.

For books on Hamas, Israel, and their relations with the United States, see Dennis Ross, *The Missing Peace: The Inside Story of the Fight for Middle East Peace* (Farrar, Strauss, and Giroux, 2005); Daniel Kurtzer and Scott Lasensky, *Negotiating Arab-Israeli Peace: American Leadership in the Middle East* (U.S. Institute of Peace, 2008); Jonathan Schanzer, *Hamas vs. Fatah: The Struggle for Palestine* (Palgrave Macmillan, 2008); Rashid Khalidi, *The Iron Cage: The Story of the Palestinian Struggle for Statehood* (Beacon, 2008); Zaju Chehab, *Inside Hamas: The Untold Story of the Militant Islamic Movement* (Nation Books, 2008); Walter Laqueur and Barry Rubin, eds., *The Israel–Arab Reader: A Documentary History of the Middle East Conflict,* 7th ed. (Penguin, 2008); Aaron David Miller, *The Much Too Promised Land: America's Elusive Search for Arab-Israeli Peace* (Bantam, 2008). For a recent article on the subject, see Walter Russell Meade, "Change They Can Believe In: To Make Israel Safe, Give Palestinians Their Due," *Foreign Affairs* (January/February 2009).

ISSUE 11

Should the United States Contribute to a NATO Peacekeeping Force to Encourage and Guarantee an Israeli– Palestinian Peace?

YES: Daniel Klaidman, from "A Plan of Attack for Peace," *Newsweek* (January 12, 2009)

NO: Montgomery C. Meigs, from "Realities of a Third-Party Force in Gaza," Washington Institute for Near East Policy, *Policy Watch*, #1451 (January 8, 2008)

ISSUE SUMMARY

YES: Daniel Klaidman, managing editor of *Newsweek*, Christopher Dickey, *Newsweek* Middle East editor, and *Newsweek* writers Dan Ephron and Michael Hirsh argue that NATO should provide peace-keeping forces as part of an overall settlement between Israel and the Palestinians.

NO: Gen. Montgomery C. Meigs (Retd.), visiting professor in the Security Studies Program at Georgetown University's Walsh School of Foreign Service, cautions that the demands upon and require-ments for a peacekeeping force between Israelis and Palestinians would be daunting, and warns that any such force would face attacks by extremist groups.

Although tensions between Israel and its Arab and Palestinian neighbors go back to Israel's founding as a state in 1948 and earlier waves of immigration, much of the contemporary confrontation between the two sides focuses on lands taken over by Israel in its 1967 war with its Arab neighbors and occu-pied in varying degrees by Israel since then: the Gaza strip, the West Bank of the Jordan River, and the Golan Heights. Many experts expect that any final peace settlement between Israel and its neighbors would involve some form of exchanging these occupied territories from Israel for credible guarantees of peace and security from the region's Arabs. One possible model for such an agreement is the Camp David Accords, a peace agreement between Israel and Egypt brokered by the United States in 1979 in which Israel returned to Egypt a fourth territory it had taken over in the 1973 War, the Sinai Peninsula. As part of this agreement, the United States and nearly a dozen other nations created a peacekeeping force, known as the Multinational Force and Observers (MFO), with the mission of verifying that both sides were following through on their commitments in the agreement. The force, currently consisting of over 400 American soldiers and troops from nearly a dozen other states, has been considered an important success, as both sides have honored their commitments and Egypt and Israel have remained at peace with one another. In addition, as part of the agreement, Israel dismantled most of its settlements in the Sinai.

Reaching peace agreements on the territories occupied in 1967 has proven far more difficult, however, and any peacekeeping force to monitor or enforce any such agreements would face far more difficult challenges. The Gaza Strip is a small, densely populated Palestinian territory that is geographically separated from the West Bank by Israeli territory. Gaza is presently controlled by Hamas, which is more radical than the Fatah party currently in power in the West Bank and which has refused to recognize Israel's right to exist and has carried out a campaign of suicide bombings and rocket attacks against Israel (see Issue 10 on Hamas). Any peacekeeping force here could have to fend off attacks from Hamas, or from even more radical groups not fully under its control, and such a force could also have to restrain Israel from any reprisals against attacks by Hamas.

The West Bank is less radicalized than the Gaza Strip and the Palestinian Authority in the West Bank has coordinated its security forces far more successfully with Israeli forces. The challenge for any peacekeeping force in the West Bank, however, is that the dramatic increase in Israeli settlements in the West Bank since 1967 has resulted in a patchwork of Israeli and Palestinian zones, often separated by security checkpoints and a large network of walls built by Israel. Wherever any boundaries might be drawn in a peace agreement—and any such boundaries would be complex and hard to police—there would be some Palestinians and some Israeli settlers who would object to the new borders, and any peacekeeping force could again be caught in the middle.

Finally, the Golan Heights include about 460 square miles of Syrian territory, and this territory is a key strategic high ground in any potential renewed conflict between Israel and Syria. Any peacekeeping force here would face the possibility of interposing itself not just between relatively small armed groups, but between the full conventional military forces of Israel and Syria.

Weighing against these challenges is the fact that the parties to any possible peace agreement have so little trust in one another that they may be unable to reach any agreement at all without the prospect of a peacekeeping force to ensure that the terms of any agreement are honored.

YES ↵   Daniel Klaidman

A Plan of Attack for Peace

In the remorseless logic of the Middle East, war is diplomacy by other means. This was true when Anwar Sadat launched a surprise attack on Israel in October 1973, a move that gave him the credibility and stature in the Arab world to make peace six years later with the Jewish state. It is also true today as Israel continues its assault on Hamas in Gaza, attacks that were prompted by Hamas missile strikes on Israel. The recent violence has reportedly cost more than 400 lives and left over 2,000 wounded; on Saturday, Israeli ground forces began moving in. Much of the outside world, not without justification, views the Gaza campaign as yet another atavistic explosion of Arab-Israeli violence that will, once again, set back the efforts for peace. But these strikes were not simply a reaction; they were a calculation.

Indeed, an Israeli source intimate with Olmert's thinking, speaking anonymously in order to speak freely, says the prime minister went into Gaza with a two-tiered set of objectives. The first was simply to stop the missiles Hamas was sending into Israel and to force a renewal of the ceasefire that existed until Dec. 19. Olmert's second goal, the source says, is far more ambitious—and risky: the prime minister wants to crush Hamas altogether, first by aerial attacks and then with a grinding artillery and infantry assault. The hope, however faint, is eventually to allow Palestinian President Mahmoud Abbas and his Fatah government to reassert control in Gaza, clearing the way in the future for a return to serious peace negotiations. With Hamas out of the way, Olmert believes there is a chance that Israel and the Palestinians can put flesh on the outlines of a comprehensive peace plan he negotiated with Abbas over the past year.

Wishful thinking? Probably. After so many failed attempts, the phrase "peace process" has little meaning. Olmert's own motives in Gaza may have as much to do with domestic politics as foreign policy. Badly weakened and facing possible corruption charges, he has been grasping to rescue his tarnished legacy. But the fact that Olmert wants to negotiate, and that Abbas wants to negotiate, underscores the stubborn, maddening fact about the Israeli-Palestinian relationship: there is only one path to peace, and both sides know what it is—and yet neither side has been willing to take it. The violence, the bombings, the threats and counterthreats are all the more exhausting and senseless because they are, essentially, an elaborate delaying tactic. The broad contours of a peace were laid out eight years ago when President Bill Clinton brought the two sides together at Camp David and tried to broker a historic deal. The current Olmert "shelf plan" is remarkably similar to the Clinton parameters: a two-state solution in which Israelis and Palestinians make painful compromises on the core issues of territory, security, Jerusalem and Palestinian refugees. The 2000 talks collapsed partly because time ran out on Clinton's term and partly because neither side had the political clout to sell the deal back home. Bush, fixated on Iraq and terror, has paid little mind to the conflict until recently.

There are many difficult details to be worked out: the exact borders of a two-state compromise; the fate of Palestinian refugees; the future of Jerusalem. President Barack Obama and his secretary of state, Hillary Clinton, will now inherit these challenges. They cannot simply pick up where Bill Clinton left off. The strategic context in the region has changed profoundly—for the worse. George W. Bush's war on terror has diminished American credibility in the Arab world. Moreover, the leaders of those Arab states that are closest to the United States have lost legitimacy, challenged by popular opposition at home. Meanwhile a Shiite government in Baghdad, the first in half a millennium, along with the rise of Iran, has increased Shiite-Sunni tensions throughout the Middle East. (On the bright side, Iran's enhanced influence in the region means that the West has a powerful incentive to break up the alliance between Tehran and Damascus. Real progress with Syria could have a positive effect on Israeli-Palestinian talks.)

At the moment, the greatest impediment to peace is Hamas, the terrorist group that won power in Gaza through elections in 2006. The rise of a rejectionist "Hamastan" in Gaza has left Palestinians divided between Abbas's more moderate Fatah government and radical Hamas leaders who encourage violence and believe Israel itself should not exist. Hamas rose by exploiting the misery and grievances of the Palestinians. The challenge for Palestinians and Israelis who desire peace is to make Hamas irrelevant in the eyes of its supporters by offering them something more tangible than revenge.

The suspicion of many Israelis—sometimes justified—that Palestinian leaders are interested not in peace but in Israel's destruction has been another powerful obstacle. Israelis warn against becoming *freiers*. The word is Yiddish for "suckers," but it carries deeper psychological freight in a country that grew out of the ashes of the Holocaust and has absorbed "never again" as its mantra. The Palestinians harbor similar resentments at having repeatedly drawn the short stick of history. As many of them see it, the land of Israel is land that the world stole from them in 1948, leaving them without a home. At Camp David, Yasir Arafat refused to finalize a peace agreement with Israel, claiming that to do so would be to court assassination by his own people.

There are no options other than a comprehensive agreement that creates two sovereign states, Israel and Palestine, warily coexisting side by side. Lately, some Palestinian intellectuals have been making the case for a single, binational state—an idea that could have even more currency in the aftermath of Israel's military action in Gaza. But from the Israeli perspective, such a one-state solution would be disastrous, for it would terminate the founding principle of the country as a Jewish homeland.

President-elect Obama may have hoped he would have time to develop an approach to peacemaking in the Holy Land. But as usual, the schedule is dictated by facts on the ground. It is unclear how engaged Obama can be in the Middle East in the early months of his administration; his first priority will be fixing the American economy. What Obama can't delay once he takes office is forcefully recommitting the United States to a two-state solution and the basic framework for peace that already exists.

During the presidential campaign, Obama's detractors tried to cast doubt on his loyalty to Israel. It was a political ploy, since Obama has spoken out forcefully in Israel's defense. Yet many Israeli and American Jews hope Obama will be willing to deliver the sort of tough love to the Israelis that Bush, reflexively defensive of Israel, refused to do for eight years. The president must be willing to pressure the next Israeli prime minister to make difficult concessions for peace. The Israelis may be more open to such pressure now than they were in the past. Time is no longer on their side. Arab birthrates are rising. By most estimates, if Israel insists on maintaining control over the West Bank, the land from the Jordan River to the Mediterranean Sea will be majority Arab in years to come. Thus, the only way for Israel to stay a Jewish state is to make way for a Palestinian state. Early signs are that Obama intends to play this role of loyal but critical friend—and in that sense will be, as the joke goes, "good for the Jews."

The new president and his team will be able to rely on ideas derived from the work of negotiators who have struggled, with the patience of Job, to find a middle ground. There is room for refinement and improvement. The haggling will be epic. But in the end (if there ever is an end), any lasting agreement for peace will probably look something like this.

Article I: Territory

Ever since Israel blitzed the Arabs in 1967's Six-Day War—taking the Sinai and Gaza from Egypt, the Golan Heights from Syria and the West Bank from Jordan—"land for peace" has been the guiding principle of any comprehensive deal. It remains the only option. Israel has already withdrawn from Gaza; it must now pull out of the vast majority of the West Bank. Palestinians will establish their homeland in these two swatches of land. In return, the Palestinians and other Arabs will formally renounce their claims on the Jewish state and recognize its right to exist. But there will have to be some adjustments to the pre-1967 borders. Israel and the Palestinians should swap equal amounts of land, allowing a majority of the roughly 270,000 Israeli settlers now residing in the largest of the West Bank settlement blocks to stay where they are while remaining under Israeli sovereignty. Israel in turn would give up a land corridor connecting Gaza to the West Bank and allowing for the free flow of people and commerce between the two. There is one additional challenge that did not exist when Clinton laid out his original proposal in 2000: the Israelis have erected a security barrier that puts a full 8 percent of the West Bank on their side of the fence. It has already changed the way Israelis think about the borders of their nation. "The security barrier is creating new conceptual and spatial contours in the Israeli imagination," says Daniel Levy, a former Israeli negotiator and now a senior fellow at both the Century and New America foundations. But for any deal to succeed, the barrier would have to be torn down or, at the very least, moved.

Article II: Security

Back in 2000, this was the most straightforward of the issues to be worked out. Both sides generally agreed that the new Palestinian state would have to be largely de-militarized. Palestinian forces would be allowed to maintain light arms to enforce domestic law and order but would not have an offensive capability that could in any way threaten Israel. The Palestinians would have sovereignty over their airspace, but it would be limited to civilian aviation. Yet the violence of the last eight years—not only between Palestinians and Israelis but also between Fatah and Hamas forces—complicates the security equation. The Israelis are now more skeptical that Fatah is strong enough to assume responsibility for security. A more feasible approach would be to put a NATO-based international force in the West Bank that would later transfer control to the Palestinians. Obama might well go for this; his designated national-security adviser, retired Gen. James Jones, developed the idea while serving as Condoleezza Rice's envoy for Palestinian-Israeli security issues. As far as Israeli forces are concerned, they would be able to withdraw from the strategically important Jordan Valley over a longer period of time, perhaps three years. Israel would be allowed to maintain a number of warning stations on Palestinian territory. Finally, Israel would allow the Palestinians to have sovereignty over their borders and international crossing points. But these borders and crossing points should be monitored by an international presence.

Article III: Jerusalem

The sacred "City of Peace" is at the very heart of the 100-year conflict: how to divvy up rights to a holy place with too much history and not enough geography. In 2000, Clinton's deft diplomatic skills helped demystify Jerusalem. He asked Israeli and Palestinian mediators to come up with a list of 60 basic municipal responsibilities they could share, from garbage collection to mail delivery. There was remarkable consensus. By moving the conversation from the sacred to the mundane, the exercise isolated the practical issues of running a city from the abstract and emotionally fraught issue of sovereignty. Clinton's seductively simple notion was this: in occupied East Jerusalem, he said, "What is Arab should be Palestinian and what is Jewish should be Israeli." This is just as relevant today. So is the principle from Camp David that Jerusalem must be divided—but shared, and it must serve as a capital to both states.

One of Clinton's solutions will likely have to be dialed back. His concept of split-level sovereignty for the holiest parts of Jerusalem are too incendiary. Jews know the area as the Temple Mount, the site where the ancient temple once stood. It is revered by Muslims as the Haram al-Sharif, the place where Muhammad ascended to heaven on a white steed. Clinton proposed Palestinian sovereignty over the Haram and Israeli sovereignty over the entire Western Wall, part of which runs beneath the Muslim quarter of the Old City.

Today, it is very unlikely that either side would accept such a division. But there are other creative solutions. One is a proposal in a new book by Martin Indyk, Clinton's ambassador to Israel at the time of the 2000 summit. Indyk recommends that the Old City be placed under a so-called "special regime," with Israeli and Palestinian governments sharing sovereignty over the territory. But the religious sites inside the Old City walls would remain under the control of the respective Muslim, Jewish and Christian religious authorities without any actual designation of sovereignty. Alternatively, Indyk suggests, the entire Holy Basin—the Old City and religious sites—could be placed under international supervision, with religious authorities controlling their holy places.

Article IV: Refugees

This may be the most difficult problem to solve. What will become of the Palestinians who fled or were forced from their territory in 1948, and their descendants? There are as many as 4 million refugees living in camps on the West Bank and Gaza and in Jordan, Syria and Lebanon. They are poor, stateless and angry. For half a century they have waited, believing that one day they will return to their homes. Throughout the years of negotiations, Palestinians have demanded a "right of return." But to Israelis, the notion implies an admission that they are responsible for the refugee crisis and the historical injustices leveled against the Palestinians. Israelis, offended at the suggestion that their country was born in sin, have drawn a clear line.

Israeli leaders have been willing to accept a partial solution: some refugees living in the camps would make homes in the newly established state of Palestine. A small, symbolic number would be permitted to move to Israel. For this to work, refugees living in camps in Syria and other foreign states would have to be allowed to stay if they chose, and be granted citizenship in their adopted countries—the Arab host countries could not demand that all of the refugees return to Palestine, where they would overwhelm the budding state. And the refugees must be granted a window of time—perhaps three to five years—to petition international courts for compensation for what they have lost, perhaps as part of a massive regional redevelopment plan.

But how to salve the wounds of Palestinian grievance? One intriguing solution is offered by writer Walter Russell Mead in an essay in the current issue of *Foreign Affairs*. Mead argues that though Israel must take some responsibility for the Palestinian tragedy, the entire *nakba*, or catastrophe, "cannot simply be laid at Israel's door." Israel must acknowledge its part in the events of 1948, but the international community must take "ultimate responsibility" for the 60-year-old crisis. In this way, the world would acknowledge that the Palestinians have indeed suffered a historic injustice, but obviate the need for Israel to bear full responsibility. "This is a way to confer dignity on the Palestinian people," says Levy—a crucial step toward securing an elusive peace.

Montgomery C. Meigs

➡ **NO**

Realities of a Third-Party Force in Gaza

$\mathbf{A}$s the conflict in the Gaza Strip rages, several international entities have called for the deployment of a third-party force to patrol the Rafah border area between Egypt and Gaza. Suggestions range from simple border monitors to a full peace enforcement operation; if configured and chartered properly, this force may offer advantages to all sides. But absent clear mission objectives, robust rules of engagement, and sufficient numbers of experienced, well-trained, and culturally sensitive personnel, the introduction of such a force in Gaza risks worsening the situation. Moreover, regardless of the mission and composition of such a force, it could operate effectively only if all parties concerned accept the premise that peace enforcement operations on their territories are required. Overcoming these many obstacles, however, may be beyond the abilities of all concerned.

The EU and Gaza

As part of the Agreement on Movement and Access negotiated after Israel's withdrawal from Gaza in 2005, the European Union provided a Border Assistance Mission (BAM) to monitor the Rafah crossing point between Egypt and Gaza. During the EU mission's peak activity from November 2005 to June 2006, nearly 280,000 people crossed the Rafah border. As a result of frequent closures and clashes after the abduction of Israeli soldier Gilad Shalit in June 2006, the Rafah border was open for only eighty-three days in the following year. Even in this short time, 165,000 people crossed. Over the years, Rafah's porosity has become an aggravating factor in the Israeli-Palestinian conflict.

Even as a limited mission, the EU BAM encountered difficulties that pale in comparison to those an international force would face after a potential ceasefire in Gaza. First, the BAM was only a monitoring mission. The European team did not operate the border terminal and had no authority beyond the Rafah passenger checkpoints. It merely oversaw the activities of Palestinian Authority (PA) border officials and liaised with the Israel Defense Forces (IDF). A future arrangement that addresses the issue of opening Gaza to the transit of goods and people will require opening not only the passenger terminal, but also Rafah's vehicle terminals for commercial goods.

From *PolicyWatch*, #1451, January 8, 2008. Copyright © 2008 by Washington Institute for Near East Policy. Reprinted by permission.

Requirements for an International Force in Gaza

Regardless of its precise mission, the international force must have a mandate that allows it to curtail the smuggling activity across and underneath the border from Kerem Shalom to the sea in order to prevent the rearmament of Hamas. To be effective, the international force's countersmuggling effort must also reach into Egypt or Gaza (or both), a prospect that is sure to complicate relations with each of those parties and perhaps nullify prospects for the force's operations. In the end, Israel may find it easier to reach bilateral agreement with Egypt. Furthermore, a mission that extends beyond smuggling, and attempts to inhibit rocket fire as well, would be even more complicated and challenging.

The following requirements must be met if an international force, mandated with curtailing smuggling activity, is to be effective:

- The force must have total authority over the border area it needs for its facilities and operations both above and below ground. This territory must have operational depth on both sides of the border that supports effective border-control operations.
- The rules of engagement (ROE) must authorize the appropriate use of lethal force (1) to counter threats to a safe and secure environment and (2) for self-defense. The force's charter must give its commander final authority on what constitutes a threat to a safe and secure environment and when to use lethal force for protection.

Given the near certainty that the force would be an international coalition, it is unlikely that all the potential contributors would have the political fortitude and the quality and type of forces needed to succeed in this type of operation. And given the current military commitments in Afghanistan and elsewhere of likely contributing nations, it will be especially difficult to assemble the necessary force. Nevertheless, nations that cannot provide the quality of troops needed, or who cannot support robust ROE, must not be included. The force commander and his cadre must be experienced in peacekeeping operations and coalition command, and must have capable U.S. and NATO political advisors. The command must be empowered to deal with senior Israeli, Palestinian, Egyptian, and perhaps other regional officials, as well as senior officials of the sponsoring international body (likely NATO).

The international peacekeeping force (PKF) would also need:

- extensive intelligence capability, requiring close cooperation with Israel, the PA, and Egypt, and the highest priority intelligence support from Washington and the capitals of the contributing nations;
- a heavy proportion of special operations forces (including a deputy commander) if the settlement includes the introduction of PA forces from the West Bank to Gaza to perform reconnaissance missions, direct action, or to train Palestinian security forces;
- engineering skills and specialized sensor technology to halt smuggling under the Rafah border;

- language, cultural awareness, and negotiating skills, since reliance on local translators would give spoilers an opportunity to infiltrate and observe the activities of the units. The PKF should include veterans of Iraq and other recent international peacekeeping operations, with a premium on speakers of Arabic.

Implications

A well-led, properly manned, well-equipped force with an appropriate mandate could manage a border-control operation, but only at significant cost and effort. From the Palestinian perspective, the force would provide them with an impartial referee that would deter future Israeli military operations into the Rafah area. Further, it could also serve as a basis for reintroducing PA forces loyal to Mahmoud Abbas back into Gaza, at least at the key border-crossing points. From an Israeli perspective, an appropriately manned, missioned, and executed force might succeed in curtailing weapons smuggling and thereby decrease the rationale for any future Israeli military operations in the area. Once a ceasefire proves durable, a PKF could ensure the access of humanitarian relief to Gaza in the short term, and reconstruction and development projects in the long term. Finally, the force and its diplomatic and political links to both sides could give the United States and its allies limited control over events, and perhaps a better sense of reality on the ground.

Even with official Israeli and Palestinian acceptance, any outside force attempting to provide security in Gaza will encounter great difficulty. The emotions and scars of the fighting in Gaza and of previous conflicts would permeate every contact with local actors, particularly when the force makes mistakes, which would be broadcast instantly throughout the Arab and Muslim world. Acceptance of the force would depend on early and continued successes in maintaining security. This dynamic will apply equally to the Palestinian population and the IDF. Given the poor record of past border monitors, however, the Israeli military will be extremely reluctant to delegate security responsibilities to foreign forces.

Most dangerously, the force would become a target for the capable rejectionist and extremist groups within or outside the Hamas umbrella. An international force must be prepared to preempt or counter well-executed, ruthless, and repetitive attacks. And if the peacekeeping forces in the Sinai and on the Golan Heights are any indicators, donor countries must accept the reality of having a PKF remain in place in Gaza for decades.

In short, knowing what the force will encounter and the certainty of frustrations and disappointments along the way, national leaders contemplating a peacekeeping operation as a means of preventing equipment and weapons from entering Gaza must approach the decision with a grounded sense of reality. To accomplish this mission, the force needs a clear mandate to use minimum lethal force to stop the smuggling, and not merely observe and report. A properly configured and supported force has a chance of success, but one not properly chartered, manned, and equipped would prove an embarrassment and, in regional political terms, very costly.

POSTSCRIPT

Should the United States Contribute to a NATO Peacekeeping Force to Encourage and Guarantee an Israeli–Palestinian Peace?

In the wake of Israel's military intervention in Gaza in late 2008 and early 2009, most observers expect slow progress at best in any negotiations on this region. In the West Bank, Israel and Fatah continued to work toward operational cooperation in providing mutual security despite tensions over the Gaza issue. Yet the complicated politics of Israeli settlements in the West Bank, and the complicated and emotionally charged issues involved in the status of Jerusalem, make dramatic progress toward any final settlement difficult here as well. Diplomatic moves by President Obama and U.S. Secretary of State Hillary Clinton early in the Obama administration suggest that they feel the prospects for a peace agreement between Israel and Syria may be slightly better than those for Gaza or the West Bank, but the history of more than four decades of conflict over this issue suggests that it is also unlikely to be resolved quickly.

For books on the theory and practice of peacekeeping, see Lise Howard, *UN Peacekeeping in Civil Wars* (Cambridge 2007); Michael W. Doyle and Nicholas Sambanis, *Making War and Building Peace: United Nations Peace Operations* (Princeton 2006); and Virginia Fortna, *Peace Time: Cease-Fire Agreements and the Durability of Peace* (Princeton 2004). For books on the United States and conflicts in the Middle East, see the sources cited in the Postscript to Issue 10.

ISSUE 12

Should the United States Continue Sanctions on Cuba?

YES: Otto J. Reich, from "Testimony Before the Senate Committee on Commerce, Science and Transportation" (May 21, 2002)

NO: Ernesto Zedillo and Thomas R. Pickering, from "Rethinking U.S.-Latin American Relations," A Report of the Partnership for the Americas Commission, The Brookings Institution (November 2008)

ISSUE SUMMARY

YES: Otto J. Reich, assistant secretary of state for Latin American affairs at the time of his 2002 testimony, argues for maintaining existing sanctions on Cuba.

NO: The report of the Brookings Institution Partnership for the Americas Commission, cochaired by former president of Mexico Ernesto Zedillo and former U.S. undersecretary of state for political affairs Thomas Pickering, proposes the lifting of all restrictions on travel to Cuba by Americans, repealing the embargo on communications equipment to Cuba, taking Cuba off the State Department's list of State Sponsors of Terrorism, and upgrading official contacts with the Cuban government.

U.S. economic and diplomatic sanctions against Cuba have been the cornerstone of U.S. policy toward that country for decades as a result of widespread American disapproval of the regime of Cuban President Fidel Castro, his suppression of dissent at home, and his ties to the Soviet Union and to revolutionary regimes more generally. Yet several developments in the last few years have renewed the long-standing debates over U.S. sanctions policies. First, Fidel Castro developed severe health problems in 2006 that have largely kept him out of public view. In July 2006, he transferred his official duties to his brother, Raul Castro, and in February 2008 Raul Castro became the official president of Cuba. Raul, who had been the longtime leader of Cuba's armed forces and has not appeared frequently in public or announced any major policy changes or reforms as president, is widely viewed as an interim leader due to his advanced age (he was born in June 1931). Second, although Cuba has continued to maintain ties to countries that are adversarial toward the United States and to foster anti-democratic movements in Latin America, these relationships do not pose a substantial strategic threat to the United States now that the Soviet Union is no more. In contrast, Cuba's relations with the Soviet Union posed a sharp strategic threat to the United States, exemplified by the Cuban missile crisis, which many experts view as the closest the United States and the Soviet Union ever came to nuclear war. Third, as the Cuban exiles who fled from Castro's revolution in 1959 to the United States have entered their fiftieth year on American soil, new generations of Cuban Americans have developed more diverse and complex views on relations with Cuba. Cuban American voters, a politically important constituent in Florida in the 2000 presidential elections, were less united in their views and voting behavior in the 2008 election. All these developments have set the context for a new debate over U.S. policies toward Cuba and created the possibility of the most fundamental changes in these policies in 50 years.

YES ↙

Otto J. Reich

Testimony Before the Senate Committee on Commerce, Science and Transportation

Mr. Chairman, members of the Committee, it is an honor for me to testify today before this committee of the United States Senate regarding the Bush Administration's trade policy toward Cuba. I want to thank the Chairman for giving me this opportunity to testify before this committee.

President Bush yesterday announced his Initiative for a New Cuba. The Initiative calls on the Cuban government to undertake political and economic reforms, and to conduct free and fair elections next year for the National Assembly. The Initiative challenges the Cuban government to open its economy, allow independent trade unions, and end discriminatory practices against Cuban workers. If the Cuban government takes these concrete steps to open up its political and economic system, President Bush will work with the Congress to ease the ban on trade and travel between the United States and Cuba.

With reform, trade can benefit the Cuban people and allow them to share in the progress of our time. Without major reform, unrestricted trade with Cuba only helps the Castro regime, not the Cuban people.

The Initiative for a New Cuba also reaches out to the Cuban people immediately by facilitating meaningful humanitarian assistance to the Cuban people by American religious and other nongovernmental groups; by providing direct assistance to the Cuban people through nongovernmental organizations; by seeking the resumption of direct mail service to and from Cuba; and by establishing scholarships in the United States for Cuban students and professionals trying to build independent civil institutions and for family members of political prisoners.

The Initiative for a New Cuba also states that the United States is not a threat to Cuban sovereignty. The Initiative for a New Cuba is not the end of the President's policy review, but the beginning of an ongoing, flexible and responsive campaign designed to generate rapid and peaceful change within Cuba.

The Initiative is important because Cuba continues to be ruled by a dictator. The regime has failed to meet the basic needs of the Cuban people and it continues to deny them the freedoms of speech and assembly as well as the ability to choose their leaders. The Committee to Protect Journalists continues

U.S. Senate, May 21, 2002, pp. 28–30.

to list Cuba as one of the 10 worst enemies of the press worldwide characterizing its actions as a "scorched earth assault" on independent journalists.

Cuba is the exception to our hemispheric family of democratic nations. It is essential that democratic development, especially through the formation of independent civil society organizations, political parties, and free elections, begin rapidly in order to maximize the prospects for a smooth transition to democracy.

The regime has shown little interest in reforming itself, or moving toward a more open or representative government. For this reason, the Administration opposes steps which would have the effect of strengthening the Cuban regime. But the Initiative encourages the Cuban government to begin addressing the concerns we share with other nations of the hemisphere.

Central to our policy is the reality of the Government of Cuba, which has continued to be hostile to the United States. Cuba remains on the list of state sponsors of terrorism, in part because Cuba harbors fugitives from U.S. justice.

Furthermore, the Cuban regime continues to violate human rights and fundamental freedoms. This was amply illustrated by the jailing of Vladimiro Roca, in the most oppressive of conditions, for over 1,700 days simply because he had the courage to call for a national dialogue. In fact, the U.N. Commission on Human Rights recently approved a resolution calling on Cuba to make progress in respecting human, civil and political rights.

As the Secretary has noted, a number of events since August 2001 also have contributed to a reevaluation of our policy toward Cuba.

First, in the wake of the tragic events of September 11, Cuba's reaction was hostile to U.S. efforts to respond to terrorism. This was clear from Cuban government statements that the war in Afghanistan is "fascistic and militaristic" and the Cuban Foreign Minister's remarks at the U.N. General Assembly, when he accused the United States of intentionally targeting Afghan children for death and Red Cross hospitals in Afghanistan for destruction.

Also in September, five agents of the Cuban government were sentenced for conspiring to spy against the United States, including efforts to penetrate U.S. military bases. One of these five also was convicted and sentenced for conspiracy to commit murder.

Further, on September 21, 2001, Ana Belen Montes, a senior analyst in the Defense Intelligence Agency, was arrested for spying for Cuba against the United States. She subsequently entered a guilty plea in March 2002.

Spying, Cuba's harboring of fugitives from U.S. justice, and its continued violation of human rights and fundamental freedoms, combine to demonstrate that Cuba continues to carry out its aggressive policies against the United States and its own people.

Moreover, we know that Cuba has a sophisticated biotechnology infrastructure capable of supporting a biological weapons program and has transferred dual-use technology to a number of countries around the world, including those with known or suspected biological weapons programs. These facts underpin our assessment that Cuba has at least a limited, developmental biological weapons research and development effort.

These incidents clearly reaffirm Cuba's hostility to the United States and the threat it represents to our national security. As a result, Administration policy considers visits by senior Cuban officials, at this time, to be inappropriate and detrimental to the national interest.

That said, the Administration is open to transforming the relationship. The President's initiative offers a serious alternative, one which we urge the Government of Cuba to weigh carefully.

Presently, sales of medicine and agricultural commodities to Cuba are, while subject to certain restrictions, legal. Sales of medicine have been legal since passage of the Cuban Democracy Act of 1992 (CDA); the Government of Cuba, however, has been reluctant to purchase medicine and medical equipment from the United States at least in part because it finds prices to be too high.

In 1999, President Clinton authorized licensing by Commerce's Bureau of Export Administration, recently renamed the Bureau of Industry and Security, of sales of food and agricultural inputs to independent entities in Cuba, including religious groups, private farmers and private sector undertakings such as family restaurants. This measure did not result in significant sales because the Cuban government opposed it.

The Trade Sanctions Reform and Export Enhancement Act of 2000 (TSRA) permitted the Cuban government to purchase, on a cash basis or with financing by third-country financial institutions, agricultural commodities from the United States. Through late 2001, Castro refused to buy "even a grain of rice" from the United States and perhaps with good reason.

Cuba is one of the most heavily indebted countries in the world, with an external debt burden of about $3000 per capita, including ruble debt. As a result of its economic performance, Moodys rates Cuba in its lowest category. Cuba is so bad off that its merchant marine leaves behind a "trail of unpaid creditors at every port they visit," according to an Amsterdam newspaper that also recently observed, "Cuba is practically bankrupt." No wonder Castro executed a 180-degree policy turn, after Hurricane Michelle last November.

Despite the Castro regime's implacable hostility, the Administration has carried out and will continue to carry out its responsibilities under TSRA. Since Cuba decided to make food purchases from the United States, Cuba has made more than $40 million in sales, with another $50 million reported to be in progress. Overall the Administration has licensed more than $1.2 billion worth of agricultural commodities for Cuba since implementation of TSRA in July 2001. These purchases demonstrate the Cuban regime's strong motivation to complete these sales, particularly taking into account that the Cuban government has chosen to use its very limited foreign exchange reserves in these transactions. This is one reason for the Administration's policy judgment that marketing visits by Cuban trade officials are not necessary to conclude purchases of U.S. agricultural commodities.

Applications for visas by Cuban officials are considered on a case-by-case basis at the time of application in accordance with existing law and in light of current policy considerations. The Department of State recognizes that visits to agricultural production facilities to address certain sanitary and phytosanitary issues may be needed so that sales can be completed. Visas have been issued to such personnel in the past and such visa applications as are received by the U.S. Interests Section will be carefully considered. In addition, representatives of American firms who wish to arrange legally permitted trade can request specific licenses from the Department of Treasury that allow travel-related transactions for visits to Cuba.

In conclusion, as the President said yesterday, quoting Jose Marti, "Barriers of ideas are stronger than barricades of stone. For the benefit of Cuba's people, it is time for Mr. Castro to cast aside old and failed ideas and to start to think differently about the future. Today could mark a new dawn in a long friendship between our people, but only if the Castro regime sees the light."

Thank you Mr. Chairman.

**Ernesto Zedillo and
Thomas R. Pickering**

➜ **NO**

Cuba and the United States: Rethinking a Troubled Relationship

U.S.-Cuban relations have disproportionately dominated U.S. policy toward the LAC region for years. Tensions generated by U.S. policies toward Cuba have affected the United States' image in the region and have hindered Washington's ability to work constructively with other countries. For this reason, addressing U.S. policy toward Cuba has implications that go beyond the bilateral relationship and affect U.S. relations with the rest of the LAC region more generally. Political change in Washington, combined with recent demographic and ideological shifts in the Cuban American community and recent leadership changes in Cuba itself, offer a valuable opportunity to change course.

Though the reforms enacted recently in Cuba have thus far been mostly cosmetic, they could create openings for grassroots political and economic activity. The removal of restrictions on access to tourist facilities and on the purchase of mobile telephones and computers may have an important psychological impact and increase contact with the outside world. Also, the Cuban government has recently lifted all wage caps, started to allow performance bonuses for certain salaried professions, liberalized the sale of farming equipment, and begun to lease idle state lands to increase agricultural output. These reforms may improve labor incentives, purchasing power, and productivity.

Economic developments in Cuba will affect U.S.-Cuban relations. Today, the United States is Cuba's fourth-largest trading partner; in 2007, it sold the island $582 million worth of goods (including shipping costs). Cuba is currently exploring its prospects for energy production in both sugarcane-based ethanol and offshore oil. Spanish, Canadian, Norwegian, Brazilian, Indian, and other international oil companies have secured contracts to explore drilling possibilities off the Cuban coast. If the ethanol and oil industries become fully operational in five to seven years, revenues of $3 billion to $5 billion annually could significantly strengthen the Cuban economy and reduce the government's vulnerability to external political pressure. With stable inflows of hard currency from oil sales, the Cuban government would have more funds to use at its discretion, further eroding the effects of the U.S. embargo on trade with Cuba.

From *Rethinking US-Latin American Relations: A Report of the Partnership for the Americas Commission* (Brookings Institution Press, November 2008), pp. 28–30. Copyright © 2008 by Partnership for the Americas Commission, Brookings Institution. Reprinted by permission.

Demographic and ideological shifts in the Cuban American community in the United States add to the prospects for reorienting U.S.-Cuban relations. The Cuban American population is getting younger demographically, and its priorities regarding Cuba have shifted from a traditional hard line to a focus on the day-to-day existence of those living on the island. According to 2007 polls by Florida International University, Cuban Americans are increasingly opposed to current U.S. policy, particularly restrictions on family travel, caps on remittances, and limitations on the sale of medical and other vital supplies to Cuba; 64 percent of those polled support a return to the more liberal policies of 2003. The Cuban American community has historically played a central role in U.S. domestic politics, with strong influence in the state of Florida. This shift in public opinion may ease the path toward reorientation for policymakers in Washington.

The view of this Commission is that U.S. policy should be reframed to enable legitimate Cuban voices to shape a representative, accountable, and sustainable transition to democracy. The Cuban people should be empowered to drive sustainable change from within by facilitating the free flow of information and expanding diplomatic networks to support human rights and democratic governance.

Recommendations

The recommendations on this issue fall into three categories: those that can be implemented unilaterally by the United States; those that require bilateral talks between Washington and Havana; and those that are multilateral, demanding cooperation among several governments. The recommendations are listed sequentially, starting with those that should be implemented immediately by the U.S. government. The timing of bilateral and multilateral recommendations would be determined by how intergovernmental negotiations and discussions evolve.

Lift all restrictions on travel to Cuba by Americans.
The ability of Americans to travel to Cuba would allow for better understanding, promote small businesses, and provide information to the Cuban people.

Repeal of all aspects of the "communications embargo" (radio, TV,
Internet) and readjust regulations governing trade in low-technology
communications equipment.
Liberalize regulations on the sale of all communications equipment, including computers, as admissible under the State Sponsors of Terrorism List under the Export Administration Act and the Foreign Assistance Act. This would encourage the transfer of information and a freer flow of ideas.

Remove caps and targeting restrictions on remittances.
The amount of money that visitors may take to Cuba should reflect the U.S. government's limits for other countries. These financial measures would help get resources directly into the hands of ordinary Cubans, empowering them, improving their standard of living, and reducing their dependence on the state.

Take Cuba off the State Department's State Sponsors of Terrorism List.
This classification is widely deemed to be factually inaccurate. There has been no evidence in the past decade to maintain this classification for Cuba, and top U.S. military leaders have called for the country's removal from the list. Doing so would reframe U.S.-Cuban relations in a less combative light, allowing for a more constructive approach to foreign policy.

Promote knowledge and reconciliation by permitting federal funding
of cultural, academic, and sports exchanges.
These exchanges would facilitate nonpolitical contact and dialogue between citizens of the two countries, bringing diverse ideas into Cuba. In parallel, U.S. nongovernmental organizations should be encouraged to establish ties with their Cuban counterparts and enhance grassroots dialogue. More broadly, the United States should work with Cuba to maximize human contacts, drawing on the full range of U.S. government programs for educational and cultural exchange, including at the high school, university, and postgraduate levels. Youth groups should be supported in establishing networks through student exchanges, home stays, video conferences, and media channels.

Provide assistance to the Cuban people in recovering from natural
and human-made disasters.
This would entail removing restrictions on the donation and sale of humanitarian goods and agricultural products to Cuba, including medicine, medical equipment, and food. It would also allow the licensing of construction and other goods needed to support postdisaster recovery efforts. U.S.-Cuban bilateral talks would be opened on responses to a variety of emergencies, including natural crises and mass migrations. The sale of medicine, medical equipment, and food would be allowed on commercial terms.

Encourage enhanced official contact and cooperation between
U.S. and Cuban diplomats and governments.
Bilateral discussions should be expanded with Cuban officials on issues of mutual security, including migration, narcotics, organized crime, disaster management, public health, and environmental protection. The U.S. government should propose a twelve-month period of intense dialogue, targeted at the exchange of defense attachés and the appointment of ambassadors. Military–military and civilian–military contacts should be fostered. Respectful and cordial relations would be resumed by allowing the Cuban Interests Section in Washington access to U.S. policymakers and expect reciprocity in Havana. Diplomatic travel for the staffs of both interests sections would be permitted, and their range of contacts would be expanded through the exchange of attachés.

End opposition to the reengagement of the international community
with Cuba in regional and global economic and political organizations
as a means to promote democracy.
This would include removing barriers to Cuba's observer status at key international financial institutions, particularly the Inter-American Development

Bank, the World Bank, and the International Monetary Fund. Cuba should be allowed to participate in relevant seminars, and the international financial institutions should be allowed to conduct fact-finding missions in Cuba. The U.S. government should ask the Inter-American Development Bank to begin engaging Cuba in areas related to the financing of strategic development projects.

A key venue for hemispheric cooperation in a wide range of issues is the Organization of American States. Cuba's membership in the organization was suspended in 1962 after a majority of its members decided that a government that self-identified as Marxist-Leninist was "incompatible with the principles and objectives of the inter-American system." The U.S. government should not object to a decision by the organization to reengage Cuba, beginning with invitations to participate in technical and specialized agencies.

Work with the members of the European Union and other countries to create a multilateral fund for civil society that will train potential entrepreneurs in management and innovation.
Providing capital to establish small businesses that improve the livelihoods of large segments of the population could increase the demand from within Cuba for expanded economic freedoms and opportunities for advancement.

POSTSCRIPT

Should the United States Continue Sanctions on Cuba?

One of the paradoxes of contemporary U.S. policies toward Cuba is that although most of the recent writings on Cuba suggest some change in U.S. policy is likely or even inevitable, U.S. policies have thus far changed very little. There may be various reasons for this: reluctance to change as long as one Castro or another is in power and Cuba's own policies have not changed; U.S. preoccupation with a global economic crisis and with more pressing foreign policy challenges in Iraq, Afghanistan, Pakistan, and elsewhere; and continuing opposition to any change in U.S. policy from many prominent Cuban Americans until circumstances in Cuba change. It is possible that resistance from U.S. economic sectors that would face losses from economic competition with Cuba plays a role as well. Depending on how long Raul Castro remains in power, the next phase of the debate is likely to be over whether it is better to wait to change U.S. policies until the future leadership of Cuba becomes clearer or to change U.S. policies first in the hope of influencing which leaders come to power in Cuba and what policies they adopt.

For recent writings on Cuba and its relations with the United States, see Daniel Erikson, *The Cuba Wars: Fidel Castro, the United States, and the Next Revolution;* Marifeli Perez-Stable, ed., *Looking Forward: Comparative Perspectives on Cuba's Transition* (University of Notre Dame Press, 2007); Julia Sweig, "Fidel's Final Victory," *Foreign Affairs* (January/February 2007); and Alex Ely, "Cuba's New Revolution," *Foreign Policy* (November/December 2008).

ISSUE 13

Is Loosening Immigration Regulations Good for the United States?

YES: George W. Bush, from "Letting the People Who Contribute to Society Stay," *Vital Speeches of the Day* (May 15, 2006)

NO: Mark Krikorian, from "Not So Realistic: Why Some Would-Be Immigration Reformers Don't Have the Answer," *National Review* (September 12, 2005)

ISSUE SUMMARY

YES: George W. Bush, the 43rd president of the United States, argues that the United States can be both a law-abiding country with secure borders and a nation that upholds its tradition of welcoming immigrants.

NO: Mark Krikorian, executive director of the Center for Immigration Studies and a visiting fellow at the Nixon Center, argues that immigration reforms promoting guest workers or amnesty are unrealistic and prone to fraud and paralysis.

T he United States of America—along with Canada, Latin America, Australia, and New Zealand—is one of the most multinational societies. Over time, about half of all of the world's immigrants have settled in the United States. Attracted by hopes of democracy, economic opportunity, and the possibility of social mobility through education and hard work, people from Europe, Africa, Asia, and the Americas have come to United States. Despite often facing difficulties in adjustment, many stay, raise families, and become part of the cultural fabric of the United States. Over time, the United States has benefited enormously from the labor, intellect, and entrepreneurship that immigrants have brought with them. Despite these benefits, once groups get settled, new immigrants are often viewed as interlopers competing for social services and threatening jobs by displacing them.

Those who want to restrict immigration argue that legal immigration undermines American jobs by providing a source of cheaper labor, and illegal immigration imposes large costs of public services. The majority of illegal immigrants in the United States are located in the Southwest, with approximately 43 percent believed to reside in California alone. To discourage illegal immigration and reduce its social costs, Californian voters enacted Proposition 187 in November 1994, which cut off undocumented aliens from medical and other public services, including education for their children. When he entered office, President George W. Bush took a more moderate view of immigration and promoted the use of temporary worker visas and other strategies for reducing the flow of illegal immigrants while enabling foreigners to work in the United States. This position was supported by large companies, such as Wal-Mart, who argued that immigrants helped address a shortage of low-wage workers.

Since the September 11 attacks, immigration policy has increasingly been embedded within debates about U.S. national security and counterterrorism policy. Those in favor of tighter restrictions argue that at least 15 of the 19 September 11 hijackers should have been denied visas based on the immigration laws of the time. Strategies to keep would-be terrorists out include the creation of a database to track all foreign students called the Student and Exchange Visitor Information System (Sevis) and a U.S. Visitor and Immigration Status Indication Technology System (US Visit) to monitor immigrants. Republican members of the House of Representatives, including Duncan Hunter of California and James Sensenbrenner of Wisconsin, have linked their support for the president's antiterrorism policy to more restrictive immigration reforms—especially tougher standards by the states to issue driver's licenses, tighter rules to grant political asylum, and the completion of the fence on California's border.

Supporters of immigration argue that increased restrictions on immigration since September 11 are already imposing costs on certain sectors of the U.S. economy, especially in higher education and the engineering and high-technology industries. In the long run, denying access to these sectors by the best and the brightest minds from around the world will decrease America's economic competitiveness and reduce its security. Many immigrants into the United States are highly skilled individuals seeking additional training or job opportunities. Once trained, many of these people remain in the United States, enhancing its companies and the strength of its economy. Others return home, taking with them an understanding of U.S. culture and society. During the Cold War, the U.S. Information Agency attracted foreigners seeking university training as a means of exposing future leaders to American culture and ideas. This practice had a profound effect on the economic and political policies pursued throughout Latin America and Asia. Today this practice is restricted to younger students from the Middle East. Beyond imposing financial costs on U.S. universities, restricting access to others seeking an American education undermines the opportunity to expose future foreign leaders to American culture and ideals.

President Bush argues that a temporary worker program would meet the needs of our economy, provide honest immigrants with a way to provide for their families while respecting the law, and promote the American tradition of the melting pot, while maintaining security. In contrast, Mark Krikorian argues that the proposals currently being considered are administratively unrealistic and impractical and, consequently, are likely to generate more rather than less fraud and abuse.

YES ◀

George W. Bush

Letting the People Who Contribute to Society Stay

Good evening. I've asked for a few minutes of your time to discuss a matter of national importance—the reform of America's immigration system.

The issue of immigration stirs intense emotions, and in recent weeks, Americans have seen those emotions on display. On the streets of major cities, crowds have rallied in support of those in our country illegally. At our southern border, others have organized to stop illegal immigrants from coming in. Across the country, Americans are trying to reconcile these contrasting images. And in Washington, the debate over immigration reform has reached a time of decision. Tonight, I will make it clear where I stand, and where I want to lead our country on this vital issue.

We must begin by recognizing the problems with our immigration system. For decades, the United States has not been in complete control of its borders. As a result, many who want to work in our economy have been able to sneak across our border, and millions have stayed.

Once here, illegal immigrants live in the shadows of our society. Many use forged documents to get jobs, and that makes it difficult for employers to verify that the workers they hire are legal. Illegal immigration puts pressure on public schools and hospitals, it strains state and local budgets, and brings crime to our communities. These are real problems. Yet we must remember that the vast majority of illegal immigrants are decent people who work hard, support their families, practice their faith, and lead responsible lives. They are a part of American life, but they are beyond the reach and protection of American law.

We're a nation of laws, and we must enforce our laws. We're also a nation of immigrants, and we must uphold that tradition, which has strengthened our country in so many ways. These are not contradictory goals. America can be a lawful society and a welcoming society at the same time. We will fix the problems created by illegal immigration, and we will deliver a system that is secure, orderly, and fair. So I support comprehensive immigration reform that will accomplish five clear objectives.

First, the United States must secure its borders. This is a basic responsibility of a sovereign nation. It is also an urgent requirement of our national security. Our objective is straightforward: The border should be open to trade and lawful immigration, and shut to illegal immigrants, as well as criminals, drug dealers, and terrorists.

Address delivered by the president to the nation from the Oval Office, Washington, DC, May 15, 2006.

I was a governor of a state that has a 1,200-mile border with Mexico. So I know how difficult it is to enforce the border, and how important it is. Since I became President, we've increased funding for border security by 66 percent, and expanded the Border Patrol from about 9,000 to 12,000 agents. The men and women of our Border Patrol are doing a fine job in difficult circumstances, and over the past five years, they have apprehended and sent home about six million people entering America illegally.

Despite this progress, we do not yet have full control of the border, and I am determined to change that. Tonight I'm calling on Congress to provide funding for dramatic improvements in manpower and technology at the border. By the end of 2008, we'll increase the number of Border Patrol officers by an additional 6,000. When these new agents are deployed, we'll have more than doubled the size of the Border Patrol during my presidency.

At the same time, we're launching the most technologically advanced border security initiative in American history. We will construct high-tech fences in urban corridors, and build new patrol roads and barriers in rural areas. We'll employ motion sensors, infrared cameras, and unmanned aerial vehicles to prevent illegal crossings. America has the best technology in the world, and we will ensure that the Border Patrol has the technology they need to do their job and secure our border.

Training thousands of new Border Patrol agents and bringing the most advanced technology to the border will take time. Yet the need to secure our border is urgent. So I'm announcing several immediate steps to strengthen border enforcement during this period of transition:

One way to help during this transition is to use the National Guard. So, in coordination with governors, up to 6,000 Guard members will be deployed to our southern border. The Border Patrol will remain in the lead. The Guard will assist the Border Patrol by operating surveillance systems, analyzing intelligence, installing fences and vehicle barriers, building patrol roads, and providing training. Guard units will not be involved in direct law enforcement activities—that duty will be done by the Border Patrol. This initial commitment of Guard members would last for a period of one year. After that, the number of Guard forces will be reduced as new Border Patrol agents and new technologies come online. It is important for Americans to know that we have enough Guard forces to win the war on terror, to respond to natural disasters, and to help secure our border.

The United States is not going to militarize the southern border. Mexico is our neighbor, and our friend. We will continue to work cooperatively to improve security on both sides of the border, to confront common problems like drug trafficking and crime, and to reduce illegal immigration.

Another way to help during this period of transition is through state and local law enforcement in our border communities. So we'll increase federal funding for state and local authorities assisting the Border Patrol on targeted enforcement missions. We will give state and local authorities the specialized training they need to help federal officers apprehend and detain illegal immigrants. State and local law enforcement officials are an important part of our border security and they need to be a part of our strategy to secure our borders.

The steps I've outlined will improve our ability to catch people entering our country illegally. At the same time, we must ensure that every illegal immigrant we catch crossing our southern border is returned home. More than 85 percent of the illegal immigrants we catch crossing the southern border are Mexicans, and most are sent back home within 24 hours. But when we catch illegal immigrants from other country [sic] it is not as easy to send them home. For many years, the government did not have enough space in our detention facilities to hold them while the legal process unfolded. So most were released back into our society and asked to return for a court date. When the date arrived, the vast majority did not show up. This practice, called "catch and release," is unacceptable, and we will end it.

We're taking several important steps to meet this goal. We've expanded the number of beds in our detention facilities, and we will continue to add more. We've expedited the legal process to cut the average deportation time. And we're making it clear to foreign governments that they must accept back their citizens who violate our immigration laws. As a result of these actions, we've ended "catch and release" for illegal immigrants from some countries. And I will ask Congress for additional funding and legal authority, so we can end "catch and release" at the southern border once and for all. When people know that they'll be caught and sent home if they enter our country illegally, they will be less likely to try to sneak in.

Second, to secure our border, we must create a temporary worker program. The reality is that there are many people on the other side of our border who will do anything to come to America to work and build a better life. They walk across miles of desert in the summer heat, or hide in the back of 18-wheelers to reach our country. This creates enormous pressure on our border that walls and patrols alone will not stop. To secure the border effectively, we must reduce the numbers of people trying to sneak across.

Therefore, I support a temporary worker program that would create a legal path for foreign workers to enter our country in an orderly way, for a limited period of time. This program would match willing foreign workers with willing American employers for jobs Americans are not doing. Every worker who applies for the program would be required to pass criminal background checks. And temporary workers must return to their home country at the conclusion of their stay.

A temporary worker program would meet the needs of our economy, and it would give honest immigrants a way to provide for their families while respecting the law. A temporary worker program would reduce the appeal of human smugglers, and make it less likely that people would risk their lives to cross the border. It would ease the financial burden on state and local governments, by replacing illegal workers with lawful taxpayers. And above all, a temporary worker program would add to our security by making certain we know who is in our country and why they are here.

Third, we need to hold employers to account for the workers they hire. It is against the law to hire someone who is in this country illegally. Yet businesses often cannot verify the legal status of their employees because of the widespread problem of document fraud. Therefore, comprehensive immigration reform must include a better system for verifying documents and work eligibility. A key part of that system should be a new identification card for every legal foreign worker. This card should use biometric technology, such as digital fingerprints, to make it tamper-proof. A tamper-proof card would help us enforce the law, and leave employers with no excuse for violating it. And by making it harder for illegal immigrants to find work in our country, we would discourage people from crossing the border illegally in the first place.

Fourth, we must face the reality that millions of illegal immigrants are here already. They should not be given an automatic path to citizenship. This is amnesty, and I oppose it. Amnesty would be unfair to those who are here lawfully, and it would invite further waves of illegal immigration.

Some in this country argue that the solution is to deport every illegal immigrant, and that any proposal short of this amounts to amnesty. I disagree. It is neither wise, nor realistic to round up millions of people, many with deep roots in the United States, and send them across the border. There is a rational middle ground between granting an automatic path to citizenship for every illegal immigrant, and a program of mass deportation. That middle ground recognizes there are differences between an illegal immigrant who crossed the border recently, and someone who has worked here for many years, and has a home, a family, and an otherwise clean record.

I believe that illegal immigrants who have roots in our country and want to stay should have to pay a meaningful penalty for breaking the law, to pay their taxes, to learn English, and to work in a job for a number of years. People who meet these conditions should be able to apply for citizenship, but approval would not be automatic, and they will have to wait in line behind those who played by the rules and followed the law. What I've just described is not amnesty, it is a way for those who have broken the law to pay their debt to society, and demonstrate the character that makes a good citizen.

Fifth, we must honor the great American tradition of the melting pot, which has made us one nation out of many peoples. The success of our country depends upon helping newcomers assimilate into our society, and embrace our common identity as Americans. Americans are bound together by our shared ideals, an appreciation of our history, respect for the flag we fly, and an ability to speak and write the English language. English is also the key to unlocking the opportunity of America. English allows newcomers to go from picking crops to opening a grocery, from cleaning offices to running offices, from a life of low-paying jobs to a diploma, a career, and a home of their own. When immigrants assimilate and advance in our society, they realize their dreams, they renew our spirit, and they add to the unity of America.

Tonight, I want to speak directly to members of the House and the Senate: An immigration reform bill needs to be comprehensive, because all elements of this problem must be addressed together, or none of them will be solved at all. The House has passed an immigration bill. The Senate should act by the end of this month so we can work out the differences between the two bills, and Congress can pass a comprehensive bill for me to sign into law.

America needs to conduct this debate on immigration in a reasoned and respectful tone. Feelings run deep on this issue, and as we work it out, all of us need to keep some things in mind. We cannot build a unified country by inciting people to anger, or playing on anyone's fears, or exploiting the issue of immigration for political gain. We must always remember that real lives will be affected by our debates and decisions, and that every human being has dignity and value no matter what their citizenship papers say.

I know many of you listening tonight have a parent or a grandparent who came here from another country with dreams of a better life. You know what freedom meant to them, and you know that America is a more hopeful country because of their hard work and sacrifice. As President, I've had the opportunity to meet people of many backgrounds, and hear what America means to them. On a visit to Bethesda Naval Hospital, Laura and I met a wounded Marine named Guadalupe Denogean. Master Gunnery Sergeant Denogean came to the United States from Mexico when he was a boy. He spent his summers picking crops with his family, and then he volunteered for the United States Marine Corps as soon as he was able. During the liberation of Iraq, Master Gunnery Sergeant Denogean was seriously injured. And when asked if he had any requests, he made two: a promotion for the corporal who helped rescue him, and the chance to become an American citizen. And when this brave Marine raised his right hand, and swore an oath to become a citizen of the country he had defended for more than 26 years, I was honored to stand at his side.

We will always be proud to welcome people like Guadalupe Denogean as fellow Americans. Our new immigrants are just what they've always been— people willing to risk everything for the dream of freedom. And America remains what she has always been: the great hope on the horizon, an open door to the future, a blessed and promised land. We honor the heritage of all who come here, no matter where they come from, because we trust in our country's genius for making us all Americans—one nation under God.

Thank you, and good night.

Mark Krikorian

→ **NO**

Not So Realistic: Why Some Would-Be Immigration Reformers Don't Have the Answer

The Senate is again considering various proposals to address our massive illegal-alien problem, and the competing bills have one thing in common: They claim to offer "realistic" solutions to the supposedly unrealistic desire to enforce the law. Writer Tamar Jacoby, perhaps the most energetic salesman of the McCain-Kennedy amnesty bill, used some form of "realistic" ten times in her testimony at a July Senate hearing. Senators Kennedy, Cornyn, Brownback, and Feingold all touted the realism of their preferred solutions at the same hearing, and the *New York Times* and *Washington Post* have done the same in numerous editorials.

The problem, of course, is that no one has checked whether our very real immigration bureaucracy is capable of implementing any of these proposals. And this is no trivial concern: The success of any proposal depends on registering and screening millions and millions of illegal aliens within a short period of time—a daunting task.

It is therefore necessary to look first at the administrative mandates of the two most popular immigration bills. The McCain-Kennedy bill would offer amnesty to the approximately 11 million illegal aliens in the United States, by re-labeling them "temporary" workers, and after six years, it would grant them permanent residence. The Department of Homeland Security would have to determine that the person was, in fact, an illegal alien on the date of the bill's introduction; that he hadn't left the United States in the meantime; that he was employed in the United States at the time of the bill's introduction— "full time, part time, seasonally, or self-employed"; that he has remained so employed, which he can prove with records from the government, employers, labor unions, banks, remittances, or "sworn affidavits from nonrelatives who have direct knowledge of the alien's work"; that he, if not employed, was a full-time student; that he has "not ordered, incited, assisted, or otherwise participated in the persecution of any person on account of race, religion, nationality, membership in a particular social group, or political opinion"; and that he is not a security threat, a criminal, a polygamist, or a child abductor. This required background check is to be conducted "as expeditiously as possible"—for potentially 11 million people.

From *The National Review,* September 12, 2005, pp. 38–39. Copyright © 2005 by National Review, Inc, 215 Lexington Avenue, New York, NY 10016. Reprinted by permission.

Now consider the better of the two major bills before the Senate, the Cornyn-Kyl bill, which has stronger enforcement provisions and isn't quite an amnesty. (It instead requires illegals to return home and sign up for its version of a "temporary" worker program from abroad, and there is no permanent-residence offer.)

A central component of the bill is "Deferred Mandatory Departure," which would give illegals who register with the government five years to get their affairs in order and leave, something you might call an "exit amnesty." The bill instructs the immigration service to determine many of the same things that McCain-Kennedy requires, including "the alien's physical and mental health, criminal history and gang membership, immigration history, involvement with groups or individuals that have engaged in terrorism, gen-ocide, persecution, or who seek the overthrow of the United States govern-ment, voter registration history, claims to United States citizenship, and tax history." And the Cornyn-Kyl bill has even more specific deadlines: All appli-cations are to be processed within one year of its enactment, and at that time the Department of Homeland Security also must have ready a new document for applicants that would be machine-readable, tamper-resistant, and have a biometric-identification component.

The point is not that these requirements are inappropriate; if you're going to be registering illegal aliens, you'd certainly want to know about their health status and involvement with terrorism. But the most pressing question remains: Is it achievable? What would happen, in the real world, if one of these "realistic" solutions were to become law?

Two words: "fraud" and "paralysis."

Will We Ever Learn?

We've attempted much smaller programs like this in the past, and the story has been the same each time: The lack of administrative capacity, combined with intense political pressure, causes the immigration service to drop every-thing else to meet impossible deadlines—and ineligible applicants get through anyway.

The closest parallel is the administration of the 1986 Immigration Reform and Control Act by the old Immigration and Naturalization Service. Some 3 mil-lion illegal aliens (out of 5 million total) applied for amnesty, and 90 percent were approved. Fraud was omnipresent, especially in the farm-worker portion, where applicants presented fake proof of employment—sometimes as flimsy as a handwritten note on a scrap of paper—and gave ludicrous stories, like, "I've picked watermelons from trees," or "harvested purple cotton."

A report from the inspector general's office of the Department of Justice noted years later that "given the crush of applications under the program and the relative fewer investigative resources, INS approved applications absent explicit proof that they were in fact fraudulent." Two of the fraudulent applica-tions that were approved were from Egyptian brothers in New York: Mahmud and Mohammed Abouhalima, who went on to participate in the first World Trade Center bombing.

We've seen paralysis before, too. On several occasions during the past decade Congress briefly opened a window for illegal aliens to apply for green cards without first returning home (by getting married to a citizen or legal resident, for instance, or by being sponsored by an employer). Hundreds of thousands applied under the program, and INS had to scramble to redirect resources. As a result, the backlog of unresolved cases ballooned to around 6 million in 2003, and wait times at some immigration offices were two years or more—even for relatively straightforward matters.

Unrealistic mandates like these are largely to blame for the backlog of immigration applications, which is now "only" 4.5 million. Since it can't work through these anytime soon, the immigration service often issues work permits and travel documents to many green-card applicants right when they submit their forms, knowing that it will be years before anyone actually reads the application. This is the present situation at the agency that is supposed to carry out extensive, complicated new responsibilities under the proposed immigration bills.

So, if an immigration package anything like McCain-Kennedy or Cornyn-Kyl were to pass, the following would almost assuredly occur: Immigration offices would be deluged by millions of applications that would need to be approved under a tight deadline; harried DHS employees would be forced to put aside their other duties to meet the onslaught; candidates for citizenship—foreign spouses of Americans, refugees, skilled workers sponsored by employers—would effectively be pushed to the back of the line; political pressure would force DHS to cut corners in adjudicating the applications; and huge numbers of ineligible applicants would be approved (in addition to the huge numbers of eligible applicants).

The workload created by any such program would be larger than the annual number of visas currently issued worldwide by the State Department (approximately 5 million), and many times larger than the annual number of green cards issued by DHS (around 1 million). Delays, mistakes, and fraud may not be what the supporters of the immigration bills have in mind, but they are nonetheless the guaranteed outcome. None of this is to pin blame on the bureaucrats charged with implementing congressional mandates. Rather, the proposals themselves are the problem, measures animated by an almost utopian spirit, one that seeks to solve an enormous and long-brewing problem with one swift masterstroke.

Things don't work that way in the real world. Instead, the illegal population needs to be decreased via muscular, across-the-board immigration enforcement over a long term. Rather than wait for a magic solution, we can implement an attrition strategy right now, using available resources. We could, for instance, immediately reject fake Social Security numbers submitted by employers on behalf of new employees (the government currently looks the other way). Or the Treasury Department could instruct banks that the Mexican government's illegal-alien ID card is no longer a valid form of identification. Or a small portion of enforcement resources could be devoted to random raids at day-labor gathering spots. This has an added advantage: As more resources become available—be they monetary or technological—they could easily bolster the attrition approach, as opposed to current proposals, which from the get-go require vast and untested programs.

An attrition strategy would adopt the conservative goal of shrinking the illegal-alien population over time by making it unappealing to be an illegal alien in the first place. As a result, fewer people would come here illegally, and those already here would be more inclined to deport themselves. Over the space of several years, what is now a crisis could be reduced to a manageable nuisance.

Now that's realistic.

POSTSCRIPT

Is Loosening Immigration Regulations Good for the United States?

Within the United States, political debate over immigration reform has often taken place within Congress. Even today, leading members of Congress tend to take a more restrictive stance on immigration than President George W. Bush. James Gimpel and James Edwards provide a good overview of the politics of immigration reform before September 11, 2001. See James G. Gimpel and James R. Edwards, *The Congressional Politics of Immigration Reform* (Allyn and Bacon, 1999), Michael Fix and Jeffrey Passel, "Immigration Debate: Myths About Immigrants," *Foreign Policy* (Summer 1994), James C. Clad, "Immigration Debate: Slowing the Wave," *Foreign Policy* (Summer 1994), and David Techenor, *Dividing Lines: The Politics of Immigration Control in America* (Princeton, 2002). For additional arguments regarding the costs of denying foreign students access to American universities, see Sylvia H. Kless, "We Threaten National Security by Discouraging the Best and Brightest Students from Abroad," *The American Chronicle of Higher Education* (October 8, 2002).

The United States Citizenship and Immigration Services provides online information regarding immigration into this country. See http://uscis.gov/graphics/index.htm. The Center for Immigration Studies provides research and policy analysis of the negative economic, social, demographic, fiscal, and other impacts of immigration on the United States. See http://www.cis.org/.

Internet References . . .

Council on Foreign Relations

The Maurice R. Greenberg Center for Geoeconomic Studies at the Council on Foreign Relations provides a useful and up-to-date analysis of the 2008–2009 financial crisis as well as a link to a wide range of books and articles on the topic.

http://www.cfr.org/

International Monetary Fund

The International Monetary Fund's home page provides a wealth of information about the organization itself as well as links to economic and financial data, analysis and articles on the international financial system, and the economic policies of its member countries.

http://www.imf.org/

World Trade Organization

The World Trade Organization is dedicated to the promotion of free trade. Its Web site provides a wealth of information about the organization itself as well as links to economic and trade data, analysis and articles on the ongoing Doha International Trade Round, and other trade-related issues.

http://www.wto.org/

The National Geographic Foundation

The National Geographic Foundation is a useful source of information about global warming, pollution, acid rain, and other environmental issues.

http://environment.nationalgeographic.com/environment/global-warming/

Pew Center on Global Climate Change

The Pew Center on Global Climate Change is a nonpartisan, nonprofit organization the provides information about climate issues and policy at U.S. federal, state, and international levels.

http://www.pewclimate.org/

U.S. International Economic and Environmental Issues

*M*any observers believe that the growth of international interdependence among countries was one of the maior developments in the latter half of the twentieth century and that this trend will not only continue but strengthen in the twenty-first century. The debates in this unit address several issues involving the global economy, energy, and the Earth's environment that present a challenge to American foreign policymakers.

- Are Free Trade and Economic Liberalism Good for the United States?
- Is Fighting Climate Change Worth the Cost?
- Is It Realistic for the United States to Move Toward Greater Energy Interdependence?

ISSUE 14

Are Free Trade and Economic Liberalism Good for the United States?

YES: Matthew J. Slaughter, from "An Auto Bailout Would Be Terrible for Free Trade," *The Wall Street Journal* (November 20, 2008)

NO: Andrew N. Liveris, from "Working Toward a (New) U.S. Industrial Policy," Speech delivered to the Detroit Economic Club, Detroit, MI (September 22, 2008)

ISSUE SUMMARY

YES: Matthew J. Slaughter, professor of international economics in the Tuck School of Business at Dartmouth College, argues that government intervention in the economy, and in the U.S. auto industry in particular, will reduce foreign direct investment in the United States, increase the likelihood of trade protectionism, reduce market access for U.S. firms abroad, and drive down the value of the dollar.

NO: Andrew N. Liveris, chairman and chief executive officer of the Dow Chemical Company, argues that a vibrant industrial and manufacturing base is indispensible to the country and this can only be achieved by developing an industrial policy targeted at rejuvenating the competitiveness of U.S. firms, bolstering economic and energy independence, and creating jobs.

One of the important political and economic changes during the twentieth century was the rapid growth of economic globalization (or interdependence) among countries. The impact of international economics on domestic societies has expanded rapidly as world industrial and financial structures have become increasingly intertwined.

The negative consequences of this interdependence became apparent in the fall of 2008 when credit shortages resulting from the financial crisis began to disrupt industry. The automobile sector was one of the first and hardest hit outside of the financial sector. Without credit, U.S. automobile companies could not secure the short-term financing needed to produce cars and would-be consumers could not secure the automobile loans needed to buy the cars that dealers had in stock, even at hugely discounted prices. Manufacturing output in the United States hit a 28-year low in December of 2008, while manufacturing in Europe and China continued its downward slide. In 2008 and 2009, the United States has joined countries in Europe, Latin America, and Asia in pursuing a variety of strategies to stimulate its economy. To date, protectionism remains low, but pressures to protect domestic industries and the jobs they provide will likely intensify as long as the economic downturn continues.

The issues here are whether free trade and economic liberalism are positive or negative trends for Americans and whether, especially in the context of a global financial crisis and recession, the U.S. government should intervene to manage the economy and, more specifically, develop an industrial policy to promote manufacturing and protect American jobs. For about 60 years, the United States has been at the center of the drive to open international commerce. Following World War II, American policy makers took the lead in establishing a new economic system based on the premise that promoting free trade and facilitating international financial relations was the best way to generate economic growth and prosperity for all. As the world's dominant superpower, the United States played the leading role in establishing the International Monetary Fund (IMF), the World Bank, and the General Agreement on Tariffs and Trade (GATT). The latest GATT revision talks were completed and signed by 124 countries (including the United States) in April 1994. Among the outcomes was the establishment of a new coordinating body, the World Trade Organization (WTO).

In the first decade of the twenty-first century, the so-called "Washington Consensus" that economic liberalism combined with prudent fiscal and monetary policies would lead to growth came under increasing scrutiny and met with increasing resistance. Trade talks that originated in an international meeting in Doha, Qatar, in 2001 and that were intended to open up trade in agricultural products (known as the "Doha Round") stalled in 2007 when the United States and Europeans failed to reach an agreement over reducing farm subsidies. Meanwhile, countries operating outside of the "Washington Consensus" continued to succeed. China's growth continued at a remarkable rate, Asian countries recovered from their late-1990s financial crisis with sufficient reserve to make them independent of the International Monetary Fund, increasing oil and commodity prices led to vast transfers of wealth from the advanced industrialized countries to energy and raw material producers, and even illiberal and undemocratic oil-producing countries like Russia and Venezuela grew dramatically. The onset of the 2008 economic crisis in the United States and its spread to Europe and then the rest of the world further undermined faith in economic liberalism and "American-style" capitalism. The result is a resurgence of the belief in the dangers of the free market and the importance of government intervention in national economies.

Given this context, the validity of free trade and economic liberalism are increasingly contested within and outside of the United States. Matthew J. Slaughter focuses on the troubled automobile industry and highlights potential negative consequences of government intervention. He emphasizes three long-term effects including declining foreign direct investment, declining access to foreign markets, and a declining willingness on the part of foreign investors to purchase U.S. debt. In contrast, Andrew Liveris contends that U.S. policy has long worked against industry and that government intervention is necessary to create a vibrant industrial and manufacturing base, spur innovation, and create jobs.

YES

Matthew J. Slaughter

An Auto Bailout Would Be Terrible for Free Trade

Congress is now considering a federal bailout for America's Big Three automobile companies. Many want to grant them at least $25 billion from the $700 billion Troubled Asset Relief Program on top of $25 billion in low-interest loans approved earlier this year.

But these figures represent only a fraction of what the total cost of the bailout could be. In a global economy, a federal bailout of the automotive industry could cost Americans jobs as well as foreign markets to trade in. There are at least three important ways an industry bailout could damage America's engagement in the global economy and hurt U.S. companies, workers and taxpayers.

The first global cost of a bailout could be less foreign direct investment (FDI) coming into the United States. On Sunday, President-elect Barack Obama asked, "What does a sustainable U.S. auto industry look like?"

Well, it looks a lot like the automotive industry run by "foreign" car companies that insource jobs into the U.S. In 2006 these foreign auto makers (multinational auto or auto-parts companies that are headquartered outside of the U.S.) employed 402,800 Americans. The average annual compensation for these employees was $63,538.

At the head of the line of sustainable auto companies stands Toyota. In its 2008 fiscal year, it earned a remarkable $17.1 billion world-wide and assembled 1.66 million motor vehicles in North America. Toyota has production facilities in seven states and R&D facilities in three others. Honda, another sustainable auto company, operates in five states and earned $6 billion in net income in 2008. In contrast, General Motors lost $38.7 billion last year.

Across all industries in 2006, insourcing companies registered $2.8 trillion in U.S. sales while employing 5.3 million Americans and paying them $364 billion in compensation. But as the world has grown smaller, today the U.S. faces increasingly stiff competition to attract and retain insourcing companies. Indeed, the U.S. share of global FDI inflows has already fallen. From 2003–2005 the U.S. received 16% of global FDI. That's down from 31.5% it received in 1988–1990.

Will fewer companies look to insource into America if the federal government is willing to bail out their domestic competitors?

The answer is an obvious yes. Ironically, proponents of a bailout say saving Detroit is necessary to protect the U.S. manufacturing base. But too many such bailouts could erode the number of manufacturers willing to invest here.

The bailout's second global cost could hit U.S.-headquartered companies that run multinational businesses. In total, these companies employ more than 22 million Americans and account for a remarkable 75.8% of all private-sector R&D in the U.S. Their success depends on their ability to access foreign customers. They do this two ways. They export goods from their U.S. parent companies. And they sell goods locally through foreign affiliates. These foreign affiliates are built by direct investment of American companies in other countries. In 2006, U.S. parent companies exported $495.1 billion to foreign markets. That same year their majority-owned affiliates earned over $4.1 trillion in sales—$8.33 for every $1 in exports.

This access to foreign markets has been good for America. But it won't necessarily continue. The policy environment abroad is growing more protectionist. Multilateral efforts to liberalize trade in the Doha Development Round died in July with no prospects for restarting. Even more worrisome are rising FDI barriers. In 2005 and 2006, the United Nations reported a record number of new FDI restrictions around the world—even in major recipient countries such as China, Germany and Japan.

Will a U.S.-government bailout go ignored by policy makers abroad?

No. A bailout will likely entrench and expand protectionist practices across the globe, and thus erode the foreign sales and competitiveness of U.S. multinationals. And that would reduce these companies' U.S. employment, R&D and related activities. That would be bad for America.

Rising trade barriers would also hurt the Big Three, all of which are multinational corporations that depend on foreign markets. In 2007, GM produced more motor vehicles outside North America than in—5.02 million, or 54% of its world-wide total. That year in China, the world's second-largest and fastest-growing automobile market by volume, GM continued to lead in market share and became the first global auto maker to surpass the one-million mark in single-year unit sales in China.

The bailout's third global cost could fall on the U.S. dollar. For 32 years the U.S. has run trade deficits and offset it with sales of U.S. assets to foreign buyers. A critical foundation of foreign-investor confidence in U.S. assets has been transparent competition in our product markets—competition that spurs economic growth and rising average standards of living. To keep that up, it is important to address concerns related to allowing foreign companies to compete on U.S. soil, not by bailing out struggling companies but by taking care of workers who are dislocated in the give-and-take of a competitive market.

Will a federal bailout that politicizes American markets bolster foreign-investor demand for U.S. assets?

Not likely. Instead, America runs the risk of creating the kind of "political-risk premium" that investors have long placed on other countries—and that would reduce demand for U.S. assets and thereby the value of the U.S. dollar.

Reduced foreign demand for U.S. assets would be troubling at any time. Its prospect is especially troubling now, when the federal government's fiscal 2009 deficit is widely forecast to reach something near or exceeding $1 trillion—up from $456 billion last year. With net saving still near zero for U.S. households and falling profits for U.S. companies, financing that deficit will require attracting foreign capital.

This week Congress is weighing the cost of the bailout. Let us hope that lawmakers realize that the true cost of such a bailout is far larger than any check the U.S. Treasury will have to write in the coming months.

Andrew N. Liveris

→ **NO**

Working Toward a (New) U.S. Industrial Policy

Thank you, Bill (Ford, Jr.) for your kind words and the invitation to be here today.

As Bill mentioned, I was here two years ago. At that time, I shared my concerns about the state of manufacturing and the weak economy. But I am an optimist and in the back of my mind I thought, surely, it can't get any worse, right?

Instead, we've witnessed two years of continual slide capped by the unprecedented meltdown in the financial sector last week. Frankly, we're just now beginning to see the repercussions of that crisis as markets respond and re-settle themselves.

Wall St. isn't the only place feeling pain, of course. Main Street USA is feeling it, too.

People in every town and city across the country are uneasy these days. And for good reason.

Since I was here last, oil has risen from the mid-$70s a barrel to around $100 today.

Housing starts are at their lowest level since 1991, and there seems to be no bottom in sight. Consumer prices are expanding at the fastest pace in 17 years, affecting every consumer item from fuel to food.

On top of that, we have the sobering news that the economy lost some half a million manufacturing jobs since the end of 2006. And I'm sure you all saw the jobs report last month for the entire nation: 84,000 jobs lost in August alone.

September, it appears, won't look any better.

And the rank and file employees who are still working? They earned three percent less last month than they had a year earlier simply because of inflation.

Even the small things are more expensive. I saw a report in the *New York Times* recently that the price for the common paper clip—this small item holding my talk together—is up 40 percent.

As that great American philosopher, Will Rogers, once said, we seem intent on showing the entire world we're prosperous . . . even if we have to go broke to do it.

Speech by Andrew Liveris delivered to the Detroit Economic Club, Detroit, Michigan, September 22, 2008. Copyright © 2008 by The Dow Chemical Company. Reprinted by permission.

Given all the doom and gloom, it really is hard to remain an optimist. But I am reminded of the advice that I've given others so many times—that often the difference between success and failure is nothing more than pure persistence and hard work.

So here we are, talking again about a difficult economy and what to do with it.

Talking . . . again . . . about a real energy crisis that will have no quick or painless solution.

Talking once more about how to return this country to a position of strength and vigor.

As Bill said, on my last visit before you I did state that the United States was THE indispensable nation in the world. As a foreign citizen who has benefited enormously from the American freedom and enterprise model, I stand by that statement today more than ever.

The world would be a much poorer—and a much more dangerous—place were it not for the United States and its global influence.

But as I travel around the world and I see other countries putting together comprehensive and well thought-out plans for energy, manufacturing and sustainable economic development—I have concerns.

I'm concerned that our economic dependence on others is continuing to increase every day. I'm concerned that we're in the midst of the greatest wealth transfer out of this country in history . . . $500 billion plus spent annually for foreign oil . . . and too few in Washington seem alarmed.

And I'm concerned—most concerned—that the U.S. is forfeiting its dominant position as THE indispensable nation because it has lost sight of what first made it strong: a vibrant industrial and manufacturing base that drives innovation, technology—and creates jobs—from the shop floor, to the engineering centers, to the R&D labs and to the white collar offices.

Ladies and gentlemen, let us never forget that the very life force and strength of this great country begins here—in America's heartland. A country can't be strong abroad if it's not strong at home. It can't be strong in China or Chile if it's not strong in places like Cleveland and Canton. It can't be strong in Dubai if it's not strong first in Detroit.

Somehow, our government has lost sight of that. Instead of implementing policies that make our industrial heartland stronger, government has made it weaker. And we've allowed bad economic policies to drive good jobs out of the country.

In fact, between the bankers in New York, the lawyers in Washington, and the actors and entertainers from Hollywood, we have allowed people who know nothing of the might and intellect of our manufacturing base to make laws and decisions on our behalf.

We've allowed them to create an industrial crisis in this country that is undermining our nation's strength . . . and they don't even know it.

If you want to do something enlightening, go to the Internet and Google for the phrase "energy crisis." You'll get over 4,000 stories.

Then search for "economic crisis." You'll get more than 5,000 hits.

Then search for the phrase "industrial crisis," something that is just as real and felt just as deeply by everyday Americans. You'll get fewer than 10 stories—and none will be about the United States.

So, yes. I am still an optimist. But I'm an impatient optimist because at Dow we know there is a better way.

So what I'd like to do today is lay out for you the broad components of a new industrial policy. Not one characterized by central planning and the picking of winners and losers. We know that approach doesn't work.

What I'm talking about is a pro-industrial policy crafted and developed by manufacturers for manufacturers, a policy that rejuvenates our economic base.

Consider it a new strategy, if you will, to make American industry competitive again, re-establish our economic and energy independence and re-grow jobs in America.

What are the components of this plan? There are two.

First, we must look with fresh eyes at the structural costs that have weakened the very foundation of our manufacturing enterprises and remove the obstacles hurting our competitiveness.

And second, we must develop a comprehensive energy policy.

Now, I will admit that some people, like the ones I referenced before, don't like the words "industrial policy." I understand.

But the truth is that in this country today we already have an industrial policy—except, in reality, it's mostly an ANTI-industrial policy—a set of contradictory, ill-planned and ultimately self-defeating laws and regulations that are creating havoc at the manufacturing base.

Consider this alarming fact: Thirty years ago, manufacturing made up nearly 22 percent of the U.S. economy. Today, it's less than 12 percent and falling.

This will be no surprise to anyone in Michigan but the number of manufacturing jobs in the U.S. has fallen by 3.7 million over the past 10 years. We're projected to lose another 1.5 million over the next eight years.

That's 5.2 million jobs—5.2 million jobs that today pay more than $17 an hour plus benefits. To put it another way, that's $190 billion in wages and $76 billion in benefits.

I ask you this: What elected official in his right mind would develop an industrial policy that destroys $190 billion in annual wages? Which politician would want to tell the American voters they just lost $76 billion in benefits?

The sad fact is that nobody intentionally sought to do this. But it's happening right under our noses. Anti-industrial policy is hurting a lot of good people.

If it were just the U.S. and nobody else, it wouldn't matter. But there are countries around the world that DO see the uplifting power of manufacturing.

I spent much of my career at Dow working in Asia. I saw first hand how the "Asian tigers" used manufacturing and trade to go from grinding poverty to growing prosperity.

Today the emerging economic powers like China and India understand that when you build an economy from the ground up—make a strong manufacturing base as its foundation—benefits flow to everyone.

Those nations are our competitors and many of them are beating us at our own game.

Do we have to change? Well . . . no. As the quality guru Edward Deming put it: Change isn't necessary. No one said survival was mandatory.

History is replete with once-great countries that have dissolved into obscurity precisely because they didn't change.

If we want to keep the economic lead we've had for a century, however, we have to re-tool a few things. If we want to keep the many benefits that accrue from a strong economy, we must change course.

Times change, and strategies have to change with them.

And we have to start, first and foremost, with the structural costs that are suffocating industry in this country. We must level the playing field by removing the artificial, ANTI-industrial policy costs that disadvantage American businesses against the rest of the world.

Think about this. The 14 million men and women who work in U.S. manufacturing created about $1.6 trillion of wealth in 2007.

That's a huge, almost mind-blowing number. But the sad fact is it could be so much larger, and we could be so much more competitive.

We're burying our manufacturers under red-tape, weighing them down with structural burdens that push our production costs a staggering 32% higher than our major trading partners.

Understand: I'm not talking about top-down economic planning in any way, shape or form. I'm talking taking into account Tom Friedman's "flat world" and using a little forethought about the policies that affect business.

I'm talking about a little more coordination with policies in place already, and a lot more coordination with reality.

And I'm talking about resolving the conflicts in law and regulation that hamper our abilities to do business efficiently and effectively.

I propose work in four areas to bring our costs in line with our competitors.

Lowering the corporate tax rate.

Re-inventing regulation.

Reforming our civil justice system.

And finding a solution to the crisis known as health care in America.

Each one of these puts U.S. industry at a competitive disadvantage above and beyond the cost of labor. And each one of these burdens could be lightened or eliminated by our own government.

I won't go into each of these for the sake of time. Besides, most of you already know, for example, that America has the second highest corporate tax rates in the world.

But did you also know that of the 30 members who comprise the Organization of Economic Cooperation and Development, nine dropped their corporate tax rates last year to attract more investments.

Germany dropped its tax rate. So did Canada and the U.K. Even the Czech Republic!

Not the U.S. Why should that be?

As one great leader said, some in this country regard private enterprise as if it were a predatory tiger to be shot. Or they look upon it as a cow they can milk. Only a handful see it for what it really is: the strong horse that pulls the whole cart.

That was Winston Churchill who fought his own battles a half century ago to keep Britain's economy unencumbered and vibrant. He was unsuccessful, if you hadn't noticed.

If you want a cautionary tale about what this economy could look like if we continue to push manufacturing out of the country, look across the great pond. The service-based economy of the U.K. rises and falls at the mercy of others.

This point is really being brought home right now as the financial crisis in the U.S. has been felt in full force in the U.K., which has no other sector available to buttress this effect.

We can't afford to follow down a path of economic malaise like U.K. by destroying our manufacturing sector.

Making things—real, tangible things—still matters.

The leaders of this country should remember that the word "industry" created this great country's might by opening up the West . . . by fighting two World Wars . . . by putting a man on the moon . . . and by improving our lives and the lives of our children by creating high paying jobs and rewarding careers.

They should remember . . . but they don't.

Instead, they've saddled it with huge corporate taxes . . . AND a crisis in health care costs . . . AND an out-of-control civil justice system that adds a huge cost burden to American enterprise.

AND an inefficient regulatory system that costs us as much as $10,000 per employee in the manufacturing sector.

Don't we owe it to America's families, and especially to the next generation, to put back in place a Pro-Industrial Policy that stimulates investments and jobs by removing the structural costs that are holding us back?

This brings me to the second key component of an Industrial Policy for the 21st Century—the need for a comprehensive Energy Plan.

I don't need to tell those of you here today that energy is the life-blood of our modern economy. But I do want to point out that the current energy crisis goes far deeper than the price of gasoline at the pump and those high heating bills on the way this winter.

Here's what I mean by way of an example. Dow is currently on track to spend $32 billion—yes, I said billion with "B"—$32 billion this year on energy and feedstock costs. That's more than the entire U.S. chemical industry spent just a few years ago.

That's just one way to measure the impact of rising energy costs. The race for affordable energy also affects where we invest and where we build plants.

Keep in mind that every dollar of energy consumed creates 20 dollars of GDP value-add. That dollar also creates five of the kind of high-paying manufacturing jobs Michigan and every other state needs so badly.

It seems like common sense to keep those kinds of investments inside our borders.

Instead, most of those investments are now occurring outside the U.S.

Dollars are flowing—in unprecedented amounts—to places like China, Saudi Arabia and Kuwait, and many other countries that want the value-add to their economy that manufacturers bring.

What I don't understand is why our political leaders don't see that.

Maybe it's because they hear TV commentators say the price of oil has "dropped" to $100 a barrel! Or that gas has "dropped" below $4 a gallon! This type of irresponsible reporting is creating a false sense of security.

It does, however, confirm what James Schlesinger, the first Secretary of Energy in the U.S., first noticed decades ago: When it comes to energy policy, he said, America has only two modes: panic and complacency.

A slight, temporary moderation in price is no excuse for complacency. $100 oil brings me no comfort. Gas at $3.70 is no cause for celebration.

Frankly, this country needs a little panic because the truth hasn't sunk in yet. We have entered a new era in energy—one driven by a new global fact of life: less supply and more and more demand.

Even with greater conservation, energy consumption is soaring. It's forecast to rise 53 percent between now and 2030. Earlier this year the International Monetary Fund put out a report projecting the number of automobiles by themselves increasing 2.3 billion by 2050.

The good news for Detroit is that somebody will have to manufacture all those cars. The bad news is that we'll still have to power them and they'll still add to our growing energy consumption.

And despite the exponential increases in the amount of wind, solar and renewable energy coming on line, the fact is that these sources won't be able to keep up with overall demand.

So the energy of tomorrow—like today—will depend predominantly on fossil fuels: oil, natural gas and coal.

Everyone in Washington knows this. So where's the policy to deal with this new reality? This country doesn't have one.

I say "this country" has no strategy. But what I really mean is that Washington has no coherent strategy. Americans everywhere else already know the solutions.

Ninety-two percent of Americans believe that developing alternative energy sources is a step in the right direction. 88 percent want cars that are more fuel efficient. 67 percent believe we need more oil refineries and 73 percent believe off-shore drilling is a good idea. And, I'm heartened to say, 82 percent believe that conservation is important to our overall energy policy.

Even in Santa Barbara—the city where 200,000 gallons of oil spilled offshore some 40 years ago and where the movement to ban off-shore drilling began—even Santa Barbara gets it. The County Board of Supervisors there voted just last month in support of new drilling off its shore.

When it comes to energy, there's no ideology among the American consumer. Almost everyone wants more conservation, alternative energy, greater fuel efficiency, and environmentally responsible offshore drilling to help us right now.

And, yet, here we are . . . constrained by the old politics, separated by silos of thinking and ill-served by politicians intent on fighting the last war instead of the one in front of us.

And what is most worrisome to me—what is most vexing—is that Washington doesn't understand that the energy crisis isn't just about energy. The energy crisis is also about jobs . . . about manufacturing competitiveness. And at its base, the energy crisis is an industrial crisis that is threatening America's strength and standing in the world.

Four years ago we at Dow proposed a way out of this. We proposed an Energy Plan with three key components.

The first is to pass comprehensive federal goals on energy efficiency and conservation. To me, this is common sense.

Now, I realize I'm in Detroit and energy efficiency goals sound like code words for new fuel standards. It's heartening to see all the Big Auto's developing new models to consume less fuel. But what I'm mostly talking about here is improving the efficiency of buildings.

Consider this: buildings are responsible for 40 percent of our total energy use, 70 percent of our electricity use and 38 percent of our CO_2 emissions. A combination of federal incentives and local energy efficiency building codes could lower all of those numbers and significantly improve this country's energy security.

A very achievable 25-percent improvement in the energy efficiency of our economy would save this country the equivalent of all of its oil purchases from the Middle East and be the foundation for a secure energy future. It's the first and easiest step to implement.

The second component is to increase and diversify our domestic energy supplies. This is simple logic.

We have the oil deposits here. We have natural gas deposits. And we certainly have the coal reserves.

We should be accessing—responsibly and safely—every source we have to produce as much energy as we can at home.

We also have the best technology in the world. Why not use that to build new, safe nuclear power facilities? Why not begin—today—an Apollo-like R&D project to solve the carbon capture and sequestration question so we can use—safely and responsibly—that 200-year supply of coal beneath our feet?

The third component of our plan is to accelerate the development of all alternative energy sources—including renewables—and provide the financial support on research and development to get us there.

Given the situation we're in today, it's amazing to me that this Congress can't even seem to pass an extension of the Renewable Energy Tax Credits and, as a result, is putting this country's renewable energy industry—along with 100,000 jobs and $20 billion in investments—at risk.

Congress should also live up to its commitment and fund the direct loan program it created last year to help lower the cost of capital so the auto industry can retool to make more fuel-efficient vehicles.

The fact is we don't need to limit our possibilities by limiting our choices. Solar. Wind. Biomass and other renewable and alternative supplies. We need them all. And we need them now.

Will these give us energy independence? No.

Energy independence is a pipe dream for the U.S. But these steps will help us achieve the more realistic goal of energy security.

And, while I'm at it, let me remind you we have to do all of this within the context of reducing our carbon footprint. That's why Dow—along with the Big Three automakers, other large and diversified companies and leading environmental groups—are members of the U.S. Climate Action Partnership and are committed to driving the Federal government to adopt measures to reduce greenhouse gas emissions.

So there are three steps to Dow's Energy Plan for America.

Improve efficiency and conservation.

Diversify domestic supplies.

Find new alternatives and renewables.

If we take these steps—in concert with one another—we can literally provide the fuel that will restore the power to American industry.

Do these sound familiar? They should.

They are now being talked about more and more . . . by more and more politicians, companies, CEOs, and yes, even the President of the United States and the two candidates that want to succeed him.

I suppose we should be pleased that this plan is finally being talked about. But it's hard to take pleasure when all we hear is talk.

We have yet to see any significant action by Congress. We have yet to see a bipartisan approach to getting it ALL put in place. And I mean ALL.

Not what partisanship brings us, but what common sense demands we do.

The right path forward is not one of "divide-and-conquer." That's what got us into this mess to begin with.

The right path forward—the only path forward—is one of collaboration and coordination: public and private sectors, Republicans and Democrats, industry and environmentalists, working together with the goal of finding and removing obstacles.

And we need to start where the major challenges of our day intersect: on manufacturing . . . on jobs . . . on energy . . . and the environment.

That's what we call the Dow Energy Plan for America—a workable plan and a real solution to rebuild the industrial base in this country and put Americans back to work.

One of the things I love about democracies—like America—like my native Australia—is that every few years we get to elect new leaders and chart a new course.

This country is entering an historic era. It will elect either its first African-American President or its first female Vice President.

And this new leadership must marshal the courage to re-establish America's place in the world as THE indispensable nation.

If this nation is going to live up to its legacy—if it's going to fulfill its potential of independent influence—our leaders must remember that its strength comes not necessarily from strong politicians . . . but from a strong economy. Not from strong words . . . but from strong, practical policies that rebuild the industrial heartland and create new jobs for Americans in every part of this great country.

We do that by removing the artificial anti-industrial policy costs that disadvantage American manufacturers.

And we do it by insisting—at every turn—on an energy policy that promotes efficiency . . . alternatives and renewables . . . AND new domestic supplies.

We at Dow are committed to this defining idea and plan. We are committed to this state and to this great country.

And I look forward to working with all of you—in the private AND public sectors—as we build this new future together and re-establish America's preeminence in the world.

POSTSCRIPT

Are Free Trade and Economic Liberalism Good for the United States?

There can be no doubt that the global economy and the level of interdependence have grown rapidly since World War II. In many ways, globalization has been extraordinarily beneficial—it has promoted economic and political liberalization, accelerated economic development, and brought people from around the world together in new and remarkable ways. For an optimistic assessment of globalization, see Thomas Freedman, *The Lexus and the Olive Tree* (Douglas and McIntyre, Ltd, 2001).

Despite its touted benefits, globalization affects different countries and different groups of people within them differently. Some benefit more than others and some are more vulnerable to the changes it generates. As a result, globalization and its effects are contentious. To learn more about the pros and cons of globalization, read Frank Lechner and John Boli, eds., *The Globalization Reader* (Blackwell Press, 2004).

One of the most remarkable shifts in political momentum in recent years has been the marked increase in the resistance to globalization. Meetings of international financial organizations such as the IMF and the WTO used to pass unnoticed by nearly everyone except financiers, scholars, and government officials. Now they often occasion mass protests, such as the riots that broke out in Seattle, Washington, in 1999 at a meeting of the WTO. For more on this and other political areas of policy dispute in the United States, see Edward S. Cohen, *The Politics of Globalization in the United States* (Georgetown University Press, 2001).

The 2008–2009 financial crisis seemingly confirmed the fears of those critical of free trade and economic liberalism. Although China, Latin America, and other countries pursuing alternative economic strategies also suffered dramatically from the crisis, doubts about the ultimate benefits of free trade and economic liberalism grew both inside the United States and abroad. There are a wide range of good books on the 2008 financial crisis. Beginning with a historical perspective, Paul Krugman's, *The Return of Depression Economics and the Crisis of 2000* (W. W. Norton, 2000), offers insights into the parallels between the financial crisis in Latin America and Asia, with a particular focus on Japan's decade-long difficulties. Alan Greenspan offers insights in his autobiography, *The Age of Turbulence* (Penguin, 2007), into the evolution of, and motivations behind, the strategy of deregulation that created the context for the financial crisis. In parallel, Robert Shiller analyzes the subprime-mortgage crisis that precipitated the financial crisis in *The Subprime Solution: How Today's*

Financial Crisis Happened and What to Do about It (Princeton, 2008). Looking at the aftermath of the crisis, George Soros blends his personal experiences as a fund manager with a call for a new theory of financial markets in *The New Paradigm for Financial Markets* (Public Affairs, 2008). Robert Samuelson warns about the dangers of inflation that may result from massive government stimuli in *The Great Inflation and Its Aftermath* (Random House, 2008).

The 2008–2009 financial crisis and subsequent global recession have rekindled a debate on the role and importance of an international mechanism—whether an enhanced International Monetary Fund or other body—for addressing resurgent concerns of liquidity, adjustment mechanisms, and confidence in the international system. In November of 2008, the Group of 20 Financial Ministers and Central Bank Governors or "G-20," including nineteen of the world's wealthiest countries plus the European Union, held a summit in Washington, DC. Information about this summit, and the G-20 generally, is available on the Web at http://www.g20.org/G20/. Labeled by some, "Bretton Woods II," this summit was notable for its timing, its participants, and its message. Following a Group of 7 (G-7) meeting in October, President George W. Bush called for the next meeting of the G-20 to focus on the global financial crisis. French President Nicolas Sarkozy and British Prime Minister Gordon Brown followed suit by calling for a special meeting of G-20 Leaders Summit on Financial Markets and the World Economy. The summit took place as the severity and negative consequences of the 2008–2009 economic crises intensified, having spread to Europe, Asia, and Latin America and having expanded from a financial crisis to a global recession in trade and manufacturing. In addition to advanced industrialized countries, its participants included countries from Asia, Latin America, and the Middle East. Its goals were both narrow—bolstering political leaders in participant countries—and quite broad—to coordinate international responses to the global financial crisis and to begin negotiations the future management of the international financial system.

The importance of this meeting and the viability of coordinated efforts to manage the international system through an enhanced International Monetary Fund or by other means are contested. Representing one viewpoint, Robert Hutchings, "A Global Grand Bargain," *Washington Post,* p. A19 (November 17, 2008), argues the IMF and Bretton Woods System are inadequate and that managing the global problems we face today will require new level of global cooperation. In contrast, representing another, Sebastian Mallaby, "Bretton Woods, the Sequel?" *Washington Post,* p. A15 (November 20, 2008), argues in favor of national solutions combined with the expansion and modernization of the International Monetary Fund.

ISSUE 15

Is Fighting Climate Change Worth the Cost?

YES: Bill McKibben, from "Think Again: Climate Change," *Foreign Policy* (January/February 2009)

NO: Jim Manzi, from "The Icarus Syndrome: Should We Pay Any Price to Avoid the Consequences of Global Warming?" *The Weekly Standard* (September 8, 2008)

ISSUE SUMMARY

YES: Bill McKibben, an environmental author and activist, argues that the science of global warming is clear and a climate catastrophe is under way, that transformational change is necessary, and that the costs of further inaction will be large and widespread.

NO: Jim Manzi, CEO of an applied artificial intelligence software company, argues that predictions about the degree and consequences of global warming are fraught with uncertainty. Consequently, the best strategy for addressing energy and the environment is to let the markets integrate known information into prices and let the consumers and producers adjust accordingly.

$\mathbf{I}$n a very short time, technology has brought some amazing things. But these advances have had by-products. A great deal of prosperity has come about through industrialization, electrification, the burgeoning of private and commercial vehicles, and a host of other inventions and improvements that consume massive amounts of fossil fuel (mostly coal, petroleum, and natural gas). The burning of fossil fuels sends carbon dioxide (CO_2) into the atmosphere. The discharge of CO_2 from burning wood, animals exhaling, and some other sources is nearly as old as Earth itself, but the twentieth century's advances have rapidly increased the level of discharge. Since 1950 alone, global CO_2 emissions have increased 278 percent, with more than 26 billion tons of CO_2 now being discharged annually. There are now almost 850 billion tons of CO_2 in the atmosphere.

Many analysts believe that as a result of this buildup of CO_2, we are experiencing a gradual pattern of global warming. The reason, according to these scientists, is the *greenhouse effect*. As CO_2 accumulates in the upper atmosphere, it creates a blanket effect, trapping heat and preventing the nightly cooling of the Earth. Other gases, especially methane and chlorofluorocarbons (CFCs, such as freon), also contribute to the thermal blanket.

In their fourth Annual Assessment Report titled "Climate Change 2007," scientists on the United Nations Intergovernmental Panel on Climate Change report that there is now "unequivocal" evidence of global warming and declare that human activity "very likely" has been the driving force in that change over the last 50 years (http://www.ipcc.ch/ipccreports/ar4-syr.htm). Their report predicts that the global climate is likely to rise between 3.5 and 8°F, leading to potential rises in sea levels between 7 to 23 inches by 2100. In combination with the publication of a growing number of other scientific reports, this assessment helped change the policy debate from whether climate change was real and how best to address it.

The 1990s saw efforts to constrain and cut back CO_2 emissions. The Earth Summit held in Rio de Janeiro in 1992 was the first of these efforts. At Rio, most of the economically developed countries (EDCs) signed the Global Warming Convention and agreed to voluntarily stabilize emissions at their 1990 levels by the year 2000. They also resolved to reconvene in 1997 to review progress under the agreement.

The 1997 meeting was held in Kyoto, Japan. Although the Kyoto Protocols went into effect in February 2005 for its more than 80 signatories, it did so without the endorsement of the United States. President George W. Bush opposed the Kyoto Treaty because of concerns regarding the domestic regulatory limits it placed on greenhouse gasses and because the treaty exempted China and India, as well as other developing countries, from its binding emissions standards.

In April 2008, President Bush signaled a change in U.S. policy by calling for a stop in the growth of U.S. greenhouse gas emissions by 2025 and calling on the U.S. Congress to develop legislation to address global warming. President Obama, in turn, emphasized his recognition of environmental concerns by appointing scientists and experts known for advocating environmental issues to key positions, including the Environmental Protection Agency, the Energy Department, the Interior Department, and the White House Council on Environmental Quality. The president and his environmental team have expressed a willingness to explore a variety of options in managing energy and environmental concerns, including carbon caps and investment in renewable energy resources, at home and in coordination with other countries.

Despite a growing consensus regarding the causes and potential consequences of climate change, the global economic downturn of 2008 and 2009 has sparked renewed debate about the potential costs of enacting transformative environmental policies versus the costs of not doing so. Bill McKibben argues that the climate change is real and already underway and that the widespread costs of inaction far outweigh the expense of transforming our energy behavior. In contrast, Jim Manzi accepts the idea that climate change is real, but argues that predictions about extent and consequences of climate change are notoriously uncertain and, like those made previously about the limits of fossil fuels like goal and oil, they are likely to be wrong. Given these uncertainties, we should be very cautious about implementing government programs that will slow economic growth and technological development. Instead, we should rely on the market, which is better than governments at integrating information about environmental changes and other unknown threats while promoting innovation.

YES ↵

Bill McKibben

Think Again: Climate Change

"Scientists Are Divided"

No, they're not. In the early years of the global warming debate, there was great controversy over whether the planet was warming, whether humans were the cause, and whether it would be a significant problem. That debate is long since over. Although the details of future forecasts remain unclear, there's no serious question about the general shape of what's to come.

Every national academy of science, long lists of Nobel laureates, and in recent years even the science advisors of President George W. Bush have agreed that we are heating the planet. Indeed, there is a more thorough scientific process here than on almost any other issue: Two decades ago, the United Nations formed the Intergovernmental Panel on Climate Change (IPCC) and charged its scientists with synthesizing the peer-reviewed science and developing broad-based conclusions. The reports have found since 1995 that warming is dangerous and caused by humans. The panel's most recent report, in November 2007, found it is "very likely" (defined as more than 90 percent certain, or about as certain as science gets) that heat-trapping emissions from human activities have caused "most of the observed increase in global average temperatures since the mid-20th century."

If anything, many scientists now think that the IPCC has been too conservative—both because member countries must sign off on the conclusions and because there's a time lag. Its last report synthesized data from the early part of the decade, not the latest scary results, such as what we're now seeing in the Arctic.

In the summer of 2007, ice in the Arctic Ocean melted. It melts a little every summer, of course, but this time was different—by late September, there was 25 percent less ice than ever measured before. And it wasn't a one-time accident. By the end of the summer season in 2008, so much ice had melted that both the Northwest and Northeast passages were open. In other words, you could circumnavigate the Arctic on open water. The computer models, which are just a few years old, said this shouldn't have happened until sometime late in the 21st century. Even skeptics can't dispute such alarming events.

From *Foreign Policy,* January/February 2009. Copyright © 2009 by the Carnegie International Peace. Reprinted with permission. www.foreignpolicy.com

"We Have Time"

Wrong. Time might be the toughest part of the equation. That melting Arctic ice is unsettling not only because it proves the planet is warming rapidly, but also because it will help speed up the warming. That old white ice reflected 80 percent of incoming solar radiation back to space; the new blue water left behind absorbs 80 percent of that sunshine. The process amps up. And there are many other such feedback loops. Another occurs as northern permafrost thaws. Huge amounts of methane long trapped below the ice begin to escape into the atmosphere; methane is an even more potent greenhouse gas than carbon dioxide.

Such examples are the biggest reason why many experts are now fast-forwarding their estimates of how quickly we must shift away from fossil fuel. Indian economist Rajendra Pachauri, who accepted the 2007 Nobel Peace Prize alongside Al Gore on behalf of the IPCC, said recently that we must begin to make fundamental reforms by 2012 or watch the climate system spin out of control; NASA scientist James Hansen, who was the first to blow the whistle on climate change in the late 1980s, has said that we must stop burning coal by 2030. Period.

All of which makes the Copenhagen climate change talks that are set to take place in December 2009 more urgent than they appeared a few years ago. At issue is a seemingly small number: the level of carbon dioxide in the air. Hansen argues that 350 parts per million is the highest level we can maintain "if humanity wishes to preserve a planet similar to that on which civilization developed and to which life on Earth is adapted." But because we're already past that mark—the air outside is currently about 387 parts per million and growing by about 2 parts annually—global warming suddenly feels less like a huge problem, and more like an Oh-My-God Emergency.

"Climate Change Will Help as Many Places as It Hurts"

Wishful thinking. For a long time, the winners-and-losers calculus was pretty standard: Though climate change will cause some parts of the planet to flood or shrivel up, other frigid, rainy regions would at least get some warmer days every year. Or so the thinking went. But more recently, models have begun to show that after a certain point almost everyone on the planet will suffer. Crops might be easier to grow in some places for a few decades as the danger of frost recedes, but over time the threat of heat stress and drought will almost certainly be stronger.

A 2003 report commissioned by the Pentagon forecasts the possibility of violent storms across Europe, megadroughts across the Southwest United States and Mexico, and unpredictable monsoons causing food shortages in China. "Envision Pakistan, India, and China—all armed with nuclear weapons—skirmishing at their borders over refugees, access to shared rivers, and arable land," the report warned. Or Spain and Portugal "fighting over fishing rights—leading to conflicts at sea."

Of course, there are a few places we used to think of as possible winners—mostly the far north, where Canada and Russia could theoretically produce more grain with longer growing seasons, or perhaps explore for oil beneath the newly melted Arctic ice cap. But even those places will have to deal with expensive consequences—a real military race across the high Arctic, for instance.

Want more bad news? Here's how that Pentagon report's scenario played out: As the planet's carrying capacity shrinks, an ancient pattern of desperate, all-out wars over food, water, and energy supplies would reemerge. The report refers to the work of Harvard archaeologist Steven LeBlanc, who notes that wars over resources were the norm until about three centuries ago. When such conflicts broke out, 25 percent of a population's adult males usually died. As abrupt climate change hits home, warfare may again come to define human life. Set against that bleak backdrop, the potential upside of a few longer growing seasons in Vladivostok doesn't seem like an even trade.

"It's China's Fault"

Not so much. China is an easy target to blame for the climate crisis. In the midst of its industrial revolution, China has overtaken the United States as the world's biggest carbon dioxide producer. And everyone has read about the one-a-week pace of power plant construction there. But those numbers are misleading, and not just because a lot of that carbon dioxide was emitted to build products for the West to consume. Rather, it's because China has four times the population of the United States, and per capita is really the only way to think about these emissions. And by that standard, each Chinese person now emits just over a quarter of the carbon dioxide that each American does. Not only that, but carbon dioxide lives in the atmosphere for more than a century. China has been at it in a big way less than 20 years, so it will be many, many years before the Chinese are as responsible for global warming as Americans.

What's more, unlike many of their counterparts in the United States, Chinese officials have begun a concerted effort to reduce emissions in the midst of their country's staggering growth. China now leads the world in the deployment of renewable energy, and there's barely a car made in the United States that can meet China's much tougher fuel-economy standards.

For its part, the United States must develop a plan to cut emissions—something that has eluded Americans for the entire two-decade history of the problem. Although the U.S. Senate voted down the last such attempt, Barack Obama has promised that it will be a priority in his administration. He favors some variation of a "cap and trade" plan that would limit the total amount of carbon dioxide the United States could release, thus putting a price on what has until now been free.

Despite the rapid industrialization of countries such as China and India, and the careless neglect of rich ones such as the United States, climate change is neither any one country's fault, nor any one country's responsibility. It will require sacrifice from everyone. Just as the Chinese might have to use somewhat more expensive power to protect the global environment, Americans will have to pay some of the difference in price, even if just in technology.

Call it a Marshall Plan for the environment. Such a plan makes eminent moral and practical sense and could probably be structured so as to bolster emerging green energy industries in the West. But asking Americans to pay to put up windmills in China will be a hard political sell in a country that already thinks China is prospering at its expense. It could be the biggest test of the country's political maturity in many years.

"Climate Change Is an Environmental Problem"

Not really. Environmentalists were the first to sound the alarm. But carbon dioxide is not like traditional pollution. There's no Clean Air Act that can solve it. We must make a fundamental transformation in the most important part of our economies, shifting away from fossil fuels and on to something else. That means, for the United States, it's at least as much a problem for the Commerce and Treasury departments as it is for the Environmental Protection Agency.

And because every country on Earth will have to coordinate, it's far and away the biggest foreign-policy issue we face. (You were thinking terrorism? It's hard to figure out a scenario in which Osama bin Laden destroys Western civilization. It's easy to figure out how it happens with a rising sea level and a wrecked hydrological cycle.)

Expecting the environmental movement to lead this fight is like asking the USDA to wage the war in Iraq. It's not equipped for this kind of battle. It may be ready to save Alaska's Arctic National Wildlife Refuge, which is a noble undertaking but on a far smaller scale. Unless climate change is quickly de-ghettoized, the chances of making a real difference are small.

"Solving It Will Be Painful"

It depends. What's your definition of painful? On the one hand, you're talking about transforming the backbone of the world's industrial and consumer system. That's certainly expensive. On the other hand, say you manage to convert a lot of it to solar or wind power—think of the money you'd save on fuel.

And then there's the growing realization that we don't have many other possible sources for the economic growth we'll need to pull ourselves out of our current economic crisis. Luckily, green energy should be bigger than IT and biotech combined.

Almost from the moment scientists began studying the problem of climate change, people have been trying to estimate the costs of solving it. The real answer, though, is that it's such a huge transformation that no one really knows for sure. The bottom line is, the growth rate in energy use worldwide could be cut in half during the next 15 years and the steps would, net, save more money than they cost. The IPCC included a cost estimate in its latest five-year update on climate change and looked a little further into the future. It found that an attempt to keep carbon levels below about 500 parts per million would shave a little bit off the world's economic growth—but only a little. As in, the world would have to wait until Thanksgiving 2030 to be as rich as it would have been on January 1 of that year. And in return, it would have a much-transformed energy system.

Unfortunately though, those estimates are probably too optimistic. For one thing, in the years since they were published, the science has grown darker. Deeper and quicker cuts now seem mandatory.

But so far we've just been counting the costs of fixing the system. What about the cost of doing nothing? Nicholas Stern, a renowned economist commissioned by the British government to study the question, concluded that the costs of climate change could eventually reach the combined costs of both world wars and the Great Depression. In 2003, Swiss Re, the world's biggest reinsurance company, and Harvard Medical School explained why global warming would be so expensive. It's not just the infrastructure, such as sea walls against rising oceans, for example. It's also that the increased costs of natural disasters begin to compound. The diminishing time between monster storms in places such as the U.S. Gulf Coast could eventually mean that parts of "developed countries would experience developing nation conditions for prolonged periods." Quite simply, we've already done too much damage and waited too long to have any easy options left.

"We Can Reverse Climate Change"

If only. Solving this crisis is no longer an option. Human beings have already raised the temperature of the planet about a degree Fahrenheit. When people first began to focus on global warming (which is, remember, only 20 years ago), the general consensus was that at this point we'd just be standing on the threshold of realizing its consequences—that the big changes would be a degree or two and hence several decades down the road. But scientists seem to have systematically underestimated just how delicate the balance of the planet's physical systems really is.

The warming is happening faster than we expected, and the results are more widespread and more disturbing. Even that rise of 1 degree has seriously perturbed hydrological cycles: Because warm air holds more water vapor than cold air does, both droughts and floods are increasing dramatically. Just look at the record levels of insurance payouts, for instance. Mosquitoes, able to survive in new places, are spreading more malaria and dengue. Coral reefs are dying, and so are vast stretches of forest.

None of that is going to stop, even if we do everything right from here on out. Given the time lag between when we emit carbon and when the air heats up, we're already guaranteed at least another degree of warming.

The only question now is whether we're going to hold off catastrophe. It won't be easy, because the scientific consensus calls for roughly 5 degrees more warming this century unless we do just about everything right. And if our behavior up until now is any indication, we won't.

Jim Manzi

NO

The Icarus Syndrome: Should We Pay Any Price to Avoid the Consequences of Global Warming?

William Ewart Gladstone, in his 1866 budget speech, warned that Britain faced the prospect of exhausting its domestic coal within a century and had poor prospects of finding sufficient alternative energy sources. This was not an idiosyncratic point of view. The year before, the economist William Stanley Jevons's influential book *The Coal Question* had made the same prediction and proposed a set of policies to conserve coal for the inevitable lean times. John Stuart Mill supported both the thesis and Jevons's proposals. Newspapers took up the "Coal Panic," and a Royal Commission on Coal was created. Eventually the issue fizzled, and Britain moved on to other, more pressing, concerns.

It was true that British coal production could not grow indefinitely, and it did not. The essential points that Jevons missed, however, were the feasibility of displacing coal with petroleum as a source of energy and the decreasing centrality of low-cost coal to the industries that were to lead Britain in the 20th century. But then again, as the great physicist Niels Bohr reportedly said, "Prediction is hard, especially concerning the future."

Successful modern economies create unprecedented wealth and material ease, but they also tend to generate characteristic anxieties. One of them is the recurring belief that the whole thing is a house of cards. Psychologically, this is the fear that there is some hidden danger that will cause modern society to collapse, and that we would have been better off if we had stayed lower to the ground and not tried to build such an overwhelming success. The most compelling of these stories often involve problems that the modern system has supposedly created itself. Call it the Icarus Syndrome.

The British Coal Panic might seem quaint from our vantage point more than a century later, but many similar fears are fashionable today. "Peak oil" is the almost perfectly analogous theory that the world is about to reach, or already has reached, maximum possible production of oil, and that we are about to experience rapid reductions in output with dire global consequences. Like Jevons, most peak oil advocates argue that we need to begin to husband our resources, rather than innovate our way around this projected problem.

The peak oil theory usually proceeds from the correct prediction in 1956 by Shell Oil geologist M. King Hubbert that oil production in the United States

From *The Weekly Standard,* by Jim Manzi, Vol. 13, no. 48, September 8, 2008. Copyright © 2008 by Jim Manzi. Reprinted by permission of the author.

would hit its high sometime in the late 1960s or early 1970s. Advocates, however, much more rarely note that in 1974 Hubbert also predicted that global oil production would peak in about 1995. Whoops. It turns out that it's more feasible to predict peak production in very well-understood geography, such as the United States, than for the world as a whole.

Unsurprisingly, the U.S. Department of Energy (DOE) has taken a serious look at this question. They project rising global production through 2030 and do not forecast beyond that date. The International Energy Agency, sponsored by the OECD in Paris, also projects rising production through 2030. So does OPEC. In 2005, Guy Caruso, the head of the Energy Information Administration, the responsible agency within the DOE, made his best guess that peak production would probably be reached "sometime in the middle of this century."

Caruso identified 36 academic forecasts for peak oil published between 1972 and 2004. There is an obvious pattern in the data. Roughly speaking, academic forecasts indicate that we are about 20 years from peak oil today, just as such forecasts generally indicated that we were about 20 years from peak oil throughout the 1970s and 1980s. What if we had reacted to these earlier, incorrect predictions of resource exhaustion with, as many advocated at the time, government coercion to force a decrease in petroleum use and to limit growth? We very likely would not have found ourselves on the other side of one of the greatest periods of wealth creation in American history, and therefore would probably not be in the happy position of paying, even at 2008 prices, a smaller share of GDP for oil than we did in 1980.

There is a finite amount of oil in the world, so we will eventually reach a production maximum. We have, however, a very poor track record in predicting when this will happen, and the world's leading experts will provide only the most general guidance that it looks like we probably have several decades of production growth in front of us. Much like the British looking forward from the 1860s, we don't have a very good idea of what the technology landscape, and much else besides, will be when or if this occurs. Almost certainly, the best course of action is the simplest: Let markets integrate this information into prices for oil and alternative energy sources, and then let entrepreneurs use this information to guide the deployment of resources through markets.

The current concern over global warming is similar to the Coal Crisis and the Peak Oil debate. It also starts with a valid observation. Modern economies emit a lot of carbon dioxide (CO_2), and all else being equal, the more CO_2 molecules we put into the atmosphere, the hotter it gets. If we were to emit enough CO_2 and drive temperatures up high enough, it would be disastrous for humanity. If you believe that such a disaster is in the offing, there is a fairly simple solution: Emit less CO_2. The typical methods that are proposed to do this are either to tax carbon emissions or to introduce a "cap-and-trade" system (in less fancy language, to ration CO_2 emissions and have the government auction off the ration cards). But this once again raises the huge question of prediction. Namely, how much hotter would our expected rate of carbon dioxide emissions make the world and how bad would this be?

The United Nations Intergovernmental Panel on Climate Change (IPCC) is the largest existing global effort to answer these questions. Its current consensus forecast is that, under fairly reasonable assumptions for world population and economic growth, global temperatures will rise by about 3°C by the year 2100. Also according to the IPCC, a 4°C increase in temperatures would cause total estimated economic losses of 1–5 percent of global GDP. By implication, if we had reached 3°C of warming by 2100, we would be well into the 22nd century before we reached a 4°C rise, with this associated level of cost.

This is a big problem for advocates of rapid, aggressive emissions reductions. Despite the rhetoric, the best available estimate of the damage we face from global warming is not "global destruction" but costs on the order of 3 percent of global GDP in a much wealthier world well over a hundred years from now.

One serious objection to this logic is that the forecasts for warming impacts might be wrong, and global warming could turn out to be substantially worse than the IPCC models predict. Now, climate and economics modelers aren't idiots, so it's not like this hasn't occurred to them. Competent modelers don't assume only the most likely case, but build probability distributions for levels of warming and associated economic impacts (e.g., there is a 5 percent chance of 4.5°C warming, a 10 percent chance of 4.0°C warming, and so on). So, the possibility of "worse than expected" impacts really means, more precisely, "worse than our current estimated probability distribution." That is, we are concerned here with the real, but inherently unquantifiable, possibility that our probability distribution itself is wrong.

The argument for emissions abatement, then, boils down to the point that you can't prove a negative. If it turns out that not just the best estimate, but even the outer edge of the probability distribution of our predictions for global-warming impacts is enormously conservative, and disaster looms if we don't change our ways radically and this instant, then we really should start shutting down power plants and confiscating cars tomorrow morning. We have no good evidence that such a disaster scenario is imminent, but nobody can prove it to be impossible. Once you get past the table-thumping, any rationale for emissions abatement that confronts the facts in evidence is really a more or less sophisticated restatement of the Precautionary Principle: the somewhat grandiosely named idea that the downside possibilities are so bad that we should pay almost any price to avoid almost any chance of their occurrence.

One could argue that we should therefore push down carbon dioxide emissions far faster than the odds-adjusted risk of global warming costs appear to justify. How much faster? One widely discussed benchmark for a "safe" level of emissions is to set a target limit for atmospheric concentration of CO_2 of no more than 150 percent of its current level. Suppose we did this via what most economists believe is the most efficient imaginable means: a globally harmonized and perfectly implemented worldwide tax on carbon. According to the modeling group led by William Nordhaus, a Yale professor widely considered to be the world's leading expert on this kind of assessment, we, humanity, could expect to spend about $17 trillion more under such a regime than the benefits that we would expect to achieve. To put that in context, the annual GDP of the United States of America is about $13 trillion. That's a heck of an insurance premium for an event so unlikely that it is literally outside of a probability distribution. But I can find major public figures who say that this level of atmospheric carbon dioxide is still too dangerous. Al Gore has proposed an even lower target for emissions that if implemented through an optimal carbon tax is expected to cost more like $23 trillion in excess of benefits. Of course, even this wouldn't eliminate all risk, and I can find highly credentialed scientists who say we need to reduce emissions even faster. Once we leave the world of odds and trade-offs and enter the Precautionary Principle zone, there is no nonarbitrary stopping point. We would be chasing an endlessly receding horizon of zero risk.

But to force massive change in the economy based on such a fear is to get lost in the hothouse world of single-issue advocates and become myopic about risk. We face lots of other unquantifiable threats of at least comparable realism and severity. A regional nuclear war in central Asia, a global pandemic triggered by a modified version of the HIV virus, or a rogue state weaponizing genetic-engineering technology all come immediately to mind. Any of these could kill hundreds of millions of people. Specialists often worry about the existential risks of new technologies spinning out of control. Biosphere-consuming nano-technology, supercomputers that can replace humans, and Frankenstein-like organisms created by genetic engineering are all topics of intense speculation. Sometimes, though, we face monsters from the deep: The cover of the June *Atlantic Monthly* said of the potential for a planet-killing asteroid, "The Sky Is Falling!"

A healthy society is constantly scanning the horizon for threats and developing contingency plans to meet them, but it's counterproductive to become paralyzed by our fears. The loss of economic and technological development that would be required to eliminate all theorized climate change risk or all risk from genetic and computational technologies or, for that matter, all risk from killer asteroids would cripple our ability to deal with virtually every other foreseeable and unforeseeable risk, not to mention our ability to lead productive and interesting lives in the meantime. The Precautionary Principle is a bottomless well of anxieties, but our resources are finite.

In the face of massive uncertainty, hedging your bets and keeping your options open is almost always the right strategy. Money and technology are the raw materials for options. The idea of the simple, low-to-the-ground society as more resilient to threats is, like the story of Icarus, a resonant myth. But experience shows that wealthy, technologically sophisticated societies are much better able to withstand resource shortages, physical disasters, and almost every other challenge than poorer societies.

Consider that if a killer asteroid were actually to approach the Earth, we would rely on orbital telescopes, spacecraft, and thermonuclear bombs to avert disaster. In such a scenario, we would be very glad that we hadn't responded to the threat of peak coal back in the 1860s by slowing our development to such an extent that we lacked one of these technologies. In the case of global warming, a much more appropriate approach than rationing energy and forgoing trillions of dollars of economic growth is to invest a fair number of billions of dollars into targeted scientific research that would give us technical alternatives if a worst-case scenario began to emerge.

We should be very cautious about implementing government programs that require us to slow economic growth and technological development in the near-term in return for the promise of avoiding inherently uncertain costs that are projected to appear only in the long-term. Such policies conceal hubris in a cloak of false humility. They inevitably demand that the government coerce individuals in the name of a nonfalsifiable prediction of a distant emergency. The problem, of course, is that we have a very bad track record of predicting the specific problems of the far future accurately.

We can be confident that humanity will face many difficulties in the upcoming century, as it has in every century. We just don't know which ones they will be. This implies that the correct grand strategy for meeting them is to maximize total technical capabilities in the context of a market-oriented economy that can integrate highly unstructured information into prices that direct resources, and, most important, to maintain a democratic political culture that can face facts and respond to threats as they develop.

POSTSCRIPT

Is Fighting Climate Change Worth the Cost?

The provisions of the Kyoto treaty include the requirement that the treaty would not go into effect until it was ratified by at least 55 countries representing at least 55 percent of the world's greenhouse gases. That requirement was met in October 2004 when Russia ratified the treaty. As a result, it became active in February 16, 2005, without U.S. ratification. By 2008, all ratifying countries are required to begin cutting their carbon emissions and by 2012 industrial nations are required to reach emission reduction targets. Since the United States is the source of approximately 25 percent of the world's carbon dioxide emissions, the U.S. refusal to ratify the treaty is of great importance.

U.S. opposition to Kyoto remained throughout the George W. Bush presidency. This opposition continued despite a 2001 report by an expert working group on climate change, appointed by the president, which argued that there is a consensus within the scientific community that the Earth's temperature is warming and that emissions of greenhouse gases and aerosols due to human activities continue to alter the atmosphere in ways that are expected to affect climate change. President Bush altered the U.S. position in April of 2008, pledging U.S. action to confront climate change and urging other nations and the U.S. Congress to develop strategies to best manage environmental concerns without reducing economic growth. President Barack Obama and his economic team have committed to exploring a federal cap-and-trade system, emissions targets, and investment in alternative, renewable and clean energies. Information on U.S. policy on climate change is available on the Web at http://www.epa.gov/climatechange/. For information on recent multilateral environmental meetings and assessments, see: http://www.unep.org/themes/climatechange/.

The United Nation's Intergovernmental Panel on Climate Change's assessment that there is "unequivocal" evidence of global warming is widely accepted (see: http://www.ipcc.ch), yet like most environmental problems, the negative impacts of global warming will be slow to build up and, therefore, are somewhat hard to see. Average temperatures will rise most years in fractions of degrees. Patterns of storms, rain, and other weather factors that strongly govern the climate of any region will also change slowly. Although some coastal cities may disappear and some now-fertile areas may become deserts, that is many years in the future. Besides, other regions may benefit. Marginal agricultural areas in northern regions may someday flourish. To make matters more confusing, the Earth warms and cools in long cycles, and some scientists believe that to the degree there is a general warming, it is all or mostly the result of this natural phenomenon. If that is true, cutting back on greenhouse gases will have little or no effect.

However, if we ignore global warming, there will only be an escalating buildup of greenhouse gases; EDCs will continue to emit them, and emissions from LDCs will rise as part of their modernization efforts. If those who are alarmed about global warming are correct, and we ignore it, there will be many devastating effects that will affect large portions of the globe.

Then there is the matter of the effects of programs to ease global warming. Those who recommend caution in responding to demands that global warming be halted also point out that significantly reducing CO_2 emissions will not be easy. It might well require substantial lifestyle changes in the industrialized countries. For example, cars might have to be much smaller, gasoline prices higher, and electricity production and consumption curtailed. Costs would also be enormous. The Union of Concerned Scientists (UCS) has concluded that a program to cut CO_2 emissions by 70 percent over a 40-year period would cost the U.S. economy $2.7 trillion.

But there will also be benefits. The UCS also projects a $5 trillion savings in fuel costs. Others have pointed to the economic stimulus that would be provided by creating alternative energy technologies. Losses from storm damages would also drop. A stabilization of the climate would stabilize the lifestyles of people in coastal and other areas that would be most strongly affected by global warming.

In the end, the question is this: Should the United States and other countries bet trillions of dollars in economic costs that emission reductions will reduce the negative consequences of global warming? For most of the George W. Bush administration, the answer was "No." The human component of global warming was considered suspect and the Kyoto treaty was "deeply flawed." While maintaining its opposition to the Kyoto treaty, near the end of its term, the Bush administration joined the international community in acknowledging human contributions towards global warming and urging national efforts at home and abroad to address its dangers. The Obama administration has expressed a willingness to work with others to address global warming, but problems remain. In addition to the importance of making a new treaty truly global by including China, India, Brazil and other large polluting countries into the agreement, the fallout from the 2008–2009 global financial crisis may reduce the willingness and ability of countries to respond as aggressively as they would otherwise to environmental concerns.

ISSUE 16

Is It Realistic for the United States to Move Toward Greater Energy Independence?

YES: **Nathan E. Hultman**, from "Can the World Wean Itself from Fossil Fuels?" *Current History* (November 2007)

NO: **Philip J. Deutch**, from "Energy Independence," *Foreign Policy* (November/December 2005)

ISSUE SUMMARY

YES: Nathan E. Hultman, assistant professor at the University of Maryland, argues that historical patterns of change in the sources of our energy and the increasing efficiency with which we consume it suggest that we can enhance energy security and address climate change without major disruptions to our society. Strategies for doing this include expanding government-sponsored research and development, establishing clear and stable long-term carbon prices, and developing new technology standards.

NO: Philip J. Deutch, director of Evergreen Solar and general partner of NGP Energy Technology Partners, a private equity firm investing in energy technology companies, argues that U.S. oil imports are so high that it would be impossible to end them in the next few decades, and that U.S. energy use is likely to continue to grow, as will oil prices, even if energy efficiency and conservation increase.

Analysts generally agree that the U.S. imports most of the oil it uses, that this creates challenges for American foreign policy, and that in the absence of policy changes the share of U.S. energy use that comes from oil imports is likely to rise. Disagreements arise, however, over how much conservation efforts and programs to stimulate alternative energy sources can reduce this dependency on oil imports, and how soon and at what cost they might do so. As Philip Deutch points out, the United States imports 4 billion barrels of oil a year, over half of the oil it uses. This slows growth in the U.S. economy and hurts the U.S. trade balance when the price of oil rises, as it has in recent years, and it also forces the United States to confront several foreign policy trade-offs.

First, dependency on oil imports, especially those from the Middle East, make the United States vulnerable to any political or military developments that disrupt the production or transport of oil and create demands for U.S. military capabilities and deployments to prevent or reverse any such disruption. Second, research suggests that countries whose economies are dependent on oil exports tend to be less democratic than other countries with comparable levels of GNP per capita. In effect, oil-rich governments are able to buy off a sufficient number of elite supporters to be able to ignore demands from their publics for greater political representation. Thus, payments for imported oil often go to undemocratic governments. Third, high use of oil and many other fuels increases the carbon dioxide emissions that contribute to global warming.

These problems are likely to intensify even if the United States becomes more energy efficient, as growing demand for oil in China, India, and elsewhere may continue to contribute to rising oil prices even if demand in the United States can be reduced below current projections. It remains unclear whether the United States can significantly reduce demand for oil and increase the use of alternative fuels, and whether government policies or market forces are the best ways to bring about these objectives. Rising prices are themselves a powerful mechanism for encouraging conservation, as is evident in the sharp decline of sales of sport-utility vehicles in the United States as gas prices rose above $3 per gallon. Higher prices also make alternative fuels more economically viable. The production of electricity from wind turbines, for example, is presently only about 2 percent of U.S. electricity generation, but is growing rapidly as the rising cost of oil and other energy sources makes the price of wind-generated power more competitive.

Even so, Nathan E. Hultman argues that addressing the problems of energy security and climate change are not as daunting as they appear. The historic transformation in energy consumption from the predominant use of coal around the world in the early 1900s to the use of oil, natural gas, and coal today demonstrates that dramatic changes in energy use can take place with relatively little social disruption. Furthermore, while energy consumption has risen over time, so too has efficiency. For example, the amount of energy used to create one dollar in national wealth has declined by 40 percent since 1975. Thus, energy transformation is possible and it can be done with efficiency gains that decrease our dependence on foreign energy sources and reduce our carbon footprint per unit of output. The key is to promote this transformation through government policies that encourage innovation, establish a credible price for carbon, and develop new technology standards. Philip Deutch, on the other hand, is pessimistic about the prospects of either government policies or higher prices to substantially reduce U.S. energy imports in the near future.

YES ↩

Nathan E. Hultman

Can the World Wean Itself from Fossil Fuels?

Climate change has moved from a niche environmental policy debate to one of central importance in current international discussions. Much of this change stems from increasing confidence in our understanding of the driving forces and probable consequences of global warming. In a recent assessment, the Intergovernmental Panel on Climate Change noted that the "warming of the climate system is unequivocal" and is "very likely" caused by humans. It further stated that continued growth in greenhouse gas emissions would likely induce climate changes in the twenty-first century far greater than those we have already seen.

At the same time, after a long period of stable energy prices and geopolitical stasis, higher oil prices and price volatility have led to increased concerns over energy security. While climate change and energy security are, in the short term, driven by independent events, their fates in the long run are intertwined.

In other words, addressing the emissions that contribute to climate change will require a fundamental restructuring of the global energy system—away from fossil fuels and toward cleaner sources like renewables, biofuels, or nuclear power—and require it at a time when many nations are worried about potential scarcities of energy supplies.

The challenge seems daunting, to say the least. Yet the fact is that shaping a pathway for global development in light of climate change and oil depletion need not imply radical disruption or widespread social harm. When it comes to addressing climate change, the way we frame the task to ourselves matters more than any speculations about specific energy-technology scenarios. Unfortunately, much of the discussion about global warming to date has focused—almost obsessively—on how different the world's future energy system must be from the present one. This perspective leads to a sense that the problem may be intractable or, at best, cripplingly expensive—in effect begging the question of whether global warming is even worth tackling.

Backward Thinking

People often frame discussions about the twin challenges of climate change and energy security by noting the sobering historical trend of steadily accelerating energy consumption. . . . [World] energy use has doubled in the past

35 years, and that much of the increase is accounted for by coal, oil, and natural gas—all of which contribute to greenhouse gas emissions when they are burned.

Such dramatic increases in energy use certainly give cause for concern about future emissions of heat-trapping gases. Making the situation even more disconcerting is the trend in coal combustion, which has recently accelerated. Just the past five years have seen a 35 percent increase, accounted for almost exclusively by aggressive Chinese expansion of coal-fired electricity generation.

In 2006, China inaugurated a new coal-fired power plant almost every week. Each of these plants has an expected lifetime of 50 years or more and will be responsible for roughly half a billion tons of carbon dioxide emissions over that lifetime. China has repeatedly stated that it will develop its energy resources according to its own needs for energy security and will not accept binding international limits on its greenhouse gas emissions. Australia and the United States also have staggeringly large coal reserves that, by all indications, they will continue to exploit.

A focus on the world's past consumption of energy can thus create deep concern about the upward momentum in energy use. Knowing that the global economy depends so fundamentally on fossil fuels, people see the task of addressing climate change as onerous and even desperate. Given that roughly 60 percent of the world's greenhouse gases are released from the burning of fossil fuels, it might seem difficult both to ensure energy security and to avoid dangerous interference with the climate without, meanwhile, stealing the promise of economic growth from the world's poor. Surely, the logic goes, this exercise will end up costing huge sums. And if the costs are prohibitive, perhaps the world should scale back what seem to be ambitious plans and consider expending effort on other urgent policy areas.

Thinking Backward

While the concern is justified, the logic is wrong. The traditional narrative brushes past two fundamentally important factors: time and efficiency. Climate change is of course a major international challenge, and addressing it will indeed require a massive restructuring of energy infrastructure. But the task need not be impossibly costly. A look at past trends shows why. Even valuable, long-lived capital stock must be replaced at some point. And on the timescale of multiple decades, history suggests that even an entrenched technology can be ousted and supplanted with relatively little pain to society as a whole. From coal's peak influence around 1910, when it accounted for 70 percent of global energy use, it took about 60 years for it to fall to about 30 percent.

The lesson of this observation is not that the problem will somehow fix itself in fourscore years. It is, rather, that conscientious and pragmatic near-term policies, if they sway long-term capital investment decisions, can lay the foundation for more far-reaching diffusion of low-carbon technologies in future decades.

Looking backward in order to take the long view, we see that long-term changes in energy sources may not be so wrenching as they might at first appear. Cleaner energy sources that we now know about and understand may expand their share of supply in the same way that oil and gas did over the past century. New technologies may also emerge that will subvert the careful capital investment plans of the entrenched technologies, like railroads did to canals.

A similar point can be made about the traditional narrative's preoccupation with the seemingly inexorable rise in energy demand over time. The twentieth century indeed witnessed a great increase in energy demand, and that demand will likely grow further. Yet historical experience suggests that energy demand several decades hence is difficult to predict. And, almost always, past forecasts of energy demand have tended to err on the high side.

Energy forecasting undoubtedly has become more refined recently with increasingly complex modeling techniques and improved input data, so perhaps this bias has been reduced or removed. Nevertheless, a number of studies have borne out the observation that complex systems linking social behavior with technology seem particularly prone to uncertainty in forecasting. In addition, forecasters tend to be overconfident in their projections and to downplay nonconforming scenarios.

The Efficiency Trend

One of the biggest uncertainties in forecasting energy demand is the degree to which energy will be used differently or more efficiently in the future. When we wake up in the morning, it does not occur to us to use a certain number of kilowatt-hours of electricity or consume a certain volume of gasoline. We do, however, wish to enjoy lighting and transportation, and therein lies an opportunity: providing the services at lower greenhouse cost.

For as long as we have historical records of energy consumption, one trend has been constant: Along with the significant increases in energy use have come significant gains in the efficiency of using that energy. . . . One measure of this efficiency is the level of carbon emitted per unit of energy consumed. Obviously, in terms of climate change, the less carbon emitted, the better. Since 1980, the amount of carbon emitted per unit of energy has dropped slightly as the fossil fuel mix in America has shifted slightly in favor of more efficient natural gas and renewables.

More striking, however, and more important, is the dramatic improvement in the energy used to create one dollar of gross domestic product. This measure, called the *energy intensity of GDP*, indicates improvements in the energy efficiency of the economy as a whole. The United States now uses 40 percent less energy and 49 percent less oil to produce each dollar of GDP than it did in 1975. Amory Lovins of the Rocky Mountain Institute points out that this efficiency increase can now be thought of as America's largest "source" of energy, equivalent to five times us domestic oil production.

Still more significant is . . . not the amount of energy used to create GDP but rather the emissions of carbon (greenhouse gases) needed to create GDP. [This] provides the most direct single indicator of the economy's "carbon footprint." Indeed, besides addressing concerns about both long-term climate change and economic growth, measuring carbon intensity of GDP has the benefit of being a straightforward calculation. The carbon productivity of the US economy has improved even faster than its general energy efficiency, in part because of a shift to natural gas.

Like other economies around the world, the United States has experienced significant improvements in both energy intensity and carbon intensity over the past 25 years. America in the past few decades has achieved a roughly 3 percent per year increase in energy productivity. This is all the more surprising because, throughout most of this time, the United States was not giving priority to this shift. For example, it did not use many policy tools to drive energy efficiency, nor was it dedicating significant public funds to research and development in energy technologies. Instead, the observed improvements have stemmed largely from the functioning of markets in reducing energy costs.

The state of California, with a more concerted set of policies and practices targeting energy use, has achieved a 4 percent per year increase in energy productivity. Other countries, including even China, have achieved improvements of 5 percent per year. By way of comparison, stabilizing the climate, according to most estimates, would require increasing energy productivity globally by only 3 percent per year. Since efficiency improvements tend to respond well to public policy interventions, further improvements in the rate of decarbonization of energy sources are almost certainly possible under a set of well-designed incentives and initiatives.

The Role of Policy

Changes in technology—both to physical artifacts and the way we use them in society—are a key driver of the world's ability to reduce emissions of greenhouse gases over the coming five decades. Unquestionably, the problem remains staggering: Despite the improvements in global energy intensity that have already occurred, greenhouse gas emissions have risen 70 percent since 1970 and are expected to continue to grow over the next few decades. Stabilizing these concentrations will require sharp reductions in the annual global rate of emissions—up to an eventual 60 percent absolute reduction worldwide despite population and economic growth.

This is not, however, beyond the realm of possibility. The challenge is to establish policies that can nudge the global economy's carbon productivity to improve by an additional 1 percent per year (from its current 2 percent rate), starting now and maintaining that moderately increased pace steadily through decades. This would translate into a 60 percent reduction in global carbon emissions, thereby stabilizing the concentrations of heat-trapping gases in the atmosphere.

There is no single way to achieve this. The long-term nature of the problem, combined with the inherent uncertainty of technological innovation, will require a portfolio of approaches ranging from the well established and well tested to the more experimental. Also required are policies that will help bring promising technologies to the market sooner, and that encourage the development of new technologies, including those not yet conceived.

Policy formation at all levels of governance—international, national, and provincial—will be needed to attain the global reductions that are necessary for climate stabilization. To be sure, experience with climate policy over the past 15 years has been sobering. The Kyoto Protocol, as a grand international agreement, was meant to impel just this kind of technological change. It made use of emissions trading—a promising tool, in combination with other approaches, for reducing the societal cost of cutting emissions. (Under this system, permits are distributed to all emitters, and those who can cut emissions more cheaply may sell their permits to those whose emissions reductions are more expensive.) The intention was sound: The Kyoto Protocol was meant to spur both long-term research and short-term deployment of new technologies. In the end, however, it seems to have done little of either.

A lesson of Kyoto—perhaps not surprising to some—is that international negotiations may prove more effective as a response to nation-states' priorities than as a cudgel to beat them into line. The European Union, for example, has been able to implement a substantial greenhouse gas cap-and-credit trading system within its own jurisdiction. The most robust climate policies are those that are aligned with the interests of individual states—especially those that solidify political support by targeting multiple benefits across different policy goals.

Fortunately, many initiatives that ameliorate the effects of climate change have other important benefits. A significant co-benefit of emission mitigation policies (ancillary to avoiding climate-related damage) is the expected improvement in human health as a consequence of reduced air pollution. Indeed, most studies of anti-emission measures suggest the health benefits alone substantially offset the costs. Additional benefits of more energy-efficient technologies could include balance-of-trade improvements, improved access to modern energy services, and higher employment.

Linking Energy and Climate

For many countries, a major overlap also exists between the goals of climate policy and the goals of energy security or energy independence. Oil price volatility and dependence on a small number of oil exporters are familiar concerns in economic and security debates. Reducing oil use, especially via greater efficiency in transportation, remains a potentially productive approach to reducing heat-trapping gas emissions as well.

This observation brings up the question of whether carefully coordinated engagement with climate change and energy security might allow more effective achievement of both. Daniel Yergin, a longtime expert on energy markets, has compiled a distillation of the principles of energy security, and these can also illuminate possible areas of overlap with greenhouse gas emissions policies. Yergin's principles include the paramount goal of diversifying supply. They also emphasize ensuring cooperative relations with energy exporters and with other importers; dealing proactively with threats to energy security;

encouraging a "healthy, technology-driven" energy industry; and supporting R&D and innovation across many technologies.

Most of these goals suggest possible synergies with climate policy. But the method of approaching energy security matters. Substitute fuels in the form of biofuels, especially biofuels produced from novel and efficient fermentation processes, square well with climate protection, for instance, since biofuel combustion produces fewer net greenhouse gas emissions than does burning gasoline.

However, the goal of energy security can, at times, work against climate goals. For example, several major greenhouse gas emitters—China, Australia, and the United States—also happen to have large coal reserves. For these countries, energy security has been interpreted as providing an imperative for expanded use of coal-fired electricity and even coal-to-liquid fuel technology for transportation. Thus, focusing myopically on only energy security or only climate policy could foil both projects. A healthy policy for each goal must acknowledge and work with the other.

A careful reading of Yergin's analysis of energy security reveals a number of dimensions shared with climate policy. Table 1 outlines 10 principles, informed by Yergin's energy goals, that focus on policies that can simultaneously advance both energy and climate policy goals. Diversity of supply can serve both goals, especially if domestic energy savings (from increased efficiency) are included as a potential source of virtual "supply." Technology development, not surprisingly, also figures importantly in both arenas.

Table 1

Ten Principles Illustrating Some Common Goals of Energy Security and Climate Policy

Ten Principles of Climate-Energy Security

1. Diversify supply and encourage efficiency

2. Ensure a long-term, credible price for carbon

3. Ensure a "security margin" of spare climate capacity

4. Recognize that the energy economy is flexible

5. Build cooperative relations with high emitters and corporations

6. Build cooperative relations with vulnerable countries

7. Deal with energy security threats proactively

8. Ensure a "healthy, technology-driven" energy industry

9. Provide credible information on climate risks

10. Support R&D and innovation across many technologies

Adapted from Daniel Yergin, "Energy Security and Markets" in: Jan H. Kalicki and David L. Goldwyn, eds., *Energy and Security: Toward a New Foreign Policy Strategy.* Johns Hopkins University Press, pp. 51–65, 2005.

Yergin's observation that markets are flexible and respond well to clear and credible price signals reveals an additional policy lever: the possibility that creating an effective price for greenhouse emissions can lead to innovative and even surprising methods to reduce the emissions. Meanwhile, in much the same way that energy security is enhanced when the world has additional production capacity, so too is climate security enhanced by ensuring that global emissions do not push the climate beyond its capacity. Early action to head off foreseeable problems can similarly reduce the chances of unpleasant scenarios.

The imperatives of energy security entail the need to maintain good relations with oil producing blocs as well as other importing countries. But adding climate change to the mix underscores the need to build cooperative relations among high-emitting countries—including major carbon emitters China, Russia, Brazil, India, Australia, and the United States, all of which are either completely outside the Kyoto framework or have zero or insubstantial emissions reduction targets. Any successful international regime for stabilizing climate change will require the active involvement of these nations.

Finally, principles for reaching climate change goals contribute another idea not usually heard in the context of energy security: that of adapting to expected climate changes. Climate policy is more than just cutting emissions. Assisting vulnerable countries in reducing their exposure to climate risks will be an important element in maintaining human wellbeing and a more cooperative and secure international community.

Decarbonizing the World

For the near term, we have already seen how improvements in efficiency can add up to a significant force in reducing emissions. Untapped efficiency options remain probably the biggest asset to draw on for reaching the necessary 1 percent improvements in global carbon productivity over the next five years. Because efficiency is modular, small, and distributed, saving electricity requires about 1,000 times less capital, and repays investments about 10 times faster, than supplying more electricity.

However, because the demand for energy has significant upward momentum, low-carbon energy supply will also have to contribute to the solution. Three of the most promising categories for near-term supply expansion are renewable energy sources, biofuels, and cleaner technologies using carbon capture and storage. Nuclear power might also play a role over a number of decades, but it is not yet clear whether the deregulated electricity supply industry will want to shoulder massive and risky investments in new nuclear plants.

In any case, enough low-carbon alternatives exist to reach even aggressive greenhouse stabilization targets at a moderate macroeconomic cost. In its most recent assessment report, the Intergovernmental Panel on Climate Change concluded that near-term options for low-carbon technology are within reach and not prohibitively expensive. The IPCC found cost-effective emissions reductions available in all sectors, with the most potential for absolute reductions in buildings, industry, energy supply, and agriculture.

The IPCC further suggested that the costs to the global economy are likely to be considerably smaller than many early studies projected. A major goal of climate policies must be to increase the price of carbon emissions—either through a tax or a trading system—to encourage reductions. Reaching stated political goals for moderate temperature rises (such as the European Union's target of 2°C) will require prices on the order of $5 to $65 per ton of carbon dioxide by 2030 and $15 to $130 per ton by 2050. These are admittedly large ranges. But, at worst, we would be looking at the equivalent of a 65-cent-per-gallon tax on gasoline—representing a 20 percent rise from current US gasoline prices, and a much smaller fraction in Europe—to be phased in over many years.

Of course, a carbon tax would pose a bigger hurdle for coal, which has a much higher carbon intensity. Yet the IPCC estimates that even its most aggressive policy target for cutting emissions would likely reduce global annual GDP by only a small amount. And this does not include the benefits of avoided climate damages, which could be much higher.

The Innovation Imperative

Reaching targets for reduced carbon emissions will require a combination of market-based innovation and public policies. The best near-term policies are those that have, or will lead to, benefits other than emissions reductions. Requiring utilities to provide a minimum portion of their electricity from renewable energy sources, for example, not only promotes renewable energy, which reduces greenhouse gas emissions. It also leads to lower local pollution and higher local employment. It encourages distributed generation, which eases pressure on transmission networks. And it has the advantage of allowing some flexibility for the market to select the lowest-cost way to comply with the regulation. Other policy tools with multiple benefits include renewable energy credits and pricing of pollutants, via a carbon tax or emissions trading system.

Pollution taxes provide what many economists consider the most effective option since the taxes can be straightforward to administer and have a well-defined price. Both carbon taxes and emissions trading also use market forces to encourage flexibility and creativity in meeting emissions standards.

In addition to encouraging near-term deployment of current technologies, the single greatest contribution of governments will be to provide a matrix that encourages innovation over time. After a period of high investment following the oil shocks of the 1970s, the energy industry stagnated for almost two decades as a combination of regulation, low oil prices, diminished government support for research, and supply-centric models reduced competition and creativity. Government-sponsored research and development worldwide dropped by half, from highs of over $2 billion per year. And American R&D dropped from 10 percent of total global R&D to less than 2 percent.

An international initiative to triple energy and low-carbon research and development in the near term would bring investments in R&D part of the way back to their levels in the 1970s. It would also lead to many benefits for climate change, energy security, and human wellbeing. Further efforts at aligning market incentives for private capital—for example, through appropriate long-term pricing of carbon and well-executed deregulation of supply—would also help.

The International Landscape

A policy that targets both energy and climate security thus would include international cooperation on technological development and investment; targeted emissions reductions by both developed and developing countries; flexible market mechanisms (like a tax or trading system) that fit the national situations of each country; and, in the words of the British economist Nicholas Stern, a "clear, credible, and long-term" signal on future carbon prices.

In recent years, a consensus has been crystallizing around these principles. This could spell the end of a long period of US disengagement. It also raises the prospect that climate regulation will soon be simply another fact of business life—a source of potential profit and innovation as well as an item of regulatory compliance, rather than only a battleground for political struggle by ideological elites.

The emerging international consensus, while potentially reinvigorating consideration of the need for coordinated policy that has been all but ignored for the past decade by four of the world's five biggest carbon emitters, remains fraught with pitfalls. Foremost among them is the possibility that the United States and the world will repeat the mistakes of the late 1990s by committing to one policy architecture at the expense of others. While the Kyoto Protocol arguably spurred activity in Europe and helped to establish a competitive advantage for a carbon-credit finance sector there, the single-policy approach of the international community created a situation in which neither the United States nor the major emitters of the developing world felt they could engage. Although these countries are now appropriately moving in the direction of emissions trading, a multi-pronged approach that would complement mandatory emissions caps remains essential.

The Long View

In a recent *New York Times* article, science writer John Tierney reviewed the arguments set forth in *Cool It: The Skeptical Environmentalist's Guide to Global Warming,* a new book by the controversial environmentalist Bjorn Lomborg. Tierney concluded, with Lomborg, that "you can't make deep cuts in emissions without affecting people in poor countries. Slowing economic growth in rich countries will have an impact on poor countries that sell to them."

Unfortunately, Tierney (and Lomborg) are repeating the backward thinking that assumes that changing the momentum of the world's energy system will require an economically painful braking, stopping, and reversal. When we pause to reflect and *think backward*—that is, review the history of change in technologies and energy sources—we can see that, given time, new technologies supplant existing ones without radical disruption to economies. We also see that energy systems, in the long view, are rather flexible and fluid. The potential readily exists to nudge them into improving carbon productivity by an additional 1 percent per year over current rates.

This long view underscores the appropriateness of immediate, incremental efforts at all levels of government wherever practical. Policies crafted to achieve many small victories soon—and to create opportunities for many more small victories later—will enable the international community to address climate change in a meaningful and successful way, without having to steal from the poor. Indeed, efficiency-focused policies may even be able to shift the orientation of capital investments from large energy-supply projects toward the human development areas about which Tierney and Lomborg are rightly concerned.

The lesson of the past 15 years of attempts at climate change policy is that many of the fundamental elements of addressing global warming—innovation, implementing current technologies, increasing efficiency, and measures to adapt to climate change and its effects—can be held hostage in an all-or-nothing policy environment. Global warming is a major but tractable challenge for the coming decades. Early engagement can preserve and create options in the future while also contributing to other social goals such as sustainable economic development, reduced vulnerability to natural disasters, and increased energy security.

Implementing these large-scale shifts in the global energy economy will require an international portfolio of policies: expanded government-sponsored R&D, innovative signals on long-term carbon prices, and new technological standards, for example. But by moving confidently on all these fronts, we can ensure that people will not look back in 50 years and marvel at both our myopic vision of future possibilities and our inability to grapple with the world's existing energy system and its effects on energy security and global climate change.

Philip J. Deutch   ➡ **NO**

Energy Independence

"The West Can Stop Relying on Imported Oil"

Not in this lifetime   When people call for energy independence, they usually mean ending reliance on imported oil. Energy independence, we are told,
would avoid dangerous disruptions in supply, ease entanglements in the Middle
East, force corrupt petrostates to reform, and dry up terrorist funds. It may be a
noble statement of ultimate intentions, but as a practical matter, energy independence is absurd. The amount of petroleum imported by the United States
and other countries is so enormous that operating without it over the next
several decades will be impossible for any advanced industrialized economy.

The trend lines clearly indicate that Americans are becoming more
energy dependent, not less so. In 1973, the United States imported 35 percent
of its oil; by 2003, that proportion had jumped to 55 percent. In 2004, the
United States consumed an average of 20.4 million barrels of oil per day, more
than half of which was imported. Ending dependence on imported oil would
mean replacing about 4 billion barrels of oil every year. To put that number
in perspective, assuming no major new discovery of oil deposits, the United
States would burn through its oil reserves in four to five years without imports.
Worse, U.S. demand is projected to grow 37 percent in the next 20 years. At
that point, oil imports will likely account for 68 percent of petroleum supply.

The picture is no different if you consider other major industrialized
countries. In 2004, Japan consumed an average of 5.4 million barrels a day—
almost all of which was imported. Ninety-three percent of Germany's daily oil
demand of 2.6 million barrels is imported. And France already imports nearly
all of its oil. Energy independence is a distant dream for all of these countries.

"Less Foreign Oil Means Lower Prices"

Wrong   Oil is a global commodity, the price of which is based on worldwide
supply and demand. Events influencing supply and demand in one country
affect prices in another. In the wake of Hurricane Katrina, gasoline prices in
Europe soared as a result of the damage to U.S. refineries, even though those
facilities send very little to Europe. Even if the United States did not import
one barrel of oil from the Middle East, the price U.S. citizens would pay at the
pump would still be a function of worldwide supply and demand. Whatever

one's opinion about U.S. or European oil policy, all indications are that worldwide demand—and global prices—will climb as China and India continue to grow. China, which imports about half its oil, is expected to double its oil consumption to 14.2 million barrels a day by 2025. India's consumption will likely jump from 1.4 to 5 million barrels a day by 2020. Global demand will cause the worldwide price of petroleum to rise nearly everywhere. No private oil company will sell oil to its domestic market for one penny less than it could realize in foreign markets, and the price that a barrel of oil commands will be based on pressures beyond any one government's control.

"The United States Should Burn Less Coal"

No   Many analysts argue that given concerns about global warming and the environment, the United States should avoid burning so much coal. Because the United States has the most technologically advanced energy sector, the argument goes, it should lead the way in giving up its coal habit. But just as independence from foreign oil is virtually impossible in the next two decades, there is no point in pretending that the United States can cease using coal. More important, why should the United States so quickly abandon a natural resource that it has in such abundance?

More than half of the electricity produced in the United States in 2004 was generated by coal. Total U.S. electricity sales are projected to increase at an average annual rate of 1.9 percent, from 3,481 billion kilowatt hours in 2003 to 5,220 billion kilowatt hours in 2025. If you want to begin to imagine reducing U.S. coal consumption, you must first account for how these growing energy needs will be met. The truth is that no other energy source could fill this gap. Wind and solar power now account for less than 2 percent of U.S. electricity generation, and nuclear power only about 20 percent.

Limiting coal also poses a dilemma for those who favor energy independence. True, coal is one of the "dirtier" fuel sources. But, for all its shortcomings, coal is a relatively cheap source of electricity. (It costs four times more to produce a kilowatt of electricity from a solar cell than from coal.) And it is plentiful: The United States has enough domestic coal to last 250 years. If the United States were to cut back on its coal consumption, its current energy needs would require it to import even more oil, reducing the country's energy independence even further.

"Nuclear Power Is Making a Comeback"

Yes, and it's a good thing   Concerns about safety, waste disposal, and weapons proliferation are very real. Nevertheless, nuclear power is an important means of diversifying energy supply and reducing carbon emissions. Electricity generated from nuclear power does not produce carbon dioxide, and nuclear energy accounts for almost 70 percent of non-carbon power produced in the United States. Reducing the use of nuclear energy means identifying other clean fuels. A recent British Parliamentary report warned that the planned closure of most of the country's nuclear plants would undermine its goal of supplying 10 percent of Britain's electricity with renewable sources by 2010.

It is because of this calculus that the nuclear power industry is ready to boom again. Last year, 16 countries generated at least one quarter of their electricity from nuclear energy. China and Brazil have plans for the construction of as many as nine new reactors. Twenty-four new nuclear plants in nine countries are under construction, with another 40 in the works. For its part, the last U.S. nuclear plant was ordered in 1973 and completed in 1996. Nuclear energy in the United States is projected to grow over the next 20 years by 9 percent. Given the projected rise in electricity demand, the use of nuclear power, like the use of coal, simply cannot be avoided any time soon. Moreover, as with oil, even if one could somehow end its use in the United States, it would still be a growing source of energy for the rest of the world.

"Energy Conservation Is the Solution"

No chance   Faced with increasing energy demands, some argue that a better alternative is to promote energy conservation. It's worthwhile to try to conserve any natural resource, but we cannot conserve our way out of today's energy bind.

Today's cars use only 60 percent of the gasoline they did in 1972, new refrigerators about one third the electricity, and it now takes 55 percent less oil and gas than in 1973 to generate the same amount of gross domestic product (GDP). Nonetheless, in the United States, national energy use has shot up 30 percent since 1973. This growth is far less than that of the economy as a whole (126 percent), but it is substantial just the same. Consumers are more interested in enjoying the goods and gadgets that require energy than in cutting energy use itself. Few people, for example, decide whether or not to buy a plasma television based on the fact that it uses as much as 10 times the electricity that a standard TV does. Nor can conservation do anything to slow demand in large, growing economies. For example, in 1973, China had an estimated GDP of $140 billion and consumed about 1 million barrels of oil a day. By 2004, China's GDP had ballooned to roughly $7.3 trillion, with demand for oil topping out at almost 6.5 million barrels a day. Thus, in a little more than 30 years, China has become far more efficient in what it gets from the oil it burns, but the needs of its economy swamped these improvements—and the country requires still more oil.

"Customers Are Willing to Pay More for Green Energy"

Prove it   Energy is still a relatively cheap commodity in the United States, but few Americans believed even pre-Katrina energy prices were reasonable. This attitude is puzzling, given that in the early 1980s, U.S. households spent approximately 8 to 9 percent of their income on energy. Today, they spend only 5 to 6 percent. And while post-Katrina oil prices are steep, they are not even close to all-time highs. When adjusted for inflation, the price per barrel of oil in January 1981 was more than $85. Today's prices would have to remain at this level for three years to have the same economic impact as the earlier oil shocks.

People want and expect cheap energy, and few people would actually pay more for clean power. More than 50 percent of U.S. consumers now have the option of buying electricity generated from renewable energy sources, but only 1 or 2 percent actually do. Hybrid car sales represent less than 1 percent of automobile sales; SUVS account for 25 percent. It is true that residential customers in Europe appear more willing to pay higher rates for green power. (Thirteen percent of people in the Netherlands are said to have chosen green power.) But that is largely a function of the natural resources that are present (such as huge hydroelectric dams) and aggressive government subsidies, which make such power far more affordable. Even with these measures, it's far from clear that a significantly greater proportion of Europeans will pay more.

"The Hydrogen Economy Is Going to Change Everything"

Misleading The so-called hydrogen economy has many people optimistic about our energy future. The idea is to provide for energy independence from fossil fuels and imported oil by developing technologies such as high-performing fuel cells that will allow clean energy to be produced from hydrogen rather than oil and natural gas. Hydrogen, of course, is plentiful—after all, every water molecule contains two hydrogen atoms. But hydrogen is a fuel that must be created. Hydrogen can be derived from water (through a process using electricity called reverse electrolysis), or directly from natural gas (using a reformer). Even if one assumes fuel cells could be manufactured at a competitive price and that a hydrogen-delivery infrastructure could be constructed (imagine the cost of replacing every gas station with a hydrogen-fueling station), natural gas or electricity produced through coal or nuclear power would still be needed to create the hydrogen. If the electricity to make hydrogen is produced from natural gas imported from Qatar, how is the United States more energy independent? If the electricity is produced by coal plants with high emissions, how is hydrogen any better for the environment? The vision of a hydrogen economy does not solve our energy dilemmas; it obfuscates them.

"New Energy Technologies Will Save Us"

In the long run Energy independence may be hopeless in the next 20 years, but there is no doubt that emerging technologies will eventually bear the brunt of our energy burden. The cost of producing electricity from wind has fallen approximately 80 percent in the last 20 years, and the cost of solar power has fallen from almost $1 per kilowatt to less than 18 cents. These efficiencies have allowed the wind and solar markets to become multibillion-dollar global markets. The markets for solar, wind, and fuel cells are projected to grow from an estimated $16 billion in 2004 to $102 billion in 2014. For the first time, there are multiple companies selling actual products based on fuel cell technologies. Danish wind manufacturer Vestas Wind Systems had revenues of almost $1.7 billion in the first half of 2005—up 47 percent from the same period in 2004. There are now companies that do nothing but maintain and fuel natural gaspowered vehicles or develop and install solar panels and wind turbines.

Earlier this year, Goldman Sachs bought Zilkha Renewable Energy, a Houston-based wind power developer, believing "wind and other renewable forms of energy will become an increasingly important part of the world's energy mix." The Carlyle Group, one of the world's most successful private equity funds, teamed up with FPL Group, a utility company, to purchase 141 megawatts of solar power in Southern California. MidAmerican Energy, majority owned by market guru Warren Buffet's Berkshire Hathaway, is undertaking a massive wind energy project in Iowa. Goldman Sachs, the Carlyle Group, and Warren Buffet are not in the business of making the world cleaner. They are sophisticated investors who believe that these technologies will offer attractive rates of return.

New energy technologies are beginning to make a difference today, and they will make a bigger difference tomorrow. But clear thinking about changes in energy supply requires a time frame measured in decades and an understanding of the trade-offs that must be made. Jettisoning the loose language about energy independence would be a good start.

WANT TO KNOW MORE?

The National Energy Policy, released by the National Energy Policy Development Group in May 2001, is a good starting point for understanding the trade-offs involved in addressing U.S. reliance on foreign oil. Ending the Energy Stalemate, produced by the National Commission on Energy Policy in December 2004, is an attempt to craft a bipartisan consensus on energy sector reform. The International Monetary Fund's April 2005 World Economic Outlook offers guidance on the interplay between energy and economic growth as well as numbers on oil prices, refining capacity, and inventories.

For a look at how corporations are taking the lead when it comes to energy and the environment, see "In Green Company," by Stuart Eizenstat and Rubèn Kraiem (FOREIGN POLICY, September/October 2005). For a more optimistic view of hydrogen's potential, see "The Hydrogen Economy" (*Physics Today*, December 2004), by George W. Crabtree, Mildred S. Dresselhaus, and Michelle V. Buchanan. A European perspective on the continent's energy future can be found in *Climate Change and a European Low-Carbon Energy System* (European Environmental Agency, 2005).

Those in search of hard data on energy supply and demand should consult BP's Statistical Reviews of World Energy and the Energy Information Administration's Annual Energy Outlook.

POSTSCRIPT

Is It Realistic for the United States to Move Toward Greater Energy Independence?

Future trends in energy dependence and energy consumption will depend on the intersection between market forces and government policies, and the proper roles of the private sector and the U.S. government in the energy market will be a subject of continued debate. Sustained oil prices above $50 per barrel can make ethanol and other alternatives economically competitive even without government subsidies, and encourage higher energy efficiency even in the absence of higher government standards. On the other hand, several kinds of "market failures" can create grounds for government involvement in energy markets. In addition to "negative externalities" like pollution and global warming, there may be collective action problems that government policies can address. For example, one justification for imposing auto efficiency standards is to reduce the incentives, whether concerns for prestige or a desire for safety, to buy heavier but less efficient cars like sport utility vehicles (heavier cars are safer for their occupants but more dangerous to other vehicles in car crashes).

Another potential market failure arises from the large "economies of scale" that are involved in some energy resources. For example, the possibility of using nuclear fusion to generate electricity requires massive, long-term, and potentially risky investments that the private sector is unlikely to undertake (currently, nuclear power plants use the relatively simpler process of nuclear fission to generate electricity). Indeed, research on fusion technology requires such a large scale of investment that a consortium of states, including South Korea, Russia, China, the European Union, the United States, India, and Japan, agreed in November of 2006 to jointly build an experimental fusion reactor in France. This reactor could begin producing electrical energy in 30 years (see http://news.bbc.co.uk/1/hi/sci/tech/6165932.stm). Alternatively, it could fail entirely, as have earlier efforts to use nuclear fusion to generate more useable energy than it uses up; as many observers have noted, scientists have always seemed to put the prospect of fusion energy 30 years into the future, whether they were writing in 1966 or 2006.

For an overview of President Barack Obama's energy plan, see: http://my.barackobama.com/page/content/newenergy. For an argument that rising oil prices will by themselves stimulate considerable conservation and investment in alternative energy resources, see Philip Auerswald, "The Myth of Energy Insecurity," *Issues in Science and Technology* (Summer 2006), pp. 65–70. For an argument that various energy resources and conservation measures can substantially reduce America's dependence on foreign oil, see Jenn Baka, Frank Ling, and Daniel Kammen, *Towards Energy Independence in 2025*, at the Web site of the Renewable and Appropriate Energy Laboratory, University of California at Berkeley, http://rael.berkeley.edu. For a report on U.S. energy policy by the National Commission on Energy Policy, a bipartisan group of energy experts, see "Ending the Energy Stalemate," December 2004, at http://www.energycommission.org/site/page.php?report=13. Finally, for an assessment of whether countries whose economies are dependent on oil exports are less likely to be democratic, see Michael Ross, "Does Oil Hinder Democracy?" *World Politics* (April 2001).

Internet References . . .

Bureau of International Organization Affairs

The Bureau of International Organization Affairs of the U.S. Department of State develops and implements U.S. policy in the United Nations, the specialized UN agencies, and other international organizations. On UN issues, the bureau works in cooperation with the U.S. Mission to the United Nations. The bureau also coordinates the U.S. Department of State's involvement in international athletic events.

http://www.state.gov/p/io/

United Nations

The United Nations home page is a gateway to information about the United Nations and its associated organizations. Click on "Human Rights" to explore categories related to human rights around the world, including the UN High Commissioner for Human Rights, the war crimes tribunals for Rwanda and the former Yugoslavia, and the Universal Declaration of Human Rights.

http://www.un.org

Coalition for an International Criminal Court

As its name indicates, the Coalition for an International Criminal Court favors ratification of the ICC treaty and full implementation of the court. This Web site has excellent information, including the full treaty text and up-to-date information on the ratification effort.

http://iccnow.org

Amnesty International

One issue related to human rights is the record of those countries with which the United States interacts. Information about the current state of human rights around the world is available at Amnesty International's Web site. The organization is a strong advocate of human rights but has been criticized by some for being too doctrinaire and for being insensitive to what may be acceptable in other cultures.

http://amnesty.org

Human Rights Watch

Like Amnesty International, Human Rights Watch is dedicated to preventing discrimination, upholding political freedom, protecting people from inhumane conduct in wartime, and bringing offenders to justice. It investigates and exposes human rights violations and seeks to hold abusers accountable. As stated on its Web site, its goal is to "challenge governments and those who hold power to end abusive practices and respect international human rights law."

http://www.hrw.org

The United States and International Rules, Norms, and Institutions

*G*lobalization involves a great deal more than the growing economic and environmental interdependence discussed in Unit 4. In these areas and in a wide range of others, the United States works with other actors— including states, international organizations, non-governmental organizations, firms, and individuals. International rules, norms, and institutions facilitate these interactions by establishing standards of conduct and shaping expectations about what others will do. As these rules, norms, and institutions evolve, some priorities—like individually based human rights—may come in conflict with others—like the primary right of states to non-intervention as codified in the United Nations charter. Similarly, these rules and norms often change following traumatic events, like the end of a great power war or, some would argue, the terrorist attacks of 9/11/2001. This section takes up two issues that reflect debates over how the United States foreign policy should respond to or perhaps try to change international rules, norms, and institutions.

- Is It Justifiable to Put Suspected Terrorists under Great Physical Duress?
- Can Humanitarian Intervention Be Justified?

ISSUE 17

Is It Justifiable to Put Suspected Terrorists under Great Physical Duress?

YES: Charles Krauthammer, from "The Truth about Torture: It's Time to Be Honest about Doing Terrible Things," *The Weekly Standard* (December 5, 2005)

NO: Andrew Sullivan, from "The Abolition of Torture," *New Republic* (December 19, 2005)

ISSUE SUMMARY

YES: Charles Krauthammer, *Washington Post* opinion columnist, argues the lives saved by information provided by those with information about terrorist incidents justify the use of torture to obtain that information.

NO: Andrew Sullivan, senior editor of *The New Republic,* argues against claims of the military utility and necessity of torture.

Conduct regarding the treatment of potential terrorists and those who may be able to provide information about potential terrorists or terrorist activity became a hot legal and political issue following the terrorist attacks of September 11, 2001. There is an extensive body of domestic and international law regarding the treatment of domestic prisoners and prisoners of war—including the Geneva Conventions of 1864, 1929, and 1949, the Hague Conventions of 1908, and the Union Army's Lieber Code of 1863—but these laws pay little attention to terrorists, paramilitaries, and other non-uniformed combatants who were not affiliated with national militaries. This created a gray legal zone in which the debate on the treatment of suspected terrorists after September 11, 2001, evolved.

The salience of this issue intensified in April 2004 following the broadcasting of photographs of abuses by U.S. soldiers of prisoners in the Abu Ghraib prison in Baghdad on nightly news programs. Although the administration asserts that the abuses were carried out by a small number of soldiers acting largely on their own, evidence of the systematic and widespread abuse of prisoners at Abu Ghraib and at prisons in Cuba and Afghanistan soon became a matter of public record.

In addition to the photographs of abuse, several internal executive branch memoranda of interrogation tactics were leaked to the press. These memoranda documented a debate between the Department of Justice, which argued that the Geneva Convention III on the Treatment of Prisoners of War did not apply to the conflict with al Qaeda, and the State Department, which urged the president to reconsider the recommendation. Although the president declared that the conventions did apply, he declared all detainees "unlawful combatants," and therefore beyond the scope of the conventions. Lt. General Ricardo Sanchez later cited the president's comments as justification for some of the interrogation techniques used in prison abuse scandal.

White House counsel (and current attorney general) Alberto Gonzales commissioned a memorandum from the Department of Justice to the president dated August 1, 2002, which provided very specific guidelines for justifying the conduct of interrogations outside the United States and for protecting the CIA from criminal prosecution for breaking U.S. laws prohibiting torture. In the memo, he argued that inflicting pain only constituted torture if it is "sufficiently intense to cause serious physical injury, such as organ failure," or death, or "psychological harm of significant duration, e.g. for months or even years." A Defense Department review board later concluded that this memo led in part to the abuses in Iraq and Cuba.

Several administration policies were overturned by the Supreme Court in June 2004, including policies that allowed the indefinite imprisonment of American citizens deemed enemy combatants without charge or access to counsel, and the policy that allowed for the indefinite imprisonment of al Qaeda and Taliban prisoners. Just prior to the confirmation hearings of Alberto Gonzales as attorney general in January 2005, the Department of Justice issued a new memorandum denouncing the policies in its previous memoranda on torture, but it left open its earlier position that the president has the authority to declare treaties null and void when he deems it necessary. The controversy continued when statements of presidential support for a congressional amendment to a defence authorization bill prohibiting the inhumane treatment of prisoners written by Senator McCain in December 2005 were followed by a signing statement reserving the president's authority to allow such actions if doing so would forestall another terrorist attack. McCain subsequently negotiated legislation that permitted the president to interpret the meaning and application of the Geneva Conventions as long as the subsequent treatment did not result in "serious" bodily or psychological injury. President George W. Bush signed this Military Commissions Act on October 17, 2006.

Charles Krauthammer argues that the prohibition of torture should not be universally applied and that captured terrorists and those with information about pending terrorist events should not be given the same rights and privileges of ordinary soldiers caught on the battlefield. In contrast, Andrew Sullivan argues that this is an unreliable means of gaining information and is thus unlikely to save lives. Furthermore, it is antithetical to freedom, indeed, the entire structure of American democracy and freedom evolved as a response against the state use of torture.

YES ↵   Charles Krauthammer

The Truth about Torture

During the last few weeks in Washington the pieties about torture have lain so thick in the air that it has been impossible to have a reasoned discussion. The McCain amendment that would ban "cruel, inhuman, or degrading" treatment of any prisoner by any agent of the United States sailed through the Senate by a vote of 90–9. The Washington establishment remains stunned that nine such retrograde, morally inert persons—let alone senators—could be found in this noble capital.

Now, John McCain has great moral authority on this issue, having heroically borne torture at the hands of the North Vietnamese. McCain has made fine arguments in defense of his position. And McCain is acting out of the deep and honorable conviction that what he is proposing is not only right but is in the best interest of the United States. His position deserves respect. But that does not mean, as seems to be the assumption in Washington today, that a critical analysis of his "no torture, ever" policy is beyond the pale.

Let's begin with a few analytic distinctions. For the purpose of torture and prisoner maltreatment, there are three kinds of war prisoners: First, there is the ordinary soldier caught on the field of battle. There is no question that he is entitled to humane treatment. Indeed, we have no right to disturb a hair on his head. His detention has but a single purpose: to keep him *hors de combat*. The proof of that proposition is that if there were a better way to keep him off the battlefield that did not require his detention, we would let him go. Indeed, during one year of the Civil War, the two sides did try an alternative. They mutually "paroled" captured enemy soldiers, i.e., released them to return home on the pledge that they would not take up arms again. (The experiment failed for a foreseeable reason: cheating. Grant found that some paroled Confederates had reenlisted.)

Because the only purpose of detention in these circumstances is to prevent the prisoner from becoming a combatant again, he is entitled to all the protections and dignity of an ordinary domestic prisoner—indeed, more privileges, because, unlike the domestic prisoner, he has committed no crime. He merely had the misfortune to enlist on the other side of a legitimate war. He is therefore entitled to many of the privileges enjoyed by an ordinary citizen— the right to send correspondence, to engage in athletic activity and intellectual pursuits, to receive allowances from relatives—except, of course, for the freedom to leave the prison.

Second, there is the captured terrorist. A terrorist is by profession, indeed by definition, an unlawful combatant: He lives outside the laws of war because he does not wear a uniform, he hides among civilians, and he deliberately targets innocents. He is entitled to no protections whatsoever. People seem to think that the postwar Geneva Conventions were written only to protect detainees. In fact, their deeper purpose was to provide a deterrent to the kind of barbaric treatment of civilians that had become so horribly apparent during the first half of the 20th century, and in particular, during the Second World War. The idea was to deter the abuse of civilians by promising combatants who treated noncombatants well that they themselves would be treated according to a code of dignity if captured—and, crucially, that they would be denied the protections of that code if they broke the laws of war and abused civilians themselves.

Breaking the laws of war and abusing civilians are what, to understate the matter vastly, terrorists do for a living. They are entitled, therefore, to nothing. Anyone who blows up a car bomb in a market deserves to spend the rest of his life roasting on a spit over an open fire. But we don't do that because we do not descend to the level of our enemy. We don't do that because, unlike him, we are civilized. Even though terrorists are entitled to no humane treatment, we give it to them because it is in our nature as a moral and humane people. And when on rare occasions we fail to do that, as has occurred in several of the fronts of the war on terror, we are duly disgraced.

The norm, however, is how the majority of prisoners at Guantanamo have been treated. We give them three meals a day, superior medical care, and provision to pray five times a day. Our scrupulousness extends even to providing them with their own Korans, which is the only reason alleged abuses of the Koran at Guantanamo ever became an issue. That we should have provided those who kill innocents in the name of Islam with precisely the document that inspires their barbarism is a sign of the absurd lengths to which we often go in extending undeserved humanity to terrorist prisoners.

Third, there is the terrorist with information. Here the issue of torture gets complicated and the easy pieties don't so easily apply. Let's take the textbook case. Ethics 101: A terrorist has planted a nuclear bomb in New York City. It will go off in one hour. A million people will die. You capture the terrorist. He knows where it is. He's not talking.

Question: If you have the slightest belief that hanging this man by his thumbs will get you the information to save a million people, are you permitted to do it? Now, on most issues regarding torture, I confess tentativeness and uncertainty. But on this issue, there can be no uncertainty: Not only is it permissible to hang this miscreant by his thumbs. It is a moral duty. Yes, you say, but that's an extreme and very hypothetical case. Well, not as hypothetical as you think. Sure, the (nuclear) scale is hypothetical, but in the age of the car- and suicide-bomber, terrorists are often captured who have just set a car bomb to go off or sent a suicide bomber out to a coffee shop, and you only have minutes to find out where the attack is to take place. This "hypothetical" is common enough that the Israelis have a term for precisely that situation: the ticking time bomb problem.

And even if the example I gave were entirely hypothetical, the conclusion—yes, in this case even torture is permissible—is telling because it establishes the principle: Torture is not always impermissible. However rare the cases, there are circumstances in which, by any rational moral calculus, torture not only would be permissible but would be required (to acquire life-saving information). And once you've established the principle, to paraphrase George Bernard Shaw, all that's left to haggle about is the price. In the case of torture, that means that the argument is not *whether* torture is ever permissible, but *when*—i.e., under what obviously stringent circumstances: how big, how imminent, how preventable the ticking time bomb. That is why the McCain amendment, which by mandating "torture never" refuses even to recognize the legitimacy of any moral calculus, cannot be right. There must be exceptions. The real argument should be over what constitutes a legitimate exception.

Let's take an example that is far from hypothetical. You capture Khalid Sheikh Mohammed in Pakistan. He not only has already killed innocents, he is deeply involved in the planning for the present and future killing of innocents. He not only was the architect of the 9/11 attack that killed nearly three thousand people in one day, most of them dying a terrible, agonizing, indeed tortured death. But as the top al Qaeda planner and logistical expert he also knows a lot about terror attacks to come. He knows plans, identities, contacts, materials, cell locations, safe houses, cased targets, etc. What do you do with him?

We have recently learned that since 9/11 the United States has maintained a series of "black sites" around the world, secret detention centers where presumably high-level terrorists like Khalid Sheikh Mohammed have been imprisoned. The world is scandalized. Black sites? Secret detention? Jimmy Carter calls this "a profound and radical change in the . . . moral values of our country." The Council of Europe demands an investigation, calling the claims "extremely worrying." Its human rights commissioner declares "such practices" to constitute "a serious human rights violation, and further proof of the crisis of values" that has engulfed the war on terror. The gnashing of teeth and rending of garments has been considerable.

I myself have not gnashed a single tooth. My garments remain entirely unrent. Indeed, I feel reassured. It would be a gross dereliction of duty for any government *not* to keep Khalid Sheikh Mohammed isolated, disoriented, alone, despairing, cold and sleepless, in some godforsaken hidden location in order to find out what he knew about plans for future mass murder. What are we supposed to do? Give him a nice cell in a warm Manhattan prison, complete with Miranda rights, a mellifluent lawyer, and his own website? Are not those the kinds of courtesies we extended to the 1993 World Trade Center bombers, then congratulated ourselves on how we "brought to justice" those responsible for an attack that barely failed to kill tens of thousands of Americans, only to discover a decade later that we had accomplished nothing—indeed, that some of the disclosures at the trial had helped Osama bin Laden avoid U.S. surveillance?

Have we learned nothing from 9/11? Are we prepared to go back with complete amnesia to the domestic-crime model of dealing with terrorists, which allowed us to sleepwalk through the nineties while al Qaeda incubated and grew and metastasized unmolested until on 9/11 it finished what the first World Trade Center bombers had begun?

Let's assume (and hope) that Khalid Sheikh Mohammed has been kept in one of these black sites, say, a cell somewhere in Romania, held entirely incommunicado and subjected to the kind of "coercive interrogation" that I described above. McCain has been going around praising the Israelis as the model of how to deal with terrorism and prevent terrorist attacks. He does so because in 1999 the Israeli Supreme Court outlawed all torture in the course of interrogation. But in reality, the Israeli case is far more complicated. And the complications reflect precisely the dilemmas regarding all coercive interrogation, the weighing of the lesser of two evils: the undeniable inhumanity of torture versus the abdication of the duty to protect the victims of a potentially preventable mass murder.

In a summary of Israel's policies, Glenn Frankel of the *Washington Post* noted that the 1999 Supreme Court ruling struck down secret guidelines established 12 years earlier that allowed interrogators to use the kind of physical and psychological pressure I described in imagining how KSM might be treated in America's "black sites."

"But after the second Palestinian uprising broke out a year later, and especially after a devastating series of suicide bombings of passenger buses, cafes and other civilian targets," writes Frankel, citing human rights lawyers and detainees, "Israel's internal security service, known as the Shin Bet or the Shabak, returned to physical coercion as a standard practice." Not only do the techniques used "command widespread support from the Israeli public," but "Israeli prime ministers and justice ministers with a variety of political views," including the most conciliatory and liberal, have defended these techniques "as a last resort in preventing terrorist attacks."

Which makes McCain's position on torture incoherent. If this kind of coercive interrogation were imposed on any inmate in the American prison system, it would immediately be declared cruel and unusual, and outlawed. How can he oppose these practices, which the Israelis use, and yet hold up Israel as a model for dealing with terrorists? Or does he countenance this kind of interrogation in extreme circumstances—in which case, what is left of his categorical opposition to inhuman treatment of any kind?

But let us push further into even more unpleasant territory, the territory that lies beyond mere coercive interrogation and beyond McCain's self-contradictions. How far are we willing to go? This "going beyond" need not be cinematic and ghoulish. (Jay Leno once suggested "duct tape" for Khalid Sheikh Mohammed.) Consider, for example, injection with sodium pentathol. (Colloquially known as "truth serum," it is nothing of the sort. It is a barbiturate whose purpose is to sedate. Its effects are much like that of alcohol: disinhibiting the higher brain centers to make someone more likely to disclose information or thoughts that might otherwise be guarded.) Forcible sedation is a clear violation of bodily integrity. In a civilian context it would be considered assault. It is certainly impermissible under any prohibition of cruel, inhuman, or degrading treatment.

Let's posit that during the interrogation of Khalid Sheikh Mohammed, perhaps early on, we got intelligence about an imminent al Qaeda attack. And we had a very good reason to believe he knew about it. And if we knew what he knew, we could stop it. If we thought we could glean a critical piece of information by use of sodium pentathol, would we be permitted to do so?

Less hypothetically, there is waterboarding, a terrifying and deeply shocking torture technique in which the prisoner has his face exposed to water in a way that gives the feeling of drowning. According to CIA sources cited by ABC News, Khalid Sheikh Mohammed "was able to last between 2 and 2 1/2 minutes before begging to confess." Should we regret having done that? Should we abolish by law that practice, so that it could never be used on the next Khalid Sheikh Mohammed having thus gotten his confession?

And what if he possessed information with less imminent implications? Say we had information about a cell that he had helped found or direct, and that cell was planning some major attack and we needed information about the identity and location of its members. A rational moral calculus might not permit measures as extreme as the nuke-in-Manhattan scenario, but would surely permit measures beyond mere psychological pressure.

Such a determination would not be made with an untroubled conscience. It would be troubled because there is no denying the monstrous evil that is any form of torture. And there is no denying how corrupting it can be to the individuals and society that practice it. But elected leaders, responsible above all for the protection of their citizens, have the obligation to tolerate their own sleepless nights by doing what is necessary—and only what is necessary, nothing more—to get information that could prevent mass murder.

Given the gravity of the decision, if we indeed cross the Rubicon—as we must—we need rules. The problem with the McCain amendment is that once you have gone public with a blanket ban on all forms of coercion, it is going to be very difficult to publicly carve out exceptions. The Bush administration is to be faulted for having attempted such a codification with the kind of secrecy, lack of coherence, and lack of strict enforcement that led us to the McCain reaction.

What to do at this late date? Begin, as McCain does, by banning all forms of coercion or inhuman treatment by anyone serving in the military—an absolute ban on torture by all military personnel everywhere. We do not want a private somewhere making these fine distinctions about ticking and slow-fuse time bombs. We don't even want colonels or generals making them. It would be best for the morale, discipline, and honor of the Armed Forces for the United States to maintain an absolute prohibition, both to simplify their task in making decisions and to offer them whatever reciprocal treatment they might receive from those who capture them—although I have no illusion that any anti-torture provision will soften the heart of a single jihadist holding a knife to the throat of a captured American soldier. We would impose this restriction on ourselves for our own reasons of military discipline and military honor.

Outside the military, however, I would propose, contra McCain, a ban against all forms of torture, coercive interrogation, and inhuman treatment, except in two contingencies: (1) the ticking time bomb and (2) the slower-fuse high-level terrorist (such as KSM). Each contingency would have its own set of rules. In the case of the ticking time bomb, the rules would be relatively simple: Nothing rationally related to getting accurate information would be ruled out. The case of the high-value suspect with slow-fuse information is more complicated. The principle would be that the level of inhumanity of the measures used (moral honesty is essential here—we would be using measures that are by definition inhumane) would be proportional to the need and value of the information. Interrogators would be constrained to use the least inhumane treatment necessary relative to the magnitude and imminence of the evil being prevented and the importance of the knowledge being obtained.

These exceptions to the no-torture rule would not be granted to just any nonmilitary interrogators, or anyone with CIA credentials. They would be reserved for highly specialized agents who are experts and experienced in interrogation, and who are known not to abuse it for the satisfaction of a kind of sick sadomasochism Lynndie England and her cohorts indulged in at Abu Ghraib. Nor would they be acting on their own. They would be required to obtain written permission for such interrogations from the highest political authorities in the country (cabinet level) or from a quasi-judicial body modeled on the Foreign Intelligence Surveillance Court (which permits what would ordinarily be illegal searches and seizures in the war on terror). Or, if the bomb was truly ticking and there was no time, the interrogators would be allowed to act on their own, but would require post facto authorization within, say, 24 hours of their interrogation, so that they knew that whatever they did would be subject to review by others and be justified only under the most stringent terms.

One of the purposes of these justifications would be to establish that whatever extreme measures are used are for reasons of nothing but information. Historically, the torture of prisoners has been done for a variety of reasons apart from information, most prominently reasons of justice or revenge. We do not do that. We should not do that. Ever. Khalid Sheikh Mohammed, murderer of 2,973 innocents, is surely deserving of the most extreme suffering day and night for the rest of his life. But it is neither our role nor our right to be the agents of that suffering. Vengeance is mine, sayeth the Lord. His, not ours. Torture is a terrible and monstrous thing, as degrading and morally corrupting to those who practice it as any conceivable human activity including its moral twin, capital punishment.

If Khalid Sheikh Mohammed knew nothing, or if we had reached the point where his knowledge had been exhausted, I'd be perfectly prepared to throw him into a nice, comfortable Manhattan cell and give him a trial to determine what would be fit and just punishment. But as long as he had useful information, things would be different.

Very different. And it simply will not do to take refuge in the claim that all of the above discussion is superfluous because torture never works anyway. Would that this were true. Unfortunately, on its face, this is nonsense. Is one to believe that in the entire history of human warfare, no combatant has ever received useful information by the use of pressure, torture, or any other kind of inhuman treatment? It may indeed be true that torture is not a reliable tool. But that is very different from saying that it is *never* useful.

The monstrous thing about torture is that sometimes it does work. In 1994, 19-year-old Israeli corporal Nachshon Waxman was kidnapped by Palestinian terrorists. The Israelis captured the driver of the car used in the kidnapping and tortured him in order to find where Waxman was being held. Yitzhak Rabin, prime minister and peacemaker, admitted that they tortured him in a way that went even beyond the '87 guidelines for "coercive inter-rogation" later struck down by the Israeli Supreme Court as too harsh. The driver talked. His information was accurate. The Israelis found Waxman. "If we'd been so careful to follow the ['87] Landau Commission [which *allowed* coercive interrogation]," explained Rabin, "we would never have found out where Waxman was being held."

In the Waxman case, I would have done precisely what Rabin did. (The fact that Waxman's Palestinian captors killed him during the Israeli rescue raid makes the case doubly tragic, but changes nothing of the moral calculus.) Faced with a similar choice, an American president would have a similar obli-gation. To do otherwise—to give up the chance to find your soldier lest you sully yourself by authorizing torture of the person who possesses potentially lifesaving information—is a deeply immoral betrayal of a soldier and country-man. Not as cosmically immoral as permitting a city of one's countrymen to perish, as in the Ethics 101 case. But it remains, nonetheless, a case of moral abdication—of a kind rather parallel to that of the principled pacifist. There is much to admire in those who refuse on principle ever to take up arms under any conditions. But that does not make pure pacifism, like no-torture absolut-ism, any less a form of moral foolishness, tinged with moral vanity. Not repre-hensible, only deeply reproachable and supremely impracticable. People who hold such beliefs are deserving of a certain respect. But they are not to be put in positions of authority. One should be grateful for the saintly among us. And one should be vigilant that they not get to make the decisions upon which the lives of others depend.

Which brings us to the greatest irony of all in the torture debate. I have just made what will be characterized as the pro-torture case contra McCain by proposing two major exceptions carved out of any no-torture rule: the ticking time bomb and the slow-fuse high-value terrorist. McCain supposedly is being hailed for defending all that is good and right and just in America by standing foursquare against any inhuman treatment. Or is he?

According to *Newsweek,* in the ticking time bomb case McCain says that the president should disobey the very law that McCain seeks to pass—under the justification that "you do what you have to do. But you take responsibil-ity for it." But if torturing the ticking time bomb suspect is "what you have to do," then why has McCain been going around arguing that such things must never be done?

As for exception number two, the high-level terrorist with slow-fuse information, Stuart Taylor, the superb legal correspondent for *National Jour-nal,* argues that with appropriate legal interpretation, the "cruel, inhuman, or degrading" standard, "though vague, is said by experts to codify . . . the com-monsense principle that the toughness of interrogation techniques should be calibrated to the importance and urgency of the information likely to be obtained." That would permit "some very aggressive techniques . . . on that small percentage of detainees who seem especially likely to have potentially life-saving information." Or as Evan Thomas and Michael Hirsh put it in the *Newsweek* report on McCain and torture, the McCain standard would "presumably allow for a sliding scale" of torture or torture-lite or other coercive techniques, thus permitting "for a very small percentage—those High Value Targets like Khalid Sheikh Mohammed—some pretty rough treatment."

But if that is the case, then McCain embraces the same exceptions I do, but prefers to pretend he does not. If that is the case, then his much-touted and endlessly repeated absolutism on inhumane treatment is merely for show. If that is the case, then the moral preening and the phony arguments can stop now, and we can all agree that in this real world of astonishingly murderous enemies, in two very circumscribed circumstances, we must all be prepared to torture. Having established that, we can then begin to work together to codify rules of interrogation for the two very unpleasant but very real cases in which we are morally permitted—indeed morally compelled—to do terrible things.

Andrew Sullivan

NO

The Abolition of Torture

Why is torture wrong? It may seem like an obvious question, or even one beneath discussion. But it is now inescapably before us, with the introduction of the McCain Amendment banning all "cruel, inhuman, and degrading treatment" of detainees by American soldiers and CIA operatives anywhere in the world. The amendment lies in legislative limbo. It passed the Senate in October by a vote of 90 to nine, but President Bush has vowed to veto any such blanket ban on torture or abuse; Vice President Cheney has prevailed upon enough senators and congressmen to prevent the amendment—and the defense appropriations bill to which it is attached—from moving out of conference; and my friend Charles Krauthammer, one of the most respected conservative intellectuals in Washington (and a *New Republic* contributing editor) has written a widely praised cover essay for *The Weekly Standard* endorsing the legalization of full-fledged torture by the United States under strictly curtailed conditions. We stand on the brink of an enormously important choice—one that is critical, morally as well as strategically, to get right.

This debate takes place after three years in which the Bush administration has defined "torture" in the narrowest terms and has permitted coercive, physical abuse of enemy combatants if "military necessity" demands it. It comes also after several internal Pentagon reports found widespread and severe abuse of detainees in Afghanistan, Iraq, and elsewhere that has led to at least two dozen deaths during interrogation. Journalistic accounts and reports by the International Committee of the Red Cross paint an even darker picture of secret torture sites in Eastern Europe and innocent detainees being murdered. Behind all this, the grim images of Abu Ghraib—the worst of which have yet to be released—linger in the public consciousness.

In this inevitably emotional debate, perhaps the greatest failing of those of us who have been arguing against all torture and "cruel, inhuman, and degrading treatment" of detainees is that we have assumed the reasons why torture is always a moral evil, rather than explicating them. But, when you fully ponder them, I think it becomes clearer why, contrary to Krauthammer's argument, torture, in any form and under any circumstances, is both antithetical to the most basic principles for which the United States stands and a profound impediment to winning a wider war that we cannot afford to lose.

From *The New Republic*, December 19, 2005, pp. 19–23. Copyright © 2005 by New Republic. Reprinted by permission.

◦◦◦

Torture is the polar opposite of freedom. It is the banishment of all freedom from a human body and soul, insofar as that is possible. As human beings, we all inhabit bodies and have minds, souls, and reflexes that are designed in part to protect those bodies: to resist or flinch from pain, to protect the psyche from disintegration, and to maintain a sense of selfhood that is the basis for the concept of personal liberty. What torture does is use these involuntary, self-protective, self-defining resources of human beings against the integrity of the human being himself. It takes what is most involuntary in a person and uses it to break that person's will. It takes what is animal in us and deploys it against what makes us human. As an American commander wrote in an August 2003 e-mail about his instructions to torture prisoners at Abu Ghraib, "The gloves are coming off gentlemen regarding these detainees, Col. Boltz has made it clear that we want these individuals broken."

What does it mean to "break" an individual? As the French essayist Michel de Montaigne once commented, and Shakespeare echoed, even the greatest philosophers have difficulty thinking clearly when they have a toothache. These wise men were describing the inescapable frailty of the human experience, mocking the claims of some seers to be above basic human feelings and bodily needs. If that frailty is exposed by a toothache, it is beyond dispute in the case of torture. The infliction of physical pain on a person with no means of defending himself is designed to render that person completely subservient to his torturers. It is designed to extirpate his autonomy as a human being, to render his control as an individual beyond his own reach. That is why the term "break" is instructive. Something broken can be put back together, but it will never regain the status of being unbroken—of having integrity. When you break a human being, you turn him into something subhuman. You enslave him. This is why the Romans reserved torture for slaves, not citizens, and why slavery and torture were inextricably linked in the antebellum South.

What you see in the relationship between torturer and tortured is the absolute darkness of totalitarianism. You see one individual granted the most complete power he can ever hold over another. Not just confinement of his mobility—the abolition of his very agency. Torture uses a person's body to remove from his own control his conscience, his thoughts, his faith, his selfhood. The CIA's definition of "waterboarding"—recently leaked to ABC News—describes that process in plain English: "The prisoner is bound to an inclined board, feet raised and head slightly below the feet. Cellophane is wrapped over the prisoner's face and water is poured over him. Unavoidably, the gag reflex kicks in and a terrifying fear of drowning leads to almost instant pleas to bring the treatment to a halt." The ABC report then noted, "According to the sources, CIA officers who subjected themselves to the waterboarding technique lasted an average of 14 seconds before caving in. They said Al Qaeda's toughest prisoner, Khalid Sheikh Mohammed, won the admiration of interrogators when he was able to last between two and two and a half minutes before begging to confess."

Before the Bush administration, two documented cases of the U.S. Armed Forces using "waterboarding" resulted in courts-martial for the soldiers implicated. In Donald Rumsfeld's post–September 11 Pentagon, the technique is approved and, we recently learned, has been used on at least eleven detainees, possibly many more. What you see here is the deployment of a very basic and inescapable human reflex—the desire not to drown and suffocate—in order to destroy a person's autonomy. Even the most hardened fanatic can only endure two and a half minutes. After that, he is indeed "broken."

⋘⟡⋙

The entire structure of Western freedom grew in part out of the searing experience of state-sanctioned torture. The use of torture in Europe's religious wars of the sixteenth and seventeenth centuries is still etched in our communal consciousness, as it should be. Then, governments deployed torture not only to uncover perceived threats to their faith-based autocracies, but also to "save" the victim's soul. Torturers understood that religious conversion was a difficult thing, because it necessitated a shift in the deepest recesses of the human soul. The only way to reach those depths was to deploy physical terror in the hopes of completely destroying the heretic's autonomy. They would, in other words, destroy a human being's soul in order to save it. That is what burning at the stake was—an indescribably agonizing act of torture that could be ended at a moment's notice if the victim recanted. In a state where theological doctrine always trumped individual liberty, this was a natural tactic.

Indeed, the very concept of Western liberty sprung in part from an understanding that, if the state has the power to reach that deep into a person's soul and can do that much damage to a human being's person, then the state has extinguished all oxygen necessary for freedom to survive. That is why, in George Orwell's totalitarian nightmare, the final ordeal is, of course, torture. Any polity that endorses torture has incorporated into its own DNA a totalitarian mutation. If the point of the U.S. Constitution is the preservation of liberty, the formal incorporation into U.S. law of the state's right to torture—by legally codifying physical coercion, abuse, and even, in Krauthammer's case, full-fledged torture of detainees by the CIA—would effectively end the American experiment of a political society based on inalienable human freedom protected not by the good graces of the executive, but by the rule of law.

The founders understood this argument. Its preeminent proponent was George Washington himself. As historian David Hackett Fischer memorably recounts in his 2004 book, *Washington's Crossing*: "Always some dark spirits wished to visit the same cruelties on the British and Hessians that had been inflicted on American captives. But Washington's example carried growing weight, more so than his written orders and prohibitions. He often reminded his men that they were an army of liberty and freedom, and that the rights of humanity for which they were fighting should extend even to their enemies. . . . Even in the most urgent moments of the war, these men were concerned about ethical questions in the Revolution."

Krauthammer has described Washington's convictions concerning torture as "pieties" that can be dispensed with today. He doesn't argue that torture is not evil. Indeed, he denounces it in unequivocal moral terms: "[T]orture is a terrible and monstrous thing, as degrading and morally corrupting to those who practice it as any conceivable human activity including its moral twin, capital punishment." But he maintains that the nature of the Islamofascist enemy after September 11 radically altered our interrogative options and that we are now not only permitted, but actually "morally compelled," to torture.

This is a radical and daring idea: that we must extinguish human freedom in a few cases in order to maintain it for everyone else. It goes beyond even the Bush administration's own formal position, which states that the United States will not endorse torture but merely "coercive interrogation techniques." (Such techniques, in the administration's elaborate definition, are those that employ physical force short of threatening immediate death or major organ failure.) And it is based on a premise that deserves further examination: that our enemies actually *deserve* torture; that some human beings are so depraved that, in Krauthammer's words, they "are entitled to no humane treatment."

Let me state for the record that I am second to none in decrying, loathing, and desiring to defeat those who wish to replace freedom with religious tyranny of the most brutal kind—and who have murdered countless innocent civilians in cold blood. Their acts are monstrous and barbaric. But I differ from Krauthammer by believing that monsters remain human beings. In fact, to reduce them to a subhuman level is to exonerate them of their acts of terrorism and mass murder—just as animals are not deemed morally responsible for killing. Insisting on the humanity of terrorists is, in fact, critical to maintaining their profound responsibility for the evil they commit.

And, if they are human, then they must necessarily not be treated in an inhuman fashion. You cannot lower the moral baseline of a terrorist to the subhuman without betraying a fundamental value. That is why the Geneva Conventions have a very basic ban on "cruel treatment and torture," and "outrages upon personal dignity, in particular humiliating and degrading treatment"—even when dealing with illegal combatants like terrorists. That is why the Declaration of Independence did not restrict its endorsement of freedom merely to those lucky enough to find themselves on U.S. soil—but extended it to all human beings, wherever they are in the world, simply because they are human.

◦◉◦

Nevertheless, it is important to address Krauthammer's practical points. He is asking us to steel ourselves and accept that, whether we like it or not, torture and abuse may be essential in a war where our very survival may be at stake. He presents two scenarios in which he believes torture is permissible. The first is the "ticking bomb" scenario, a hypothetical rarity in which the following conditions apply: a) a terrorist cell has planted a nuclear weapon or something nearly as devastating in a major city; b) we have captured someone in this cell; c) we know for a fact that he knows where the bomb is. In practice, of course, the likelihood of such a scenario is extraordinarily remote. Uncovering a terrorist plot is hard enough; capturing a conspirator involved in that plot is even harder; and realizing in advance that the person knows the whereabouts of the bomb is nearly impossible. (Remember, in the war on terrorism, we have already detained—and even killed—many innocents. Pentagon reports have acknowledged that up to 90 percent of the prisoners at Abu Ghraib, many of whom were abused and tortured, were not guilty of anything.) But let us assume, for the sake of argument, that all of Krauthammer's conditions apply. Do we have a right to torture our hypothetical detainee?

According to Krauthammer, *of course* we do. No responsible public official put in that position would refuse to sanction torture if he believed it could save thousands of lives. And, if it's necessary, Krauthammer argues, it should be made legal. If you have conceded that torture may be justified in one case, Krauthammer believes, you have conceded that it may be justified in many more. In his words, "Once you've established the principle, to paraphrase George Bernard Shaw, all that's left to haggle about is the price."

But this is too easy and too glib a formulation. It is possible to concede that, in an extremely rare circumstance, torture may be used without conceding that it should be legalized. One imperfect but instructive analogy is civil disobedience. In that case, laws are indeed broken, but that does not establish that the laws should be broken. In fact, civil disobedience implies precisely that laws should *not* be broken, and protesters who engage in it present themselves promptly for imprisonment and legal sanction on exactly those grounds. They do so for demonstrative reasons. They are not saying that laws don't matter. They are saying that laws do matter, that they should be enforced, but that their conscience in this instance demands that they disobey them.

In extremis, a rough parallel can be drawn for a president faced with the kind of horrendous decision on which Krauthammer rests his entire case. What should a president do? The answer is simple: He may have to break the law. In the Krauthammer scenario, a president might well decide that, if the survival of the nation is at stake, he must make an exception. At the same time, he must subject himself—and so must those assigned to conduct the torture—to the consequences of an illegal act. Those guilty of torturing another human being must be punished—or pardoned ex-post-facto. If the torture is revealed to be useless, if the tortured man is shown to have been innocent or ignorant of the information he was tortured to reveal, then those responsible must face the full brunt of the law for, in Krauthammer's words, such a "terrible and monstrous thing." In Michael Walzer's formulation, if we are to have dirty hands, it is essential that we show them to be dirty.

What Krauthammer is proposing, however, is not this compromise, which allows us to retain our soul as a free republic while protecting us from catastrophe in an extremely rare case. He is proposing something very different: that our "dirty hands" be wiped legally clean before and after the fact. That is a Rubicon we should not cross, because it marks the boundary between a free country and an unfree one.

Krauthammer, moreover, misses a key lesson learned these past few years. What the hundreds of abuse and torture incidents have shown is that, once you permit torture for someone somewhere, it has a habit of spreading. Remember that torture was originally sanctioned in administration memos only for use against illegal combatants in rare cases. Within months of that decision, abuse and torture had become endemic throughout Iraq, a theater of war in which, even Bush officials agree, the Geneva Conventions apply. The extremely coercive interrogation tactics used at Guantánamo Bay "migrated" to Abu Ghraib. In fact, General Geoffrey Miller was sent to Abu Ghraib specifically to replicate Guantánamo's techniques. According to former Brigadier General Janis Karpinski, who had original responsibility for the prison, Miller ordered her to treat all detainees "like dogs." When Captain Ian Fishback, a West Point graduate and member of the 82nd Airborne, witnessed routine beatings and abuse of detainees at detention facilities in Iraq and Afghanistan, often for sport, he tried to stop it. It took him a year and a half to get any response from the military command, and he had to go to Senator John McCain to make his case.

In short, what was originally supposed to be safe, sanctioned, and rare became endemic, disorganized, and brutal. The lesson is that it is impossible to quarantine torture in a hermetic box; it will inevitably contaminate the military as a whole. Once you have declared that some enemies are subhuman, you have told every soldier that every potential detainee he comes across might be exactly that kind of prisoner—and that anything can therefore be done to him. That is what the disgrace at Abu Ghraib proved. And Abu Ghraib produced a tiny fraction of the number of abuse, torture, and murder cases that have been subsequently revealed. The only way to control torture is to ban it outright. Everywhere. Even then, in wartime, some "bad apples" will always commit abuse. But at least we will have done all we can to constrain it.

⌘

Krauthammer's second case for torture is equally unpersuasive. For "slow-fuse" detainees—high-level prisoners like Khalid Sheikh Mohammed with potentially, if not immediately, useful intelligence—Krauthammer again takes the most extreme case and uses it to establish a general rule. He concedes that torture, according to almost every careful student and expert, yields highly unreliable information. Anyone can see that. If you are screaming for relief after a few seconds of waterboarding, you're likely to tell your captors anything, true or untrue, to stop the agony and terror. But Krauthammer then argues that, unless you can prove that torture *never* works, it should always be retained as an option. "It may indeed be true that torture is not a reliable tool," he argues. "But that is very different from saying that it is *never* useful." And if it cannot be deemed always useless, it must be permitted—even when an imminent threat is not in the picture.

The problem here is an obvious one. You have made the extreme exception the basis for a new rule. You have said that, if you cannot absolutely rule out torture as effective in every single case, it should be ruled in as an option for many. Moreover, if allowing torture even in the "ticking bomb" scenario makes the migration of torture throughout the military likely, this loophole blows the doors wide open. And how do we tell good intelligence from bad intelligence in such torture-infested interrogation? The short answer is: We cannot. By allowing torture for "slow-fuse" detainees, you sacrifice a vital principle for intelligence that is uniformly corrupted at best and useless at worst.

In fact, the use of torture and coercive interrogation by U.S. forces in this war may have contributed to a profound worsening of our actionable intelligence. The key to intelligence in Iraq and, indeed, in Muslim enclaves in the West, is gaining the support and trust of those who give terrorists cover but who are not terrorists themselves. We need human intelligence from Muslims and Arabs prepared to spy on and inform on their neighbors and friends and even family and tribe members. The only way they will do that is if they perceive the gains of America's intervention as greater than the costs, if they see clearly that cooperating with the West will lead to a better life and a freer world rather than more of the same.

What our practical endorsement of torture has done is to remove that clear boundary between the Islamists and the West and make the two equivalent in the Muslim mind. Saddam Hussein used Abu Ghraib to torture innocents; so did the Americans. Yes, what Saddam did was exponentially worse. But, in doing what we did, we blurred the critical, bright line between the Arab past and what we are proposing as the Arab future. We gave Al Qaeda an enormous propaganda coup, as we have done with Guantánamo and Bagram, the "Salt Pit" torture chambers in Afghanistan, and the secret torture sites in Eastern Europe. In World War II, American soldiers were often tortured by the Japanese when captured, But FDR refused to reciprocate. Why? Because he knew that the goal of the war was not just Japan's defeat but Japan's transformation into a democracy. He knew that, if the beacon of democracy—the United States of America—had succumbed to the hallmark of totalitarianism, then the chance for democratization would be deeply compromised in the wake of victory.

No one should ever underestimate the profound impact that the conduct of American troops in World War II had on the citizens of the eventually defeated Axis powers. Germans saw the difference between being liberated by the Anglo-Americans and being liberated by the Red Army. If you saw an American or British uniform, you were safe. If you didn't, the terror would continue in different ways. Ask any German or Japanese of the generation that built democracy in those countries, and they will remind you of American values—not trumpeted by presidents in front of handpicked audiences, but *demonstrated* by the conduct of the U.S. military during occupation. I grew up in Great Britain, a country with similar memories. In the dark days of the cold war, I was taught that America, for all its faults, was still America. And that America did not, and constitutively could not, torture anyone.

If American conduct was important in Japan and Germany, how much more important is it in Iraq and Afghanistan. The entire point of the war on terrorism, according to the president, is to advance freedom and democracy in the Arab world. In Iraq, we had a chance not just to tell but to show the Iraqi people how a democracy acts. And, tragically, in one critical respect, we failed. That failure undoubtedly contributed to the increased legitimacy of the insurgency and illegitimacy of the occupation, and it made collaboration between informed Sunnis and U.S. forces far less likely. What minuscule intelligence we might have plausibly gained from torturing and abusing detainees is vastly outweighed by the intelligence we have forfeited by alienating many otherwise sympathetic Iraqis and Afghans, by deepening the divide between the democracies, and by sullying the West's reputation in the Middle East. Ask yourself: Why does Al Qaeda tell its detainees to claim torture regardless of what happens to them in U.S. custody? Because Al Qaeda knows that one of America's greatest weapons in this war is its reputation as a repository of freedom and decency. Our policy of permissible torture has handed Al Qaeda this weapon—to use against us. It is not just a moral tragedy. It is a pragmatic disaster. Why compound these crimes and errors by subsequently legalizing them, as Krauthammer (explicitly) and the president (implicitly) are proposing?

Will a ban on all "cruel, inhuman, and degrading treatment" render interrogations useless? By no means. There are many techniques for gaining intelligence from detainees other than using their bodies against their souls. You can start with the 17 that appear in the Army Field Manual, tested by decades of armed conflict only to be discarded by this administration with barely the blink of an eye. Isolation, psychological disorientation, intense questioning, and any number of other creative techniques are possible. Some of the most productive may well be those in which interrogators are so versed in Islamic theology and Islamist subcultures that they win the confidence of prisoners and pry information out of them—something the United States, with its dearth of Arabic speakers, is unfortunately ill-equipped to do.

_⚜_

Enemy combatants need not be accorded every privilege granted legitimate prisoners of war; but they must be treated as human beings. This means that, in addition to physical torture, wanton abuse of their religious faith is out of bounds. No human freedom is meaningful without religious freedom. The fact that Koran abuse has been documented at Guantánamo; that one prisoner at Abu Ghraib was forced to eat pork and drink liquor; that fake menstrual blood was used to disorient a strict Muslim prisoner at Guantánamo—these make winning the hearts and minds of moderate Muslims far harder. Such tactics have resulted in hunger strikes at Guantánamo—perhaps the ultimate sign that the coercive and abusive attempts to gain the cooperation of detainees has completely failed to achieve the desired results.

The war on terrorism is, after all, a religious war in many senses. It is a war to defend the separation of church and state as critical to the existence of freedom, including religious freedom. It is a war to persuade the silent majority of Muslims that the West offers a better way—more decency, freedom, and humanity than the autocracies they live under and the totalitarian theocracies waiting in the wings. By endorsing torture—on anyone, anywhere, for any reason—we help obliterate the very values we are trying to promote. You can see this contradiction in Krauthammer's own words: We are "morally compelled" to commit "a terrible and monstrous thing." We are obliged to destroy the village in order to save it. We have to extinguish the most basic principle that defines America in order to save America.

No, we don't. In order to retain fundamental American values, we have to banish from the United States the totalitarian impulse that is integral to every act of torture. We have to ensure that the virus of tyranny is never given an opening to infect the Constitution and replicate into something that corrupts as deeply as it wounds. We should mark the words of Ian Fishback, one of the heroes of this war: "Will we confront danger and adversity in order to preserve our ideals, or will our courage and commitment to individual rights wither at the prospect of sacrifice? My response is simple. If we abandon our ideals in the face of adversity and aggression, then those ideals were never really in our possession. I would rather die fighting than give up even the smallest part of the idea that is 'America.'" If we legalize torture, even under constrained conditions, we will have given up a large part of the idea that is America. We will have lost the war before we have given ourselves the chance to win it.

POSTSCRIPT

Is It Justifiable to Put Suspected Terrorists under Great Physical Duress?

The issue at stake was summarized nicely by Alberto Gonzales during his confirmation hearings for the position of attorney general on January 7, 2004. He argued, "After the attacks of 9/11, our government had fundamental decisions to make concerning how to apply treaties and U.S. law to an enemy that does not wear a uniform, owes no allegiance to any country, is not a party to any treaties and—most importantly—does not fight according to the laws of war. As we have debated these questions, the president has made clear that he is prepared to protect and defend the Untied States and its citizens, and will do so vigorously, but always in a manner consistent with our nation's values and applicable law, including our treaty obligations."

Ultimately, the treatment and interrogation of prisoners involves an interpretation of the spirit as well as the letter of domestic and international law. Even if the narrow definition of torture specified by White House counsel to the president in August 2002 holds up to judicial scrutiny, the brutality of U.S. interrogations of potential terrorists and other nontraditional or unlawful combatants challenges the spirit of existing laws. This suggests that the Geneva Conventions may indeed need to be updated to account for the role terrorists and other non-state actors play in matters of international security. The practices established by the United States are significant because they may set precedent against which negotiations over such future conventions may take place and against which others may justify their use of various techniques in the interrogation of others—including U.S. citizens and military personnel.

Details and evidence supporting Alan Dershowitz's arguments that torture is appropriate under given circumstances are available in his book, *Why Terrorism Works* (Yale University Press, 2002). A counterpoint is offered by Anthony Lewis in his article, "Making Torture Legal," *New York Review of Books* (July 15, 2004).

The ACLU has posted an extensive collection of records regarding torture that have been released as the result of a request under the Freedom of Information Act. See http://www.aclu.org/safefree/torture/torturefoia.html. Additional materials may be found at http://findlaw.com/ and the National Security Archive, George Washington University at http://www2.gwu.edu/~nsarchiv/nsa/the_archive.html.

ISSUE 18

Can Humanitarian Intervention Be Justified?

YES: Kenneth Roth, from "Setting the Standard: Justifying Humanitarian Intervention," *Harvard International Review* (Spring 2004)

NO: Alan J. Kuperman, from "Humanitarian Hazard: Revising Doctrines of Intervention," *Harvard International Review* (Spring 2004)

ISSUE SUMMARY

YES: Kenneth Roth, executive director of Human Rights Watch, argues that while humanitarian intervention is extremely costly in human terms, it can be justified in situations involving ongoing or imminent slaughter, but that it should only be considered when five limiting criteria are met.

NO: Alan Kuperman, resident assistant professor of international relations at Johns Hopkins University, argues that the benefits of humanitarian intervention are much smaller and the costs much greater than are generally acknowledged because violence is perpetrated faster than interveners can act to stop it and the likelihood of humanitarian intervention may actually make some local conflicts worse.

The question of whether humanitarian intervention is justified hinges on the nature of human rights and the question of intervention. The United Nations reaffirms "faith in fundamental human rights" and "encouraging respect for human rights and for fundamental freedoms for all" through the 1948 Universal Declaration of Human Rights and a variety of other covenants, protocols, and agreements. There is also a growing number of regional and group-specific human rights commissions and treaties like the European Commission on Human Rights and the World Conferences on Women.

Despite the growing number of agreements on human rights, there is no consensus on what rights constitute human rights and which of these are sufficient to justify intervention if they are violated. The United Nations specifies two fundamental sets of rights as specified in the Covenant on Civil and Political Rights and the Covenant on Economic, Social and Cultural Rights. The

United States and others in the West tend to define human rights in terms of civil liberties, including the right to freedom of thought, religion, expression, peaceful assembly, movement, and the right to take part in periodic and genuine elections with universal and equal suffrage. Others emphasize the relative importance of economic, social, and cultural liberties, including rights to food and a standard of living adequate for health and well-being; right to work, rest, and leisure; rights to access to a free education; and social security.

There is also disagreement about whether international human rights agreements should be interpreted as guidelines or moral standards that define good behavior, or whether they provide a regulative entitlement one can demand. The former interpretation provides a much weaker basis for humanitarian intervention than the latter.

Furthermore, there is no global consensus on whose rights are most appropriately considered human rights, nor whose take precedence when they conflict with one another. Indeed, defining human rights in terms of the rights of individuals is a relatively recent phenomenon. The rights of groups and those of states have historically taken precedence over those of individuals. For example, the 1907 Hague Conventions, one of the earliest international agreements regarding human rights, limited what a state could do to foreign nationals, but did not limit what states did to their own people; even slavery was not outlawed by international treaty until 1926. The indictment of "crimes against humanity" was applied for the first time only in 1945–1946 at the Nuremberg War Crimes Trials following the holocaust in World War II.

Despite its support for human rights, the United Nations has historically considered human rights to be the internationally protected prerogative of sovereign states. Article 2(7) denies the United Nations jurisdiction in domestic matters and, therefore, in the way that states treat their citizens. Furthermore, Article 2(4) of the Charter explicitly forbids members from engaging in the threat or use of force against the territorial integrity or political independence of any state except in self-defense. And, should any state pose such a "threat to the peace," Chapter VII of the UN Charter allows for the Security Council to adopt military and economic sanctions against that state if peaceful settlement procedures have failed. Thus, the United Nations prohibits states from attacking others for violations of human rights. International legal scholars like Thomas Franck have justified this prohibition by arguing "in very few, if any, instances has the right [to humanitarian intervention] been asserted under circumstances that appear more humanitarian than self-seeking and power seeking." There are arguable exceptions, however, including U.S. intervention in Somalia in 1992–1993 and NATO intervention in Kosovo in 1997, both of which were clearly motivated by humanitarian concerns.

Despite these difficulties, there is a growing recognition in the United States and the world community that basic human rights are of high moral importance and that states are increasingly using humanitarian grounds to justify or at least bolster their arguments for intervention. Kenneth Roth argues that intervention may be justified, but only under a very limiting set of criteria. In contrast, Alan Kuperman argues that even if practiced under those criteria, humanitarian intervention would be ineffective at best and may even be counterproductive.

YES ↵

Kenneth Roth

Setting the Standard: Justifying Humanitarian Intervention

Humanitarian intervention was supposed to have gone the way of the 1990s. The use of military force across borders to stop mass killing was seen as a luxury of an era in which national security concerns among the major powers were less pressing and problems of human security could come to the fore. Somalia, Haiti, Bosnia, Kosovo, East Timor, and Sierra Leone: these interventions, justified to varying degrees in humanitarian terms, were dismissed as products of an unusual interlude between the tensions of the Cold War and the new threat of terrorism. The events of September 11, 2001, supposedly changed all that by inducing a return to more immediate security challenges. Yet surprisingly, even with the campaign against terrorism in full swing, the past year has seen four military interventions that their instigators describe, in whole or in part, as humanitarian.

In principle, one can only welcome this renewed concern for the fate of faraway victims. What could be more virtuous than to risk life and limb to save distant people from slaughter? But the common use of the humanitarian label masks significant differences among these interventions. The French intervention in the Democratic Republic of Congo in 2003, later backed by a reinforced UN peacekeeping presence, was most clearly motivated by a desire to stop ongoing slaughter. In Liberia and the Ivory Coast, West African and French forces intervened to enforce a peace plan but also played important humanitarian roles. A handful of US troops briefly joined the Liberian intervention, but with little effect. All of these African interventions were initially or ultimately approved by the UN Security Council. Indeed, in each case the relevant government consented, though under varying degrees of pressure.

By contrast, of the various grounds used by the US-led coalition forces to justify the invasion of Iraq, only one—and a comparatively minor one at that—was humanitarian. The UN Security Council did not approve the intervention, and the Iraqi government, its existence on the line, violently opposed it. Moreover, unlike the relatively modest African interventions, the Iraqi invasion involved an extensive bombing campaign and some 150,000 ground troops.

The sheer size of the Iraqi invasion, the central involvement of the world's superpower, and the enormous controversy surrounding the war meant that it overshadowed the other aforementioned military actions. For better or worse,

From *Harvard International Review,* Spring 2004, pp. 58–62. Copyright © 2004 by the President of Harvard College. Reprinted by permission of Harvard International Review.

that prominence gave it greater power to shape public perceptions. As a result, at a time of renewed interest in humanitarian intervention, the effort to justify the Iraq war even in part in humanitarian terms risks giving humanitarian intervention a bad name. If that breeds cynicism about the use of military force for humanitarian purposes, it could be devastating for people in need of future rescue.

Since the Iraq war was not mainly about saving the Iraqi people from mass slaughter, there was little serious pre-war debate about whether it could be justified in purely humanitarian terms. Indeed, if Iraqi President Saddam Hussein had been overthrown and the issue of weapons of mass destruction reliably dealt with, there clearly would have been no war, even if the successor government were just as repressive.

Over time, however, the original justifications for war lost much of their force. More than seven months after the declared end of major hostilities, weapons of mass destruction still have not been found. No significant prewar link with international terrorism has been discovered. The difficulty of establishing stable institutions in Iraq is making the country an increasingly unlikely staging ground for promoting democracy in the Middle East. More and more, the Bush administration's remaining justification for the war is that Hussein was a tyrant who deserved to be overthrown—an argument for humanitarian intervention. The administration is now citing that rationale not simply as a side benefit of the war but as a prime justification for it.

Does that claim hold up to scrutiny? This is not a question about whether the war was justified on other grounds; my organization, Human Rights Watch, is explicitly neutral on that point. Rather, it is a question about whether humanitarianism alone can justify the invasion. Despite the horrors of Hussein's rule, it cannot.

A Time for War

War's human cost can be enormous, but the imperative of stopping or preventing genocide or other systematic slaughter can sometimes justify the use of military force. Human Rights Watch has thus, on rare occasion, advocated humanitarian intervention—for example, to stop ongoing genocide in Rwanda and Bosnia.

Yet military action should not be taken lightly, even for humanitarian purposes. Such force might be used more readily when a government facing serious abuses on its territory invites military assistance from others, as in the three recent African interventions. But when military intervention on asserted humanitarian grounds occurs without a government's consent, it should be used with extreme caution.

Given the death, destruction, and disorder that are often inherent in war and its aftermath, humanitarian intervention should be reserved as an option only in situations of ongoing or imminent mass slaughter. Only the direst cases of large-scale slaughter can justify war's deliberate taking of life.

If this high standard is met, one should then look to five other factors to determine whether the use of military force can be characterized as humanitarian. First, military action must be the last reasonable option. Second, the intervention must be primarily guided by a humanitarian purpose. Third, it should be conducted to maximize respect for international human rights law. Fourth, it must be reasonably likely to do more good than harm. Finally, it should ideally, though not necessarily, be endorsed by the UN Security Council or another body with significant multilateral authority.

Mass Slaughter

The most important criterion in legitimating humanitarian intervention is whether mass slaughter is underway or imminent. Brutal as Hussein's reign was, the deaths being directly caused by his government in March 2003 were not of the exceptional magnitude that would justify humanitarian intervention. Granted, during the previous 25 years of Baath Party rule, the government murdered some 250,000 Iraqis. There were times in the past when the killing was so intense that humanitarian intervention would have been justified—for example, during the 1988 Anfal genocide, in which the Iraqi government slaughtered some 100,000 Kurds. But by the time of the March 2003 invasion, the government's killing had ebbed. On the eve of war, no one contends that Baghdad was engaged in murder of anywhere near this magnitude. "Better late than never" is not a justification for humanitarian intervention, which should be countenanced only to stop mass murder, not to punish its perpetrators, desirable as punishment is.

It might be argued that if Hussein committed mass atrocities in the past, his overthrow was justified as a way to prevent his resumption of such atrocities in the future. However, humanitarian intervention may be undertaken preventively only if slaughter is imminent. There must be evidence that large-scale slaughter is in preparation and about to begin unless militarily stopped. No one seriously claimed before the war that Hussein's government was planning imminent mass killing, and no evidence has emerged that it was. There were claims that the government, with a history of gassing Iranian soldiers and Iraqi Kurds, was planning to deliver weapons of mass destruction to terrorist networks, but no supporting proof of these allegations has yet emerged. There were also fears that the government might respond to an invasion with the use of chemical or biological weapons, perhaps even against its own people, but no one seriously suggested such use as an imminent possibility in the absence of an invasion.

The Last Reasonable Option

The lack of ongoing or imminent mass slaughter in March 2003 was itself sufficient to disqualify the invasion of Iraq as a humanitarian intervention. Nonetheless, in light of Hussein's ruthless past, it is useful to examine the other criteria for humanitarian intervention. For the most part, they too, were not met.

As noted, because of the substantial risks involved, an invasion qualifies as a humanitarian intervention only if it is the last reasonable option to stop mass killings. Since there were no ongoing mass killings in Iraq in early 2003, this issue technically did not arise. But it is useful to explore whether military intervention was the last reasonable option to stop what Iraqi abuses were ongoing.

It was not. At least one other option should have been tried long before resorting to the extreme step of military invasion—criminal prosecution. There is no guarantee that prosecution would have worked, and one might have justified skipping it had large-scale slaughter been underway. But in the face of the Iraqi government's more routine abuses, this alternative to military action should have been tried.

To be sure, an indictment is not the same as arrest, trial, and punishment. A piece of paper will not stop mass slaughter. But as a long-term approach, an indictment held some promise. The experiences of former Yugoslav President Slobodan Milosevic and former Liberian President Charles Taylor suggests that an international indictment profoundly discredits even a ruthless, dictatorial leader. That enormous stigma tends to undermine support for the leader, both at home and abroad, often in unexpected ways. By allowing Hussein to rule without the stigma of an indictment for genocide and crimes against humanity, the international community never tried a step that might have contributed to his removal and a parallel reduction in government abuses.

Humanitarian Purpose

A humanitarian intervention should be conducted with the aim of maximizing humanitarian results, since an intervention motivated by purely humanitarian concerns probably cannot be found. Governments that intervene to stop mass slaughter inevitably act for other reasons as well, but a dominant humanitarian purpose is important because it affects numerous decisions that can determine the intervention's success in saving people from violence.

Humanitarianism, even understood broadly as concern for the welfare of the Iraqi people, was at best a subsidiary motive for the invasion of Iraq. The principal justifications offered in the prelude to the invasion were the Iraqi government's alleged possession of weapons of mass destruction, its alleged failure to account for them as prescribed by numerous UN Security Council resolutions, and its alleged connection with terrorist networks. US officials also spoke of a democratic Iraq transforming the Middle East. In this tangle of motives, Hussein's cruelty toward his own people was mentioned, sometimes prominently, but, in the prewar period, it was never the dominant factor. This is not simply an academic point; it affected the way the US attacks were carried out, to the detriment of the Iraqi people.

Most significant, if invading forces had been directed to maximize the humanitarian impact of an intervention, they would have been better prepared to fill the security vacuum that predictably was created by the toppling of the Iraqi government. It was entirely foreseeable that Hussein's downfall would lead to civil disorder. The 1991 uprisings in Iraq were marked by large-scale summary executions. The Iraqi government's Arabization policy raised the prospect of clashes between displaced Kurds seeking to reclaim their old homes and Arabs who had moved into them. Other sudden changes of regime, such as the Bosnian Serb withdrawal from the Sarajevo suburbs in 1996, have been marked by widespread violence, looting, and arson.

In part to prevent violence, the US Army Chief of Staff before the war, General Eric K. Shinseki, predicted in 2003 that "several" hundred thousand troops would be required. But the civilian leaders of the US Pentagon dismissed this assessment and launched the war with considerably fewer combat troops—some 150,000. Coalition troops were quickly overwhelmed by the enormity of the task of maintaining public order in Iraq. Looting was pervasive. Arms caches were raided and emptied. Violence was rampant.

The problem of understaffing was only compounded by the failure to deploy an adequate number of troops trained in policing. Regular troops are trained to fight—to meet threats with lethal force. But that presumptive resort to lethal force is inappropriate and unlawful when it comes to policing an occupied nation. The consequence was a steady stream of civilians killed when coalition troops, on edge in the face of common but unpredictable attacks by resistance elements, mistakenly fired on civilians. That only increased resentment among Iraqis and fueled further attacks. Troops trained in policing—that is, trained to use lethal force as a last resort—would have been better suited to conduct occupation duties in a humane fashion. But the US Pentagon has not made a priority of developing policing skills among its troops, leaving relatively few to be deployed in Iraq.

Compliance with Humanitarian Law

Every effort should be made to ensure that a humanitarian intervention is carried out in strict compliance with international human rights and humanitarian law. Compliance is required in all conflicts—no less for an intervention that is justified on humanitarian grounds. The invasion of Iraq largely met this requirement, but not entirely. Coalition aircraft took extraordinary care to avoid harming civilians when attacking fixed, pre-selected targets. But the coalition's record in attacking targets that arose unexpectedly in the course of the war was mixed.

As described in Human Rights Watch's December 2003 report, US efforts to bomb leadership targets were an abysmal failure. The 0-for-50 record reflected a targeting method that was dangerously indiscriminate, allowing bombs to be dropped on the basis of evidence suggesting little more than the presence of a leader somewhere in a community. Substantial civilian casualties were the foreseeable result.

Coalition ground forces also used cluster munitions near populated areas, with a predictable loss of civilian life. After Human Rights Watch found that roughly a quarter of the civilian deaths in the 1999 NATO bombing of Yugoslavia were caused by the use of cluster bombs in populated areas, the US Air Force substantially curtailed this practice. But the US Army apparently never learned this lesson. In responding to Iraqi attacks, US Army troops regularly used cluster munitions in populated areas, causing substantial losses of life. Such disregard for civilian life is incompatible with a genuinely humanitarian intervention.

Better, Rather Than Worse

A humanitarian intervention should be reasonably calculated to make things better rather than worse for the people being rescued. One is tempted to say that anything is better than living under the tyranny of Hussein, but unfortunately, it is possible to imagine scenarios that are even worse. Vicious as his rule was, chaos or abusive civil war might well become even deadlier, and it is too early to say whether such violence might still emerge in Iraq.

Still, when the war was launched in March 2003, the US and British governments clearly hoped that the Iraqi government would topple quickly and that the Iraqi nation would soon be put on the path to democracy. Their failure to equip themselves with the number of troops needed to stabilize post-war Iraq diminished the likelihood of this rosy scenario coming to pass. However, the balance of considerations before the war probably supported the conclusion that Iraqis would be better off if Hussein's regime were ended. But that one factor does not make the intervention a humanitarian one.

UN Approval

There is considerable value in receiving the endorsement of the UN Security Council or another major multilateral body before launching a humanitarian intervention. Convincing others of the validity of a proposed intervention is a good way to guard against pretextual or unjustified action. An international commitment also increases the likelihood that adequate personnel and resources will be devoted to the intervention and its aftermath. And approval by the UN Security Council, in particular, ends the debate about the legality of an intervention.

However, in extreme situations, UN Security Council approval should not be required. In its current state, the UN Security Council is simply too imperfect to make it the sole mechanism for legitimizing humanitarian intervention. Its permanent membership is a relic of the post-World War II era, and its veto system allows those members to block the rescue of people facing slaughter for the most parochial of reasons. In light of these faults, one's patience with the council's approval process would understandably diminish if large-scale slaughter were underway. However, because there was no such urgency in early 2003 for Iraq, the failure to win the UN Security Council's approval, let alone the endorsement of any other multilateral body, weighs more heavily in assessing the intervenors' claim of humanitarianism.

Of course, the UN Security Council was never asked to opine on a purely humanitarian intervention in Iraq. The principal case presented to it was built on the Iraqi government's alleged possession of and failure to account for weapons of mass destruction. Even so, approval might have ameliorated at least some of the factors that stood in the way of the invasion being genuinely humanitarian. Most significant, an invasion approved by the UN Security Council is likely to have seen more foreign troops join the predominantly US and British forces, meaning that preparation for the post-war chaos might have been better.

Failing the Humanitarian Test

In sum, the invasion of Iraq fails the test for a humanitarian intervention. The killing in Iraq at the time was not of the dire and exceptional nature that would justify military action. In addition, intervention was not the last reasonable option to stop Iraqi atrocities. It was not motivated primarily by humanitarian concerns. It was not conducted in a way that maximized compliance with international humanitarian law. It was not approved by the UN Security Council. And while at the time it was launched it was reasonable to believe that the Iraqi people would be better off, it was not designed or carried out with the needs of Iraqis foremost in mind.

Hussein certainly presided over a coercive, undemocratic, and brutal regime, and few shed tears at his overthrow. But in the interest of preserving popular support for a rescue option on which future potential victims of mass slaughter will depend, proponents of the Iraqi war should stop trying to justify it as a humanitarian intervention.

Alan J. Kuperman

→ NO

Humanitarian Hazard: Revisiting Doctrines of Intervention

No foreign policy seems more inherently benign than humanitarian military intervention. It is rooted in the altruistic desire to protect innocents from violent death. It appears feasible, given the military superiority of Western forces over those in developing countries where most violent conflict occurs. And the only obvious costs are a modest financial commitment and the occasional casualty.

For these reasons, in the wake of the world's failure to prevent violence in the Balkans and Rwanda, US President Bill Clinton declared in June 1999 the doctrine that bears his name: "If the world community has the power to stop it, we ought to stop genocide and ethnic cleansing." In December 2001, a distinguished international panel went a step further and declared the existence of a "Responsibility to Protect"—suggesting that the failure to intervene by those capable of doing so might even breach international law.

But a more sophisticated analysis calls into question the value of humanitarian military intervention, even when judged by its own explicit standard of saving lives. For two reasons the benefits of such intervention are much smaller, and the costs much greater, than commonly recognized. First, most violence is perpetrated faster than interveners can realistically arrive to stop it. Second, as economists could have predicted, but few humanitarians have acknowledged, the intervention regime actually exacerbates some conflicts through what I have labeled "the moral hazard of humanitarian intervention." In light of these two dynamics, an increase in intervention does not save as many lives as commonly claimed. Unless the West adopts a number of reforms outlined at the end of this article, more intervention might actually lead to a net increase in killing.

Killers Are Quicker Than Interveners

In the high-profile conflicts of the 1990s, most violence was perpetrated far more quickly than commonly realized. In Bosnia, although the conflict dragged on for more than three years, the majority of ethnic cleansing was perpetrated in the spring of 1992. By the time Western media arrived on the scene later that summer, Serb forces already occupied two-thirds of the republic and had displaced more than one million residents. In Rwanda, at least half of the eventual half-million Tutsi victims were killed in the first three weeks of genocide. When Croatia's army broke a three-year cease-fire in August 1995, it ethnically cleansed virtually all of the more than 100,000 Serbs from the Krajina region in less than a week. In Kosovo, when Serbian forces switched from a policy of counter-insurgency to ethnic cleansing in March 1999, in response to NATO's decision to bomb, most of their cleansing occurred in the first two weeks, and they managed to cleanse 850,000 Albanians, half the province's total. In East Timor, following a 1999 vote for independence, Indonesian-backed militias damaged the majority of the province's infrastructure and displaced most of the population in little more than a week.

Even less well recognized is the fact that logistical obstacles impose significant delays on military intervention, humanitarian or otherwise, even where a strong political will exists. For example, after Iraqi President Saddam Hussein invaded Kuwait in August 1990, and US President George Bush ordered an immediate deployment to defend Saudi Arabia (Operation Desert Shield), it took nine days for the first unit of 2,300 US troops to reach the area of conflict. Another week was required before the unit was sufficiently prepared to venture beyond its makeshift base. Thus, even with the vital national security interest of oil at stake, it took the United States more than two weeks to deploy and begin operations of a relatively tiny force. The reasons are numerous, but stem mainly from three factors: modern militaries cannot operate without their equipment, their equipment is extremely heavy, and there are limits to the rate at which such equipment can be airlifted to remote countries.

Indeed, the airlift to Saudi Arabia was much easier than a typical humanitarian intervention because the Arabian peninsula is closer to the United States and has better airfields than most conflict zones. Even short-distance interventions can be bedeviled by the combination of poor airfields and weighty forces. For example, when the United States deployed just 24 Apache helicopters from Germany to nearby Albania (Task Force Hawk) for the 1999 Kosovo intervention, it required 17 days. Two factors explain this: poor Albanian airfields and a US Army doctrine that mandated a force of 5,350 personnel and their equipment to operate, maintain, and protect the helicopters. In total, this task force weighed 22,000 tons, necessitating 500 flights of large, modern C-17 cargo aircraft.

Intervening in Africa, where most of today's violent conflicts take place, is even harder due to bad airfields and the farther distance from western military bases. Had the United States tried to stop the Rwandan genocide, it would have required about six weeks to deploy a task force of 15,000 personnel and their equipment. This time estimate is conservative, because analogous past interventions to Haiti, Panama, and the Dominican Republic actually required somewhat larger forces. Unfortunately, this means that by the time Western governments learned of the Rwandan genocide and deployed an intervention force, the vast majority of the ultimate Tutsi victims would already have been killed.

The fact that much civil violence is carried out more quickly than intervention forces can arrive is by itself no excuse for failing to intervene; some lives can be saved even by belated intervention. However, it does mean that the benefits of humanitarian intervention are far smaller than commonly realized. This is important to remember as we turn to the unexpected costs of humanitarian intervention.

Intervention Exacerbates Violence

The most counterintuitive aspect of humanitarian military intervention is that it sometimes may cause the very tragedies it is intended to prevent. The explanation for this starts from the little known but empirically robust fact that genocidal violence is usually a state retaliation against substate groups for launching armed secession or revolution. Most groups are deterred from such armed challenges by the fear of state retaliation. In the 1990s, however, the regime of humanitarian military intervention changed this calculus, convincing some groups that the international community would intervene to protect them from retaliation, thereby encouraging armed rebellions. As events played out, these armed challenges did provoke genocidal retaliation, but intervention arrived too late to save many of the targets of retaliation. Thus, the intervention regime—intended to insure against risks of genocide and ethnic cleansing—inadvertently encouraged risk-taking behavior that exacerbated these atrocities. This is the classic dynamic of moral hazard, which is an inherent drawback of insurance systems.

For example, in the early 1990s, Bosnia's Muslims wanted their republic to secede from Yugoslavia so that they could establish their own state. However, they knew Serbs in Bosnia and the rest of Yugoslavia, who possessed considerably greater military power, opposed secession, so they initially eschewed secession as suicidal. By 1992, however, the international community had pledged to recognize Bosnia's independence if it seceded. This led the Muslims to believe that they had a guarantee of humanitarian military intervention if they armed themselves and seceded from Yugoslavia—which they did (with the support of Croats, who mainly hoped to join Croatia). The Serbs retaliated as expected in April 1992, but the international community did not intervene with significant force for more than three years—by which time an estimated 100,000 Bosnian Muslims had been killed and more than 1,000,000 displaced.

A similar scenario played out a few years later in the Serbian province of Kosovo. There the local ethnic Albanian majority sought independence but prudently had hewed to peaceful resistance throughout the early 1990s. Even after an influx of light weapons from neighboring Albania in 1997, most of Kosovo's ethnic Albanians, including the rebel Kosovo Liberation Army, believed they were no match by themselves for heavily armored Serb forces. However, the rebels expected that if they could provoke the Serbs into retaliating against Albanian civilians, the international community would intervene on their behalf, thereby facilitating independence. The plan played out almost perfectly. The rebels began shooting large numbers of Serb police and civilians in 1997, the Serbs retaliated with a brutal counter-insurgency in 1998, and NATO bombed the Serbs and occupied the province in 1999, establishing Kosovo's de facto independence. As noted above, however, the intervention also compelled the Serbs to initiate last-ditch ethnic cleansing—displacing about half the province's Albanians and killing more than 5,000. After Serbia's defeat, the Albanians took revenge by ethnically cleansing 100,000 Serbs, about half those in the province, while killing hundreds more.

All of this death and displacement on both sides was a direct consequence of the promise of humanitarian intervention. Research in both Bosnia and Kosovo, based on interviews with senior Muslim and Albanian officials who launched the suicidal armed challenges, indicates they would not have done so except for the prospect of such foreign aid. The unavoidable conclusion is that the regime of humanitarian intervention helped to cause the tragic outcomes it intended to prevent, at least in these two cases.

In the wake of the terror attacks of September 11, 2001, the international community—and especially the United States—has switched its military focus from altruistic humanitarian intervention to a self-interested war against terrorism and proliferation. One unintended side benefit is that rebels no longer expect that they can attract humanitarian intervention by launching provocative armed challenges against states. In today's security environment, the United States is more likely to view such rebels as international terrorists and to support state retaliation against them. As a result, nascent rebellions by Albanian rebels in Macedonia and southern Serbia have fizzled out, rather than replicating the dynamics of Bosnia and Kosovo. However, when and if the terrorist threat wanes, the international community is likely to pick up the gauntlet of humanitarian intervention once again, and recreate the problem of moral hazard.

A Lesson Learned

The shortcomings of humanitarian military intervention do not mean it should be abandoned as a policy tool. The goal should be to enhance its beneficial potential, while reducing its unintended costs. The conflicts of the 1990s present three major lessons: the speed of violence, the moral hazard of intervention, and the limits of coercive diplomacy. Formulating reforms to address these lessons, however, requires a sober consideration of both the costs and the trade-offs.

The first lesson, based on the lightning pace of the recent violence, is that we need intervention forces that can deploy more quickly. Lighter forces, with fewer heavy weapons and less armor, require fewer cargo flights and thus can save more lives by deploying quicker. However, shedding protective armor and weaponry also would increase casualties among the interveners. Such a trade-off cannot be made lightly.

An alternative is to pre-position troops and their heavy equipment at forward bases closer to where they are most likely to be needed for humanitarian intervention: in Africa. Interventions could be launched from these bases using small military cargo aircraft, which are more plentiful and better able to land at rudimentary African air fields than wide-body inter-continental models. The cargo aircraft could also make several round-trips per day to an intervention from forward bases, rather than one trip every few days from distant US or European bases—radically reducing deployment time from weeks to days. One obstacle, however, is that many Africans oppose foreign military bases as a form of neo-colonialism. An even bigger obstacle is that western states so far have been unwilling to invest in military forces dedicated to missions other than defending their own interests.

In recognition of the West's lack of will to deploy ground troops to Africa, the United States launched a project in the mid-1990s to train indigenous African forces for humanitarian intervention. This initiative had a reasonable premise—that African states would be more willing to risk the lives of their troops to stop conflict on the continent—but it has several shortcomings. First, there has been little provision of weaponry or combat training, so the African forces are suitable only for the permissive environment of peacekeeping after a conflict ends—and even then only so long as violence does not re-ignite, a common risk. Second, the initiative so far has failed to pre-position heavy weapons, armored personnel carriers, or helicopters at African bases, so that in the event of a crisis such equipment would have to be transported and joined up with intervention forces on an ad hoc, protracted basis. Third, most training has been conducted within national units, so that the few trained forces are unprepared for multi-national coalition operations that would be necessary in any large-scale intervention. In light of these shortcomings, if major civil violence were to break out again in Africa in the future, an all-African force would have little hope of quickly or effectively stopping the killing.

Another option is a UN rapid response capability, as proposed several years ago by an international commission headed by Algerian diplomat Lakhdar Brahimi in 2000. This panel called for expanding UN standby arrangements "to include several coherent, multinational, brigade-size forces and the necessary enabling forces, created by Member States working in partnership, in order to better meet the need for the robust peacekeeping forces." One problem is that the report makes no provision for the coordination of airlift operations. Only the US military has a large, long-haul cargo air fleet; rapid reaction to most parts of the world is impossible unless the United States participates. A further problem is that even if UN member states were willing to commit troops in advance for humanitarian intervention, it is uncertain they would actually deploy them when called upon. Relying on a UN force that might not materialize when needed could prove even worse than today's ad hoc system—in which states at least know that the buck stops with them.

Reduce Moral Hazard

As noted, some sub-state groups have been emboldened by the prospect of humanitarian intervention to launch armed challenges against states, provoking genocidal retaliation. One superficially attractive solution would be for the international community to launch timely humanitarian military intervention in every case of genocidal violence. However, this is unfeasible for two reasons. First, even if the political will for such extensive intervention existed (which it does not), the number of actual cases of such violence would soon exhaust our resources. The 1990s alone witnessed major civil violence in at least 16 areas (some on several occasions): Albania, Algeria, Angola, Azerbaijan (mainly in Nagorno-Karabakh), Bosnia, Cambodia, Congo Republic, Croatia,

Ethiopia, Liberia, Kosovo, Sierra Leone, Somalia, Sudan, Tajikistan, and Zaire (and its successor, the Democratic Republic of Congo). Moreover, by the logic of moral hazard, each instance of humanitarian intervention raises expectations of further intervention and thus encourages additional armed challenges that may provoke still more genocidal retaliation—further overwhelming the international capacity for intervention.

Two means exist to mitigate moral hazard. First, the international community should reward non-violent protest movements, rather than armed rebellions. In Kosovo, it did the opposite, ignoring a non-violent ethnic Albanian resistance for eight years and then rewarding its violent counterpart with military assistance. So long as disgruntled ethnic groups believe they can attract Western intervention with violence rather than with passive resistance, Western states encourage rebellions that provoke genocidal retaliation.

The second solution is drawn from the economics literature on moral hazard, which suggests we should not pay claims that arise solely because of the provision of insurance coverage. In other words, the international community should not intervene on behalf of groups that provoke retaliation in the hope of garnering humanitarian intervention. If the West adopted this policy, and stuck to it, such cynical rebellions would likely peter out fairly quickly. Such a policy still would permit humanitarian intervention on behalf of groups that suffer genocidal violence through no fault of their own—for example, at the hands of leaders like Adolf Hitler or Pol Pot—as the concept originally envisioned.

A policy of not intervening in cases of intentionally provoked genocide is open to criticism as being hard-hearted. This is especially true in cases where the victims of retaliation did not endorse the armed challenge or did not know it would provoke a backlash. However, if the theory of moral hazard is correct, a policy of not intervening in response to deliberate provocations eventually would reduce the number of such cases—and thereby the overall incidence of genocidal violence. If so, such a policy would not be hard-hearted, but actually compassionate, at least from a long-term perspective.

Avoid Pyromaniac Diplomacy

A third lesson is that the international community needs to better coordinate its diplomacy with military intervention. Since the end of the Cold War, the West has tried to coerce authoritarian governments (or rebels) to hand over power to opponents by applying economic or military sanctions. However, in several cases, including Rwanda, the former Yugoslavia, and East Timor, the targets of coercion have responded instead by ethnically cleansing their opponents. To prevent this eventuality, the West needs to preventively deploy robust intervention forces, prior to exercising coercive diplomacy. Unfortunately, most preventive deployments so far have been feeble. When violence breaks out, as in Rwanda and Srebrenica, they provide little protection and then are withdrawn. Such half-hearted deployments lend a false sense of security that encourages vulnerable groups to let down their guard so that they ultimately die in greater numbers, making this type of intervention worse than nothing.

If the West is unwilling to deploy robust forces preventively, it must temper its use of coercive diplomacy aimed at compelling rulers or rebels to surrender power, because of the risk of inadvertently triggering massive violence. So long as the West lacks the will for adequate preventive deployments, its diplomats should focus instead on carrots, rather than sticks—offering incentives to oppressive governments and rebels, including economic assistance, in exchange for gradual power-sharing. The West also should be prepared to offer "golden parachutes"—monetary rewards, asylum, and immunity from subsequent prosecution—to entrenched leaders willing to peacefully yield power. While human rights groups abjure the prospect of cutting deals with leaders who have blood on their hands, in some cases forgiving past crimes may be the price of preventing future ones.

It may be a noble endeavor to use military force to protect victims of genocidal violence. But it is infinitely preferable to prevent the outbreak of such violence in the first place. To do so requires adoption of more enlightened policies of humanitarian intervention, tempering altruistic instincts with the stubborn realities of human nature and military logistics.

TO MOVE A GIANT

Ground forces, while required for effective humanitarian intervention, are the slowest to deploy. The US Army is dependent upon support from US Air Force or Navy units for mobility. Such deployments are subject to availability of transportation, quality of ports or landing zones, and the need for heavy machinery.

While various technological improvements can be made on current transportation mezthods, a more effective means of facilitating mobilization is efficient prepositioning. Efficient prepositioning would allow for the rapid transfer of soldiers and equipment as well as expedite the establishment of a base of operations.

Current positioning of US forces is inefficient and could be substantially improved. US forces in Central Europe, for instance, could be transferred to Italy, close enough to assure NATO of US priorities in the area, but also closer to the Mediterranean for quick deployment. Additional forces in the Pacific should be moved onto Theater Support Vessels and placed off the West Coast of Australia and near Japan to support the brigade already in Korea. Coverage of South and Central America could be improved by placing better naval transport options in the Gulf of Mexico.

An examination of the main conflicts involving US troops in 2002 reveals that most occurred as sudden urban conflicts. Since 75 percent of major urban areas are within 150 miles of coastline, a naval prepositioning such as the one mentioned here could theoretically move a medium brigade anywhere in the world in four days, an entire division in five days, and five divisions in 30 days.

POSTSCRIPT

Can Humanitarian Intervention
Be Justified?

The debate over humanitarian intervention is not simply an academic exercise. As Kenneth Roth points out, the preservation of human rights has been offered as part of the justification for the recent U.S. intervention in Iraq. The degree to which that justification is accepted will affect the perceived legitimacy of U.S. actions and, as a consequence, the ease or difficulty with which the United States can build local and international support for its efforts there. Samantha Powers is critical of the United States for not doing more to fight genocide and violations of human rights abroad. See Samantha Powers, *"A Problem from Hell": America and the Age of Genocide* (HarperCollins, 2003). Powers and others have also criticized the United Nations, the United States, and other states for not taking stronger action to stop what they characterize as an ongoing episode of genocide in Darfur, Sudan. For a review of U.S. interventions in general, see Richard Haass, *Intervention: The Use of American Military Force in the Post–Cold War World* (Brookings Institution Press, 1999). The failure of the United States and the international community to take action against genocide in Rwanda was also the subject of a movie, *Hotel Rwanda*.

U.S. conduct following humanitarian interventions has also been a matter of dispute. In particular, U.S. actions involving the interrogation of prisoners following the terrorist attacks of September 11, 2001, in Afghanistan, Cuba, and Iraq could be interpreted as violations of human rights. If so, these actions could be used to justify the equally poor treatment of U.S. combatants in foreign conflicts. They may also undermine the symbolic role of the United States as the purveyor of civil and political liberties, thereby greatly complicating its efforts to democratize Iraq and other countries. In such instances, nongovernmental organizations like Human Rights Watch (http://www.hrw.org/) and Amnesty International (http://www.amnestyusa.org/) play a key role in monitoring human rights violations and providing documentation of human rights abuses.

Other nongovernmental organizations play a key role in humanitarian interventions. David Rieff provides a critical assessment of humanitarian intervention and the roles played by relief organizations like Oxfam, CARE, and Doctors without Borders. He also rejects "the false morality play" that, in any given conflict, there are victimizers and innocent victims, and that it is always clear who is who. See David Rieff, *A Bed for the Night: Humanitarianism in Crisis* (Simon & Schuster, 2002). In contrast, Martha Finnemore argues that there is a growing norm of humanitarian intervention and an important role played by nongovernmental organizations. She argues that long-term trends suggest

342

the steady erosion of force's normative value in international politics, the growing influence of equality norms in many aspects of global political life, and the increasing importance of law in intervention practices. See Martha Finnemore, *The Purpose of Intervention: Changing Beliefs About the Use of Force* (Cornell, 2003).

Contributors to This Volume

EDITORS

ANDREW BENNETT, Ph.D., is professor of government at Georgetown University. He has written or edited books on military interventions, alliance burden sharing, and research methods, and he teaches courses on international relations theory, research methods, and the American foreign policy process. Professor Bennett has also worked as a staff aide in the U.S. Senate, a special assistant to the Assistant Secretary of Defense for International Security Affairs, and a foreign policy advisor on several presidential campaigns. His Web site can be found at: http://www8.georgetown.edu/departments/government/faculty/bennetta/.

GEORGE E. SHAMBAUGH, IV, Ph.D., is an associate professor in the Edmund A. Walsh School of Foreign Service and chairman of the department of government at Georgetown University. He has written numerous articles and taught classes on international politics, foreign policy, international political economy, and the environment. He is author of *States, Firms, and Power: Successful Sanctions in U.S. Foreign Policy,* co-author of *The Art of Policymaking: Tools, Techniques, and Processes in the Modern Executive Branch,* and co-editor of *Anarchy and the Environment: The International Politics of Common Pool Resources.* His articles have appeared in a range of journals including *American Political Science Review, International Politics, Environmental Politics, International Interactions, International Studies Quarterly, The Journal of Peace Research, Review of International Studies,* and *Security Dialogue.* Dr. Shambaugh received a B.A. in government and physics from Oberlin College, an M.I.A. in international affairs, and an M.Phil. and Ph.D. in political science from Columbia University. His departmental Web page is http://explore.georgetown.edu/people/shambaug/?PageTemplateID=156.

AUTHORS

HUSSEIN AGHA is senior associate member of St. Antony's College at the University of Oxford. He is the author, with A. S. Khalidi, of *A Framework for a Palestinian National Security Doctrine*. He has been an advisor for the Palestinian delegation in Middle East peace negotiations.

GEORGE W. BUSH is the 43rd president of the United States, inaugurated on January 20, 2001, and re-elected in the 2004 U.S. presidential election. Bush is the eldest son of the 41st U.S. president, George H. W. Bush, grandson to Prescott Bush, the former U.S. senator from Connecticut, and older brother to Jeb Bush, former governor of Florida. George W. Bush became the 46th governor of Texas in January 1995, resigning in December 2000, after being elected president.

VICTOR D. CHA holds the D. S. Song-Korea Foundation Chair in Asian Studies in the department of government and the Edmund Walsh School of Foreign Service, Georgetown University and is the Asia director in the National Security Council of the U.S. government. He is the author of *Alignment Despite Antagonism: The United States-Korea-Japan Security Triangle* and has written articles on international relations and East Asia in journals including *Foreign Affairs, International Security, Political Science Quarterly, Survival, International Studies Quarterly, Journal of Strategic Studies, The Washington Quarterly, Orbis, Journal of Peace Research, Security Dialogue, Australian Journal of International Affairs, Japanese Journal of Political Science, Korean Studies*, and *Asian Survey*.

DAVID COLE is the legal affairs correspondent for *The Nation* and a professor at Georgetown University Law Center. He is the author of *No Equal Justice: Race and Class in the American Criminal Justice System*; co-author, with James X. Dempsey, of *Terrorism and the Constitution: Sacrificing Civil Liberties for National Security;* and author of *Enemy Aliens: Double Standards and Constitutional Freedoms in the War on Terrorism*.

JOSEPH J. COLLINS is a retired U.S. army colonel who teaches at the National War College.

STEVE A. COOK is senior fellow for Middle Eastern studies at the Council on Foreign Relations.

CHARLI E. COON is senior policy analyst for energy and environment at the Heritage Foundation in Washington, D.C. Before moving to Heritage, she was a research and budget analyst for Republicans in the Illinois state assembly. She earned her M.A. in public administration from the University of Illinois–Springfield in 1976 and her law degree from Loyola University of Chicago in 1992.

PHILIP DEUTCH is a member of the board of directors of Evergreen Solar and is a former board member of Beacon Power Corp., Northern Power Systems, and International Marketing Concepts. Mr. Deutch has spoken or been on panels at energy conferences held by Goldman Sachs, Bank of America, Credit Suisse First Boston, Salomon Smith Barney, the American Council for Renewable Energy, Bear Stearns, Montreux Energy, McIntire School of Commerce at the University of Virginia, and the FRA Renewable Energy Finance & Investment Summit. Mr. Deutch served on the Advisory Committee for the 2005 Energy Venture Fair and the selection committees for the 2005 Cleantech Venture Forum and 2005 National Renewable Energy Laboratory Industry Growth Forum.

CHRISTOPHER DICKEY is Middle East editor for *Newsweek*.

DAN EPHRON is a writer for *Newsweek*.

AARON L. FRIEDBERG is a professor of politics and international affairs at Princeton University and director of Princeton's Research Program in International Security.

NIKOLAS GVOSDEV is senior editor of *The National Interest* and adjunct senior fellow at the Nixon Center.

RICHARD N. HAASS is president of the Council on Foreign Relations.

MICHAEL HIRSH is a writer for *Newsweek*.

NATHAN E. HULTMAN is assistant professor at University of Maryland.

AMBASSADOR ROBERT HUTCHINGS is diplomat-in-residence at the Woodrow Wilson School of Public and International Affairs at Princeton University and former chair of the U.S. National Intelligence Council from 2003 to 2005.

JOSEF JOFFE is editor and publisher of *Die Zeit*, a weekly German newspaper, the Marc and Anita Abramowitz Fellow in International Relations at the Hoover Institution, a fellow at the Freeman Spogli Institute for International Studies and adjunct professor of political science at Stanford University, and an associate of the Olin Institute for Strategic Studies at Harvard University. His essays and reviews have appeared in a wide number of publications including the *New York Review of Books*, *Times Literary Supplement*, *Commentary*, *New York Times Magazine*, *New Republic*, *Weekly Standard*, and the *Prospect* (London). He is a regular contributor to quality daily newspapers in the United States and Britain.

DANIEL KLAIDMAN is managing editor of *Newsweek*.

CHARLES KRAUTHAMMER is a Pulitzer Prize–winning columnist and neo-conservative commentator. Krauthammer appears regularly as a guest commentator on *Fox News*, and his print work appears in the *Washington Post*, *Time* magazine, and *The Weekly Standard*. In 2006, the *Financial Times* named Krauthammer America's most influential commentator.

MARK KRIKORIAN is the executive director of the Center for Immigration Studies (CIS), a think tank that promotes stricter immigration standards and enforcement. Before joining CIS in February 1995, Krikorian was an editor at the Winchester (Va.) *Star*, as well as editor of a publication on marketing via electronic media and of the monthly newsletter of the Federation for American Immigration Reform. Mr. Krikorian is a regular contributor to the conservative publication *National Review* as well as a regular participant of *National Review*'s "The Corner." Krikorian received his B.A. from Georgetown University and his M.A. from the Fletcher School of Law and Diplomacy at Tufts University.

WILLIAM KRISTOL is editor of the Washington-based political magazine, *The Weekly Standard*. Mr. Kristol regularly appears on *Fox News Sunday* and on the Fox News Channel. Mr. Kristol recently co-authored *The War Over Iraq: America's Mission* and *Saddam's Tyranny*.

ALAN J. KUPERMAN is resident assistant professor of International Relations at Johns Hopkins University, based at Bologna Center. He has also served as fellow at Brookings Institution, Harvard University, University of Southern California, and U.S. Institute of Peace; was legislative director for U.S. Representative Charles E. Schumer, legislative assistant to Speaker of the U.S. House of Representatives Thomas S. Foley, and chief of staff for U.S. Representative James H. Scheuer. His publications include *The Limits of Humanitarian Intervention* and articles on genocide and intervention in the *Journal of Genocide Research, Foreign Affairs, The SAIS Review, The Washington Post, The Wall Street Journal*, and *USA Today*.

CHRISTOPHER LAYNE is a professor at Texas A&M University's George H.W. Bush School of Government and Public Service.

ROBERT J. LIEBER is professor of government at Georgetown University.

ANDREW N. LIVERIS is chairman and chief executive officer of the Dow Chemical Company.

MARC LYNCH is associate professor of political science and international affairs at George Washington University.

SEBASTIAN MALLABY is director of the Maurice R. Greenberg Center for Geoeconomic Studies and Paul A. Volcker senior fellow for international economics for the Council on Foreign Relations.

MICHAEL MANDELBAUM is the Christian A. Herter Professor of American Foreign Policy at The Johns Hopkins School of Advanced International Studies in Washington, D.C. He is also the author or co-author of ten books. Mandelbaum writes a regular column for *Newsday*.

JIM MANZI is the chief executive officer of an applied artificial intelligence software company.

BILL McKIBBEN is an author and environmental activist.

JOHN J. MEARSHEIMER is the R. Wendell Harrison Distinguished Service Professor of Political Science and the co-director of the Program on International Security Policy at the University of Chicago, where he has taught since 1982. During the 1998–1999 academic year, he was the Whitney H. Shepardson Fellow at the Council on Foreign Relations in New York, and in 2003 he was elected to the American Academy of Arts and Sciences. Professor Mearsheimer has written extensively about security issues and international politics more generally.

GEN. MONTGOMERY C. MEIGS (Retd.) is a visiting professor in the Security Studies Program at Georgetown University's Walsh School of Foreign Service.

GEN. DAVID H. PETRAEUS is commander of U.S. Central Command and former commander of the Multi-National Force in Iraq.

THOMAS PICKERING is former U.S. undersecretary of state for political affairs.

NORMAN PODHORETZ is editor-at-large for *Commentary* magazine.

DAVID POLLOCK is senior fellow at the Washington Institute for Near East Policy.

AHMAD RASHID is a Pakistani journalist and fellow at the Pacific Council on International Policy.

OTTO J. REICH is former assistant secretary of state for Latin American affairs.

KENNETH ROTH is the executive director of Human Rights Watch. Previously, he was a federal prosecutor for the U.S. Attorney's Office for the southern district of New York and the Iran-Contra investigation in Washington. He also worked in private practice as a litigator. Mr. Roth has conducted human rights investigations around the globe, devoting special attention to issues of justice and accountability for gross abuses of human rights, standards governing military conduct in time of war, the human rights policies of the United States and the United Nations, and the human rights responsibilities of multinational businesses. He has written over 70 articles and chapters on a range of human rights topics in such publications as *The New York Times, The Washington Post, Foreign Affairs,* the *International Herald Tribune,* and the *New York Review of Books.*

BARNETT R. RUBIN is director of studies and senior fellow at the Center on International Cooperation at New York University.

SCOTT D. SAGAN is professor of political science and director of the Center for International Security and Cooperation at Stanford University.

STEPHEN SESTANOVICH is professor of international diplomacy at Columbia University and senior fellow at the Council on Foreign Relations.

JOSEPH SIEGLE is Douglas Dillon Fellow at the Council on Foreign Relations. Dr. Siegle has worked on international development and humanitarian assistance projects in Africa, Asia, and the Balkans. He was the country director for the international NGO, World Vision, in Eritrea from 1995 to 1997 and promoted aquaculture as a Peace Corps volunteer in Liberia in the mid-1980s. His publications include *Democratization and Economic Growth: The Contribution of Accountability Institutions;* "Understanding Food Security: A Conceptual Framework for Programming"; "Operationalizing Reconciliation: Strategies for Rwanda and Burundi"; and "Botswana's Approach to Drought: How Disaster Relief Can Be Developmental."

MATTHEW J. SLAUGHTER is a professor of international economics in the Tuck School of Business at Dartmouth College.

JACK SNYDER is the Robert and Renée Belfer Professor of International Relations in the department of political science and Institute of War and Peace Studies at Columbia University. His research focuses on international relations theory, post-Soviet politics, and nationalism. Snyder received his B.A. from Harvard University, his certificate from the Russian Institute at Columbia University, and his Ph.D. also from Columbia University.

ANDREW SULLIVAN is a journalist and political commentator. Sullivan is the former editor of *The New Republic,* known for both his unusual personal-political identity (HIV-positive, homosexual, self-described conservative often at odds with other conservatives, and practicing Roman Catholic), as well as his successful and pioneering efforts in the field of blog journalism. He is also the author of three books.

SHIBLEY TELHAMI is professor of peace and development at the University of Maryland.

STEVE WALT is a professor of international affairs at Harvard University's John F. Kennedy School of Government. In 1983, he received a Ph.D., in political science, from the University of California, Berkeley. Dr. Walt developed the "Balance of Threat" Theory, which defined threats in terms of aggregate power, geographic proximity, offensive power, and aggressive intentions.

TAMARA COFMAN WITTES is a research fellow in the Saban Center for Middle East Policy at the Brookings Institution, where she analyzes U.S. policy toward democratization in the Arab world and the challenge of regional economic and political reform. She has also served as an adjunct professor of security studies at Georgetown University and a consultant for the RAND Corporation, the U.S. Institute of Peace, and the Middle East Institute. Her publications have appeared in *Political Science Quarterly*, the *Weekly Standard*, the *Chronicle of Higher Education*, and *National Security Studies Quarterly*.

ERNESTO ZEDILLO is former president of Mexico.